CW01617679

BOOK ONE: LIBERA
RECONSTRUCTION 1

The Open University
Walton Hall, Milton Keynes MK7 6AA

First published 2000

Edited, designed and typeset by The Open University

Printed in the United Kingdom by The Alden Group, Oxford

This text is a component of the Open University course AA304 *Politics, Culture and Society in France and Italy, 1943–1973*. Details of this and other Open University courses can be obtained from Course Reservations and Sales Office, PO Box 724, The Open University, Milton Keynes MK7 6ZS, United Kingdom: telephone (0044) (0)1908 653231, e-mail ces-gen@open.ac.uk.

For availability of this or other course components, contact Open University Worldwide Ltd, The Berrill Building, Walton Hall, Milton Keynes, MK7 6AA, United Kingdom: telephone (00 44) (0)1908 858785, fax (00 44) (0)1908 858787, e-mail ouwenq@open.ac.uk

Much useful course information can also be obtained from The Open University's website: http://www.open.ac.uk

ISBN 0 7492 8792 6

009497B/AA304B1i1.1

UNIT 1 Introduction to the Course Italo Calvino: *Adam, One Afternoon*

Prepared for the course team
by Geoffrey Warner, revised by Bernard Waites

Study materials

For your work on this unit you will need to refer to the following materials:

Ginsborg, *A History of Contemporary Italy*

Gildea, *France since 1945*

Documents and Texts 1

Calvino, *Adam, One Afternoon*

Aims

This unit is divided into three main sections. Firstly, it provides a general introduction to Part One of AA304, explaining what you will be studying and why. Secondly, it tells you how to make best use of the histories of post-war France and Italy which we have adopted as set books: Paul Ginsborg's *A History of Contemporary Italy: Society and Politics 1943–1988* (1990) and Robert Gildea's *France since 1945* (1996). (These will be referred to as Ginsborg and Gildea throughout AA304.) We will ask you to read passages relating to the Resistance movements and to the Liberation of France and Italy. Thirdly, it examines in some detail the short stories by the Italian writer, Italo Calvino, collected in your set book, *Adam, One Afternoon*.

By the end of this unit you should be able to:

1. describe the nature and composition of the Resistance movements;
2. describe the political, economic and cultural background to Liberation and reconstruction;
3. understand what is meant by such critical concepts as 'realism', 'neo-realism' and 'fantasy';
4. discuss how Calvino's short stories relate to these concepts and to the historical context in which he was writing.

1 Introduction

Welcome to AA304, an interdisciplinary course dealing with politics, culture and society in France and Italy in the three decades after the Second World War. We have organized the course into two parts, and each combines historical and social analysis with textual case studies. To avoid confusion, we should say immediately that the term 'texts' includes paintings and feature films as well as literary works. The course should deepen your knowledge of two major European countries during a period of rapid development and change, and foster a range of disciplinary skills. Part One (Units 1–16) deals with the sub-period of Liberation and post-war reconstruction between 1943 and the mid 1950s; it incorporates material from a previous half-credit course which we have revised and updated.[1] Part Two (Units 17–32) deals with the years of rapid economic growth and 'cultural revolution' between the later 1950s and 1973. We have put quote marks around that phrase because it begs the question 'What do we mean by a cultural revolution?' Much more is said about the concept of cultural revolution in the introduction to Part Two and in Unit 18, and the quote marks will henceforth be dropped.

Little justification is required for the comparative historical study of France and Italy in the post-war decades. We cannot understand how contemporary western Europe evolved without knowing something about the political and economic development of France and Italy in this period. They became major industrial economies, were founder members of the European Union, and

[1] A324 *Liberation and Reconstruction: Politics, Culture and Society in France and Italy, 1943–1954* (Open University, first published 1990).

their national cultures attracted world-wide attention. As a method of study, comparison enables us to identify what was unique in one country's history and what was common to the development of a larger group of countries with similar economies and political institutions. France and Italy were part of the liberal, capitalist West during the Cold War; they combined democratic institutions with market economies and, by joining the Atlantic Alliance in 1949, accepted the military protection of the United States. Part of their history can be subsumed under that of the West: accelerated economic growth, a rising proportion of manufactures going to export markets, greater welfare spending, the achievement of full employment – these were near-universal phenomena in the western industrialized nations in our period.

Nevertheless, certain political and cultural factors set France and Italy apart from their allies and trading partners, and made them a distinctive 'pair' of societies. Without going into too great detail, some are worth mentioning here to signpost what lies ahead in this course. Perhaps the obvious socio-cultural difference between them and the Anglo-Saxon democracies was that the overwhelming majority of French and Italian people were baptised into the Catholic Church, and Protestants were tiny minorities. The strength of Catholicism in Italy lay behind the most successful religiously-based political party in post-war Europe: the Christian Democrat Party (or Democrazia Cristiana, hence DC). French Christian Democracy was important immediately after the war but its electoral support dwindled fairly quickly. Comparing them should help you understand the different relationship between religious culture and politics in the two societies. Again, in stark contrast to the other western democracies, France and Italy contained powerful Communist Parties: at national elections, Communist voters were between one in five and one in four of the electorate throughout our period. In no other western European democracy did electoral support for communism reach 5 per cent of voters in the 1950s and 1960s; in Britain, it was 0.2 per cent. The non-Communist left was also electorally significant in France and Italy, and – on paper at least – as committed to radical social change as the Communists. So it behoves us to ask why so many French and Italian people identified with the left, but also why – given this basis of support – the left was out of office for most of the period of our study.

In terms of their economies and social structures, France and Italy in the 1940s and 1950s differed sharply from Britain in having substantial proportions of their labour forces occupied in agriculture. Peasants – small farmers relying on family labour – constituted large social classes. Many of them did not speak standard French or Italian in the home and their ways of living varied from region to region. You will get a sense of two Italian regional cultures in the post-war years from Cesare Pavese's novel, *The Moon and the Bonfires* (the story is located in the valley of the Belbo in Piedmont), and from the extracts from Luchino Visconti's film, *La Terra Trema* (set in Sicily). With the contraction of agricultural employment, millions migrated to the cities. Italy was a comparatively undeveloped economy around 1950, and the social upheaval was more wrenching and traumatic than in France, but the rural exodus was *the* great transformation in both societies in our period.

Periodization

Our periodization is not rigid. Liberation is an obvious starting point because it represented a unique opportunity in French and Italian twentieth-century history for social renewal. The Fascist and Vichy regimes were morally bankrupt, and the élites and institutions that had allowed Mussolini and Marshal Pétain to come to power were scarcely less discredited. Businessmen stood accused of economic collaboration with the Nazi occupiers. The Catholic hierarchy was tainted by its open support for Hitler's anti-Bolshevik crusade and its muted response to the Holocaust. Resistance to fascism had empowered many ordinary people who believed they could participate in a 'remaking' of political and social institutions. Part One of the course is largely concerned with the frustration of these aspirations. There was a 'fresh start' in the sense that France and Italy were endowed with new constitutions (discussed in Unit 2) and both adopted universal adult suffrage by enfranchising women. Significant reforms were instituted on behalf of working-class families in France and landless peasants in Italy, and government acquired new powers of economic management. But the innovations fell far short of the radical social reconstruction many had anticipated in 1944. Inequalities of economic class and region in France and Italy in 1950 were little changed from the inter-war period.

We chose 1973 as the terminal date for the course because the energy crisis of that year brought to a close the great economic boom that underlay the social and cultural transformation of the preceding decades. We have occasionally ignored this end-point when to do otherwise would have left certain crucial developments 'hanging in the air'. It would have been perverse, for example, when discussing the changing status of French women in the 1960s and early 1970s, not to mention the Veil Law of 1975 legalizing abortion (Unit 23). Equally, no analysis of the role of Catholicism in Italy at the end of our period could ignore the divorce law referendum of May 1974, when the Church put its moral authority behind the campaign to repeal the law permitting divorce, and lost (Unit 29).

A bigger problem was deciding the historical watershed between the two parts of the course. The period covered in the predecessor course, A324 *Liberation and Reconstruction*, terminated in 1954, but in terms of this course a more appropriate date is 1958. That year saw the obvious 'break' in French political and constitutional history. The Algerian War, which had broken out in November 1954, destroyed the 'parliamentary' political system of the Fourth Republic. General de Gaulle returned to power on 29 May 1958 with the authority to draw up a new 'presidential' constitution, which the electorate endorsed by a large majority in the referendum of 28 September. 1958 was also a pivotal year economically because of the ratification of the Treaty of Rome (signed 25 March 1957), which instituted a common market among the founding states of the European Economic Community (France, Italy, Federal Germany, Belgium, the Netherlands and Luxemburg). The Italian economy entered the boom known as the 'industrial miracle' in 1958, although as in France the origins of rapid economic growth can be traced back much earlier.

In the history of the Catholic Church, 1958 is a 'watershed' date because of the death of Pope Pius XII and the election, in October, of John XXIII, the Pope who convoked the Second Vatican Council. Quite unexpectedly, John XXIII initiated profound changes in Catholic doctrine and worship, and in the Church's relations with the wider world.

A substantial part of your studies on AA304 will be devoted to the cinema, and in film history the 'watershed' came in 1959 with the release of two key 'New Wave' films (Alain Resnais' *Hiroshima mon amour*, and François Truffaut's *Les 400 coups* (*The 400 Blows*)). Jean-Luc Godard's *A Bout de souffle* (*Breathless*) went into production in 1959, but was released in 1960. The Italian cinema also produced masterpieces by Federico Fellini, Luchino Visconti and Michelangelo Antonioni at the turn of the decade: *La Dolce Vita*, *Rocco and his Brothers*, and *L'Avventura* were all released in 1960.

There are, therefore, compelling reasons for making the later 1950s the chronological break between the two halves of AA304, and you will find this reflected in the structure of the examination paper. That is not to claim that the schema 'fits' all historical developments, nor to deny the significance of prior turning points. The events of 1956 in the communist world and in international affairs had a momentous impact on France and Italy, as they did on Europe more generally. In February, at the Soviet Communist Party Congress, Nikita Khrushchev denounced the crimes of the Soviet dictator Joseph Stalin (who died 5 March 1953) in a secret speech that fairly soon leaked to the West. The revelations embarrassed the leaders of the French and Italian Communist Parties – who had participated in the 'cult' of a man now vilified as a mass murderer – and had a very sobering effect on 'fellow travelling' intellectuals. Most of them became totally disillusioned with Soviet Communism when Warsaw Pact forces crushed the Hungarian uprising in November. Almost simultaneously, French and British forces invaded Egypt in an attempt to topple Colonel Nasser's nationalist regime and (in the case of France) cut off external support for the Algerian insurrection. Under American pressure, France and Britain were forced into a humiliating withdrawal. For both states, it was a bitter lesson in the limits of their power in a world dominated by two superpowers.

2 Using Ginsborg and Gildea

We have prescribed Ginsborg and Gildea as set books for three reasons: firstly, to give you the background information necessary to put the cultural texts in historical context; secondly, to provide a narrative framework within which to make sense of the often bewildering political history of France and Italy after 1945. They offer authoritative explanations of why events unfolded as they did and not in some other way. (Why, for example, the immense desire and potential for radical reform in Italy between 1943 and 1945 was frustrated; why the Fourth Republic failed to survive the crisis generated by the Algerian War.) But they are not narrow political histories and the third reason for prescribing them is to help you understand the economic and social processes that transformed France and Italy into urbanized, prosperous and increasingly secularized societies. Economic and social modernization did *not* begin in 1945, but in the next decade or so it entered a new phase characterized by the mass consumption of hitherto élite luxuries (such as motor cars) and new durables (such as televisions). Women came to live more emancipated lives and young people constituted a new social actor. The chronology of this transformation was not identical: France entered it with a stronger industrial base, higher per capita income, and without the deadweight of agrarian poverty and backwardness found in the Italian south and islands. What the French call *laïcité* (the 'lay' tradition) was already a guiding principle of public institutions: Church and state had been separated in 1905 and organized religion excluded from state education; civil divorce – a key index of secularization – had been instituted in the nineteenth century. But there was a process of convergence which Ginsborg and Gildea will enable you to trace without blurring the distinctiveness of each society.

Ginsborg and Gildea are very different in style, presentation and length. Ginsborg was published to great acclaim in 1990, and is unlikely to be superseded as the outstanding history of post-war Italy. It combines continuous narrative, searching analysis of broad social and political forces, and rich local detail. An important theme of the book is the relationship of the Italian family to society and politics, and individual family histories illuminate the larger, national history. Gildea is much more succinct, has none of the local detail found in Ginsborg, and is organized into thematic chapters, not a continuous narrative. This has had unconventional results: the German Occupation and French Resistance are covered on pages 55–61 *after* an account of the May 1968 'events' on pages 51–5. But this makes sense in terms of Gildea's chapter organization: Chapter 3 is devoted, not to the Occupation, Resistance and Liberation in themselves, but to how the memory of these events resonated in French politics and culture up to the 1990s, when a former Vichy police official, Paul Touvier, was tried for crimes against humanity, and President Mitterand's youthful flirtation with the far right and his recruitment by the Vichy regime were closely scrutinized. You can always find your way around Gildea by referring to his chapter outline in the introduction.

Exercise In this exercise, we want you to 'fill out' your knowledge of Italy and France in the latter part of the Second World War by reading pages 8–17 and 39–59 of Ginsborg, and pages 30–5 and 57–62 of Gildea. Then answer the following questions.

1. Why was 8 September 1943 such a significant date in Italian history?
2. Both authors make clear that attacking the German Occupation forces was not the only dimension to violent resistance. What was the other dimension?
3. What were the different strands within the Italian and French Resistance movements?
4. What was the distinctive feature of French Resistance that made the situation at the Liberation very different in France as compared with

Italy? How were the divisions within the French Resistance expressed during the Liberation itself?

5 The Italian Communist leader, Palmiro Togliatti, returned home from exile in Moscow in March 1944, as did the French Communist leader, Maurice Thorez, in November: what political strategy did they persuade their respective parties to adopt? What impact did this have on the political situation in each country?

6 In what terms does Gildea describe the relationship between the Vichy regime and the Fourth Republic? Would the same terms be applicable to the relationship between the Fascist regime and the Italian state in 1944–46? (Bear in mind that Italy remained a monarchy until the referendum of June 1946. In considering this last question, look up the entries on 'judiciary' in Ginsborg's index.)

Specimen answers

1 On this day, King Victor Emmanuel and Marshal Badoglio made public the armistice they had secretly negotiated with the Allies. It concluded the turbulent 'forty-five days' since the fall of Mussolini on 25 July, during which the end of Fascism had been celebrated by enormous popular demonstrations. Unfortunately, protracted, supposedly secret, armistice negotiations had given the German army the opportunity to pour troops into Italy, and the peninsula was invaded from both north and south. (The Allied landings on the Italian mainland had begun on 8 July.) The 'blackest moment' in the history of the unified state (Ginsborg, p.13) nevertheless provoked a 'new spirit' of resistance, a refusal to submit.

2 The other dimension was civil war. In France, the Resistance forces engaged in a brutal struggle with the Vichy Militia in the months following the Allied landings. In the Salò Republic in the north of Italy, the Resistance struggle was as much against Italian blackshirt troops as against German divisions. The terrorization of the population in the north in December 1944, following General Alexander's unfortunate radio broadcast, was primarily the work of the Fascist national guard (Ginsborg, p.56).

3 Ginsborg identifies three strands of Italian armed resistance: the Communist Garibaldi Brigades (who comprised more than 70 per cent of the partisans in the early months), the 'Justice and Liberty' Brigades of the Action Party, and the Socialists. Other anti-Fascist parties contributed almost nothing. The French Resistance was divided between those who had rallied to de Gaulle's Free French movement (and who fought against Vichy forces in the French empire) and those who joined the clandestine movement within metropolitan France. In the latter, Communists were the most numerous element, but not as preponderant as in Italy. Catholics, Socialists and social conservatives also participated. Jean Moulin, de Gaulle's representative, had tried to tie together the 'external' and

'internal' strands but the underlying rivalry between Communist and non-Communist resistance could not be disguised (Gildea, p.58).

4 De Gaulle's presence made the Liberation of France fundamentally different from that of Italy. No Italian leader had his prestige and none could claim to represent his nation in the way de Gaulle represented France. He had the ambition to restore France's great power status and defend the integrity of its empire which no Italian leader could seriously entertain. De Gaulle was heartily disliked by the Allies, but they had grudgingly recognized his authority, armed his forces (recruited mainly in North Africa) and could see no alternative to recognizing him as Head of the Provisional Government (though he was greatly angered by their delay in so doing). He commanded a sizeable conventional army which took a notable part in the war's final phase and occupied part of defeated Germany. In terms of the domestic situation, it represented a considerable counterweight to the Communists in the *milices patriotiques*. They viewed the Liberation as an opportunity to settle scores with collaborators and to purge the administration and judiciary of Vichy sympathizers; revolutionary courts were set up by Committees of Liberation to dispense rough justice. De Gaulle insisted that the proper procedures of law and order and state power be re-established as quickly as possible.

5 The Communist leaders persuaded their parties to forswear revolutionary action and co-operate with the other anti-fascist forces in coalition governments. This was in accordance with the partition of Europe into Soviet and western spheres of influence agreed at Yalta, and Stalin had a powerful influence on the strategy followed by Thorez and Togliatti. It was in the Soviet interest to see France restored as a great power because this would tend to divide the western Allies. But in Togliatti's case the strategy was also influenced by the evolution of Italian Communist thinking during the years of repression, especially with regard to the argument put forward in Gramsci's *Prison Notebooks* that western Communists had to pursue a long 'war of position' in civil society, in alliance with other social forces, before they seized control of the state (Ginsborg, p.45). The impact of Communist strategy was to defuse a potentially revolutionary situation, and it meant that Communists became junior partners in the provisional governments formed in 1944. It is most unlikely that revolution would have succeeded in either country, so the strategy allowed the Communists to avoid debacle and build mass organizations in conditions of legality. Ginsborg argues that a very high price was paid for this achievement: national unity during Liberation crowded out all other objectives for the Communists, and they did not press for radical social reforms when the popular anti-fascist forces were at their strongest and conservative elements (such as the monarchy) utterly discredited.

6 Gildea draws a distinction between a sharp discontinuity between Vichy and post-war France in the 'political class' of elected representatives, and considerable continuity in the public administration, the judiciary and business élite. The vast majority elected to the first Constituent Assembly in October 1945 had not sat in parliament before the war (the thirty-two women elected had not, of course, been eligible) and four out of five claimed a record in the Resistance movement. Collaborators had been declared ineligible for election, and it was a convention of the Fourth Republic that only those who had gained some honour in the Resistance could legitimately hold office. As Gildea makes clear, men like Antoine Pinay, who had served Vichy and resisted only 'at the eleventh hour', fairly soon wangled their way back into national politics, but the turnover in parliamentary personnel was sweeping. Not so in the civil service: only a tiny proportion of administrators – 0.5 per cent – were dismissed after the Liberation (Gildea, p.60). Businessmen also escaped the purge very lightly.

From your reading of Ginsborg so far, you should have inferred considerable continuity between the Fascist regime and the 'Kingdom of the South': Togliatti swore allegiance to the king (as had Mussolini) and under Ivanoe Bonomi the old bureaucracy – a formidable obstacle to radical reform – was resurrected. There was a 'real restoration' under the very eyes of the left-wing parties (Ginsborg, p.53). The Allies' determination that no Committee of Liberation should have the slightest degree of executive or administrative authority reinforced the continuity in state personnel (p.70). Subsequently, Ginsborg informs us that the judges who had served under Fascism kept their posts and that the Fascist penal code remained in force (p.149; you should have picked this up using Ginsborg's index). This was a vital element in state continuity. Fascist Italy had dispensed with a 'political class' by suppressing parliamentary democracy, and free general elections were not held until June 1946, so the issue of political discontinuity did not arise in the same way as in France. There was, of course, a major new element in the political situation with the emergence of the Christian Democrats under Alcide De Gasperi, but they became the principal governing party in a state where most public institutions were unreformed. ❑

3 Culture, your cultural texts and the role of the intellectual

This course is, we must emphasize, not just about political and economic history. All that we associate with that imprecise term 'culture' is just as important. No single definition will satisfy everybody working in the humanities but most would agree there are two basic aspects to any national community's culture. One is the meanings, attitudes and values current within the community (though not necessarily shared; values are often contested, and attitudes vary according to social location). The other aspect is the symbolic forms and practices in which meanings, attitudes and values are expressed and/or embodied. (A symbolic form is any text or artefact that communicates its meaning through language or a sign-system akin to language. It could, for example, be a poem, a painting or a melody.) Cultures – even national cultures – differ from states in not having fixed boundaries, and many cultural networks 'spill over' national borders and language barriers. Catholicism is a pertinent example: the international community of believers share meanings and values, and participate in the same religious practices. In the 1940s and 50s, communism was akin to an international counterculture, though the events of 1956 accelerated the process by which western Communist parties defined 'national' roads to socialism.

The approach to culture in AA304 is quite conventional. Our starting point is the texts produced in 'the arts', including the so-called popular arts: literature, drama, the visual and plastic arts, music and the cinema. Regrettably, not all forms of art are represented – there is no poetry and only a 'taste' of music – but you will study a range of accessible and rewarding texts. Those adopted for Part One were selected as examples of 'political' – or, to use the term that became current after the Liberation, 'engaged' – art. We do not mean they are political propaganda (and therefore not worth serious analysis as art) but that they deal with political issues in a literary form and idiom (or dramatic or cinematic or painterly). For many in the 1940s, the paradigm form of political commitment was engaging in the resistance to fascism, and several texts reflect the centrality of that experience in making a generation of committed writers, artists and film makers. They include some short stories by Italo Calvino which you will study later in this unit, Pavese's *The Moon and the Bonfires,* and Roberto Rossellini's film *Rome, Open City,* which you will encounter in the units on Italian neo-realist cinema. Some of the paintings you will study can be interpreted as images of resistance. One of your tasks will be to analyse these texts as art (or as cultural constructs). This entails understanding their formal properties, relating them to a particular creative practice (whether it be painting, film making, writing for the stage, and so on) and situating them within aesthetic traditions and conventions. ('Realism' is one such tradition, which figures large in the first part of the course.) Your other task will be to use these texts as evidence for the formative historical experiences of resistance: being exposed to betrayal, torture and death; summarily executing informers in a brutal civil war; making comrades across social classes and ideologies; believing that resistance presaged social renewal.

The role of the intellectual

This emphasis on 'engagement' means we have to give some attention to the role of the intellectual in French and Italian society. Our word 'intellectual', when used to refer to someone with a scholarly or critical vocation, is borrowed from the French, *un intellectuel* (or in the case of a woman *une intellectuelle*). It only became widely used from 1898 when the writer Emile Zola intervened in the Dreyfus affair to accuse the military and civil authorities of deliberately denying justice to an innocent man. Interestingly, it was as much a term of opprobrium as of praise: nationalist writers dismissed their Dreyfusard opponents as *intellectuels*, simpletons or foreigners – as if they were much the same thing. In subsequent decades, *un intellectuel* came to be associated with a particular social role or even duty: that of intervening in public debate when basic political or social values were being contested. The intellectual did not just deal in abstractions; he or she communicated them.

This conception of the intellectual's role was especially powerful in the years following the Liberation. In Italy it owed a great deal to the posthumous reputation of Antonio Gramsci (d. 1937) the Communist leader imprisoned by Mussolini whose ideas and influence you have already encountered in Ginsborg. Central to Gramsci's thought is an extension of the concept of 'hegemony': he believed that a dominant class did not just exercise power through coercion, but also by persuading society generally that its way of seeing the world and human nature and relationships are the most 'natural'. It is the role of intellectuals to articulate and disseminate such a 'world view', to make it part of the 'common sense' of society. Gramsci never supposed that intellectuals were merely the spokespersons for class interests. For him, the 'exemplary' intellectual was the philosopher, historian and literary critic, Benedetto Croce (1886–1952), whose reputation and influence was such that Mussolini judged it unwise to exile him or to ban the bimonthly review he edited, *La Critica*. This does not mean Gramsci approved of Croce's thought and influence: simply that he considered Croce the prime example of how an intellectual could impose his authority on a nation's culture. Until 1943 Croce was the unwilling leader of the internal opposition, the only person who could say openly what he thought. His books on modern Italian literature and contemporary history influenced the post-war generation enormously. Even Togliatti, who disliked him, conceded that 'the whole intellectual life of the last half-century, the entire culture, is indebted to him. He was the inspiration, the leader of the last two generations of Italian intellectuals' *(Rinascita*, 1 May 1965). Croce was the great spokesman for liberalism and philosophical idealism – they comprised a 'world view' that Gramsci regarded as part of the 'common sense' of bourgeois society. In the 'war of position', the Italian Communist Party's task was to constitute an 'anti-Croce': a body of socialist thinking and values that would permeate through civil society prior to the seizure of power.

The French Communist Party did not produce a theorist of Gramsci's stature until Louis Althusser (1918–90) began to publish on Marxism in the mid 1960s. Before then, the 'model' intellectual in post-war France was Jean-Paul Sartre (1905–80), who was never a member of the Communist Party though extremely close to it between 1951 and 1956. Sartre only became a political animal after he was called up in 1939 and taken prisoner of war during the fall of France. Before then he was preoccupied with philosophy and literature, and indifferent to politics. Imprisonment politicized Sartre, partly by forcing him into the company of ordinary men, partly because camp life obliged him to 'live out' what had hitherto been an abstract philosophy of human freedom. When released because of bad eyesight he moved towards the intellectual resistance through membership of the Comité national des écrivains (though he was never exposed to physical danger). As the war drew to a close, Sartre entered a phase of exceptional creativity, and his growing influence stemmed partly from the ease with which he moved between different cultural forms. As well as a major philosophical treatise, *L'Être et le néant* ('Being and Nothingness') (1943), he published a trilogy of novels, *The Roads to Freedom,* wrote a string of successful plays, edited *Les Temps modernes* (an avant-garde monthly review), gave lectures on existentialism to packed audiences, and even appeared in films to publicize his ideas (you will see him in an extract from *La Vie commence demain* on Video-cassette 1). Sartre was only briefly involved in organized politics through participation in the Rassemblement démocratique et révolutionnaire (RDR) – a pressure group of dissident socialists formed in early 1948 as the Cold War opened a schism within the French intelligentsia that mirrored the division of Europe. The RDR wanted to construct a socialist Europe independent of the superpower blocs. Having preached commitment, Sartre felt he could scarcely avoid joining the RDR's executive when asked, though he anticipated it being a talking shop. In fact, Sartre's political interventions went far beyond his association with the RDR. He lent his name to several campaigns to right miscarriages of justice: one case was that of Ethel and Julius Rosenberg, executed in the USA in June 1953, after two years on 'death row', for spying for the Soviet Union. Not since the Dreyfus affair were French national passions so aroused by a judicial process; it provoked furious anti-Americanism in the French press. Another case was that of Henri Martin, a Communist sailor sentenced to five years' solitary confinement for distributing propaganda leaflets against the war in Indo-China. Sartre's prestige and his eloquent denunciations of McCarthyism and imperialism helped turn these cases into *causes célèbres.* As he moved closer to the Communist Party, Sartre became part of the public face of the Communist-inspired peace movement. He allowed himself to be put forward for the presidency of the Association France-USSR. In spite of the often virulent criticism levelled against him, he had an extraordinary authority in the post-war years as the 'conscience' of the broad left.

Communism and culture

Sartre's ambivalent attitude towards communism in the 1940s and 1950s, his public soul-searching on how far he should co-operate with the French Communist Party (PCF, Parti Communiste français) on major issues of the day, made him very representative of his milieu. After 1945 many workers and intellectuals believed that international communism represented the best hope for social progress, but a history of ruthless *realpolitik* had tainted its progressive reputation. Whether to support communism because of what it promised or reject it because of its unsavoury methods was a real quandary. In France only a narrow circle of intellectuals was sufficiently committed to communist ideals to join the Party, even briefly, but they included artists and writers of great distinction, such as Pablo Picasso, Fernand Léger and the poet,

Paul Eluard. In Unit 7 you will explore how painters drawn into the Communist orbit were caught in the tension between their revolutionary politics and the conservative pictorial style prescribed by the doctrine of 'socialist realism' – a stultifying orthodoxy imposed on Soviet art from the 1930s.

In Italy, the fact that all opposition parties had been outlawed under Mussolini actually made co-operation between the Communist and non-Communist left easier than in France, where political quarrels in the late 1940s and 50s were filled with echoes of the Communists' pre-war and wartime history. The memories of two events still rankled: in 1931, Stalin had surmised that capitalism was on the point of collapse, and ordered the western European Communist parties to treat the democratic socialists as the main political enemy (a disastrous strategy known as 'class against class'). Léon Blum, leader of the French Socialists in the 1930s, never again trusted the PCF; nor did other socialists of his generation. Even the formation of a Popular Front in 1934–35 (when Communists, Socialists and Radicals agreed on an electoral pact) did not remove the bitterness. The second event was the Nazi-Soviet alliance of August 1939, and the subsequent denunciation by the Communist International (wholly controlled by Stalin) of the war as 'an imperialist war'. The PCF was thrown into complete confusion: it voted for war credits, but it was declared an illegal organization. More than a quarter of its deputies and senators left the party and the main trade union federation, the CGT (Confédération Générale de Travail), severed its links. The Party's underground press took the line that imperialist fratricide was of no concern to the workers. Until June 1941, Communists were regarded as little better than traitors by many French people; Maurice Thorez was especially suspect because he had deserted the French army in early 1940 and made his way to Moscow via Belgium.

A further factor blighting the reputation of Communism was Stalinist political repression in the Soviet Union and in central Europe after 1945, and the revelations from defectors concerning the 'Gulag archipelago'. This became a much publicized and divisive issue in France after *Les Lettres françaises* (a Communist journal) attacked Victor Kravchenko's *I Chose Freedom* (the best-known account by a defector) as a concoction of the US Central Intelligence Agency. Kravchenko sued for libel, and between the offending article in November 1947 and the actual trial, the French press was full of the affair. It was against this background that Jean-Paul Sartre wrote *Les Mains sales* (published in English with the title *Crime passionnel*; you will study this in Unit 4), which had its first theatrical run between April and September 1948. The events in the play hark back to the assassination of Trotsky and it dramatizes to telling effect the ruthlessness with which communist party apparatuses had disposed of internal opposition. Yet the play's most attractive character is the party boss who is convinced that the objective of realizing socialism warrants any Machiavellian stratagem. 'History', he feels, is on his side. The play subtly explores why communism was a source of attraction to bourgeois intellectuals, and a source of despair.

Albert Camus' *Les Justes,* which you will study in conjunction with *Crime passionnel,* though in less detail, has a similar theme, for it deals with the circumstances in which a political assassination is morally warranted. The play is set in Tsarist Russia, but there can be no doubt as to its relevance for Camus' own time. He returned to the theme in an extended political essay *L'Homme révolté* ('The Rebel') (published in 1951), which provoked an acrimonious rupture with Sartre and prolonged controversy among French intellectuals. To his admirers Camus spelt out the moral nihilism and political cynicism of communism more clearly than any other writer; to Sartre and most of the intellectual left, he had simply become an apologist for the status quo. We have selected passages for you to study in Unit 12, although for our purposes the controversy over *The Rebel* is as important as the text itself. Some signposting as to its most controversial claim will be helpful. Camus traced the totalitarianism of communism, and its amoral subordination of means to ends, to the historical determinism of Marxist doctrine. That is to say, Marx's claim to have discovered the 'natural laws of capitalist production' had been twisted by his followers into the pseudo-scientific dogma that the triumph of socialism was historically inevitable. The golden age promised by Marxist prophecy had served to justify dictatorship and violence. Camus concluded by reasserting the values of liberal individualism – which damned him as a 'bourgeois moralist' in Sartre's eyes.

4 The themes of Part One of the course

We have organized Part One around four nodal points or themes: (1) reconstruction; (2) the left; (3) the Roman Catholic Church; and (4) the United States. We will now say a little more about each of them.

Reconstruction

Exercise Reconstruction covers the process of rebuilding the political, social and economic systems in France and Italy after 1945. It is best introduced by looking at the social expectations entertained by key intellectuals as the war drew to a close. Turn to the booklet *Documents and Texts 1* and find items 1(a) and (b). These consist of extracts from two editorials by Albert Camus, which appeared in the French Resistance newspaper, *Combat* ('Fight' or 'Battle'), at the time of the Liberation of Paris. Your reading of Gildea should have given you the broad context for this document. Do you think Camus believed that there was more to Liberation than getting rid of the Germans and, if so, why?

Discussion The answer to the first part of the question, of course, is 'yes'. Camus actually says as much when he writes (in the first extract): 'But if it [the fight against Nazi Germany] is the toughest of the battles for which the whole of France is mobilized, it is not the only one we must fight'. The reason, as he goes on to make clear in both extracts, was that Liberation ought to involve changes inside France as well as the expulsion of the enemy forces from its soil. It was no use simply going back to the old order which had existed before the war. Not only was the latter unjust, but it was also to blame for the defeat and

Occupation. The opportunity afforded by the Liberation had to be used, in Camus' view, to rebuild France on a more democratic and egalitarian basis. As we shall see, similar sentiments existed in Italy, and indeed almost everywhere else in liberated Europe. ❑

The rebuilding process referred to by Camus is covered in Units 2 and 10 (which deal with changes in the political systems and economies) and in Unit 13, which is devoted to the role of women in society. You will be given most of the background you need to understand these developments when you come to study the units in question, but you may find it helpful if we make one or two general points here. First of all, at the end of the Second World War, France and Italy were 'balanced' economies in the sense that employment in agriculture was roughly equal to employment in industries and services. According to the 1954 census, 26 per cent of men in France worked in agriculture, and in Italy no fewer than 42 per cent (1951 census). For comparative purposes we might note that in Britain the proportion was only 6.5 per cent. We should add that there is nothing sexist about restricting the analysis to men in this instance. The inclusion of women, unfortunately, produces statistical complexities which would take too long to unravel. France and Italy were also poorer countries by comparison with Britain. Economists use the concept of Gross National Product (GNP) per head to give a rough idea of the comparative wealth of different countries. This is arrived at by dividing the value of the total output of goods and services in a particular country by the number of inhabitants, and expressing the answer in a common currency, which is usually US dollars. In 1948, annual GNP per head in Italy is reckoned to have been $229, as compared with $417 in France and $773 in Britain. Were we to look at other indices of economic development – such as the output of iron, steel, electricity and motor vehicles – we would have the same broad picture confirmed: Italy was comparatively 'backward' in economic terms, with a narrow industrial base, and a domestic market restricted by low purchasing power. France was wealthier and more industrialized, but average income was substantially below the British level. Not surprisingly, government-inspired attempts to raise industrial output were a basic aspect of reconstruction in France and Italy.

Reconstruction had political aspects, chiefly because parliamentary and liberal institutions had to be restored in both states. In Italy, these had never taken deep root. The country had been unified more as a result of conquest by the kingdom of Piedmont in the north-west than by a democratic process. Italy's democratic base had been simply too weak to bear the strain imposed by participation in the First World War, and the great social and political turmoil of the post-war years. In 1922 the king had invited Mussolini to become Prime Minister after the so-called march on Rome, and by 1926 the latter had suppressed all political opposition and established a single-party dictatorship. As you will have gathered from Ginsborg, Mussolini's decision to enter the Second World War was a disaster for Italy and the undoing of his regime.

France had a sturdier democratic and republican tradition. After 1871 the French political community had found in the Third Republic the regime that divided it least. Under the Republic, France was endowed with a great colonial empire, a compromise was reached in the conflict between Church and state, and the nation survived the ordeal of the First World War. The French fascist leagues had threatened the parliamentary regime with mob violence in February 1934, but had insufficient popular support to topple the Republic, or to prevent the return, in 1936, of a left-wing, Popular Front government led by Léon Blum. The relationship of the authoritarian Vichy regime with the Third Republic was constitutionally problematic. De Gaulle denied that Vichy had any legitimacy. When he was asked on 26 August 1944 to proclaim the inauguration of a new Republic from the balcony of the Hotel de Ville in Paris, he refused on the grounds that he himself incarnated the continuity of the Third Republic. Since it had not ceased to exist, there was no need to resuscitate it. This was a loftily personal reading of recent history. Marshal Pétain had been asked to form a *union nationale* government in June 1940 in a perfectly constitutional way, and the decision to seek an armistice had been greeted with almost universal relief. The National Assembly which had been elected in 1936 voted overwhelmingly to amend the constitution in July, and to grant full powers to Pétain (including the power to draft a new constitution). Public support for the new state seems to have been virtually unanimous; it faced no serious dissent before the summer of 1941. After the Liberation most people affected to despise the Vichy regime, but they tacitly endorsed the deputies' decision of July 1940 that had brought it into being. Very few wanted to restore the Third Republic, but there was no consensus on the type of constitution best suited for post-war France. In many ways political reconstruction was delayed until 1958, when de Gaulle won a popular mandate for a 'presidential' constitution that he had been unable to impose on the political parties between 1944 and 1946.

The left

Were this a single-discipline course in political history, the emphasis given to the left would seem perverse. Between 1943 and 1973, left-wing parties in France and Italy had only brief periods in office: the most important was the three years between the Liberation and the onset of the Cold War when Communists and Socialists participated in coalition governments alongside Christian Democrats. Democratic Socialists continued to participate in the governing coalitions of the Fourth Republic, but they represented only about a third of the left-wing electorate. After 1958 the Gaullists and their allies – who occupied the centre-right of the political spectrum – dominated national politics. In Italy the DC was the hegemonic political party from 1948 until the 1990s. They did form centre-left coalitions with the democratic socialists in the 1960s, but always as the dominant party.

But from the point of view of a multidisciplinary course looking at cultural history, and the connections between culture and politics, privileging the left makes a great deal of sense. All the writers, artists and film makers considered in Part One of the course were on the left at the Liberation, and most retained their left-wing sympathies. Despite his anti-Communism and the rupture with

Sartre, Camus continued to see himself as a democratic socialist, and energetically supported left-wing causes.

The Roman Catholic Church

At the Liberation, Catholicism was a primordial source of the meanings, values and attitudes shared (and contested) by the French and Italians. For most, it still defined the rites of passage from baptism to extreme unction. Artists of all kinds continued to draw on the rich resources of Catholic imagery and symbolism. Probably the most esteemed French novelist at this time was François Mauriac, a self-consciously Catholic writer. Alongside its traditional role as a cultural and moral source, Catholicism acquired a new – or at least reinvigorated – political role during Liberation and reconstruction. You will learn more about the organization and doctrine of the Church in Unit 5, and it suffices to say here that it was a more 'imperious' organization than it has become since the Second Vatican Council of 1962–65. It was more dogmatic in matters of doctrine and less tolerant in its attitude towards other denominations and faiths. Most importantly, it did not regard religion and the state as 'separate spheres'. The papacy and the Catholic bishops believed that instructing the faithful politically was as much part of a priest's vocation as giving spiritual and moral guidance. Coupled with its disciplined and strongly hierarchical organization, which extended its influence into all walks of society, this attitude made it a force to be reckoned with in most aspects of French and Italian life.

Not surprisingly it had been chronically difficult to accommodate Catholicism in the secular nation state, and anti-clericalism was a strong presence in both countries. Recent history seemed to demonstrate that the Church was happiest cohabiting with right-wing authoritarianism. In 1929 Mussolini had reached an agreement (or concordat) with the Pope which, among other things, recognized Catholicism as the state religion and the Vatican City as a sovereign state. While relations between Fascism and the Church were never entirely smooth, the papacy's blistering condemnations of 'atheistic communism' confirmed the view of many on the left that, as far as official Catholicism was concerned, Fascism was definitely the lesser of two evils. The initial support of the French Church for the Vichy regime was interpreted in much the same way.

In Unit 5 we will examine how Catholicism came to terms with the aspirations unleashed by Resistance and Liberation, and how far it was able to influence the process of reconstruction in ways that would preserve its own position.

The United States

'It meant so many things, America!', wrote Simone de Beauvoir in the volume of her autobiography covering the period just after the Liberation. '[I]ts jazz, cinema and literature had nourished our youth [...] [It] was also the country which had sent our deliverance; it was the future on the march; it was abundance and infinite horizons; it was a crazy magic lantern of legendary images' (*Force of Circumstance*, p.25). Similarly, Cesare Pavese wrote that, around 1930,

> [...] a lot of young Italians looked in their books and discovered America. [...] For many, the encounter with Caldwell, Steinbeck, Saroyan, and Lewis broke open the first breathing-hole to liberation, offered the first hint that not everything in the culture of the world finished with Fascism. [...] After several years of study we comprehended that America was not *another* land, *another* historical beginning, but merely the gigantic theatre where, with more frankness than was possible anywhere else, the drama of everybody was being enacted.
>
> ('Yesterday and today', *L'Unità*, 3 August 1947; translated in Heiney, *America in Modern Italian Literature*, pp.245–8)

These two quotations will give you a good idea of what the United States meant to many French and Italian intellectuals during the 1930s and 1940s: an exhilarating example, a beacon of freedom in the darkness of fascism and occupation, and a deliverer.

The United States had an economic power that eclipsed that of all other industrialized countries and was in a position to reshape the international economic order. Already the richest country in the world before the Second World War, the United States increased its wealth by almost two-thirds in real terms between 1938 and 1945, and its GNP per head in 1948 stood at $1,523, double that of Britain. It was inevitable that the war-ravaged countries liberated by the Americans would turn to them for help in the process of reconstruction, as indeed Britain itself was forced to do.

It was equally inevitable that such help would have enormous influence on the countries concerned. The Soviet leader, Joseph Stalin, said in April 1945: 'This war is not as in the past; whoever occupies a territory also imposes on it his own social system. Everyone imposes his own system as far as his army can reach. It cannot be otherwise.' He was not far wrong. The division between communist and capitalist Europe, or between the eastern bloc and the 'free world' if you prefer, did indeed roughly coincide with the division between those countries liberated by the British and the Americans and those liberated by the Russians. And it was American influence, in all spheres, which soon became predominant in the former.

For this reason it is vital that this influence be examined. Why and how was it exercised – in literature, films, art and popular culture, as well as in politics and economics – and to what extent did it modify the vision of reconstruction held by those pressing for radical change? Units 6 and 15 in particular will be devoted to this issue, but references to it will appear throughout the course.

5 Italo Calvino: *Adam, One Afternoon*

For the rest of this unit we shall study a collection of Italian short stories in two ways: firstly as artistic creations in their own right, but secondly, also as expressions of the period in which they were produced. It is, of course, impossible completely to separate the two. A work of art is bound to bear the stamp of its time and cannot be fully understood in isolation from it. We shall, however, go beyond the acquisition of sufficient 'background' information to aid the comprehension of the individual work of art. We shall also try to use the latter as a means of understanding the entire period we are studying. In this way we hope to help you come to grips with the perennially fascinating problem of the relationship between art and society.

Italo Calvino (1923–85) is one of Italy's best-known post-war writers. We have chosen as a set text for this course one of his early works, a collection of short stories written between 1945 and 1952. Most of Calvino's early short stories were originally published in periodicals. Some of these, like Elio Vittorini's *Il Politecnico* (of which more will be said in Unit 3), were of some significance in Italian political and cultural life, but none of them enjoyed a large readership. In 1947 Calvino published his first novel, *Il sentiero dei nidi di ragno*, translated into English as *The Path to the Nest of Spiders*. The novel was a minor literary sensation in Italy and won for its young author one of the lesser known literary prizes. It was this success that doubtless prompted Calvino and his publisher to issue a collection of his short stories, which they did in 1949, albeit with the relatively small print run of 1,500 copies. This collection forms the basis of the text you are about to study.

You should be aware, however, of some important differences between the original Italian collection and the one you are reading. In the first place, the title is different. Although the story 'Adam, One Afternoon' was also the first in the Italian collection, the latter appeared under the title of one of the other stories, *Ultimo viene il corvo*, or 'The Crow Comes Last'. Secondly, only two-thirds of the original thirty stories which appeared in *Ultimo viene il corvo* are contained in *Adam, One Afternoon*. Moreover, the final (and longest) story in the English translation, 'The Argentine Ant', was not in the Italian collection at all, not having been written until 1952, three years after the Italian volume was published. Your guess as to the reasons for these differences is as good as ours.

If you have not done so already, you should now read *Adam, One Afternoon*. Reading the complete volume will give you the necessary background for the discussion of 'realism' and 'neo-realism' that follows. Further on in the unit, we will look more closely at particular stories. Since the stories are not printed in chronological order, you will find it helpful to pencil in the date of each one, either in the contents list of your copy, or at the beginning or end of the story itself. These dates are important, not only for 'situating' a story in its historical context, but also because ignorance of them can lead to error. One critic, for example, wrote that *Ultimo viene il corvo* (published in 1949) contained a more disillusioned portrait of the Italian Resistance than *Il sentiero dei nidi di ragno* (published in 1947).

Unfortunately, one of the stories cited in support of this judgement, which appears in your edition as 'Going to Headquarters', was written in 1945, two years before *Il Sentiero*! Anyway, the dates are as follows:

Adam, One Afternoon	1947
The Enchanted Garden	1948
Father to Son	1946
A Goatherd at Luncheon	1948
Leaving Again Shortly	1946
The House of the Beehives	1947
Fear on the Footpath	1946
Hunger at Bévera	1947
Going to Headquarters	1945
The Crow Comes Last	1946
One of the Three is Still Alive	1947
Animal Wood	1948
Seen in the Canteen	1946
Theft in a Cake shop	1946
Dollars and the Demi-Mondaine	1947
Sleeping like Dogs	1947
Desire in November	1948
A Judgment	1947
The Cat and the Policeman	1948
Who put the Mine in the Sea?	1948
The Argentine Ant	1952

Figure 1.1 *Italo Calvino at a meeting of the* Circolo della stampa *('press club'), Palermo, 6 July 1955. Photo: Giulio Einaudi Editore.*

Italo Calvino was actually born in Cuba, but his parents, who were both scientists, brought him back to San Remo on the north-western coast of Italy in 1925. His father was the director of a horticultural experimental station and readers of Calvino's work will soon notice the influence of this background in the precision with which he customarily describes plants and trees. His earliest political sympathies were with anarchism, but in 1944 he applied to join the Communist Party and, evading the call-up of Mussolini's Italian Social Republic, he went off to join a Communist Resistance unit in the Ligurian foothills which he had earlier explored with his father. After the Liberation he enrolled as a student at the University of Turin. Initially, he followed in his parents' footsteps and studied agriculture, but he soon switched to literature and in 1947 graduated with a dissertation (which all Italian undergraduates have to write) on the novelist, Joseph Conrad. He then joined the staff of the famous Italian publishing house of Einaudi and also wrote regularly for the

Communist Party's daily newspaper, *L'Unità* ('Unity'), and other left-wing periodicals.

Calvino was so enthusiastic a Communist during this period that he was asked to take over the running of a weekly paper for young Communists, but he refused. One reason, apparently, was that the then secretary of the Italian young Communists (and later of the whole party), Enrico Berlinguer, had told him: 'If you start out on that task, if you become an official, don't kid yourself that you'll be able to go on writing novels' (Spriano, *Le Passioni di un decennio*, p.17). He resigned from the Communist Party in July 1957, in the wake of the Russian suppression of the Hungarian revolt the previous November, but continued to vote for it. In the meantime he achieved even greater success with his stories and novels and, at the time of his death from a stroke in 1985, was regarded by many as Italy's greatest contemporary writer.

To go back to Turin and the Liberation, Giuseppe Bonura, an Italian authority on Calvino, has written that the city was the place 'in which the resistance atmosphere was breathed more deeply and where the possibility of creating a new culture was scented with a full understanding of all its implications' (Bonura, *Invito alla lettura di Calvino*, p.23). Some might argue that Milan was equally, if not more, important. But there is no disputing the 'new culture' that was being created in Italy at the time; it was associated with the term 'neo-realism'. It is clear from the very word that neo-realism cannot be properly understood without reference to realism. So what is realism and how does it relate to neo-realism?

Exercise Turn to *Documents and Texts 1* and read item 2, the 'Introduction' to Millicent Marcus's book, *Italian Film in the Light of Neorealism*. This is quite long and its argument may well strike you as dense and complex. Don't worry if you feel you have not fully come to grips with the issues it discusses, for they will be discussed again later in the course in Units 8–9 and 16, so you will have other opportunities to think about them. For the moment, just try to answer the following three questions:

1. What does Marcus tell us about realism as an artistic theory and, in particular, to what extent does it simply mean 'true to life'?
2. Where did the nineteenth-century Italian realists, and especially the novelist, Giovanni Verga, fit into this picture?
3. What, according to Marcus, is the essential difference between Italian realism and neo-realism and why did the latter develop? Note that although Marcus's book deals with the cinema, and there are therefore repeated references to film, she clearly believes that you cannot divorce the discussion of neo-realism in the cinema from that of neo-realism in literature. As she puts it, 'Despite the scarcity of cross-influences between the literature and cinema of neorealism, the two media shared enough common source material to enable us to consider them parallel manifestations of the same aesthetic and ideological impulses.' What you are doing in this exercise, basically, is trying to discover what these 'aesthetic and ideological impulses' were.

Discussion

1 Marcus argues that realism is a highly elusive term, capable of many and occasionally contradictory meanings. It is therefore best understood in a specific context and stylistically, indeed, it 'is always defined in opposition to something else, be it romanticism in nineteenth-century literature, modernism in twentieth-century art, nominalism in medieval philosophy, or idealism in eighteenth-century thought'. This is more important than what Marcus calls 'mimetic accuracy', and which we would describe, in accordance with the terms of the question, as meaning 'true to life'.

According to Marcus, there is a conflict between what she calls 'classical realism', based on the ideas of the Greek philosopher Aristotle, which relates less to surface manifestations of reality than to some underlying ideal pattern which it is the artist's duty to express, and nineteenth-century realism (especially in France), which professes a scrupulous 'warts and all' objectivity, rooted in the scientific advances and theories of the period and which later became known as 'naturalism'. Indeed, Marcus argues that:

> [...] the survival of classical realism goes far to explain the inconsistencies and contradictions of modern realist theory, which demands that art be at once objective and politically *engagé*, that it be disinterested yet didactic, limited to the phenomena of empirical experience yet attuned to the underlying patterns that determine it, a styleless record of material reality yet formed and harmonized by human reason. These disparate claims on the artwork testify to the continual pull of classical realism on the one hand, and nineteenth-century scientism on the other. The quest for an ideal movement toward perfection in the world order and the role of the work of art to bear witness to, and convince us of, its presence would explain the didactic, politically interested, synthetic impulse of the tradition. Nineteenth-century realism, with its denial of preconceived systems of meaning and its insistence on a scientifically verifiable, objective approach to the material world, would explain the disinterested, styleless, superficial tendencies of the theory.

Marcus's reference, just before this passage, to the ideas of the Hungarian Marxist critic, George Lukács, reminds us that there is yet another brand of realism to add to classical realism and nineteenth-century realism: namely, socialist realism. The outgrowth of Marxist theory, the Russian Revolution and the experience of the Soviet state, this concept is much closer to the classical than to the nineteenth-century variant. Speaking at the first all-Soviet Congress of Writers in August 1934, one of the Communist Party's leading ideologists, Andrei Zhdanov, of whom you will hear more in Units 3, 7 and 11, told his audience that Soviet writers must depict life 'not scholastically, not lifelessly, not simply as "objective reality ", but [...] in its revolutionary development'. '[T]he truthfulness and historical concreteness of artistic description', he went on, 'must be combined with the task of the ideological transformation and education of the working people in the spirit of socialism.' It was this approach, which explicitly harnessed art to the aims and objectives of the Communist Party, that Zhdanov defined as socialist realism.

2 Nineteenth-century Italian realism, and particularly the ideas of Verga discussed by Marcus, seem to have been a mixture of the classical and modern approaches. On the one hand, Verga insists on the need for scientific accuracy in writing. On the other, he also speaks of the necessity of representing reality 'as it ought to have been'.

3 Towards the end of the introduction, Marcus draws what she sees as the fundamental distinction between the nineteenth-century Italian realists and their neo-realist successors. The former, she argues, were essentially passive in their attitude. Even when they discovered reality 'as it ought to have been', they did not appear to believe that they could influence events so as to bring this reality about. The neo-realists, on the other hand, were active in their approach. They believed that they could, and should, do something about it. Marcus suggests that the experience of the Resistance was responsible for the change from the resignation of the nineteenth-century realists to the dynamism of the neo-realists. She writes:

> This movement gave its generation the confidence to believe that the ideal could impinge upon the real and that man could forge his own destiny in accordance with his highest moral promptings. Art, which for Verga bore passive witness to the underlying dynamism of the historical process, becomes the instrument for motivating radical change in the hands of the neorealists.

Marcus does not go into detail, but Doug Thompson has explained at more length why the Resistance was the catalyst which produced neo-realism. He points out, for example, that just as Italian unification was the work of a small ruling class, so Italian culture had been the exclusive possession of that minority. Even the use of the Italian language had cut it off from the bulk of the population. What the Resistance did, says Thompson, was first of all to unite the Italian people more effectively than they had ever been before, and secondly, through the medium of a whole host of individual accounts of experience in the Resistance, whether fact or fiction, to take the first steps towards the creation of a genuinely mass culture. He writes:

> The political parties of the Left, in particular, though by no means exclusively, were determined that art in all its forms should be made, and remain, accessible to the people as a whole, which meant ensuring that its language should remain common to all, for the creation of metalanguages and mystiques – the possessions always of élites – was one of the traditional manifestations of the divide-and-rule principle which had always operated in Italian society.
>
> (Thompson, 'The historical and literary premises of "neo-realism"', p.46)

In conclusion, it is necessary to say something about the relationship between neo-realism and socialist realism. At the risk of over-simplification, we would argue that while there was a basic similarity between the two, in that both forms of realism were intended to assist in that process of radical transformation which it was hoped the Resistance would bring about, there was also the potential for considerable conflict. This was because neo-realism was rooted in individual experience and reflection, whereas socialist realism was rooted in the needs and dogmas, not only or even mainly of the Italian Communist Party, but in those of the Communist Party of the Soviet Union.

Calvino set out his own relationship to neo-realism in an important Preface to the 1964 reprint of his first novel, *The Path to the Nest of Spiders*. In the light of our previous discussion, two points in particular emerge which clearly place his early works in the neo-realist canon. First of all, there is the crucial significance of the Resistance experience. As Calvino put it:

> We had experienced the war, and we younger people – who had been barely old enough to join the partisans – did not feel crushed, defeated, 'beat'. On the contrary, we were victors, driven by the propulsive charge of the just-ended battle, the exclusive possessors of its heritage [...] Having emerged from an experience – a war, a civil war – that had spared no one and had established immediacy of communication between the writer and his audience, we were face to face, equals, filled with stories to tell.

(Calvino, 'Preface', p.v)

Much of Calvino's early work was indeed about the Resistance itself. Six of the stories in *Adam, One Afternoon* have a Resistance setting: 'Fear on the Footpath', 'Hunger at Bévera', 'Going to Headquarters', 'The Crow Comes Last', 'One of the Three is Still Alive' and 'Animal Wood'. In the original Italian edition, *Ultimo viene il corvo*, there were four more. Moreover, *The Path to the Nest of Spiders* was a novel about the Resistance.

Secondly, there is the concern with ordinary people, with their environment, and with their everyday language. According to Calvino:

> 'Neo-realism' was not a school [...] It was a collection of voices, largely marginal, a multiple discovery of the various Italys, even – or particularly – the Italys previously unknown to literature [...] We had drawn a line, or rather a triangle – Verga, Vittorini, Pavese – from which to set out, each on the bases of his own local vocabulary and his own landscape.

(Calvino, 'Preface', pp.vii–viii)

Regional influence is very marked in *Adam, One Afternoon*. Stories like 'Hunger at Bévera' and 'Fear on the Footpath' are peppered with local allusions and the landscape is lovingly described in these and many of the other stories. As for 'local vocabulary', Calvino does use a number of dialect words and expressions, while there is a specific reference to dialect and its social connotations in 'A Goatherd at Luncheon' (see pp.30–1).

There is, however, a third point which also needs to be made because it bears upon one of the themes of the course: the influence of the United States.

Calvino freely acknowledges the influence of American writers. As he wrote in the Preface to *The Path to the Nest of Spiders*:

> We had just ended our partisan activity when we discovered (first in fragments published in magazines, then the whole book) a novel about the [civil] war in Spain that [Ernest] Hemingway had written six or seven years before: *For Whom the Bell Tolls*. It was the first book in which we recognized ourselves. This was where we began transforming into narrative themes and sentences that [which] we had seen, felt, lived.
>
> (Calvino, 'Preface', p.xvi)

It was not just Hemingway's subject, which dealt of course with another struggle against fascism, that appealed to the Italian neo-realists, but also his narrative style. For example, in both his novels and short stories Hemingway makes extensive use of dialogue. This is not usually of an elaborate kind, but consists of relatively brief exchanges, with a minimum of explanatory comment. For comparison with Calvino, look at the dialogue between Maria-nunziata and the gardener's boy, Libereso, in the title story of *Adam, One Afternoon*.

Literary analysis of *Adam, One Afternoon*

Let us begin in this section with a closer look (written by Dennis Walder of the course team) at the title story from *Adam, One Afternoon* in order to get some idea of the kind of thing it is, and how it works. 'But', you may object, 'I know what it is. It's a short story, and what it does is entertain and perhaps inform me.' This is fair enough, but are things really quite as simple as that? Not only can you read something with more or less care as to what the words on the page actually mean; you can also read it with more or less thought as to how far your habits of mind are enabling you to see what is there and what is not. We all, often quite unconsciously, adopt an approach to what we read which depends on what we think we are reading for. This determines not only how we read, but what we find when we do so.

Later in the unit, we shall be looking at these stories from the viewpoint of the historian, trying to discover what they tell us about Italy during the period we are studying. But for the moment let us concentrate on these stories as literary texts. What is special about them? First of all, they are fiction and so, literally, not true. But, as you will be aware if you have studied literature, there is an assumption that what literature conveys is another kind of truth, which may be harder to uncover, but which is, if the literary text is any good, worth uncovering. And the way to do this is to begin by laying out the story *as a text* and to examine, not only the words on the page, but also our own approach to them, in order to uncover things that we failed to notice before and also things we did not recognize before in ourselves and the world in which we live, especially things we usually take for granted.

Some literary critics and theorists suggest that *all* our responses to a text are determined by more or less unconscious social assumptions or 'ideology'. We are not working on that assumption, but it is a possibility you should keep in mind. We assume that there is a more active, indefinable or at least *changing* relationship between readers and texts, which does not leave us with fixed or simple responses to the questions we ask. It is one of the more obvious features of worthwhile and lasting cultural products that they have a potential for unceasing reinterpretation, a continuing openness, which prevents us from definitively tying them down to one meaning or another. We also need to remember all the time that what we are dealing with is artefacts (stories, novels, plays, films, pictures, and so on), and not 'real life'. Concentrating on the detail – in this case the words on the page – helps us to see all this.

Exercise We might as well start right at the beginning, with the first two pages of the title story, *Adam, One Afternoon*. Let us ask ourselves: what kind of writing is this, and how does it work? To help, try noting down points about how the story is told, from what point of view, and what sort of tone it has. Remembering that this is a translation, jot down any features of the language that strike you as odd, anything unexplained. What do you think the title means?

Discussion To begin with, this struck me as precise and succinct descriptive prose: 'The new gardener's boy had long hair which he kept in place by a piece of stuff tied round his head with a little bow.' (By the way, according to the original Italian, he is a boy-gardener, *ragazzo-giardiniere*, and not a gardener's boy.) The first paragraph gives us a character observed by another: it is a partial view, which entices us to want to know more about him, as does the oddity of his appearance mentioned in the first line. He is *different*: why? The point of view is what is called 'omniscient', yet it is also *selective*. The narrator tells us what Maria-nunziata thinks and observes, but not Libereso. Indeed, that is also what keeps up our interest, isn't it? The boy's actions, feelings and thoughts are not reported or explained at all, except in so far as they are implicit in his behaviour and dialogue, whereas we are taken inside the girl's consciousness. In other words, we are encouraged to identify with her and, perhaps, sympathize with her. The boy we view from outside; he is as enigmatic as his name. 'D'you want to see something nice?' the boy asks. Is there any erotic implication in this question? After all, these are adolescents, aren't they? And although the girl's legs are described as 'thin and childlike', her body 'under the folds of her apron, was already round and ripe'. Like a fruit perhaps, in a garden? But it is perhaps anticipating the conclusion of the story, when a frog and a lot of little frogs suddenly appear between her legs, as if by magic. What we make of this depends partly on the tone, but that in which the exchanges between the two adolescents is conveyed seems cool, dispassionate and possibly amused. It is hard to be sure, since the narrator sticks so closely to description, dialogue and to one character's point of view.

The language is ordinary, everyday prose. Indeed, its 'everydayness' is emphasized by such little touches as the sharply observed image of the boy watering the nasturtiums 'as if pouring out coffee and milk' (in the original: *come versasse caffelatte*). What could be more ordinary? We believe in its reality. On the other hand, there is the strangeness, even mystery, of the boy's appearance, his name – which is then explained – and his behaviour: mysterious to the girl and therefore mysterious to us. Finally, what has the story to do with *Adam, One Afternoon*? Who is 'Adam'? It is another mystery.

The key surely lies in the strange, mysterious resonance to what is happening, the feeling conveyed throughout of things left hidden and unsaid. This is a garden. That is emphasized from start to finish. In it are two young people, adolescents who seem innocent of sex. At least, he may be knowing, but the girl is not. This is confirmed by their names: his representing freedom and hers the Virgin Mary. The garden is full of plants and animals. It is fertile, and its fertility is confirmed by the ending. In other words, what we are witnessing is a little fictional reworking of the Adam and Eve story – hence the title. Ironically, however, it is the story *reversed*, for on this occasion Adam tempts Eve, who remains a virgin. On another level, the story could be interpreted as showing that left-wing freethinkers tempt Christians and fail. Or do they? What about those little frogs? ❑

There is a lot going on here within a short space of narrative. The point is that we have to concentrate on this narrative very closely even to begin to get to grips with it. This is quite independent of whatever historical information we may derive from it, or even of the fact, revealed by an Italian critic, that the characters of both Libereso and Maria-nunziata were based on real people and the story on an actual incident. It is, after all, primarily a short story asking to be read as such. This means attending first to the words on the page, the language. But it also involves attending to such matters as narrative technique, tone, characterization, dialogue, mental processes, action, image or symbol, and finally, theme or 'moral'. With Calvino this last is characteristically obscure, enigmatic or playful. We have made some suggestions as to the story's meaning, but in his work it is always difficult to tell where the everyday ends and the strange or mysterious begins.

Calvino's use of fantasy

Dennis Walder's reference in the last section to this tension between the everyday and the strange or mysterious brings us back to Millicent Marcus's discussion of the nature of realism. Do you remember that she said that realism, as a stylistic term, was always defined in terms of opposition to something else? Well, another 'opposite' to realism is fantasy, and Calvino later became well known for his 'Fantasies'. Indeed, it would probably be safe to say that he is now much more widely known for his fantastic than for his neo-realist works.

Studies of fantasy are now an important field of literary criticism because of the popularity of the genre itself and of an allied type of fiction known as 'magic realism'. None of them has succeeded, however, in coming up with a generally accepted definition of what fantasy is. One, by the British scholar Colin Manlove, at least possesses the virtue of comprehensiveness. His definition in his book *Modern Fantasy* is:

> A fiction invoking wonder and containing a substantial and irreducible element of supernatural or impossible worlds, beings or objects with which the mortal characters in the story or the readers become on at least familiar terms.

Manlove's definition, unlike those of some other critics, deliberately includes the fairy story, which is a matter of some importance for Calvino, who was very interested in this genre. In fact, during the early 1950s he spent a great deal of his time collecting fairy stories from all over Italy and rendering them into standard Italian. The fruits of his labours were published in 1956 in a two-volume collection entitled *Italian Folktales*, which was subsequently translated into English.

A handy definition of a fairy story is as elusive as one of fantasy. However, that by J.A. Cuddon in the *Penguin Dictionary of Literary Terms* is as good as any. He writes:

> In its written form the fairy tale tends to be a narrative in prose about the fortunes and misfortunes of a hero or heroine who, having experienced various adventures of a more or less supernatural kind, lives happily ever after. Magic, charms, disguise and spells are some of the major ingredients of such stories, which are often subtle in their interpretation of human nature and psychology.

We would add that fairy stories tend to make use of stock settings and specific narrative techniques. An example of the first is the wood or forest, which in fairy tales is usually a place of enchantment and/or danger (for example, 'Little Red Riding Hood', 'Hansel and Gretel', 'Goldilocks and the Three Bears'). As for narrative techniques, one of the most common is repetition, which undoubtedly derives from the fairy story's oral roots ('Grandma, what big arms/legs/ears/eyes/teeth you've got!' and 'Who's been eating my porridge/ sitting in my chair/sleeping in my bed?').

To return to Calvino, it must be stressed that he did not perform a 180-degree turn from writing neo-realist fiction to writing fantasy, for there was always a fantastic element present in his work. Cesare Pavese drew attention to this as early as 1947, when he wrote that *The Path to the Nest of Spiders* reminded him of 'a woodland fable' (*una favola di bosco*), and our discussion of *Adam, One Afternoon* has also hinted at this element.

Exercise We should now like to turn to a more detailed examination of Calvino's use of fantasy and propose to do so by considering those stories in *Adam, One Afternoon* which, on the face of it, you might think would be the least likely to contain elements of fantasy: the six Resistance stories. Remind yourself of these stories: 'Fear on the Footpath', 'Hunger at Bévera', 'Going to Headquarters', 'The Crow Comes Last', 'One of the Three is Still Alive', and 'Animal Wood', and then note down your answer to the following question. In the light of our discussion of fantasy and the fairy story, which of these stories strikes you as the most fantastic and why?

Discussion We would choose 'Animal Wood', because although its point of departure is a frighteningly real event – a Fascist round-up – it soon takes on the appearance of a fairy story. Note in particular the following points:

1 The wood itself is a magical place. '"What a strange wood", [the German] thought, "with pigs in bushes and lambs in caves"' (p.88). And his further amazement is recorded on the same page.

2 There is a strong repetitive element in the narrative structure of the story. The hero, Giuà Dei Fichi, is asked in succession not to kill the pig, the lamb, the turkey, the rabbit and the hen.

3 The story has the traditional 'happy ever after' ending: 'So it was that Giuà, a hopeless shot, was fêted as the greatest partisan and huntsman in the village. And poor Girumina was bought a brood of newly-hatched chicks at the expense of the community' (p.91).

It is surely not too fanciful, moreover, to compare the German soldier to the traditional ogre – compare his counterpart, Gund, in 'Fear on the Footpath' – and Giuà to a superannuated Jack the Giant-Killer.

But what about 'The Crow Comes Last'? The storyline of this has been described by the Italian critic, Germana Pescio Bottino, as 'a typical, fairy-tale situation: an apple-cheeked boy possesses the talent to pass a test with the talisman, which is the instrument capable of destroying the enemy and of freeing him by freeing the rest' (Pescio Bottino, *Calvino*, p.13).

There are also fantastic elements in some of the other stories. The wood in 'Fear on the Footpath' almost takes on a life of its own, while the deliverance of the German soldier from the appropriately named Witch's Hole (even though the Italian original, *Culdistrega*, would be more accurately translated as 'Witch's Arse') in 'One of the Three is Still Alive' bears traces of the miraculous. ❑

Before leaving this discussion of the fantastic element in Calvino's short stories – and you can doubtless find many other examples – it is important to emphasize that, as far as Calvino was concerned, fantasy was not to be equated with escapism. In the 'Introduction' to his collection of *Italian Folktales*, he wrote that folktales were 'real': they followed the life cycles of ordinary human beings; they reflected the arbitrary division of inherently equal people into kings and poor; they dealt with the persecution of the innocent and their subsequent vindication; and they confronted the trials and tribulations of love. Even the use of spells and magic mirrored the reality of 'having one's existence pre-determined by complex and unknown forces'. The folktale's preoccupation with struggle, moreover, merely illustrated the need 'to free oneself, to determine one's own fate'. But this could only be achieved – and this echoes the interpretation of 'The Crow Comes Last' cited above – if others are liberated too, 'for this is a *sine qua non* of one's own liberation' (Calvino, *Italian Folktales*, pp.xviii–xix). Calvino's defence of the relevance of the folktale thus brings us back, as does much of his early writing, to the reality and significance of the Resistance.

Adam, One Afternoon and its historical period

As we mentioned earlier, you will study works of art not only as artistic creations in their own right, but also as expressions of the period in which they were produced. Fictions, paintings and feature films are all evidence for the attitudes, ideas and feelings – what are called the 'mentalities' – current when they were produced. Our discussion of neo-realism has, of course, taken us some way along this road as far as *Adam, One Afternoon* is concerned, but we now propose to go a stage further and look at some of the stories as a way into the history of the period. This means reading them in a different way from that which we used when analysing them from a literary point of view. Thus, we shall not be concerned with narrative technique or point of view, but with contemporary references, not with tone or style, but with the unspoken assumptions that reflect the common knowledge of both author and reader at the time.

Exercise As in the case of our literary analysis, we shall begin with an exercise based on the title story, 'Adam, One Afternoon'. In addition to the story itself, you will probably find it helpful to re-read the section of this unit on the Roman Catholic Church (p.20). What do you think the story tells you about the nature of religious belief and practice in Italy in the period in which it was written?

Discussion In their way, Maria-nunziata and Libereso represent respectively the Catholic and the anti-clerical traditions in Italy. Maria-nunziata's very name, with its reference to the Annunciation (that is, when the angel Gabriel told Mary that she would bear God's son; see Luke 1:26–38), is a sign of her parents' piety. She is, moreover, aware of the allusion (see p.9) and adds that her brother is named after Mary's husband, Saint Joseph. Her birthday falls on Assumption Day (15 August), which commemorates the ascent of Mary into heaven after her death, and this probably accounts for her name in the first place. As you will see in Unit 5, the cult of the Virgin Mary was very strong in the Catholic Church at this time, and Pope Pius XII actually proclaimed the Assumption as an infallible dogma on 1 November 1950. You may also have noticed Maria-nunziata's reference to the fact that the mass, which is the principal Roman Catholic service, was conducted in Latin (p.14). This was the case throughout the world at that time, but since the reforms of the Second Vatican Council it is usually conducted in the appropriate local language. (The Council is discussed in Unit 29.)

Libereso, on the other hand, is totally ignorant of all this. He comes from an anarchist background, and anarchists would have regarded the cult of the Virgin Mary, and indeed all religion, as so much superstitious nonsense. His own name, as explained in the text, is the Esperanto word for 'freedom'. Esperanto, an artificial international language designed on rational principles in the 1880s, would no doubt have appealed to anarchists and other free-thinkers as a particularly fitting vehicle in which to express human solidarity.

The name of Libereso's brother – Germinal – is also a political statement, being one of the months in the French revolutionary calendar of 1793. Anarchism was not a very powerful political movement in Italy at the time of Liberation, although it certainly existed. Indeed, Italy was the only western European country, apart from Spain, where it had ever had much impact. It had been a driving force in the creation of the working-class movement in the 1880s and 1890s, and remained influential up to about 1920. It was an anarchist who in 1900 assassinated Umberto I, the second king of united Italy. Anarchist trade unions also played an important part in the social agitation which had taken place in Italy during the First World War.

Collect some bonus points, by the way, if you noted the fact that Maria-nunziata came from Calabria, the backward region which forms the toe of the Italian boot. Peasant piety was deeply entrenched in the south and Maria-nunziata's presence in Calvino's Liguria is an instance of the internal migration in search of work which was a feature of Italian life, despite attempts to regulate it (this is discussed further in Units 2 and 10). ❑

Calvino's Resistance stories

We want now to look at the six Resistance stories, to see how they can be used to increase our historical knowledge of the Italian Resistance. Since the course also deals with France, we shall make frequent comparisons with the situation in that country.

The first point to be stressed is that we get a more intimate sense of the Italian Resistance as a civil war against the Fascists as much as a war of liberation against the Germans. 'All winter it was a game of hide and seek', we read in 'Fear on the Footpath', 'the Bersaglieri at Baiardo, the Militia at Molini, the Germans at Briga' (p.48). The first two were formations of Mussolini's Italian Social Republic – the Bersaglieri being mountain troops in the regular army and the Militia a Fascist Party fighting unit. 'Hunger at Bévera' and 'Going to Headquarters' introduce us to two more Fascist military forces: the Black Brigades, set up in June 1944 under the control of the party secretary, Alessandro Pavolini; and the Decima Mas, or Tenth Motor-Torpedo-boat Flotilla (see the footnote on page 66), which, since the Italian Social Republic had hardly any navy, was employed like a marine unit in land operations against the Resistance.

Although it was undoubtedly true that many of the Italian Social Republic's hapless conscripts lacked any stomach for fighting their fellow Italians, some were dedicated Fascists – note the slogans painted by the Black Brigade in 'Hunger at Bévera' – and little quarter was sought or given on either side in their conflict with the predominantly left-wing Resistance. The sheer brutality of this civil war is brought out very well in 'Going to Headquarters', in which the Resistance man shoots down in cold blood a compatriot whom he suspects of working with the Germans and the Fascists.

There was a similar situation in France. In January 1943 the Vichy government had set up a paramilitary organization known as the Milice française (French Militia) under the leadership of the arch-fascist, Joseph Darnand. A year later, as a result of German pressure, Darnand was appointed

Secretary-General for the Maintenance of Order in the Vichy government, and on 20 January 1944 he was empowered to set up special courts martial to try on the spot those caught in acts of assassination or other violent crimes against the state – in other words, members of the French Resistance. As an American scholar, Bertram Gordon, has written: 'Bloody incidents became commonplace as members of the Milice were shot down in ambushes by the Resistance and Darnand's forces retaliated with ever larger forays against the maquis [...] By June 6 [1944], when Allied forces landed in Normandy, France was already in the throes of full-scale civil violence' (Gordon, *Collaborationism in France*, p.294).

How strong was the Resistance in France and Italy? Reliable figures are hard to come by, but the British scholar, Roger Absalom, who based his calculations on Allied estimates, comes up with a total of 290,000 for Italy at the moment of total Liberation in April 1945. This figure is composed of 250,000 in the regular partisan units which fought in the countryside and in the mountains, and 40,000 members of the Gruppi d'Azione Patriottica (Patriotic Action Groups),

Figure 1.2 *France divided, June 1940. (Redrawn from H. Michel,* La Seconde Guerre mondiale*, PUF, 1968, vol.1, p.190.)*

Figure 1.3 *Italy, showing areas of Resistance and the stages of Liberation, September 1943–December 1945. (Redrawn from C.R.S. Harris,* Allied Military Administration of Italy 1943–1945, *HMSO, 1957, and from A. Polcri,* Le cause della resistenza italiana, *Istituto Editoriale Internazionale, 1977, p.169.)*

who were urban guerrillas based in the major cities. The French scholar, Henry Rousso, argues that the only firm basis for an estimate of the strength of the French Resistance is the number of identity cards issued to former members of the Resistance by the government after the war. This gives us a total of 220,000. The French figure represents a proportion of between 1 and 1.5 per cent of the working population and the Italian figure around 0.9 per cent, but you should be extremely wary of drawing the conclusion from this that the French were more 'Resistance-minded' than the Italians. Those joining the Resistance were tiny minorities in both countries but, considering the risks involved, is that really surprising?

When we come to look at the composition of the resisters, we find that the vast majority of them were men, around nine out of ten in various Italian and French local studies, on which we have to rely in the absence of any national breakdown. They were also predominantly young. Almost half the resisters in the French *département* of Île-et-Vilaine (between Brittany and Normandy in the north-west of France) were aged between 13 and 29, while those under 30 represented nearly three-quarters of resisters in the north-eastern Italian province of Bologna. Two in every hundred were below 16, so the boy marksman of 'The Crow Comes Last' is not an example of poetic licence. It is not hard to account for the overwhelmingly male and predominantly youthful character of the Resistance. Combat troops in most societies consist largely of young men and, as we have seen, the Resistance was engaged in a particularly nasty form of combat. It is also true that young men in France and Italy were subject to conscription by 'the other side' at the time: Frenchmen to the compulsory labour service and Italians to the armed forces of the Salò Republic. For many, like Calvino, the Resistance was a more acceptable alternative.

It is for these reasons that we should be careful about limiting opposition to fascism and the Germans to membership of the Resistance. Joining the Resistance was a particular form of opposition: armed force. Many expressed their opposition in other ways, by taking part in strikes and demonstrations, by refusing supplies to the authorities, and by harbouring and feeding resisters and escaping Allied servicemen. Even simply listening to Allied radio broadcasts and repeating their contents represented a form of opposition.

The social composition of the Resistance in both Italy and France was undoubtedly skewed in the direction of the lower end of the social scale. As Henry Rousso has written of France: 'The Resistance was not a class phenomenon in the strict sense of the term: its influence extended into all social groups, even the upper middle class, although the latter was in a tiny minority. It is nevertheless the case that workers and middling groups supplied the greatest numbers' (Rousso, 'Où en est l'histoire de la Résistance', pp.119–20). That this was also true of Italy can be seen from the figures for the Bologna province. Manual workers, white-collar employees and artisans and tradesmen provided almost four-fifths of all resisters; employers, managers, rentiers and members of the liberal professions only one in ten.

This in turn is certainly related to the political complexion of the Resistance. As was indicated above, since fascism was a right-wing phenomenon, opposition to it came mainly from the left (p.10). In 'Fear on the Footpath' there is a reference to 'the commissar' of the partisan unit to which the hero is bringing his message (p.52). This shows that the unit in question was Communist, for the Italian Communist Party appointed political commissars to its Resistance units to educate the rank-and-file in the political context of the struggle in which they were engaged, just as its Soviet counterparts had done with the Red Army. As we have seen, the Communists were the largest single component of the Resistance in both France and Italy, partly because communist parties had become skilled in operating in conditions of illegality. After the German invasion of the Soviet Union in June 1941, the organizational and propagandist skills of the Party machines were harnessed to the Resistance cause. Although regular soldiers and 'non-Party' people participated, the organization of the Resistance was dominated by the political parties. In Italy this was so from the start. The Italian Resistance was co-ordinated by a network of Comitati di Liberazione Nazionale (Committees of National Liberation, or CLNs for short). You will have noted from Ginsborg (p.16) that the first was set up in Rome on 9 September 1943, and presided over by the veteran politician, Ivanoe Bonomi. It consisted of representatives of the five anti-fascist parties, plus Bonomi's own tiny Democratic Labour Party. They had begun to co-operate even before Mussolini's overthrow in July.

In the north, the leading role there was soon assumed by the Milan CLN, subsequently renamed Comitato di Liberazione Nazionale – Alta Italia (Committee of National Liberation for Upper Italy), which consisted of representatives of the same six political parties as its Roman counterpart. In addition, as indicated in the story 'Hunger at Bévera' (pp.54–5), dozens of smaller CLNs, modelled on those in Rome and Milan, proliferated in the regions, towns and cities of northern Italy.

To some extent, therefore, it could be said that the Resistance in Italy grew from the top downwards. The main difference between the organization of the Resistance in France and in Italy is explained by the role of General Charles de Gaulle, which has already been mentioned (p.10).

A number of independent Resistance movements also sprang up inside France. Initially, most of them were not directly affiliated to any political party. In January 1942 de Gaulle sent one of his most trusted aides, Jean Moulin, to France in order to unify these internal Resistance movements and to bring them under Free French control. This dual aim was achieved on 27 May 1943, when the Conseil National de la Résistance (National Resistance Council, or CNR) held its first full meeting with Moulin in the chair and acknowledged the leadership of General de Gaulle. Moulin was arrested by the Gestapo in the following month and was later tortured to death, but the CNR survived. Although its membership, unlike that of its Italian counterpart, was weighted in favour of the individual Resistance movements as opposed to representatives of political parties, the latter soon came to predominate. Among them the Communist Party, as in Italy, was the most important. It was reckoned that at the time of the Liberation in 1944 the Communists controlled getting on for a third of the Comités Départementaux de la Libération (Departmental Liberation Committees, or CDLs) which the CNR had established throughout the country.

The importance and revolutionary potential of this network of Resistance organizations in Italy and France can be more readily appreciated by reference to the situation in Russia in 1917. After the February Revolution in that country there was what the Communist leader, Lenin, called a situation of 'dual power', with the Provisional Government on the one hand and the soldiers' and workers' councils (or soviets) on the other. Lenin called for 'all power to the soviets', even though his party was not yet in control of them. The existence of this 'dual power' was one of the key factors leading to the paralysis and eventual overthrow of the Russian Provisional Government. Might not Resistance 'dual power', in the shape of the various Liberation committees, produce the same result in France and Italy? You will find consideration of this question in Unit 2.

References

ABSALOM, R., 'The armed resistance in Italy (1943–45): the politics of history and the recovery of "national legitimation"' in Eric Cahm and Vladimir Claude Fisera (eds), *Socialism and Nationalism in Contemporary Europe (1848–1945)*, vol.3, Nottingham, Spokesman, 1980, pp.87–109.

ARDIGÀO, A. (ed.), *Società Civile e Insorgenza Partigiana: Indagine sociologica sulla diffusione dell'insorgenza partigiana, nella provincia di Bologna*, Bologna, Nuova Universale Cappelli, 1979.

BEAUVOIR, S. DE, *Force of Circumstance*, Harmondsworth, Penguin, 1968.

BONURA, G., *Invito alla lettura di Calvino*, Milan, Mursia, second edition 1985.

CALVINO, I., 'Preface' to *The Path to the Nest of Spiders*, New York, The Ecco Press, 1976, pp.v–xxv.

CALVINO, I., *Italian Folktales*, translated by George Martin, Harmondsworth, Penguin, 1982.

CUDDON, J.A. (ed.), *Dictionary of Literary Terms*, Harmondsworth, Penguin, second edition, 1982.

GORDON, B.M., *Collaborationism in France during the Second World War*, Ithaca/London, Cornell University Press, 1980.

HEINEY, D., *America in Modern Italian Literature*, New Brunswick, New Jersey, Rutgers University Press, 1964.

MANLOVE, C., *Modern Fantasy: Five Studies*, Cambridge, Cambridge University Press, 1987.

PESCIO BOTTINO, G., *Calvino*, Florence, La Nuova Italia, 1976.

ROUSSO, H., 'Où en est l'histoire de la Résistance' in *Etudes sur la France de 1939 à nos jours*, Paris, Editions du Seuil, 1985, pp.113–37.

SPRIANO, P., *Le Passioni di un Decennio, 1946–1956*, Milan, Garzanti, 1986.

THOMPSON, D., '"Andremo se mai verso l'uomo": the historical and literary premises of "Neorealism"', *Association of Teachers of Italian Journal*, 39, Summer 1983, pp.37–52.

UNIT 2 Political and economic reconstruction, 1943–48

Prepared for the course team
by Clive Emsley and Bernard Waites

PART ONE: THE POLITICS OF RECONSTRUCTION

CLIVE EMSLEY

PART TWO: ECONOMIC RECONSTRUCTION, 1943–48

BERNARD WAITES

Study materials

For your work on this unit you will need the following materials:

Ginsborg, *A History of Contemporary Italy*

Gildea, *France since 1945*

Documents and Texts 1

Video-cassette 1, part 1, 'Archive film'

Audio-cassette 1, side A, 'The Italian Resistance: aspirations and delusions'

Cassette Notes 1

PART ONE: THE POLITICS OF RECONSTRUCTION

1 Introduction and aims

The aims of this part are very straightforward. It consolidates much of your work in Unit 1 and you may want to refer back to the reading from Ginsborg and Gildea which you did for that unit. We shall also refer you to some other sections of these set books. After completing this part you should:

1. have a broad knowledge of the chronology of French and Italian history between 1943 and 1947;
2. be aware of the principal groups that participated in the Resistance in the two countries and what they sought to achieve;
3. have an understanding of the political problems that preoccupied the provisional governments in the aftermath of the war;
4. be able to offer some explanation for the voting patterns in the elections and referenda of 1945–47.

2 Resistance

Unit 1 gave you a brief account of the process of Liberation in France and Italy. Here we will look in more detail at who the resisters were, and what they wanted.

Italy

Exercise Let's start with some visual images of the Resistance. You will need Video-cassette 1. Please watch the first two extracts in part 1, the 'Archive film' compilation (items 2.1 and 2.2). These consist of extracts from two films shot by Don Pollarolo. Remember that Don Pollarolo was an amateur film maker and in consequence you may find some difficulties in 'reading' the films. Information about the films is printed in the supplementary booklet *Cassette Notes 1*, and you should study this before answering the following questions:

1. What is the essential difference of form between the two films?
2. What do the two films tell you about (a) the enemy, and (b) the aspirations of the partisans?

Discussion

1. The first film has all the attributes of a home movie; the images strike me rather as the kind of pictures you would find in a photograph album if they moved. *Campane a stormo* is different in that it sets out to tell a story, and a story with a message at once patriotic and reassuring to the young women whose young men are off fighting with the partisans.

2(a) The 'home movie' really tells us little about the enemy, who are never seen, though there may be some unwitting testimony here – the partisans seem to be moving fairly freely and everyone seems to be having a good time, which may suggest a lack of enemy activity in the area. *Campane a stormo* portrays the enemy as lascivious and brutal; it is also interesting that Italian blackshirts are shown as the enemy, not Germans.

2(b) I doubt if you considered that there was much in these extracts showing partisan aspirations, though the idea of young people fighting for a better Italy might be said to be implicit in the conclusion of *Campane a stormo*. There is one point which I do not expect you to have noted in either film, but it is worth some comment – the Italian tricolour displayed by the partisans does not have the royal coat of arms in the centre. The 'better tomorrow' of this band does not, therefore, appear to have included the monarchy, though it clearly did include the Church. ❑

Exercise I want you now to turn to Audio-cassette 1, side A, and listen to the talk by Paul Ginsborg, 'The Italian Resistance: aspirations and delusions'. As you listen, take notes on the following questions.

1 What did the resisters hope to achieve by their actions?

2 Why, according to Ginsborg, were these aspirations thwarted?

Discussion

1 Some men joined the partisans for immediate, short-term reasons – to avoid arrest, conscription, and so on. They could be termed 'spontaneous resisters', and some of the strikers of March 1944 could also be included in this category since they seem to have gone on strike, essentially, for peace and an end to war production for Germany. At the same time, however, there were committed political activists in the Resistance, notably the Communists (and remember the division between the leadership with its programme for 'progressive democracy' and some of the rank and file who perceived the chance for socialist revolution), the Actionists and the Socialists. In different ways, and to different degrees, each of these groups wanted to change society.

2 Ginsborg argues that there was no significant change in Italian society at the end of the war because, for the sake of national unity, the PCI (Communist Party) leadership decided to postpone any attempt to pursue social and political objectives until the calling of a Constituent Assembly after the war. Furthermore, the German counter-offensive against the partisans at the end of 1944 prompted the northern partisan delegates to agree to the Protocols of Rome, which were, in effect, a defeat for the radical aspirations of resisters in the north. ❑

France

As you saw in Unit 1, the French Resistance had been unified by General de Gaulle and the CNR (Conseil National de la Résistance) during 1943. The following year this body produced a programme for Liberation and post-war reconstruction.

Exercise Turn now to *Documents and Texts 1* and read the Charter of the CNR (item 3). Then answer the following questions.

1 Do the plans of the CNR stop with the Liberation of France?

2 Does the CNR propose the re-establishment of the Third Republic?

Specimen answers

1 The Charter states explicitly that the CNR would remain united (and hence in existence) after Liberation, and outlines a major programme of political freedoms to be established and economic and social reforms to be achieved.

2 There is no mention of the re-establishment of the Third Republic in the Charter, but the implication behind the continuance of the CNR and its programme of reform is that the Resistance aspired to the creation of a new political order.

Discussion As in Italy there were considerable differences among the resisters. In the eyes of de Gaulle, while the *Third* Republic had ceased to exist, the Republic of France continued wherever he and his Free French were based. There was also, as in Italy, a division within the Communist Party between the leadership which was prepared to go along with the restoration of parliamentary democracy, and some of the rank and file who were prepared to push for more revolutionary change, and who were subsequently to regard 1944 as a missed opportunity.

Internal and external resistance was united following the Allied landings in France in June 1944, but the process of Liberation was confused. Some areas were liberated by Allied troops, with a significant number of de Gaulle's Free French soldiers fighting at their side. In a few instances Liberation followed a rising by French people against the German Occupation; the most celebrated example of this being the Liberation of Paris, which began with the Paris police turning their headquarters into a fortress against the Germans and which was completed by the arrival of the Free French Armoured Division. In most of the south-west, however, and in the Jura and Corsica, Liberation was the work of partisan forces (Forces Françaises de l'Intérieur – FFI) (see Figure 2.1). In contrast to the role of the Italian partisans, however, in many instances French *maquisards* had little more to do other than to enter a town, declare it liberated and establish their own administration in the wake of the withdrawing German army. Yet even if France was liberated in a much shorter time and with much smaller losses among the Resistance fighters, the punishment of collaborators was ferocious; at least 4,500 were executed summarily. ❑

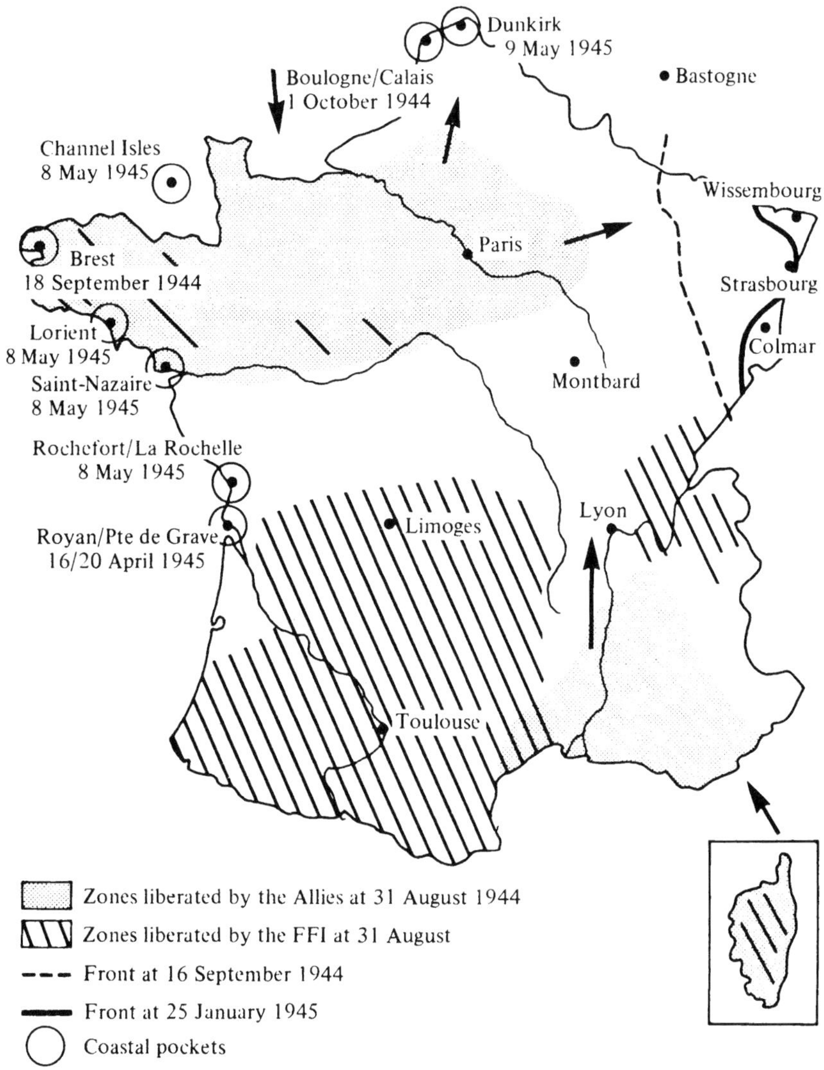

Figure 2.1 *France: stages of the liberation. (From Jean-Pierre Rioux,* The Fourth Republic, 1944–1958, *Cambridge, CUP, 1987.)*

Exercise Now I want you to look at some more film. Watch item 2.3 on Video-cassette 1, which consists of extracts from *La Grande Épreuve* ('The Great Ordeal').

Look at the accompanying notes about the film and then answer the following questions.

1 The first section of the film deals with the maquis.

(a) How does this extract differ from Don Pollarolo's film of Italian partisans?

(b) What image does it give of the Resistance?

(c) Who appears as the enemy?

2 The second brief section deals with Liberation:

(a) How does the filming of these sequences differ from those of the maquis?

(b) Who is doing the liberating?

(c) What is the difference between these acts of Liberation and those in the south-west, the Jura and Corsica?

(d) What popular attitudes towards Liberation can be detected in these sequences?

Specimen answers

1(a) Unlike Don Pollarolo's 'home movie', this is carefully edited and is a mixture of original film, film probably posed for the camera after the event (no cameraman is likely to get slightly forward of men engaged in a battle), and film used to illustrate events with which it probably had little connection (possibly some of the destruction in the railyards shown here was the result of Allied bombing; the German machine gunners could have been filmed anywhere, probably by a German army film crew). This recounts a piece of history, using whatever film can be found (or shot) to illustrate that story.

(b) A very heroic and largely successful image.

(c) German soldiers.

2(a) While these sequences are edited like those discussed above, they appear to have been taken from film shot during the events which they describe: for example, people are keeping their heads down under fire.

(b) Regular troops. (In fact most of the troops shown in these sequences were from General Leclerc's Free French Armoured Division.)

(c) Clearly hard fighting was involved here. (The scale of destruction in northern France following the invasion will be discussed later in this unit.)

(d) Many people came out to cheer the liberators, but some sequences hint at a darker side: German prisoners were roughly handled and collaborators fared worse.

Discussion In general, this sequence probably overemphasizes the success of the French Resistance before the Allied landings. Also, in an interesting contrast to *Campane a stormo*, its emphasis on the German enemy might be said to underplay the wartime division within France; there is no sign here of Vichy *milice*. ❑

3 Provisional governments

Italy

Exercise Ginsborg describes how Marshal Badoglio's government came into being (pp.11–12). How could this government justify its legitimacy? How might its origins undermine its legitimacy?

Discussion Badoglio's government could justify its legitimacy on the grounds that it had been formed at the request of the constitutional head of state – the king. The problem with this claim was, of course, that the constitution had been in abeyance during the years of Fascist rule, that the monarchy had compromised itself by collaborating with the Fascists, and that the new head of government himself had held high military office under Mussolini. One might also add that Badoglio's government had no electoral mandate, it depended on the Allies, and it only had direct jurisdiction over a small (though increasing) area of Italy. ❑

Six political parties had come together in the Committees of National Liberation (CLN): the Action Party (PdA), which was the only one to spring directly from resistance to Fascism, not having existed before the destruction of the parliamentary system; the Communist Party (PCI); the Socialist Party (PSIUP); the Democratic Labour Party (PDL); the Liberal Party (PLI); and the Christian Democratic Party (DC). These parties will be discussed in more detail later, but a few points should be noted. The first four were opposed to the monarchy on both ideological grounds and for the way in which Victor Emmanuel had compromised with Mussolini. The Liberals and some of the DC were keen to see the monarchy preserved, but even they objected to the reigning monarch and had reservations about his son and heir. When the Allies suggested that Victor Emmanuel broaden the base of Badoglio's government by bringing in representatives from the CLN, the parties were lukewarm and the king only yielded finally under persistent Allied pressure. In January 1944 a congress of the CLN was held in Naples; it was attended by representatives from the Central CLN in Rome, who were more radical than most of those present, and under their encouragement the congress confronted the monarch, proposing that Victor Emmanuel abdicate and that his son, Umberto, delegate all his powers to a body which would, in turn, appoint a cabinet made up of all parties in the CLN. The Allied authorities in Italy accepted the proposal, but it was strongly opposed by Winston Churchill who declared his support for the monarchy. The problem was shelved by an agreement that Victor Emmanuel would not abdicate but retire from public life, and that Umberto would take over as Lieutenant General of the Realm. The Socialists and the Action Party disliked the agreement but were brought into line by the moderating influence of the Communists and their leader, Palmiro Togliatti, who returned from long exile in Moscow in March 1944. Togliatti justified his position in a lengthy speech to party militants at Salerno. Since he thereby reversed what had hitherto been the PCI's own republicanism, the episode has been dubbed *La svolta di Salerno* ('the Salerno turning point'). On 22 April a new government, still led by Badoglio, was formed with members drawn from all parties in the CLN; it was to be short lived. When Rome fell to the Allies, the city's Central CLN, in league with Actionists and Socialists, obliged Umberto to endorse the CLN's choice of prime minister – Ivanoe Bonomi, a former socialist and now a leader of the PDL. On 25 June Bonomi's government, as its first act, issued a decree promising that, as soon as the war ended a Constituent Assembly would be established to prepare a new constitution. ❑

France

While de Gaulle did not acknowledge that the Republic in France had ceased to exist between 1940 and 1944, he did accept that the government-in-exile established in Algiers needed broadening to include men who had spent the war years in France and who had participated in internal Resistance. The provisional government announced on 9 September combined traditional forces in French politics with men of the Resistance who had no overt political affiliations. There were twenty-two ministers: two-thirds were from the Algiers group, the rest from metropolitan France. Nine men, including de Gaulle, had no party affiliation; the others were Socialists (4), Mouvement républicain populaire (MRP) (3), Radicals (3), Communists (2) and one from a small 'moderate' party. But it also became increasingly clear that de Gaulle wanted to make the important decisions: Georges Bidault, the president of the CNR whom de Gaulle made Foreign Minister, had not set foot outside France for four years, and Adrian Tixier, who became Minister of the Interior, had not been in France for four years. One final point ought to be noted about de Gaulle and his provisional government: relations between the general and his Anglo-American Allies were often strained during the war, and while his government was announced on 9 September, it was not formally recognized by the Allies until 23 October. (De Gaulle's relations with the Allies are discussed further in Unit 6.)

Aims of the provisional governments

Exercise What do you consider were likely to have been the administrative and political priorities of these provisional governments when they were established?

Discussion The key priorities, not in any particular order, were, I think, as follows:

1. to bring the war to a successful conclusion;
2. to bring the administrative and governmental system of the country under the unified control of the central, albeit provisional government;
3. to endeavour to heal the divisions created by the previous regime, by Occupation and by civil conflict, yet, at the same time 'punish' the most compromised members of the old regime and the most compromised collaborators;
4. to prepare the way for establishing, or re-establishing, the constitutional foundation on which post-war governments could function.

While you may not have listed it, it is also worth noting here that de Gaulle placed a high priority on:

5 re-establishing France's credentials as a great power (look again at the last phrase of point 1 of the CNR Charter). ❑

We will now discuss each of these issues in turn, except for the last, which will be dealt with in Unit 6.

1 Concluding the war

In many respects, bringing the war to a successful conclusion was the easiest of these priorities; it did not depend solely on the actions of the provisional governments, and while they maintained armies in the field, the bulk of the effort in men and material was British and, primarily, American.

2 Re-establishing unified government

In Italy the provisional government faced the threat of national fragmentation with an independence movement in Sicily, the acute isolation of Sardinia, and difficult northern neighbours casting greedy eyes over parts of its territory. In the north-west there was the threat of French annexation of Valle d'Aosta and in the north-east the Yugoslavs argued over the position of the frontier. In both Italy and France the provisional governments faced a serious problem arising from the situation of 'dual power' outlined in Unit 1. In some areas liberated by Resistance partisans, the local liberators had installed their own administrations and they greatly resented the instructions, and the bureaucrats, sent by central government. The local men, moreover, were often Communists and were far more radical than the provisional governments; for such men Liberation was the prelude to socialist revolution and they regarded their local organizations as the vanguard. No central government could countenance such a state of affairs, especially since the radicals in the localities were armed.

In both countries the provisional governments found support for the suppression of dual power from an unexpected source – the leadership of the Communist Party. Neither Togliatti nor Maurice Thorez, the French Communist leader who also returned from Moscow in 1944, had revolution on the agenda. Both Italy and France had been allotted to the western sphere of influence and both had large numbers of western Allied troops stationed in them. But apart from this, both Togliatti and Thorez believed that their parties could achieve legitimate domination through the existing political systems. They had a three-pronged strategy for achieving this: an alliance, even a merger with the Socialists; taking control of the trade unions; using their position in government to infiltrate those departments of government that they controlled as ministers. Supporting rival alternatives to the existing state would only serve to undermine their aspirations and the legitimacy of that state which they expected, ultimately, to control.

3 Healing divisions; punishing the 'guilty'

The victors of any civil conflict face the difficulty of having both to heal divisions and to deal with their opponents without making those divisions any worse.

In France, following the Liberation and the summary justice administered by various individuals and groups, 124,750 persons were tried in the courts, of whom 767 were formally sentenced to death and executed, and over 38,000 were sentenced to terms of imprisonment. There seems to have been a parallel between the traditional economic and social divisions in French society and the outcomes of these cases. In Valenciennes, for example, the court acquitted one-third of the employers, a quarter of those from the liberal professions, shopkeepers, soldiers and policemen, but only a tenth of the peasants or workers. Ninety per cent of those accused of military offences were convicted, 50 per cent of those accused of political offences, and only 33 per cent of those accused of economic offences. The legal purge was not simply an official way of punishing everybody who had collaborated. Key figures were singled out for trial: Pétain was condemned to death, but the sentence was commuted to life imprisonment; Pierre Laval, the chief minister of Vichy, was tried, condemned and shot. Louis Renault's car works had built tanks for the Germans; he died in prison before his trial and his factories were confiscated by the state. While thousands of officials in public service were expelled or demoted, an analysis of the men holding the higher offices in the civil service reveals that a very high percentage remained in post.

In France the group that is most closely identified with a particular regime is the prefectoral corps; the prefect is the principal government representative in the provincial *département*. Vichy purged prefects; the Liberation purged prefects; but nearly half of the professional prefectoral corps survived through the years 1939–46. In Italy too several of the leaders of the Fascist regime received short shrift. Mussolini was summarily shot by partisans and several thousand Fascists suffered similarly in the closing weeks of the war. But as Paul Ginsborg explained, the purge was limited. A fissure rapidly developed within the CLN itself. The Liberals and the DC were happy to support the prosecution of leading Fascists but they were opposed to the thorough-going purge of the bureaucracy, army, and industrial and commercial groups proposed by parties on the left. The Liberals and the DC pointed out that, under the Fascist regime it had been impossible to hold a government post without being a member of the party. The Socialists and Actionists in particular insisted that overt allegiance to Fascism should be punished. The argument reached a climax in November 1944 when the High Committee for Measures against Fascism requested the dismissal of a number of leading officials in the Navy and the Treasury. Both of these departments had Liberal ministers who responded to the request by threatening to resign. Bonomi backed the Liberal ministers and resigned himself. Discussions over a new government dragged on for two weeks until the Lieutenant General asked Bonomi to form another government. This he did, but both the Socialists and the Actionists refused to serve.

4 Preparing for a post-war constitution

In neither France nor Italy did the provisional governments consider it their task to determine the constitutional structure of their countries in the post-war world. However, they did make some significant moves with reference to the manner in which these structures would be decided; most notably, in both countries women were given the vote. Generally speaking, the provisional governments saw it as their task to fill the gap between Liberation and the meeting of the first elected assemblies. But this did not prevent the parties with members in the governments jockeying for position, falling out with each other, and urging their preferred constitutional structure on the electorates.

4 Parties, referenda and constitutions

For this section you will need to read Gildea, pages 35–39. The whole of Ginsborg's chapter 3, 'The Post-war Settlement 1945–8', is relevant to this unit, but for political and constitutional developments concentrate on pages 89–93, 98–104.

The years 1945–46 witnessed considerable activity and debate in both France and Italy as post-war constitutional structures were hammered out, as referenda were held and elections fought. You will find details of these elections and referenda in the statistical tables in *Documents and Texts 1*, and you will need to have them to hand.

France

There were four principal political parties at the end of the war.

1. The Communist Party (PCF) had been formed in 1920 following a breach within the Socialist Party. It was rigidly hierarchical and tightly disciplined from the bureaucrats at the top down to the small, local cells. The Communists had used the Resistance movement to penetrate agricultural areas and to extend and strengthen their position within the trade unions. There is considerable debate over the size of the Party in 1945, but there seems to have been a membership of about 700,000.
2. The Socialist Party (Section française de l'internationale ouvriére, SFIO) had been created in 1905. It was Marxist, but not Leninist, and was less authoritarian than the Communist Party. Its reputation had been tarnished in 1940 when some of its members had accepted that Pétain be entrusted with 'full power'. In 1945 the membership was only about half that of the Communists. A group of revisionists sought to persuade the party to break publicly with its Marxist creed and to bring in new men via the Resistance; others wanted a close alliance, even merger with the Communists; while the conservative rank and file clung to their traditional ideas and also ensured that the party maintained its anti-clerical tradition, which alienated many potential supporters who were Catholics.

3 The MRP (Mouvement républicain populaire) was formed in 1944 out of progressive Catholic groups involved in the Resistance; its continuing relationship with the Catholic Church will be discussed in more detail in Unit 5. Self-consciously the MRP styled itself a 'movement' rather than a party; it wanted to reconcile workers and Catholics, uniting them solidly behind the Republic; it also hoped to introduce a new level of moral principle and idealism to public life. There were about 100,000 members in 1945, but its electoral support was greatly swollen by right-wing voters who, after the collapse of Vichy, had no other party to turn to.

4 The Radical Party liked to perceive itself as the inheritor and guardian of the Jacobin tradition of the great Revolution of 1789. It had held the balance of power for most of the Third Republic, but it had made a poor showing in the Resistance, and its membership had fallen by perhaps two-thirds to about 30,000 in 1946.

In addition to these four main parties there were a variety of smaller groups often catalogued as 'moderates'.

On 21 October 1945 a general election and a referendum were held in France. Two questions were posed in the referendum. Firstly, did the electors want the new assembly for which they were voting to prepare a new constitution? If the answer was 'no', the constitution of the Third Republic would remain in force. Secondly, if the electors did want a new constitution prepared, did they want the powers of the assembly limited? The proposed limitations were a life of only seven months, the requirement that the new constitution be submitted to a new referendum, and the requirement that the new constitution establish a parliamentary system in which the head of the government was responsible to the assembly.

Exercise

Turn now to the statistical tables in *Documents and Texts 1* and study Table 16, the election and referendum results in France, 21 October 1945.

1 What do the results of both the election and the referendum suggest about French attitudes to the Third Republic in 1945?

2 On the evidence of the election results, where might a majority be found for establishing a government?

Specimen answers and discussion

1 Both results suggest that, in the minds of the French people, the Third Republic and the men who had dominated it were totally discredited. Whatever French electors wanted, it was not a restoration of the system that had collapsed in 1940. The PCF did particularly well compared with the last time France had gone to the polls in 1936; however, it did not have an overall majority.

On the other hand, while the Communists campaigned for a 'no' vote to the second question in the referendum, a majority favoured the limitations on the constituent assembly and appear, in consequence, to have favoured the continuance of a bicameral parliamentary system.

All the other parties, together with de Gaulle, had urged a 'yes' vote to both questions in the referendum.

2 On paper there was the potential for a Marxist government with a coalition between the PCF and the SFIO.

In practice, for a variety of reasons, such a coalition was not possible. Few in the new assembly could imagine a provisional government which was not led by de Gaulle, and there were members of the SFIO concerned about being outflanked by the Communists – note the change in their respective electoral fortunes since 1936. In spite of attempts to build bridges between the two parties, these concerns grew more acute in the following months. ❑

The new assembly invited de Gaulle to form a government and friction promptly developed between the General and the Communists when he refused their demand for all three key ministries of Foreign Affairs, Interior and Defence. A government was eventually formed with de Gaulle at its head and the three largest parties each holding five ministries. It was short lived. De Gaulle intensely disliked the political in-fighting and squabbling that developed, and he regarded much of the criticism in the assembly as personal betrayal. On 20 January 1946 he resigned. In the wake of his departure the three main parties agreed a charter of tripartism, promising to avoid offensive and injurious polemic and to develop a spirit of solidarity for common decisions of government.

On 5 May the assembly presented its draft constitution to the country for ratification. This constitution was backed by the PCF and the SFIO; it proposed a single, all-powerful national assembly elected for five-year terms; this assembly would choose the president of the republic and the head of the government. The MRP and most of the smaller parties strenuously opposed the proposal; they warned of the danger of a single assembly dominated by Marxists and urged the need for a bicameral legislature. Against general expectation, the constitution was rejected. This verdict required the election of a second constituent assembly to draft a different constitution.

Exercise Turn to Tables 17 and 18 in *Documents and Texts 1*. What appears to you to be significant in the results of the May referendum and the June election?

Discussion A majority shared the concerns expressed by the non-Marxist parties about an all-powerful single-chamber assembly. This attitude was reflected in the June election when both the MRP and the Radicals received a significant boost at the expense of the PCF and, to an even greater extent, the SFIO. The MRP was the largest party in the second constituent assembly, but the tripartite agreement on government continued. You can see clearly from the figures the way in which the MRP, while it sought to be a progressive party, was manifestly picking up votes from people who were essentially moderate and concerned about the strength of the Marxist parties.

The second assembly drafted a constitution on the lines favoured by the MRP. There was to be a bicameral legislature composed of a national assembly elected for five years and a council of the republic; the constitution did not explain how this second chamber was to be selected and it was left to electoral legislation, passed on 27 October, to outline an extremely complicated system. The president of the republic was to be elected by the two chambers every seven years; one of his tasks was to recommend a head of government to the national assembly; of course, this head of government still needed a majority in the assembly. The new constitution was put to the nation on 13 October; it was accepted and an election for the new national assembly followed on 10 November. ❑

Exercise Turn now to Tables 19 and 20 in *Documents and Texts 1*.

1 Do the numbers of abstentions and spoiled papers in October and November 1946 suggest anything to you when compared with those for elections and referenda in the preceding twelve months?

2 Given the pattern of voting for different parties during 1945–46, how could a majority government be formed for the new Fourth Republic?

Specimen answers and discussion

1 The vote that accepted the new constitution does not suggest overwhelming support for the proposals among the population, but given the steady decline in the numbers who turned up at the polls for the elections and referenda of 1945 and 1946, it is arguable that familiarity with the polls was breeding, if not contempt, increasing apathy.

Incidentally, of some significance in the lack of enthusiasm for the new constitution, though its precise impact cannot be measured, was the forceful condemnation of the proposals which was made by de Gaulle on 22 September.

2 No party achieved an absolute majority in this election (or its immediate predecessors), and consequently the government would have to be a coalition or a minority. There was no likely coalition with an overall majority in the assembly, but the Socialists' anxieties about being swamped by the Communists were increased by their ever-declining support at the polls. ❑

It took a month for the new national assembly to find a man who could form a government acceptable to the majority. Even though the tripartite accord was still generally adhered to, the MRP had fought the election campaign with the slogan 'Bidault without Thorez', and the PCF had responded in kind. In the event, the first government of the Fourth Republic was composed entirely of members of the SFIO and was headed by Léon Blum, seventy-four years old and the former head of the 1936 Popular Front government of the Third Republic. Blum's government lasted from 16 December 1946 until 16 January 1947. While it was only intended to be a caretaker government, its brief duration set the trend for the Fourth Republic. There were three new governments before the end of 1947:

22 January to 30 April: Paul Ramadier (SFIO) with ministers drawn from all the major parties;

9 May to 11 November: Paul Ramadier, as before but without the PCF;

22 November to 19 July 1948: Robert Schuman (MRP), all major parties except PCF.

The PCF continued to command the largest electoral following throughout the Fourth Republic. But after Ramadier's first government the PCF never again held ministries in the Republic's lifetime. The international climate of the developing Cold War made the situation difficult for all Communist parties in the western democracies, and in the early months of 1947 the PCF fell out with its partners in government over matters of policy. Following a nationalist insurrection in Madagascar, the Communists were critical of the repressive policies of the French army. In March Communist deputies voted against the military credits which the government proposed for the war in Indo-China; Communist ministers in the government abstained. At the beginning of May, the Communist ministers voted against Ramadier's government over a strike at the Renault works.

De Gaulle was a further problem for the Republic. On 14 May he launched the Rassemblement du Peuple Français. The RPF was not intended to be a conventional political party but a mass movement of the French people which, like the Resistance, crossed party divisions. De Gaulle saw himself at one with sentiments which he detected in the French people – an opposition to the revived party system, and to the Republic as established by the new constitution, and a hostility to Communism both in its external and internal manifestations. The three main parties in the assembly condemned the RPF, but while it never grasped the popular imagination in the way that de Gaulle had hoped, by the end of the year there were about a million members.

Italy

There were five principal political parties in Italy in this period.

1. The Liberal Party (PLI) had claims to being the party that united Italy during the nineteenth century. While its stranglehold on power had been weakened by the introduction of universal manhood suffrage (1912) and proportional representation (1919), it had continued to dominate parliaments and governments until the Fascist take-over. Like the other parties, it was suppressed in 1926, re-emerging in 1943 as largely conservative and pro-monarchy. Numerically, it was very small and its involvement in the Resistance was minimal.
2. The Socialist Party (PSIUP) had been founded in 1892; by 1919 it was the largest single party in the Italian parliament. The party was always divided between those seeking complete change through revolutionary action, and those supporting gradual change within the parliamentary system. This division re-emerged within the party itself in 1943 and became complicated by divided attitudes towards the

Communists; as in France, there were disagreements between those who wanted to work with the Communists and those who did not.

3 The Communist Party (PCI) was established in 1921 by a breakaway faction of socialists. For much of the Fascist period the party's leader, Togliatti, was in exile in Moscow where he became a member of the Presidium of the Comintern and a key figure in the development of the idea of the Popular Front. Some of Togliatti's subordinates fought for the Spanish Republic where they learned tactics which they subsequently employed as partisans. The Communists were largely responsible for organizing the anti-Fascist strikes in Milan and Turin in the spring of 1943. By 1946 the party had close on two million members.

4 The Action Party (PdA) was created during the Fascist period by exiles in Paris. It had close links with (and really grew out of) the Giustizia e Libertà (Justice and Liberty) movement, which in some areas had a decisive effect on the partisan war. It was mainly a party of intellectuals – artists, teachers, writers and professional men – who sought to link liberal ideas of freedom and political democracy with socialist demands to achieve a thorough-going reform of Italian society. Their socialism was free from what they considered to be Marxist determinism.

5 The Christian Democrats (DC) had their origins in the old Catholic party, the Partito Popolare Italiano, a significant force in the years between the end of the First World War and the coming of Fascism. The DC was first organized in 1942–43. Its emphasis was on moderate reform (regional governments, land reform, progressive taxation, freedom for workers to organize and participate in the management of enterprises) and Christian values. Its close relations with the Roman Catholic Church will be examined in Unit 5. Its right wing was pro-monarchy.

Among the smaller parties it is worth noting the Partito Democratico del Lavoro, founded in 1912 by reforming socialists, including Bonomi, which had support only in the south and centre. Also notable was the Partito Repubblicano Italiano, which had small areas of support across the whole country; its programme was similar to that of the Action Party, but had greater emphasis on the idea of a republic and positive demands for a federal structure.

Italy experienced many similar problems to France in the reconstruction of political life, but there was no outstanding figure like de Gaulle. When Bonomi was forced to resign in June 1945, the Lieutenant General of the Realm turned, eventually, to a Resistance leader. Ferruccio Parri was a leader of the Action Party and former head of the partisans in Milan. The invitation to Parri to form a government was one aspect of the *vento del nord* ('the wind from the north'), the phrase used to describe the spirit and aspirations of the northern partisans which swept into Rome with the Liberation of the north and the end of the war. Parri was a popular choice as head of government. His government was made up of ministers drawn from the six major parties.

But the problems he faced were colossal. In February 1945 the Displaced Persons and Repatriation Subcommittee of the AMG (Allied Military Government) estimated that there were about a million Italians to be returned to Italy from outside its northern frontiers: these were former soldiers, prisoners of war and deported men and women workers. At the end of June the refugee centres on the Brenner Pass were processing 5,000 persons a day. There were also soldiers and partisans who had fought in Italy returning to their homes. Given the disrupted state of the Italian economy, there was little work for these people, and the consequent discontent occasionally flared into riots and violence. Many of the partisans had kept their guns and this was a source of an additional anxiety. Members of the propertied classes and people with positions of privilege were convinced that the left was exploiting the discontent and there was fear of a Communist uprising. Within the government itself there were increasingly serious divisions. The Liberals and Christian Democrats wanted resolute action to crush disorder; Parri, Minister of the Interior as well as Prime Minister, was reluctant to order the police to turn on his former Resistance comrades. There were other divisions over the extent to which the purge of Fascists in government and industry should be pursued, the extent to which the state should involve itself in the economic life of the country, and the timescale before the election and the referendum on the monarchy. In November the coalition broke up and Parri's government fell.

Parri denounced the Liberals and Christian Democrats as a 'Fifth Column' within his government, and accused them of 'preparing to restore to power those political and social forces that had formed the basis of the Fascist regime'. Nevertheless, it was the leader of the Christian Democrats, Alcide De Gasperi, who was next invited to form a government, and who was to form eight successive governments up until July 1953. De Gasperi had begun his political career before the First World War as a representative of the Austrian province of Trentino in the parliament at Vienna. After the First World War, when Trentino became part of Italy, he represented the same area in the Italian parliament. He had been imprisoned during the Fascist era and, on his release in 1939, had gone to work as a librarian in the Vatican. Here he wrote political articles under a pseudonym and helped to organize the new Christian Democrat Party. The government which De Gasperi organized in December 1945 was the last to contain representation of all six parties in the CLN. In contrast to Parri, De Gasperi leaned much more to the right; he terminated the purge of Fascists and Fascist sympathizers, and he began to replace CLN appointees in local administrative posts in the north with bureaucrats of a more traditional type. It was this first government headed by De Gasperi that presided over the elections to the constituent assembly and the referendum on the monarchy.

Exercise Turn to Tables 22 and 23 in *Documents and Texts 1*. Study the results of the election and referendum and answer the following questions.

1 Who were the obvious losers and winners as indicated by the votes in (a) the referendum and (b) the election?

2 Do you detect any clear geographical divisions in the voting?

3 Given the pattern of voting, where might a workable majority be found for the government of the new republic?

Specimen answers and discussion

1(a) The clear loser in the referendum was the monarchy.

Recognizing the likelihood of such a vote, Victor Emmanuel's advisors had finally persuaded him to abdicate in favour of Umberto on the eve of the referendum. It was hoped that such a move would influence the electorate in the monarchy's favour since Umberto was less compromised with Fascism and, as Lieutenant General, had demonstrated his ability to work alongside progressive politicians. Monarchist propaganda had also, and unsuccessfully as it turned out, attempted to play up the 'Red Threat'. When the votes were counted there were predictable cries of 'Foul' by the monarchists who protested about fraud and procedural irregularities; they also attempted to claim the void votes.

1(b) The most successful parties in the election were the DC, the PCI and the PSIUP; but you should note that the DC, a new party in these elections, had received a much higher percentage of the vote than that given to its Catholic predecessor in 1921. The PCI also had greatly improved on its percentage of the 1921 vote and, as in France, there was some reason for supposing that this was at the expense of the Socialists – this trend was confirmed by local elections later in the year, and the resulting divisions in the PSIUP over the extent to which the party should make a common electoral front with the Communists led to a split in the party in January 1947. Support for the Liberal Party was revealed to have fallen greatly, but the greatest loser was the Action Party. This was perhaps the most surprising outcome, given that by its origins the PdA had a very real claim to being *the* party of the Resistance. (The PdA never recovered from the fall of Parri and, indeed, did not long survive as a separate entity.)

2 There was a clear geographical division in the voting between north and south: in the election the parties of the left were revealed to be much stronger in the north, the Liberals and the right were strongest in the south. The referendum showed the north supporting the republic by two to one, and the south supporting the monarchy by the same margin.

The conclusion that might seem obvious from this is that the 'backward' peasant was more conservative and more easily swayed by traditional social superiors than the 'progressive' factory proletarians of the north – but beware the obvious conclusion. If you look closely at the pattern of the voting you will see that the largest communes in the south (notably the city of Naples) were as strong for the monarchy as the smallest communes. Left-wing voting in Italy was not the simple result of urbanization and industrialization: indeed there were peasant districts with long traditions of radicalism which became staunchly Communist.

3 As in France, no single party had an overall majority and, consequently, coalition government was necessary to ensure a working majority in the assembly. The DC had 207 seats, but the PCI and the PSIUP, combined by their 'Unity of Action' agreement, had 219 seats.

Again as in France, the belief that some kind of national unity was required in the aftermath of war, and during the crucial period in which the constitution was being drafted, led to coalitions involving the main parties. As leader of the party that had secured the most seats, De Gasperi was invited to form a government; Communists, Socialists and Republicans agreed to join him. The Actionists were in complete disarray; while the Liberals, smarting at the referendum verdict and protesting about the procedures that had been followed, refused to participate. ❑

Major problems beset De Gasperi's new government. The economy remained weak and the result of this was continued unrest. The restoration of former functionaries of the Fascist state to positions of authority in the republic provoked disorder, notably when former policemen, released under an amnesty, replaced the demobilized partisans who had taken over police tasks. These disorders were all the more serious because of the vast quantities of arms which still remained in private hands. The compromises reached between De Gasperi and the left in dealing with these problems provoked furious condemnation in the right-wing press. On the international front, Italy was still in something of a political and diplomatic no-man's-land since it had yet to sign a peace treaty with the victorious Allies. In the hopes of improving Italy's international position, as well as securing aid, De Gasperi travelled to the United States at the beginning of 1947. In America the trip was a great success, but political problems continued in Italy. The PSIUP split in early 1947 with just under half of the Socialist deputies elected to the constituent assembly forming the breakaway Socialist Party of the Italian Workers (PSLI; later the Social Democrat Party, PSDI). De Gasperi's government was compelled to resign, but he was invited to form a new one. Again he looked for support from other parties, especially as a peace treaty with the Allies was on the point of signature and he recognized that it would be folly for such a treaty – which was bound to provoke protest in some quarters – to be the responsibility of only one party. He formed a coalition with the PCI and those Socialists (now reverting to their old title of PSI) who were still prepared to co-operate with the Communists. The government lasted from 2 February to 12 May. Friction over how to handle the economy and continuing unrest, together with increasing international tension, combined to bring about its collapse.

After several other politicians had failed to form a new government, De Gasperi finally proposed a one-party minority government of Christian

Democrats, which was accepted by the assembly on 21 June by a vote of 274 to 231, the Liberals, *Qualunquists* and various monarchist and right-wing factions being prepared to back it now that the Communists had gone. This government, reshaped in December, remained in power until the elections under the new constitution the following year. Significantly, it marked the end of the wartime and post-war collaboration of anti-Fascist parties, as well as the end of PCI participation in central government.

Throughout the months of ministerial change, of economic difficulties, disorder, negotiations over the peace treaty and increasing Cold War tension, the constituent assembly had continued drafting the new constitution. On 22 December, the assembly finished its work and approved the constitution by 457 votes to 62; only the extreme right voted against. The new constitution came into effect on 1 January 1948.

5 Conclusion to Part One

Exercise What key parallels were there between France and Italy in the achievement of Resistance aspirations and the direction of political reconstruction by the end of 1947?

Discussion We suggest the following:

1. The rapid disintegration of Resistance unity and the emasculation of the aspirations of many resisters. In France, a significant part of the administrative and industrial élites maintained their position and pre-war political squabbling re-emerged under the new constitution. In Italy, where the closing stages of the war had been even more traumatic than in France, many Fascist functionaries were restored to authority, the anti-Fascist coalition crumbled and the true party of resistance and renewal, the Action Party, broke up in disarray.

2. The strength of the left in both countries is worth emphasizing, especially the increasing strength of the Communists at the expense of Socialists. Again, in both countries the Communist parties, in spite of their electoral strength, were out of government (permanently, as it turned out) two years after the end of the war. This was partly because of disagreements over national policy, but also because of international developments in which both France and Italy were eventually allied with the United States.

3. As well as the strength of the left, it is important to note the strength of the Church as manifested in new political parties – the MRP in France, the DC in Italy. Both parties began with progressive aspirations but increasingly became conservative and certainly appear to have picked up votes because of concern about the 'Red' menace. ❑

We will return to the Church and the United States in Units 5 and 6.

PART TWO: ECONOMIC RECONSTRUCTION, 1943–48

1 Introduction

The set reading for this part is Gildea, chapter 4, which provides essential background to the post-war French economy (the discussion of the Monnet Plan for economic modernization, pp.83–4, is particularly useful), and Ginsborg, chapter 3, which has a section on the economic and social problems of post-war Italy (pp.93–8). There is a discussion of agrarian problems in Ginsborg's section on social struggles, pages 105–10.

By 1945 the economies of France and Italy had been devastated by military operations and Nazi depredations, and it appeared to many that the task of reconstruction would take at least a decade. Yet, even though the Second World War was far more materially destructive than the First, both France and Italy recovered more rapidly after 1945 than they had after 1918. Taking 1937 as 100, by 1948, the index of industrial production in France was 103. Italy had not quite recovered its pre-war level of industrial output by 1948, but by 1949 the index was 109 (again 1937 = 100). France was refurbishing its industry under the guidance of state planners (*dirigisme*). Italian economic policy was more 'classically' orthodox, and planning for structural change in agriculture and industry, the development of the south and the revitalization of basic industries like steel, were delayed until after 1948. Though it would be foolish to predate the origins of the Italian 'economic miracle' of the 1950s, there were, none the less, signs of a remarkable vitality in 1948, notably recovery of the export trade to a real value significantly above that of 1938. However, both societies did face acute economic problems in the later 1940s, some of which were inherent in the unbalanced trade relationships between western Europe and the United States, while others were peculiar to their national economies.

Aims

After completing this part of the unit you should:

1. have an estimate of the scale of French and Italian losses due to the war;
2. be able to assess the causes and scope of the economic problems of shortage and inflation which persisted in both societies up to 1948;
3. be able to examine the measures taken to control inflation and reconstruct the French and Italian economies between 1945 and 1948, and in particular to consider the purposes and effects of Marshall Aid and French state planning.

We will be pursuing two of our course themes, reconstruction and the role of the United States, which were indeed intimately linked in this period. Though there are many valid comparisons to be made between France and Italy, we do not intend to make direct, detailed comparisons. The political and cultural similarities between France and Italy masked profound economic differences, basically attributable to the lateness of Italian industrial 'take-off', the generally deleterious effects of Fascist economic policies between 1922 and 1940, and the chronic and severe disparity between the backward south and the industrially advanced triangle around Genoa, Turin and Milan. This disparity and the under-development of Italian society are discussed in detail in Unit 10. Two points worth stressing here are that in 1950 the north–south differential was wider than ever; nevertheless, the north was poor by European standards.

French economic development was based on more abundant natural resources, was more deeply rooted, and had avoided Italy's acute 'dualism'. The picture of French industrial retardation, and of entrepreneurs afraid of expansion, that used to be drawn by Anglo-Saxon economic historians, has been challenged by French authorities who now stress the underlying continuities between the rapid growth of 1906–29 and the post-1945 resurgence. In the 1920s, France led the vanguard of European industrial progress, becoming the leading European car manufacturer, and in the Alpine region using hydro-electricity to develop substantial chemical and metallurgical industries. Its export trade fared exceptionally well, unlike Britain's and Germany's. It is true that the French economy suffered a severe industrial defeat during the depressed 1930s, when the nineteenth-century staples (such as textiles, iron and steel) were particularly hard hit. Industrial output declined at a rate of more than 1 per cent annually over the decade 1929–39 and real income per head was 12 per cent lower at its end. Some of this poor performance is attributable to the determination of successive French governments to maintain the franc at an artificially high rate of exchange.

It is evident from this glance at French inter-war economic history that the late 1920s (rather than 1938) would be taken by planners as a baseline by which to measure 'reconstruction' and growth; the 'success stories' of 1906–29 were bound to influence planning; and the economic and monetary policies of the 1930s were to be avoided.

Let us now turn to a detailed consideration of each country.

2 France

War losses – demographic

Economic decline in the 1930s was exacerbated by demographic decline. The birth rate reached a low point of 14.8 per 1,000 between 1935 and 1939, and the death rate was more than fifteen per 1,000. France faced the prospect of a diminishing population, the situation made especially grave by a century's restricted population growth and grievous losses of young men (and potential fathers) during the First World War. Total demographic losses between 1939 and 1945 are variously estimated at between 1.395 and 1.45 millions. The lower estimate is given in Table 1(a) of the 'Statistical tables' in *Documents and Texts 1*. Turn to it and let us see how it was composed.

The largest item is the excess of deaths over births, but this excess was not entirely due to deaths caused directly by the war. Some occurred simply with the lapse of time; because of the demographic profile of France, deaths would have exceeded births over the six-year period even if war had not broken out. However, the 'natural' death rate did rise with wartime privations and because the absence of young men (as prisoners of war and deported workers) altered the age structure of the population. Those who remained were, on average, more elderly and less healthy. Increased infant mortality was a significant feature of the 'war-related' excess of deaths, with the civilian flight of 1940 (*l'exode*) taking a severe toll. The appalling figure for 1945 (see Table 1(b)) was the result of an outbreak of infantile intestinal disorders, coupled with the disruption of the milk supply by warfare.

The war had positive, as well as negative, demographic effects. Under the Vichy regime, there were distinct incentives to marrying and having children (in the form of family allowances and favourable rations), and it was in this period that a remarkable demographic revival began. Though the number of births fell in 1940 and 1941, the fall was less than to be expected given the absence in Germany of 1.5 million prisoners of war. In 1942 the birth rate revived, and in the last years of the war total births were above the pre-war figure. There was a change in the size of the average 'completed' family which suggests that throughout the 1940s and 1950s children were less of an economic burden than they had been in the past.

Table 2.1 Average number of children after ten years' marriage

Years of marriage	
1920–24	1.86
1930–34	1.82
1940–44	2.29
1950–54	2.28

Such figures obviously have a crucial bearing on the social roles of women in post-war France; they help explain why, for example, female participation in paid employment declined after the war (although the contraction of agriculture was a more important factor). The decline in the female workforce also suggests a greatly increased demand placed on the productive effort of the working population which was *smaller* in 1946 than in 1921, and remained so until the mid 1960s.

Those who began the work of rebuilding were scarcely fit (at least physically) to do so: 70 per cent of men and 55 per cent of women were, in March 1945, officially reckoned to be underweight. In the large cities one child in three was identified as suffering stunted growth.

Material losses

Exercise Please watch item 2.4 on Video-cassette 1, Part 1, 'Archive film'. This consists of two extracts from a French government documentary made in late 1945, *Les Ponts renaissants* (literally 'The Re-born Bridges', although the English language version you will see was entitled 'The French Highway Lives Again'). Assess the value of the film evidence for your understanding of the task of physical reconstruction facing France in 1945 and the zeal with which the French undertook it.

Specimen answer I think this is a good example of moving pictures being worth a thousand words and a dozen statistical tables. The impact of war on France's road transport system – which left 7,500 bridges destroyed and made every important river an obstacle to traffic – is here for you to see. The 'recycling' of steel structures shown on the film is evidence of the desperate shortage of metals; the use of German POWs reminds us of one of the very few assets at the disposal of the French government. The film is undoubtedly propagandist but still convincing evidence of France's determination to restore the material infrastructure of economic life as quickly as possible. ❑

The total cost of restoring France to 'normality' was calculated as 4,900 milliard francs in 1946, a sum equivalent to about two to three years the pre-war national income (though the hyper-inflation of the time makes comparison with pre-1939 extraordinarily difficult). Much of this was accounted for by the destruction of the railway system, a particular target of Allied bombing and the Resistance. At the end of 1944, only 18,000 of the 40,000 kilometres of railway track were in service. We have already seen what the war did to France's bridges. Road freight, which before the war had amounted to two-thirds of that carried by rail, was in any event crippled by shortages of lorries, diesel and petrol. Consequently food was difficult to move from the countryside to the towns, and restoring industrial production was delayed by the inability to move coal, the major source of power. Because the Atlantic ports and harbour facilities had all been badly damaged, imports were severely restricted; and the loss of the merchant fleet made France entirely dependent on foreign carriers. The importance the government attached to restoring the means of transport can be judged from the fact that 20 per cent of the 1945 budget was allocated to the road network, and by the end of that year the railways had been re-established at their 1938 level.

The loss of buildings, due directly to their damage and destruction, and indirectly to the cessation of most civilian construction during the war, was much less quickly remedied. 460,000 dwellings were destroyed, a further 1.9 million damaged, and more than a million families left homeless in the 74 French *départements* ravaged by war. Nearly a quarter of all immobile capital was wiped out. The government made the repair of factories and offices – indispensable for the revival of production – a priority, but the nation's housing stock was denied the resources needed for renovation. France had experienced nothing like Britain's inter-war housing boom and in the later 1940s families seeking accommodation faced the consequences of years of under-investment in housing as well as the losses of war. Throughout north-east France houses at the end of the war were, on average, 120 years old and mostly devoid of what we now consider basic amenities. In 1946, only 37 per cent of all French dwellings had indoor running water, only 12 per cent mains drainage, and only 5 per cent had a bathroom.

Lack of investment and maintenance during the war in French industrial plant were, in aggregate, more serious problems than the outright losses of factories and machinery. Bombing was inefficient against industrial targets and all countries found making good bomb damage easier than had been envisaged. The value of productive capital destroyed was considerable – 393 milliard francs at 1938 prices – and a further 160 milliard was lost because of wartime disinvestment. But the hidden costs of the total subservience of the French economy to the German war effort were greater. French firms became 'metal bashing' subcontractors to the Reich, working with increasingly obsolescent machine tools and cut off from the technical evolution that took place in other war economies. Industrial production and labour productivity fell steeply. Workers were undernourished and slacking was often a form of passive resistance. When 40 per cent of French industrial output was being extorted by Germany in 1944, the good patriot played 'ca'canny'.

From the point of view of the revival of industry, the most critical shortage in 1945 was that of coal. France was poorly endowed with coal and had been before the war the world's leading importer, looking to Germany and Britain to provide one-third of its needs. Daily production had fallen to less than half its pre-war level by the autumn of 1944. Output of the Lorraine iron and steel industry, which was normally dependent on Ruhr coking coal, was about one ninth of the pre-war figure by December 1944. Because of transport and other difficulties coal imports in 1946 were 10 million tonnes as against 23 million in 1938.

This energy shortage, the outcome of natural deficiencies and the impact of war, was a central consideration for both the economic planners and foreign policy makers of post-war France. It dictated the priorities of the Monnet Plan for the modernization and re-equipment of industry and led the French to demand the internationalization of the Ruhr. It also made France an early and enthusiastic proponent of atomic power.

The last of the material losses we will consider were those affecting agriculture. Total production did not fall as steeply as in industry, but nor did it recover so quickly in post-war years. This reflects the exhaustion of the soil, which was starved of chemical fertilizers and manure during the war, the depletion of livestock (many horses were requisitioned by the German army), the shrinking of the area of cultivated land, and the shortage of labour. A post-war revival was hampered by severe winters and the Saharan summer of 1949. Given the soaring black market prices of the post-war years and the shortage of consumer goods on which to spend agricultural profits, there was, moreover, little incentive for producers to increase output.

Monetary and financial losses and post-war inflation

Inflation was one of the most destructive forces unleashed on Europe by the war; it wiped out savings and investments, lowered wage earners' and employees' standards of living, made domestic daily life a constant struggle, and set consumers against producers. For some there were benefits: holders of stocks found their value soaring (which encouraged hoarding); debts and mortgages were written off; firms were saved from bankruptcy by demanding payment in advance and settling with their suppliers on long-term account; employment was kept high (or at least higher than deflation would have allowed). French inflation aggravated class hostility and was a source of the bitter strife of 1947.

The roots of inflation lay in the great increase in deficit public financing and paper money during the war, combined with the loss of production. The Vichy regime could not impose wage and monetary restraint without provoking popular discontent, but most people were no better off, for shortages pushed up prices, and a great gap opened between incomes and the cost of living. While the index of wages rose from 100 in 1938 to 163 in April 1944, the cost of living rose nearly three times. Liberation accelerated the inflationary process. The purchasing power of weekly wages had declined to just over half its pre-war level by the end of the war, and remained substantially below it until the 1950s, although some of the difference was made good through social welfare supplements to income (see Table 2 in *Documents and Texts 1*). During the post-war reconstruction, a new inflationary dynamic arose from the irreconcilable desires of government and industrialists to invest and consumers to consume.

Escalating food prices meant that the burden of inflation was carried disproportionately by the less well-off. Vichy France used subsidies and price controls with some success, but with the Liberation prices rose steeply up to 1949, and at a lesser but still considerable rate in the early 1950s (see Table 3 in *Documents and Texts 1*). Restoration of price stability was hindered by the disequilibrium between agricultural and industrial prices; between the summer of 1946 and the end of 1948 the former rose much more quickly than the latter.

Inability to control inflation was the most signal failing of post-war governments. Admittedly, price control was not altogether in the power of government, but measures that would have alleviated the situation and were successfully applied elsewhere were not taken. A currency reform, freezing of assets, and a capital levy – such as were implemented in Belgium – were advocated by Pierre Mendès France, Minister for the National Economy in the Provisional Government, and would have been popular with the left and the working classes. The proposals were defeated by the opposition of René Pleven, Minister of Finance, and de Gaulle's failure to support Mendès France. Instead, the more financially orthodox measure of launching the Liberation Loan was taken. It mopped up 164 milliards and substantially reduced the amount of money in circulation. But in appeasing the hoarders of notes, particularly peasant producers, the government threw away the opportunity to seize the illicit profits of black marketeers and 'economic collaborators' which a freezing of deposits and other assets would have given it.

The issue exposed the division between those who saw economic reconstruction as taking place in a planned regime of strict controls in which an enlarged public sector would provide the dynamic element, and those who regarded a restoration of business confidence as a prerequisite for reconstruction in a much more liberal context. The resignation of Mendès France in April 1945 signalled the defeat of the policy of strict controls. The government's easygoing financial policy unleashed the inflationary forces in the economy: in January 1946 the index of retail prices stood at 481 in relation to 1938's 100; by the end of the year, it was 865.

Enlarging the public sector

Exercise Return to the CNR Charter, item 3 in *Documents and Texts 1*, and say what economic measures were pledged in it.

Answer The CNR Charter promised 'the setting up of a true economic and social democracy' and called for 'the return to the nation of the great monopolies in the means of production, the sources of energy, mineral wealth, insurance companies, and the large banks'. ❑

These specific pledges were the warrant for the nationalization of part of French industry and most financial services by the Provisional Government. The Renault motor company, which had supplied the German army with armoured and other vehicles, was nationalized without compensation in January 1945, and major aero-engine manufacturers were also taken over because of economic collaboration. The coal mines were nationalized in two stages in December 1944 and April 1946, and the gas and electricity industries in March 1946. The majority of the insurance companies and the largest banks were taken over by the state in early 1946. Air transport was nationalized in June 1945 and the state acquired a majority shareholding in the merchant marine. Under pressure from the trade unions and the Parisian Liberation committee, the Paris transport system was municipalized. How far these measures went towards instituting economic democracy is debatable. Employees were represented on the board of the nationalized Renault firm and they participated in the management of the confiscated Berliet motor lorry works. Organized labour acquired a role in the direction of the nationalized coal mines – production would not have restarted without this concession. But the majority of nationalized companies retained their former management structures and the imaginative experiments in employee participation in management were short lived. As Gildea notes (p.83): 'The state [...] was keen both to assert itself against the power of the trusts and to limit workers' control, and ensured this by a strategy of orderly nationalization.'

The revival of industrial production

The index in the statistical tables in *Documents and Texts 1* – Table 6(a) – shows a startlingly quick restoration of industrial production, made possible in the first instance by a continuation of the Resistance consensus. Until the Communists were dismissed from the government of Paul Ramadier in May 1947, it appeared that the revival was to be accompanied by the forward march of collectivism: as well as the enlargement of the public sector, compulsory national insurance was instituted and welfare rights were established. The Social Security system made it possible to distribute a larger share of national income to the workforce. Though the measures were not part of a policy of socialist transformation, they all suggested that national economic revival would be carried on the flood tide of the left. Their passage helps explain why there was a popular willingness to raise productivity (in part by lengthening the working week) and to see postponed non-productive investment in housing.

While this popular will was necessary for industrial resurgence, it was not sufficient. France had to maintain a high level of 'basic' investment in its transport system, energy resources and capital goods. The finance capital market – which had never been very important in France – had dwindled to insignificance and the state took on the role of facilitating investment. More importantly, the government allocated credits from the loans floated abroad up to 1947 and, after that date, from Marshall Aid. As a percentage of national income, gross domestic capital formation rose from 17 per cent in 1938 to 22 per cent in 1947. Much of this investment took the form of capital goods and metals imported from the United States, and it is a measure of the French determination to reconstruct their economy that they continued on the course of high investment and such imports in the face of bankruptcy in 1947.

This investment was deliberately targeted and the overall index of industrial production masks extraordinary progress in some sectors and stagnation in others. A comparison of the production indices for selected industries will give you a broad idea of the overall pattern of post-war growth, which favoured the industries in which France had already made great strides up to 1929 and discriminated against older industries, such as textiles. Behind this disparate growth lay a redistribution of industrial labour away from textiles, clothing and leather towards engineering and chemicals. There were also differences in productivity gains.

Table 2.2 Some comparative production indices (1938 = 100)

	1929	*1949*
Motor cars	107	240
Tractors	107	990
Chemical industries	113	126
Rubber	90	155
Paper, cardboard	63	100
Textiles	120	101
Leather	117	67

The Monnet Plan

Many on the left hoped that the two waves of nationalization, during the winter of 1944–45 and between December 1945 and May 1946, would give the state control of the commanding heights of the economy and the ability to fulfil the Resistance programme of equality and freedom. In practice, the public sector was composed of disparate elements, many of which behaved little differently from private institutions, and was a poor instrument for a policy of long-term state intervention. That instrument was provided by a small team of functionaries headed by Jean Monnet, who produced an overall plan (the 'Monnet Plan') for economic modernization and equipment which was intended to develop national production and foreign trade, increase the productivity of labour, conserve full employment and raise the standard of life of the population.

Though in general terms the Plan expressed the Resistance desire for social renewal, it also owed something to a long tradition of state intervention in France and to the activities of the Vichy regime itself. Post-war planners drew upon the work of Vichy's statistical service which had started GNP accounting – indispensable for macro-economic planning. There were, too, institutional links between Vichy corporatist organizations and the *modus operandi* of post-war planning. Moreover, the pragmatism with which Monnet and his team approached national planning made the connection with Resistance ideology still more tenuous. Monnet was not ideologically wedded to *dirigisme*, and conceived his task as 'concerting' and providing long-range objectives for a capitalist economy too weakened by war and restrictive in outlook to perform these functions itself. The Four-Year Plan adopted in January 1947 projected a recovery to the 1929 level of production by 1949, and to 25 per cent above that level in 1950. It gave absolute priority to investment in energy industries (coal and electricity), steel, cement, tractors and transport, to which were later added motor fuels and nitrate fertilizers. Housing, agriculture and consumer goods were given low priority. The Plan set production and productivity norms which were imperative for the public sector, but were negotiated with the private sector on the basis of the government assuring firms the regular supply of raw materials, such as coal and steel, and providing credit from foreign loans.

The Plan was not an unqualified success. Its global production target was not attained and a comparison of the projections and the achieved production figures reveals serious shortfalls (for example, in coal, steel and tractors). But to judge the Plan a failure would be harsh. It did not follow the Soviet model, but was designed for a predominantly capitalist market economy whose investment priorities it sought to *indicate*, not dictate. Planners had negligible executive power and when we bear its purpose and context in mind the Plan appears eminently successful.

The role of American aid

National planning and American aid presupposed each other. When the wartime system of US economic assistance known as Lend-Lease was wound up in September 1945, the Americans made it clear that further aid to France was dependent on some overall plan for modernization to which it could be directed. On his part, Monnet knew that the huge investment programme envisaged by the Plan could not be realized without American aid. When Léon Blum went to Washington in March 1946 to negotiate credits for economic recovery, he did so with a draft of the Plan in his pocket, and Monnet later joined his delegation. American experts spent six weeks scrutinizing the draft. Whatever its quantitative contribution to French recovery – which is a matter of some dispute – American aid had a crucial *psychological* influence because without it the ambition to modernize was inconceivable.

The Americans made available a $650 million credit over the years 1946–49 'to facilitate the restoration, reconstruction, and modernization of the French economy', and persuaded the World Bank to make a $250 million reconstruction loan in 1947. Fear of Communist electoral advances influenced them, but they were also anxious to see a quick return to free trade and an end to the economic and financial restrictions which post-war France had, of necessity, maintained. Though considerable, these sums represented only a tiny fraction of the investment capital, estimated at between 23 and 25 per cent of national income, which the Plan's fulfilment required. Much bigger amounts came under the European Recovery Programme (ERP), which put into effect Secretary of State Marshall's offer of co-ordinated aid to Europe, made in June 1947. Though the eastern bloc was offered aid, there can be no doubt that the powerful political motive behind the Marshall Plan was the closer political integration of western Europe under American hegemony.

Marshall's offer was made in an atmosphere of crisis, when many Americans were persuaded that Europe faced starvation. It has, however, been argued that what western Europe faced was merely a crisis of international financing, brought on by the speed of post-war industrial recovery, which sucked in American capital goods and metals, and the refusal of national governments to deflate (i.e. restrict credit and investment). In the case of France, this interpretation of the crisis can be substantiated by looking at the use to which Marshall Aid was put. ERP aid between mid 1948 and mid 1949 added about 6 per cent to national income, and about one-fifth of all imports were covered by it in 1949. The Aid-covered imports were geared to reconstruction rather than relief. Thus, while food accounted for 12.5 per cent of ERP shipments (but 24 per cent of total imports), machinery, vehicles and fuel amounted to nearly 30 per cent of ERP shipments (as against 19.2 per cent of all imports). In other words, France was using 'normal' imports of food to cover its shortages to a far greater extent than it was using Marshall Aid, and conversely using Aid for industrial growth to a greater extent than it was using normal trade. In fact, France could not have acquired the capital goods it did acquire without Aid, and to this extent the speed and rhythm of reconstruction depended on it. This pattern was continued over the whole period of Marshall Aid. If we break down the distribution of the counterpart funds which the Modernization and Equipment Fund (FME – Fonds de modernisation et d'équipement) made available under ERP, then we find that the largest allocations went to the nationalized coal and energy industries.

The mechanism of Aid distribution can best be followed in Figure 2.2.

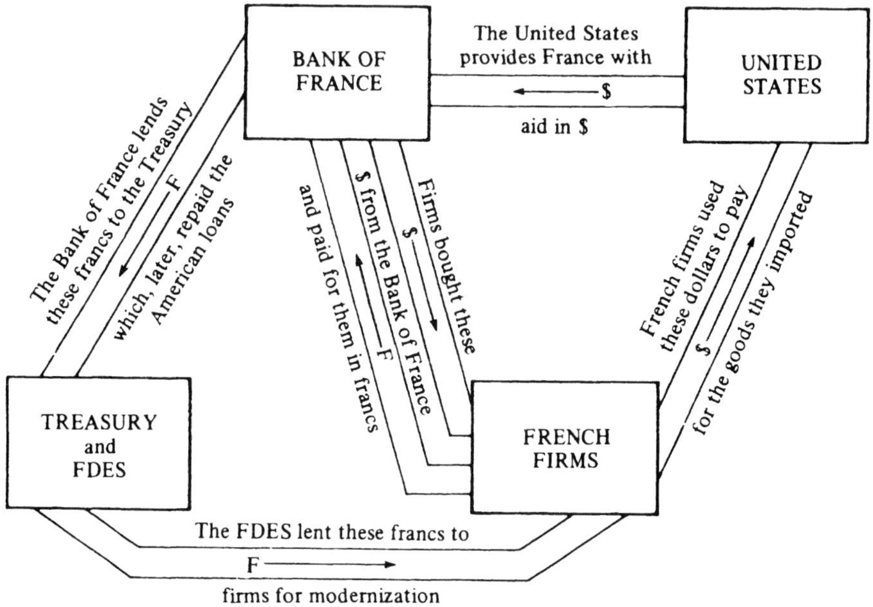

Figure 2.2 *The mechanism of Marshall Aid. (From J. Guynard,* Le Miracle français, *Éditions du Seuil, 1965, as reproduced in Jean-Pierre Rioux,* The Fourth Republic, 1944–1958, *Cambridge, CUP, 1987, p.176.)*

Exercise Using the diagram and the discussion so far, describe how Marshall Aid was distributed, how it interconnected with national planning, and evaluate its contribution to post-war reconstruction.

Specimen answer The United States provided the Bank of France and the Exchange Stablisation Fund with dollars which were then (a) bought with francs by French businesses to import goods from America; (b) lent as francs to the French Treasury and FME in order to furnish loans to businesses so that they could modernize. The Treasury-FME control over the disbursement of loans was the chief link with national planning. The *prospect* of Aid made the planning of modernization thinkable, but actual receipts of Aid contributed more to the *continuation* of industrial revival than its inception. Whether the revival would have (a) continued at a slower rate in 1948 had Aid not been forthcoming, or (b) turned into deep depression (as occurred when the post-First World War 'restocking' boom burst) is a difficult question. Outcome (a), at least, is virtually certain, and Aid was therefore important but not vital. If you consider (b) to have been likely, then you will consider Aid to have been indispensable to long-term reconstruction. ❑

Controlling inflation

The policy of investment 'at all costs' accelerated the galloping inflation, for although the volume of credit and money income grew with the influx of foreign aid and other investment funds into the economy, consumers' demands for food, clothing and household goods were unsatisfied. Official price fixing merely drove goods on to the black market and led to wage claims that were difficult to resist. The absence of competition among producers meant that, in reality, they could dictate prices and demand payment in advance. Industrial wage earners were the chief victims of the price spiral: they increased their hours and productivity to meet the nation's need, only to find the purchasing power of their wages falling rapidly. By November 1947 their patience was exhausted, and the Communist Party sought to capitalize on their industrial militancy by organizing a wave of strikes (this is analysed in Unit 3). At the time, Jean Monnet wrote:

> The French economy is in danger of real dislocation. Food prices are shooting up madly. Speculative hoarding is growing more and more widespread. Even rising prices contribute to supply difficulties, because producers prefer to consume or keep their own products rather than sell them for money which is depreciating. The lowering of the worker's standard of living makes France live under the threat of strikes. Budgetary attempts to redress the balance are swept away in the flood of rising prices.
>
> (quoted in Caron, *An Economic History of Modern France*, p.275)

The measures proposed by the Minister of Finance, René Mayer, in December 1947, decelerated the inflationary spiral. He introduced exceptional taxation to reduce liquidity and began to dismantle the rigid system of price controls which had facilitated the rapid diffusion of increases. Above all, he sought stability through the operation of market laws which the liberalization of the economy would bring. The first effect of his measures was to reduce the gap between industrial and agricultural prices (which slowed down the rise in the workers' cost of living). In 1948 prices began to stabilize with the restoration of competition, stocks started to accumulate and vendors had to accept payment on account or even at discount. In the years 1948–51, mean annual inflation ran at considerably less than half the rate which had prevailed between 1939 and 1947.

The year 1948 witnessed not just price stabilization, but a more pervasive economic and social stabilization. With self-financing by firms and some revival of private investment, growth became less dependent on the state. The period of simple reconstruction of a war-devastated economy was over, with the significant exception of domestic building. The French had been offered a choice between 'modernization or decadence'; they had chosen the first, and begun a national revival barely conceivable in 1940 or 1944.

3 Italy

War losses – demographic and territorial

Italy did not 'lose' demographically overall during the Second World War: between 1939 and 1945, its population increased by 4 per cent from 43.6 million (within the post-1945 boundaries) to 45.34 million. This was in spite of 444,523 war deaths, of whom 291,376 were military personnel. The war did slow down the natural rate of increase because the birth rate fell during

1940–44 from an annual pre-war average of 23.2 per 1,000 of the population to 20.6. To a considerable extent, this was a continuation of a long-term trend, but accelerated by the absence of husbands on military service and working abroad. At the same time, the death rate (excluding deaths directly due to war) rose from 13.9 to 14.5. Malnutrition of the civilian population and lowered resistance to disease were the basic causes of the increased death rate. By 1944 Italians had one of the lowest per capita food rationing levels in Europe (lower, even, than that of Poland). The blockade, which cut off food imports and fertilizers, and the lower productivity of land and labour, meant that annual per capita expenditures of civilians on food at 1938 prices fell from 1,372 lire in 1940 to 826 lire in 1945. Increased infant mortality was a factor in the greater death rate. The infant mortality rate increased from 103 deaths per thousand live births during 1935–39 to 110 during 1940 – 44. Between 1945 and 1949, the 'hidden' demographic loss to Italy – a result of the slowing down of the natural rate of increase by the abnormal wartime conditions – was made good. The birth rate rose temporarily as couples who had postponed marriage and parenthood started families, the general death rate and infant mortality fell.

The adverse demographic impact of the war was further eased by two factors: the repatriation of Italians between 1939 and 1945 exceeded gross emigration for the first time since the great exodus abroad began in the late nineteenth century. This trend was given a further impetus with the territorial changes imposed on Italy by the peace settlement of February 1947, which deprived it of colonies in Africa, the Dodecanese Islands and the Istrian peninsula. Italian settlers returned from North Africa and the ceded regions. The colonial losses were deeply resented, particularly in the light of the southern kingdom's participation in the Allied war effort and the partisan struggle in the north, but were an economic godsend: Liberal and Fascist Italy had squandered scarce resources on a largely barren empire, and it was spared the expensive colonial conflicts subsequently experienced by France and Portugal.

Population and employment

The course of Italian economic history was closely related to its demography and it is essential to consider longer term demographic trends, particularly in relation to labour supply. From 1900, Italy suffered chronic serious unemployment and hidden agricultural under-employment. The net migration of six million before the First World War was, of course, unemployment 'in disguise'. The Fascist regime attempted to hold down visible unemployment by restraints on internal migration (which were not lifted until 1961) but this only exacerbated difficulties on the land, particularly in the south. Post-war Italy failed to solve the problem it had inherited: the demand for labour collapsed in the disastrous crystallization of adverse economic forces of 1945. Unemployment rose to two million and remained near or at this figure for more than a decade. The official statistics, reproduced in Table 5 in *Documents and Texts 1*, are thought to underestimate the real level of unemployment which probably did not fall below 10 per cent of the labour force until 1959. Among industrial workers the percentage was much higher.

Given the extraordinary propensity of Italians to emigrate (and seasonally migrate in search of work), there has been an understandable belief that the country has been burdened with a population beyond its resources: birth control and population decrease were advocated as solutions to the labour surplus. (On the other hand, some economists attributed the economic miracle of the 1950s to excess labour supplies, arguing that they kept wages low and Italian exports highly competitive.) Undoubtedly much of the land is poor and there are strict limits to the numbers of rural workers it will support, but this demographic explanation of unemployment is, at best, incomplete. Developed societies can sustain much higher population densities than are to be found in Italy, and often have to look elsewhere to overcome labour scarcities (as did Britain, France and West Germany in the 1950s and 1960s). The persistence of high unemployment long after the onset of the Italian economic miracle suggests that some factors in addition to the under-development of the south were in force.

Some argued that statutory control of internal migration created a geographic imbalance in the labour market, with the south bearing a disproportionate burden of unemployment. This cannot, however, have been the major factor. As we shall see in later units, large-scale internal migration did take place in the 1950s and many Italians emigrated. At the root of the unemployment problem lay the failure to industrialize the southern economy during and after the period of unification, and the social legacy of chronic under-investment. The flight from the land, accelerated by increasing agricultural productivity, directed many towards the southern services and handicraft sectors, which simply could not absorb such an influx. Although the northern industrial sector expanded its output continuously from the later 1940s, it did so principally by increasing productivity. Rather than taking on more workers, firms invested in labour-saving equipment. The demand for labour in the strongest part of the economy never matched its supply in the weakest. The result was economic 'dualism' – or the coexistence of advanced manufacturing in the north with poverty and high unemployment in the south – which persisted in an acute form until the early 1960s, and in a somewhat ameliorated form for long after.

War losses – material

Exercise Turn to Video-cassette 1, part 1, 'Archive film', and watch item 2.5, which consists of extracts from an assembly of silent film material on the immediate post-war months in Italy. The 'AMG' you will see is an acronym for Allied Military Government and shots include their Naples headquarters. List in brief phrases the economic and social problems facing Italy in the first post-war months that are indicated by the film.

Specimen answers

- Harbour facilities destroyed – importing/exporting severely restricted where this is typical.
- Abject poverty among ruined dwellings.
- Food shortages – large numbers seemingly dependent on Allied handouts.
- Food aid arriving – Italy not able to sustain itself without foreign succour?
- A problem of social control suggested by the shots of struggling queues. ❑

Naturally this is fleeting, impressionistic evidence. We have to use it conjointly with aggregate statistics. The destruction of the Italian economy in 1945, a result not simply of the devastation of war but also distortions imposed by Fascist policy since 1935, can be gauged by the indices of agricultural and industrial production (see *Documents and Texts 1*, Tables 6(a) and (b)).

The 1945 wheat harvest was half its pre-war level; sugar production had fallen from 560,000 tons in 1940 to 18,000. The steep decline of industrial output was due less to quite modest outright losses of industrial plant (estimated at 8 per cent of the whole) than to crippling shortages of raw materials, power and the means of transport. In particular sectors, however, plant losses were severe: 67 per cent of pig-ironmaking capacity was destroyed, 34 per cent of steel and 50 per cent of shipbuilding. With the destruction of a quarter of all railways, 60 per cent of locomotives, half the freight cars, as well as extensive damage to roads, bridges and ports, Italy did not have a national transport network. Sinking had reduced the merchant marine to one seventh of its pre-war size. Basic industries were virtually inoperative; steel output fell from 2.3 million tons in 1938 to 395,000 in 1945; shipbuilding and auto-engineering experienced corresponding declines in output. In the post-war years, the problems of these (and other industries) were magnified by legislation which compelled employers to retain workforces far in excess of capacity or demand. High wage costs made their products uncompetitive. The housing stock had been reduced by the destruction of seven million rooms; no replacement building had taken place.

In addition to these material losses, Italy suffered the less tangible effects of ten years autarky begun when Mussolini placed the economy on a war footing in 1935. The Fascist state had over-invested in agricultural self-sufficiency (restrictions on labour mobility had been partly motivated by its agrarian production drives) and armaments. Engineering had expanded rapidly, but in technical isolation, and it was ill-adapted to the domestic and foreign demands of peace. The consumer goods industries – such as clothing and textiles – had, by contrast, been starved of investment.

There were glimmers of light in the post-war economic gloom. The destruction of productive capital and enforced scrapping through obsolescence in effect 'wiped the technological state clean', enabling entrepreneurs to rebuild industry with the latest imported innovations. Furthermore, as a defeated and decolonized power, Italy was denied the economically wasteful expenditure on armaments and empire such as Mussolini had imposed (and post-war Britain undertook). The mass psychological effects of the complete defeat inflicted on the Axis powers were economically influential too. The break with the past and the need to construct a new future were obvious to all, and despite deep political and social cleavages, this created a broad consensus in Italy (as in Germany) that economic growth was the prime objective of national policy. Even Italian Communists agreed that socialism would not be achieved in an under-developed society.

Exercise From reading Ginsborg, pages 93–8, you should have noted that there was a policy failure by the Italian government in 1945 comparable to one in France at this time, and that they had very similar consequences. What was the failure? What were the consequences?

Answer The Communist Minister of Finance, Mauro Scoccimarro, planned to choke off inflation by a currency reform and a progressive tax on wealth. His proposals were similar to those put forward by Mendès France in early 1945, and the fact that they were frustrated by bizarre delaying tactics on the part of the Bank of Italy had similar consequences. The public authorities were simply unable to restrain the inflationary pressures in the economy.

Discussion The fate of Scoccimarro's plan revealed two opposing views on the best policies for the reconstruction of the economy and, more importantly, its *long-term development.* On the one side were economic 'liberals', who identified controls, protectionism and autarky with Fascism, excessive bureaucracy, and ample scope for corruption. They believed that only a rapid restoration of a free market mechanism and the opening up of international trade could cure the structural faults of the economy. They wanted to control government expenditure, which they regarded as the main source of inflation, and they did not believe the state administration should have a major role in planning economic growth and development. In the 'liberal' camp were many industrialists from the technologically advanced sector (such as motor vehicles) who saw exports – and readily available imports of raw materials – as essential for business expansion. Opposing the 'liberals' were those arguing for the maintenance of economic controls in the short term and a managed and planned economy in the longer run. They wanted to maintain rationing to guarantee an equitable distribution of scarce consumer goods, and foreign exchange controls so that hard currency earnings could be allocated to priority imports. They envisaged a positive role for the state administration in economic management and believed that government could generate rapid growth by directing investment to the large public sector that Italy had inherited from Fascism.

As Ginsborg makes clear (p.93), it would be simplistic to portray this division simply in terms of right and left. The Communists and Socialist parties as such did not have coherent economic strategies, and in August 1945 Togliatti dismissed the idea of national economic planning as utopian. Many businessmen were content with a controlled and protected economy which gave them a monopoly position. However, between 1945 and 1947 the 'liberal' view came to dominate the Italian approach to economic reconstruction, and this was reflected in the key policy choices made in the early summer of 1947 (discussed below). None the less, it would be a mistake to imagine that the predominance of 'liberalism' led to a *laissez-faire* political economy. The giant public holding company, Istituto per la Riconstruzione industriale (IRI) was preserved, and certain industries (such as steel) were developed by public sector planning and investment. ❑

The monetary and financial effects of the war and post-war inflation

The Second World War began an Italian price inflation, the intermeshing causes of which were the explosion of deficit public financing, the great increase in the money supply and the drastic decline in output. The general index of prices (taking 1938 as 100) jumped to 273 in 1943, to 1,215 in 1944, and 2,392 in 1945, with some goods forty times the 1938 level. Although prices were held stable between late 1945 and mid 1946, they began to shoot up again in June. At the peak of this new (or renewed) inflation, in September 1947, wholesale prices were 62 times their pre-war level, rising at an average 9.4 per cent a month. Food prices were rising slightly less rapidly and, because of statutory rent controls, the rise in the cost of living at 7.7 per cent a month lagged behind the general price index. Since wages were index-linked through the *scala mobile* (see Ginsborg, p.97) they rose automatically, exerting a feedback effect on costs and prices. The depreciation of the external value of the lira was an inevitable consequence of such a giddy price rise. Inflation became the biggest obstacle to long-term reconstruction, for it made imported materials and machines – without which industrial revival could not begin – extremely costly to obtain, and it encouraged the speculative hoarding of imported goods rather than their speedy despatch to industry. In 1945 the official exchange level was 100 lire to the dollar (19.0 in 1938). In January 1946 importers were authorized to offer 225 on certain goods, and a great gap opened up between the free and the official rates of exchange. In May 1947 the free rate reached 906 as against the official rate of 350; only when inflation began to come under control and speculators became apprehensive that they would burn their fingers did the gap narrow.

Inflation arose, basically, from monetary causes – namely the excess creation of notes and credit accounts – although circumstances differed somewhat in its wartime and post-war phases. Apart from other factors, during the division of the country prices were more stable in the German-dominated north, but real wages lower (only about half their 1938 level as compared with three-quarters in the south). The Allied military authorities in the south paid well the workers rebuilding roads and other facilities which kept the wage level up. Fascist government borrowing to cover war costs rose from 11.2 billion lire in 1938 to 572 billion by 1944–45; an increase due in part to the inelasticity of the easily evaded tax system. As a proportion of expenditure, tax receipts fell from nearly 70 to just over 20 per cent. The government treasury looked to the Bank of Italy, the central bank, for its funds, which were supplied by advances on treasury account and the purchase of short-dated treasury bills. The nominal value of these volatile forms of credit rose forty-seven fold during the war. As the government drew on them, the Bank's note issue soared. The amount of currency increased nearly nineteen times between 1938 and the end of the war, and the face value of current accounts over eight times. This growth in the supply of money far outstripped the nominal growth in GNP (i.e. its total in current prices; as we have seen, in real terms, GNP fell). As a proportion of GNP, money supply rose from 28.5 per cent in 1938 to 70.7 per cent in 1944, falling back to 50.2 per cent in 1945. The war ended with the liquid resources of the banks and of some sections of the public bloated by government deficit financing.

During the renewed inflation of July 1946 to September 1947, deficit public financing was no longer the primary factor in building up the money supply. Rather, the needs of reconstruction and industrial revival gave rise to private demands for credit which the commercial banks, with their legacy of extreme liquidity bequeathed by war finance, were able to advance. Credit extensions to the private sector totalled 431 billion in this period, and 159 billion to the public sector. The soaring demand for private credit reflected both the recovery of investment, production and imports, and speculation in commodities and on the increasingly feverish stock market.

The solution to the inflationary process lay in orthodox measures of monetary deflation, and they were favoured by Alcide De Gasperi, the dominant figure in post-war Christian Democracy, and Luigi Einaudi, Governor of the Bank of Italy until May 1947, when he joined De Gasperi's reconstructed ministry as deputy premier and budget minister. These men were strict liberals in economics, believing that the state's primary duty was to ensure sound money and public financing so that the market could function healthily. Though the new Italy inherited an extensive public-holding sector, it was not looked on as the motor force of reconstruction, nor did *dirigiste* concepts generally find much favour with the leading figures of the centre. Monetary deflation was delayed until May 1947 by the opposition of Communists in the government, who feared that credit restriction would increase unemployment and who demanded greater spending on relief for the jobless. Keynesian-influenced American officials of the relief agencies who, too, believed that mass unemployment would result from lowering aggregate demand also opposed deflation. In June, De Gasperi was able to form a ministry without Communist participation and Einaudi began instituting a workable system of credit control.

Exercise The measures implemented by Einaudi had a considerable impact on the development of the Italian economy. Using Ginsborg, pages 112–13, summarize them and say what their social consequences were.

Answer Einaudi intervened in the economy to bring inflation under control by 'classic deflationary policies'. One major social consequence was the exacerbation of unemployment because employers responded to credit restrictions by cutting back on investment and laying off workers. On the other hand, the urban middle classes dependent on fixed incomes were immensely relieved to see inflation brought under control and their standard of living protected. The DC started to recover the electoral support that had been draining away to the Uomo Qualunque movement. ❑

The chief instrument of monetary control implemented by Einaudi was enforcing of stricter reserve requirements on the commercial banks by the Bank of Italy, so that their liquidity was sharply reduced. Statutory limits were also placed on the treasury's resort to financing by the central bank, and under the new constitution any law entailing new or increased expenditure now had to set out the means by which this spending was to be covered. Though government expenditure did not decrease, its rate of growth slowed down. A series of measures was taken towards liberalizing foreign exchange and trade which had the effect of reducing import costs at the 'free' rate.

The measures aimed to strike a balance between the socially destabilizing effects of spiralling prices and the equally perilous consequences of greater unemployment, between restricting the growth of credit and not hindering the growth of output. They were certainly successful in the first of their objectives: the wholesale price index fell 17.1 per cent between September 1947 and July 1948, and the cost of living by 13.7 per cent. The price fall was accelerated by the disgorging of commodities hitherto hoarded by speculators, and now convinced of the government's determination to control prices. The money supply continued to grow, but to circulate more slowly, for it increasingly took the form of cash balances. What came to be known as the 'Einaudi line' ensured monetary stability in Italy for the next decade, and economists have argued that this was an essential condition for business confidence and industrial growth in the 1950s. At the time, however, it seemed to many that the unemployed and the impoverished south were paying a desperately high price for monetary orthodoxy. ERP officials, for example, were deeply critical of the priority the Italian government gave to monetary stabilization over the launching of a co-ordinated investment programme.

Though acknowledging the success of credit restraint in bringing down prices, they argued that private investment could not be counted on to expand industrial plants rapidly or to build housing. Wholehearted government action in this direction was, they believed, being impeded by an exaggerated lack of confidence in official Italian circles that any new inflationary pressures generated by such a programme could not be controlled.

Industrial revival and the role of American aid

Whether the monetary restraint followed by Italian governments in the late 1940s and 1950s created a deficiency in effective demand and, therefore, unnecessarily *prolonged* high employment is a more debatable matter. The indices show what to Keynesian economists is a peculiar combination of rapid industrial growth and high unemployment. The pre-war level of industrial output was surpassed in 1949 and growth slowed down only with the Korean war recession. It is doubtful whether faster growth could have been attained without the feared inflationary effects. What stopped per capita gross domestic product surpassing its 1938 level before the early 1950s was the much slower revival of agriculture. (Note that total national product exceeded gross domestic product because of remittances from Italians working abroad, and other external earnings.) In many ways, Keynesian spectacles are inappropriate for viewing the Italian scene and what lay beneath the paradoxical indices was the 'dualism' of the economy (discussed in Unit 10), which gave rise to two relatively insulated sectors, one advanced and the other backward. The mutual insulation of these sectors meant that the great increases in output of the advanced sector were achieved by quite extraordinary gains in labour productivity, rather than by taking on more workers.

A later unit will discuss attempts to lessen this dualism by the creation of a government fund for southern development (Cassa per il Mezzogiorno, 'Fund for the South') and land reform aimed at breaking up inefficient *latifundi* and consolidating landholdings among the peasantry. Suffice to note here that the destructive impact of the war accentuated the dualism (for the south suffered more devastation than the north), and so did the measures of economic reconstruction taken up to, and even beyond, 1948. Despite the strong preference of centrist leaders for a market economy, the scale of the losses and the weakness of private investment obliged post-war governments to make extensive use of the public sector in reviving industry. A Fascist agency, Istituto per la Riconstruzione Industriale (IRI), which became a holding company and survived the Liberation, played an important role in protecting the over-expanded engineering industry and channelling public investment into selected sectors. In 1947 an Engineering Industry Fund was established to finance the reorganization and modernization of engineering, with the state as the major contributor. In 1948 engineering output already exceeded that of 1938 (itself a buoyant year for engineering) by 5 per cent, while other industries – such as leather and building materials – lagged substantially behind their pre-war levels of output. However, the industry which, by 1948, had made the greatest gains on pre-war output was power, which increased by 46 per cent over 1938. This was indicative of considerable state investment, particularly in hydro-electricity. This industrial revival was heavily weighted towards the north.

Post-war American relief and economic aid were indispensable to ensure the physical well-being of the population and significant in the industrial revival, although aid appears to be relatively less important in the latter respect than it was in France. In 1946 the USA provided $380 m. through the United Nations Relief and Rehabilitation Administration (UNRRA), $98 million through the Foreign Economic Administration (FEA) and $110 million through gift parcels and emigrant remittances. In the next year, the USA granted further aid and, conjointly with Argentina, credits for the purchase of ships and food. The bulk of this aid was directed to *ad hoc* relief, and unconnected to any plan for modernization.

Marshall Aid – distributed by the Organization for European Economic Cooperation – was allocated roughly according to the size of a country's trade and dollar deficits, and for this reason Italy received a smaller proportion than

France, though its population was larger. (Whereas France received 20.6 per cent of all ERP aid, Italy received 11 per cent between 1948 and 1950, and 12.7 per cent in 1950–51.) Marshall Aid to Italy in 1948–49 was a somewhat smaller proportion of Italian national income (5.3 per cent as against 6.5 per cent in France) and its different items were differently weighted. 35 per cent of ERP shipments to Italy in 1949 comprised food aid (as against 12.5 per cent in France); only 6.9 per cent was accounted for by machinery and vehicles (as against 21.1 per cent in France). In 1950 food became a much smaller proportion of ERP aid to Italy and machinery and vehicles much larger, but there was still a very significant difference in their weightings as compared with France. The contrast should not be exaggerated (for the great bulk of payments out of Italian 'counterpart funds' went into industry, railways and public works), but the figures do indicate that France used ERP aid rather more single-mindedly for modernization than did Italy.

4 Conclusion to Part Two

Exercise What would you say was the basic difference between the French and Italian approaches to economic reconstruction between 1945 and 1948?

Specimen answer We would say the basic difference lay in the role of the state. Far-sighted members of the French political and administrative élites saw post-war reconstruction as an opportunity to inaugurate an *économie concertée*, one in which there would be a new balance between liberalism and interventionism. The Italian political class did not make this choice; state interventions in the economy were chiefly intended to restore free market disciplines. ❑

In some respects 1948 is an unsatisfactory point at which to break off our discussion of post-war economic reconstruction, for Marshall Aid and the Monnet Plan were just beginning and the full effects of Italian deflationary policies were yet to be felt. If we accept the interpretation of the 1947 crisis advanced earlier (p.71) then there was an unbroken economic movement from 1945 through the great post-war boom. Why the Europe devastated by the most costly war in its history stood on the threshold of its longest period of constantly increasing prosperity is a question to which we will return in Unit 10.

Reference

CARON, F., *An Economic History of Modern France*, trans. B. Bray, London and New York, Methuen and Columbia University Press, 1979.

UNIT 3 The Left, 1943–48

Prepared for the course team
by Stephen Gundle and Bernard Waites

Preface

This unit deals with the second of the themes in Part One, the left. For reasons you will appreciate when you work through the unit, the chronology of each part is slightly different. Part One, on the French left, ends with the great strike wave of November–December 1947; Part Two, on the Italian left, covers the period up to the general elections of April 1948 and the assassination attempt on Palmiro Togliatti, the Communist leader, in July. There is, too, a difference in emphasis with respect to the topics covered. Stephen Gundle – whose doctoral research was into the cultural politics of Italian communism – writes fully on the left and the intellectuals. Bernard Waites refers more briefly to the relationships between Marxism, Communism and intellectual opinion in France. This issue is discussed more fully in Units 4 and 12 where you will study the politics of Sartre and Camus, and reverted to in Unit 16, *Liberation and Reconstruction Reviewed.*

Study materials

For your work on this unit you will need to refer to the following material:

Gildea, *France since 1945*

Documents and Texts 1

Video-cassette 1, part 1, 'Archive film'

Audio-cassette 1, side A, 'The Italian Resistance: aspirations and delusions'

Audio-cassette 5, side A, 'Agrarian struggles and reform in Italy, 1943–50'

PART ONE: THE LEFT IN FRANCE, 1944–47

1 Introduction

This part of the unit is concerned with the political parties of the French left – the Communist Party (PCF) and the Section française de l'internationale ouvrière (SFIO) – and their relations with organized labour. In the period we will examine, these two parties moved from a close alliance within the Resistance movement, to an increasingly tense relationship as fellow members of the tripartite governments formed between November 1945 and May 1947, and finally to rancorous conflict when the Communists left office and the reverberations of the Cold War produced bitter divisions within French politics and society. In this movement from Resistance unity to Cold War disunity, the Communists won and maintained a position as the largest party, not just of the left, but of France itself. The Socialists' electoral strength declined markedly in 1945 and 1946, and it is evident that their participation in 'Third Force' governments (i.e. coalitions with the Radical Party of the centre and the Catholic MRP) both further undermined their popularity and shifted them ideologically to the right. After 1947 the great rift between Communism and anti-Communism overlay the historic division between left and right.

Aims

1. To *explain* the shift from alliance to schism within the left, and to show how it was 'mirrored' in the labour movement.
2. To outline the *social and geographic bases of support* for parties of the left.
3. To analyse the *organization, ideologies* and political *strategies* of the Communist and Socialist parties.
4. To examine briefly the attraction of Marxism and communism for the French intelligentsia.

The reading you did from Gildea in connection with Unit 1 will have given the background to tripartism and the expulsion of the Communists from government in May 1947. We will refer you back to certain passages from Gildea where appropriate. You will also need to read pages 147–51 in connection with out fourth aim.

2 Liberation and the options for the left

Liberation was the hour of the left, for the Resistance had been either the work of men and women from left-wing parties or a politically radicalizing experience for Christian Democrat resisters. The programme of the CNR (National Resistance Council), discussed in Unit 2, expressed the social radicalism of Resistance ideology. The right was utterly discredited by its association with Vichy while the Communist Party enjoyed an unusual integration into the national political community. This was a result both of a Resistance record second to none and the strategy towards other Resistance groups which it pursued. As we have seen (Unit 1), up to the Nazi attack on the Soviet Union the Party's official line was to denounce the 'imperialist war', endorse the Nazi-Soviet pact and even encourage Franco-German collaboration. However, after 22 June 1941 the Party's dedication to Resistance enabled it to win back support lost between 1939 and 1941, to gain many new adherents and to extend its influence beyond pre-war strongholds (principally the industrialized *départements* of Seine, Nord and Pas-de-Calais) into rural regions. Because of its organizational ruthlessness and the collaboration of several labour leaders with Vichy, it was able to capture control of the trade unions. Its advances were made easier by a strategy of promoting the unity of all resisters – Catholic, Republican, Socialist, Communist – in the *Front national* and wrapping itself in the mantle of patriotism.

Though many Socialists played an active and creditable part in the Resistance, the SFIO had been compromised by a large pacifist element and the decision of three-quarters of its deputies to vote in favour of full powers for Pétain in 1940. Its November 1944 congress agreed to an exceptionally drastic purge of collaborators. French socialism had, however, taken credit from the courage and dignity with which its pre-war leader, Léon Blum, defended himself at his trial by Vichy at Riom. (He was charged with responsibility for the defeat of 1940. It is worth noting that prominent Communists wrote to Marshal Pétain offering to give evidence *for the prosecution*.) Blum himself came to believe that the war was accelerating the socialization of human life. In *À l'Échelle humaine* ('On the Human Scale') – written in captivity – he declared 'It is on the foundation of socialist principles that societies, whether consciously or not, are everywhere being re-constituted', and when he addressed the party congress in August 1945 he proclaimed: 'It is socialism which is master of the hour; it is socialism which will one day be master of the Earth.'

In its context, this hyperbole was understandable: a socialist state had liberated east and central Europe, a Labour government was in power in Britain, at home the CNR programme was still widely accepted as the charter of national reconstruction (although, as we shall see, public opinion had very rapidly become indifferent to its social radicalism). What seemed much more uncertain than the substance of Blum's claim was the party political form a triumphant socialism would take in France, and the precise character of its ideology. As noted in Unit 2, the SFIO tended to divide between a moderate faction, led by the general secretary Daniel Mayer (and much influenced by Blum's *À l'Échelle humaine*), which sought to alter the party's self-proclaimed character as 'a party of the class struggle and of revolution', and a more traditionalist faction, led by Guy Mollet, which clung to the 'class' principles first adopted in 1905. The strategic options open to the party (and the left more generally) further complicated matters by creating divisions which did not coincide with the 'moderate'/'traditionalist' factions.

For simplicity's sake we can enumerate these options for the left as:

1 the creation of a new 'parti de la Résistance' around the CNR programme;

2 the fusion of the Socialists and Communists (but not their erstwhile Resistance partners in the MRP) in a joint party;

3 the revival of the 'Popular Front' of the late 1930s – which had embraced the SFIO, the PCF and the Radical Socialists – around a minimum programme of national reconstruction;

4 the continuation in peacetime of the 'Resistance Front' (i.e. Communists, Socialists and Christian Democrats) on an agreed government programme;

5 a 'half-way' stage to (2) in which the Socialists and Communists would preserve their separate identities but institute formal procedures for achieving unity of action.

Option 1 attracted many patriotic idealists within the Resistance and was briefly favoured by the PCF leadership, but it did not long survive the Liberation. A major obstacle to its realization was that the members of the metropolitan and Algiers-based Resistance movements had never lost their party political identities and though party loyalties were subordinated to patriotism they were not obliterated, any more than the social and doctrinal divisions which gave rise to party politics. The formation of the Catholic MRP – which convened its constitutive congress in November 1944 – was clear evidence of the way the fundamental division between practising Catholics and anti-clericals in French society was still determining the structure of its politics. Though at its inception the new movement embodied progressive Catholic social thought, it owed its rapid electoral growth to middle-class fear of communism and the apprehension of the devout that reconstruction would bring a renewed attack on Catholic schooling. The issue of religious education was a serious source of dispute with the SFIO, many of whose militants were fiercely anti-clerical, and was exploited by both Communists and Gaullists to drive a wedge between the MRP and the Socialists. Furthermore, the very pre-eminence of Communists in the *Front national*, other Resistance bodies and the CGT (General Confederation of Labour) was a great spur to the revival of 'normal' party politics after Liberation and, consequently, a decisive blow against 'le parti de la Résistance'. Moreover, popular support for the CNR programme (and, by implication, any party created to put it into effect) was perhaps less than the great efflorescence of radical journalism and progressive 'cultural politics' at the Liberation would give us to believe.

Exercise An opinion poll taken in March 1945 showed the French responding to the question 'Do you approve, yes or no, the CNR programme?' in the following proportions:

Table 3.1 French opinion towards the CNR programme, March 1945 (in %)

	Yes	*No*	*No opinion*
France	40	7	53
Paris	48	12	40
Other towns	40	7	53
Countryside	35	3	62

(Rioux, *The Fourth Republic, 1944–1958*, p.476)

What do these results tell us about popular attitudes to the idea of radical social reconstruction?

Specimen answers

They show that far more people were for it than definitely against it, but the great body of public indifference – suggesting, perhaps, extensive public cynicism about radical reconstruction – is even more striking. The differences in opinion between Paris and the countryside are notable too. Parisians were more positively for or against the programme; peasants preserved their habitual reserve towards political utopias. In the following month, we must add, only 12 per cent of those polled still wished that the Resistance would found a new party. ❑

Exercise

Given party policy between late September 1939 and June 1941, it is clear that the PCF would – in the absence of contagious political amnesia – face a problem in establishing itself in many French people's eyes as a patriotic party independent of a foreign power. When de Gaulle formed a government in November 1945, he resolutely denied Communists the key ministries of National Defence, Foreign Affairs and the Interior precisely because he thought them susceptible to foreign influence. What could the Party do to allay this suspicion? Which of the options 1 to 5 would it try to follow in the non-revolutionary situation in which it found itself after the Liberation? An interview given by Thorez to the London *Times* on 18 November 1946 (see *Documents and Texts 1,* item 4) should enable you to answer these questions.

Specimen answers

1. The Party could suggest that there was a 'French road to socialism' and present itself as a *national* Communist party, with an ethos and organization distinct from the 'Bolshevik model' provided by Leninism, and more in accord with French political traditions.
2. Option 2 had clearly emerged by this date as central to party strategy.

Discussion

Thorez's interview was a clear signal that the PCF had abandoned the insurrectionary route to power and was committed to coalition politics. Some party militants opposed this strategy. The most prominent was André Marty, a party veteran who had led a mutiny in the French fleet stationed in the Black Sea in 1919 in protest against intervention in Bolshevik Russia, and was a hero to the revolutionary rank and file. Marty and his following were rumoured to have pressed for insurrection at the Liberation (though he later denied this) and believed the compromises involved in being part of a governing coalition would corrupt the party leadership. Thorez's authority, and the rigid discipline observed within the PCF, silenced the dissentients. The great majority accepted that the Party would capture state power via the electoral system. In this they were no different from Communists throughout western Europe who had learned the dangers of political isolation and the advantages of participating in national coalitions. The experience of fascism had taught them the value of 'bourgeois' freedoms, and they now used the term 'people's democracy' to denote a regime led by coalition government in which Communists would have a significant share of power. The regime's policies would include enlarging a public sector, strengthening the labour movement, and a foreign policy generally oriented towards friendship with the Soviet Union (Sassoon, *One Hundred Years of Socialism*, p.99). Only later, with the development of the Cold War, did 'people's democracy' become a euphemism for Communist dictatorship in central and eastern Europe. ❑

When Thorez gave his interview, the prospects for the 'democratic road to socialism' must have seemed good. A week before (10 November) the Communist share of the vote in the general elections had risen to 28.2 per cent (an advance on the 25.9 per cent achieved in June), and Communist ministers had won plaudits for their responsible behaviour in office since September 1944. Marcel Paul, Minister of Industrial Production, and Thorez himself had impressed on workers the patriotic duty of raising productivity and refraining from strike action. The election results had strengthened Thorez's claim on the highest political office and, following the resignation of Georges Bidault on 28 November, he made a bid to become premier in a coalition with the Socialists (but excluding the MRP). Though the SFIO leadership concurred, a minority of Socialist deputies refused to support a proposal that would further strengthen their Communist rivals. Thorez was unable to secure a parliamentary majority for a Communist-led government. After an interlude in which Blum (who was not even a deputy) led an all-Socialist caretaker ministry, a broad coalition was re-formed on 22 January 1947 under the premiership of the Socialist, Paul Ramadier. Thorez was reappointed Minister of State and Vice-President of the Council. The government was predominantly 'Tripartite', with nine ministries going to the SFIO, five to the MRP and five to the PCF, and the rest allocated among minor centrist parties. But even as the government was being constructed, the continued viability of 'Tripartism' began to look doubtful. Whatever Thorez's protestations, the PCF was deeply distrusted by its coalition partners who feared that key ministries would be 'colonized' by men whose primary loyalty was to international communism, not to France. Though a Communist was made Minister of National Defence, his powers were deliberately neutered by awarding 'flanking' ministries for the armed forces to the MRP and the Radicals. It was evident that the socio-economic problems of inflation and wage restraint would put strains on tripartism, but in the spring of 1947 the worsening international situation interacted with domestic politics to open the 'great schism' in the French left. Before examining this, we must follow the evolution of Socialist strategy.

Within the SFIO a strong movement in favour of the unification of the parties of the left had arisen out of the Resistance alliance, and towards the end of 1943 the SFIO proposed the establishment of a joint-party committee to discuss reunification and a common radical programme. The SFIO's clandestine leadership was composed of 'new men' – like Mayer – who had not experienced the bruising conflicts with the PCF of the early 1930s and did not share the almost pathological anti-Communism of the older, imprisoned leaders, Blum and Vincent Auriol. The influence of this new generation was evident at the SFIO's November 1944 congress which agreed to invite the Communists to join a committee to discuss the unity of the proletarian parties.

Nothing came of this. Why not? The return of Blum from a German prison in March 1945 helped articulate the distrust many Socialists had for the rigid authoritarianism of the PCF, which contrasted with the 'openness' and factionalism of their own party. Moreover, the growth of the MRP had the indirect consequence of cooling the enthusiasm of those Socialists who had envisaged unity with the PCF being achieved on the basis of SFIO preponderance. The MRP was the focus for progressive Catholic voters whom Auriol and others had hoped to attract to a social democratic party not unlike the British Labour Party. With its broad constituency, and the confessional issue shelved, such a party could have contemplated fusing with the PCF without fear of being devoured. At its August 1945 congress, the SFIO resolved that unity of the labour movement was one of its prime objectives, but that no merger with the PCF could develop before a prolonged period of successful joint activity enabled the generation of an atmosphere of loyalty and mutual trust. The electoral success of the MRP in October scotched the prospects of both a broad-based social democratic party and PCF–SFIO unity. A period of prolonged joint activity never materialized.

Exercise French Socialists faced a cluster of strategic and ideological dilemmas unwittingly expressed in a SFIO statement of February 1946, which is included as item 5 in *Documents and Texts 1*. Read it and summarize those dilemmas.

Specimen answer Ideologically, French Socialism faced the dilemma of being both 'revolutionary' and 'democratic' in a real world where actual socialist revolution had been violently anti-democratic. This dilemma was carried over into its long-term strategy, for while part of its rhetoric committed it to a fundamental social transformation through the class struggle, another part expressed a commitment to social reform through democratic means. This dilemma affected its internal coherence and relations with other parties, most notably the PCF. Its democratic traditions opened it to many who just didn't believe a revolutionary transformation through the class struggle was on the political agenda and for whom democratic reformism was all. Moreover, these traditions made the ideology and political methods of Leninism and Stalinism abhorrent.

Discussion The dilemmas of French Socialism and the emergence of the MRP meant that the form of government under which the Fourth Republic was inaugurated was a version of option 4. The parties of the left had sufficient support to establish a government independent of the MRP, but the Socialists insisted on tripartism in order to maintain a Christian Democrat counterweight to the Communists. The PCF would have preferred option 3 as a 'second best' to option 2, for the weakness of the Radicals would have been a source of Communist strength in a 'Popular Front' government; which is why the Socialists refused to consider it. ❑

3 The geographic and social distribution of support for the left[1]

Since the early nineteenth century there has been a persistent electoral geography in France. The extreme left has been supported in parts of southern and central France since the 1790s; the Communists, in the 1940s, were particularly strong in those regions which had voted for 'the Mountain' (social radicals) of 1849. After 1945, the Communist electorate was to prove more stable and more *national* than that of any other party. In the elections of 1946, the PCF was the only party never to poll less than 6 per cent of the registered votes, and the one to poll more than 24 per cent in the largest number of districts. Its expansion into rural and hitherto solidly conservative *départements* was remarkable. In clerical Vendée, for example, party membership rose from 170 to 3,000 between 1936 and 1946, and Communist voters increased from 2,600 to 26,900. Nevertheless, the Party's post-war electoral strength continued to be limited by the regionalism of French voting.

Exercise Using the maps showing the Communist vote in November 1946 and the distribution of industry in France (Figures 3.1 and 3.2), identify the main areas of Communist strength and weakness and their broad socio-economic character.

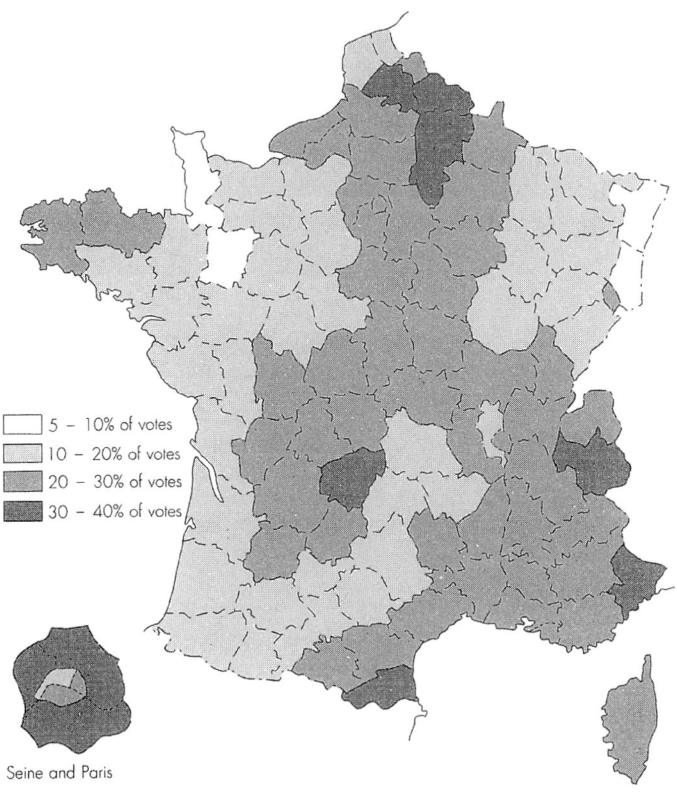

Figure 3.1 *Distribution of the PCF vote in the November 1946 elections for the first assembly of the Fourth Republic. (Redrawn from F. Goguel,* Géographie des élections françaises sous la IIIème et IVème république, *Paris, Armand Colin, 1970, p.113.)*

[1] The issue of gender and political affiliation is discussed in Unit 13.

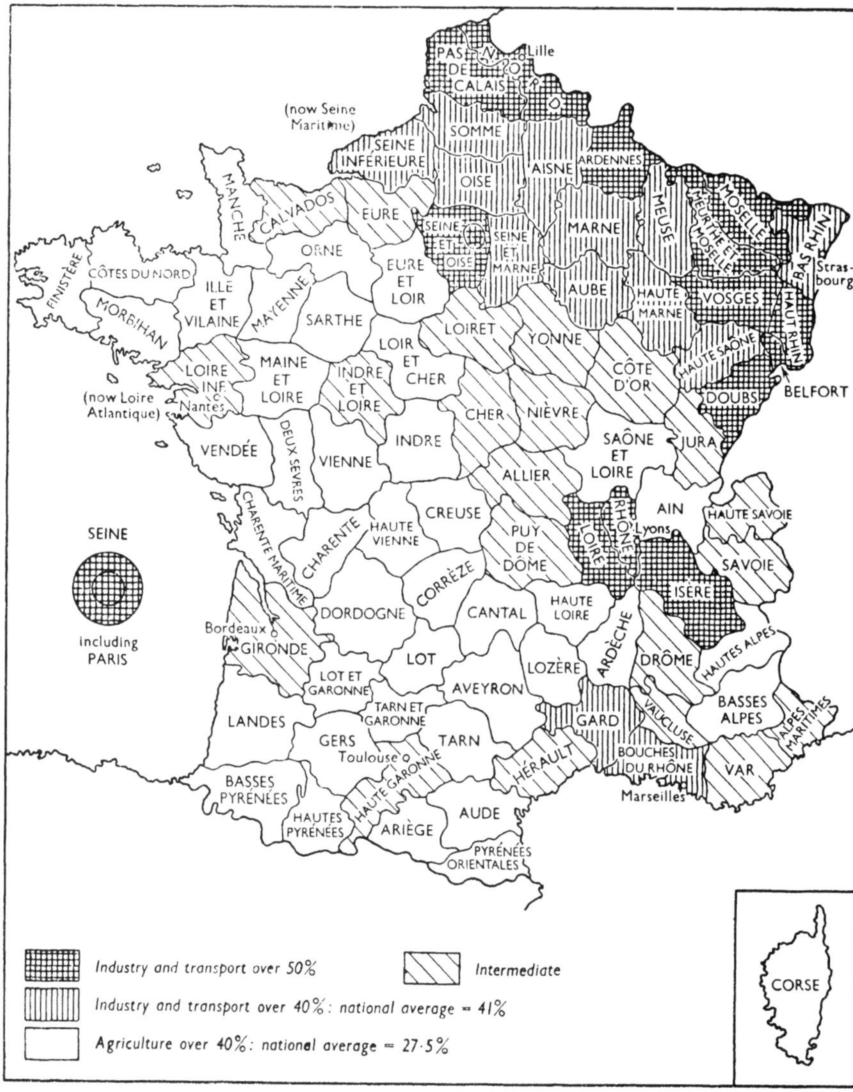

Figure 3.2 *French départements and distribution of industry (working population), 1954. (From Philip M. Williams,* Crisis and Compromise: Politics in the Fourth Republic, *Longmans and Green, third edition 1964, p.461.)*

Specimen answer The 'three bastions' of Communist electoral strength were the northern industrialized region running from the Belgian frontier to the industrial suburbs of Paris, the central region from Berry to Agenais (an area of mixed industry and agriculture), and the predominantly agricultural Midi, especially the Meridional and Rhône regions. The three 'deserts' or areas of weakness were the west (largely agricultural), the east (which included some of the heavily industrialized regions of France), and part of the Massif Central (which was largely agricultural).

Discussion It is clear that there was no straightforward correlation between the industrial character of a region and Communist electoral strength. The influence of the Church in Alsace-Lorraine stopped the PCF making greater advances among the metal workers and miners whom we might have thought a 'natural' part of the Communist constituency. Conversely, many peasant proprietors in the south were voting Communist as they had once voted anti-clerical and republican. In 1951 the 'reddest' *département* in France (with a PCF vote of 40.4 per cent) was Corrèze, where over 80 per cent of the agricultural population were small landholding peasants. The post-Liberation gains were predominantly rural and in some of its pre-war urban strongholds the PCF actually retreated in 1945 (in southern Paris, for example, its vote was 40 per cent as compared with 43.9 per cent in 1936). This rural expansion tended to correspond with the areas of Communist-led Resistance. ❑

Exercise Now look at the map below showing the SFIO vote in November 1946 (Figure 3.3). Identify the SFIO's main areas of electoral strength and weakness and compare them with those of the Communists.

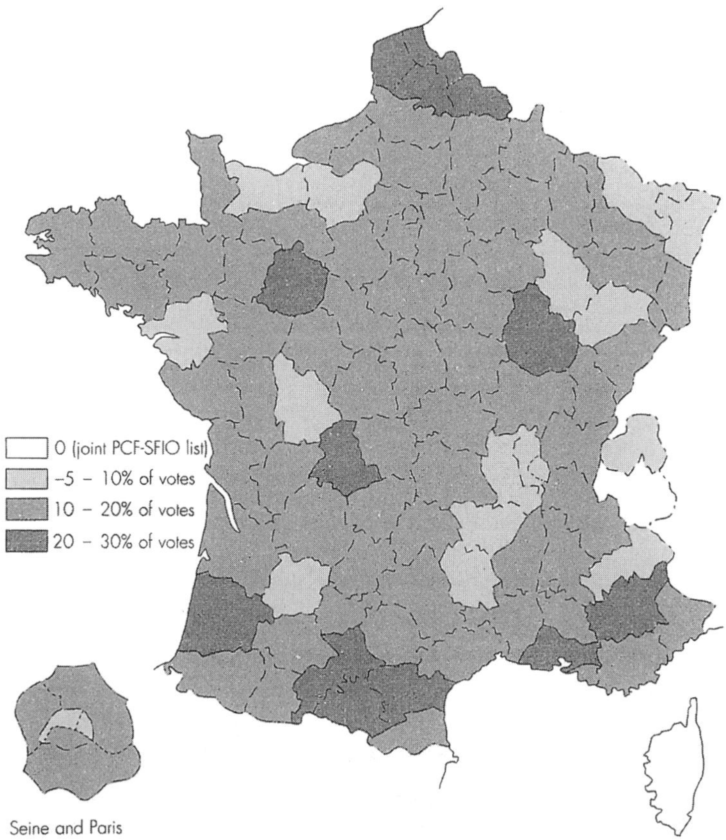

Figure 3.3 *Distribution of the SFIO vote in the November 1946 elections for the first assembly of the Fourth Republic. (Redrawn from F. Goguel,* Géographie des élections françaises sous la IIIème et IVème république, *Paris, Armand Colin, 1970, p.111.)*

Specimen answer The Socialists' chief regions of support were the *département* of Haute Vienne to the north-west of the Massif Central, the Protestant south-east, the *départements* of Landes and Aude near the Pyrenean frontier, Sarthe in western Loire, and in the central zone of the Nord and Pas-de-Calais industrial region. There was a chain of *départements* running north-east from the lower left bank of the Rhône to Alsace-Lorraine where Socialist support was negligible. The greater geographic 'evenness' of Socialist support in comparison with the Communists is noticeable.

Discussion Were we to compare this map with the electoral situation in 1945, then we would be struck by the fact that the regional distribution of Socialist support had been more concentrated and by 1946 it was picking up between 10 and 20 per cent of the vote in more *départements*. There was also a noticeable decline in the industrial north; here it had clearly lost the struggle for workers' political allegiance to the Communists. Like the PCF, the SFIO had regional strongholds, and since these were not predominantly industrial areas it is clear that the Socialist constituency was in many places discrepant with its 'class' ideology.

What our map does not bring out in sufficient detail is the dependence of the SFIO on rural and small-town France. It had, by 1946, lost the battle for the industrial working class either to the PCF or the MRP and even in the 'Jacobin' Mediterranean was losing out to the Communists. In electoral terms, the Socialists were tending to occupy the terrain held by the Radicals of the Third Republic, and as the pivotal party of tripartism they were taking on a similar governmental role. ❑

Unlike most French parties, the PCF did not exist primarily to contest elections. The strength of Communism lay in the number and still more the quality of committed militants. After the Liberation, the growth in party membership was very rapid: in January 1945, 387,000 accepted their party cards; a year later over 800,000. But this expansion lasted only so long as the PCF was seen to be adopting a policy of collaboration with the non-Communist left around a national and democratic platform. Although the Party has often been described as 'massive' and 'solid', its steady decline from a peak post-war strength in 1947 and the constant turnover in membership belies this description. Total numbers were, strictly speaking, a party secret, but some estimate of their falling trend can be gauged from the decline in the number of party cards delivered by the central committee to the departmental federations: from a peak of 907,785 in December 1947 these fell to a low of 389,000 in 1955 but then recovered in the following years (despite the Soviet repression in Hungary). Real membership was much below these figures. This decline in political commitment was not peculiar to the PCF, for it affected all parties, just as it affected the sales of all political newspapers.

What the global figures for party membership hide – and we can only guess at – is the high rate of turnover through defection or lapses of membership. It is probable that, in the later 1940s, the Party would have had to recruit the equivalent of 10 per cent of its membership each year simply to compensate for turnover. Far from being a solid political phalanx, it was more like a sieve through which a large proportion of the politicized passed.

The PCF was a workers' party, if not the party of the working class. Skilled industrial factory workers (particularly from the metal-working and engineering trades) and railwaymen made up the largest segment of its membership. Poorer, less skilled workers tended to be under-represented in the Party. After the war, membership included quite a substantial minority of peasants and agricultural workers, and the Party's rural weekly newspaper *La Terre* ('The Land') sold about 200,000 copies. When the Party was 'Bolshevized' in 1924–25, it had followed Comintern practice of attempting to organize into 'cells' formed at the point of production (usually the factory). In 1946 it had 12,060 rural cells, 8,363 factory cells and 15,860 local cells. The comparative failure of factory cell organization can be traced to the generally under-organized character of French industrial labour which, in the organized employers *(Le patronat)*, encountered a ruthlessly anti-union body. The high proportion of engineering workers among party members cannot be traced to any tradition of strong trade unionism. On the contrary: the weakness of organized labour drove class-conscious workers into the PCF for, apparently, it was only through revolutionary politics that a society of just rewards could be achieved. Many workers paid dearly for their membership when, after the 1947 strikes, the bosses purged French industry of militants.

The leadership and parliamentary group of the Party faithfully reflected the social composition of its membership. Despite the attraction of Communism for a minority of bourgeois intellectuals, they were rarely promoted to positions of political leadership within the Party whose Central Committee was dominated by workers and former workers. Of its 166 deputies in 1947, 61 were occupationally classified as 'workers' (as against only seven in the MRP and four in the Socialist group). Party discipline required deputies to pay their parliamentary salaries into party funds from which they were returned the equivalent of a skilled worker's wage. Parliamentarians and leaders were untainted by the customary venality of French politics and the austerity of their private lives helped sustain the proletarian ethos which bound the rank and file to the leadership.

Between Liberation and the inauguration of the Fourth Republic, the SFIO was transformed from a workers' party to a party of white-collar employees and petty functionaries. Manual workers still provided a great deal of Socialist voting strength (an estimated 40 per cent in the early 1950s) and a third of party members were working class, but both voters and members tended to come from small plants and secondary industries or the public sector. Civil servants (a category which in France includes postmen and school teachers) and their families figured in the Socialist electorate, their membership and leadership in a way quite disproportionate to their numbers in society as a whole. With their wives and retired colleagues, civil servants made up 30 per cent of the Socialist vote in 1951; 15 per cent of members were civil servants and they were heavily over-represented in the national and local leadership. While the SFIO never sent more than a handful of working-class deputies to a Fourth Republic Assembly, it never sent fewer than thirty teachers. Like the civil service, the

Party adopted the 'Buggins' turn' policy to promotion and – with the exception of younger men from the Resistance – leaders and parliamentarians tended to be middle aged or elderly.

4 'Le parti de l'intelligence française': communism and the intellectuals

At its tenth congress in 1945, Georges Cogniot, who was responsible for the political education of party cadres, proudly described the PCF as 'le Parti de l'intelligence française'. What he was alluding to was not an entirely post-Resistance phenomenon, since several distinguished intellectuals had been strongly attracted by communism before 1939. But, on the whole, the political affiliations of the pre-war intelligentsia lay with the right: the 'Manifesto of the Intellectuals', signed by over 850 writers and academics in October 1935, was a protest *against* the sanctions imposed on Fascist Italy for invading Abyssinia. The special relationship between communism and the intelligentsia in the 1940s arose partly from the 'de-legitimization' of the intellectual right and the purging of the publishing industry and the press after the Liberation. A few notorious collaborators were prosecuted for treason, but the large majority was unofficially blacklisted by the Comité national des écrivains (in which the majority sympathized with the left). For some years, writers who had compromised themselves with Vichy and the Nazi occupiers had great difficulty getting their work published. The notion of the intellectual as someone detached from the political fray was itself discredited: the editorial boards of the major publishing houses and prestigious journals were dominated by 'new men' (and a few token women) preaching the duty of 'engagement'. For at least a decade, the left-wing intellectuals would have the ideological field to themselves.

In strictly numerical terms, the PCF's claim to embody the nation's 'intelligence' was a myth. True, many of 'the generation of 1925' who entered university in the 1940s spent their formative political years in the PCF. They included historians such as François Furet and Emmanuel Le Roy Ladurie, the sociologist Edgar Morin, and the political scientist Annie Kriegel. But they made their impact on French national culture in the 1960s and 70s (when they had all long departed the PCF). In the 1940s, card-carrying Communists were only a narrow circle among intellectuals with established reputations. The well-publicized membership of a few outstanding figures in the arts and sciences has given an exaggerated impression of the Party's success in recruiting the intelligentsia.

Few of these 'stars' were Marxists out of deep conviction, and most had gravitated to the Party through participating in the intellectual resistance to fascism. Fairly typical in this respect was the brilliant physicist, Frédéric Joliot-Curie (1900–58) who, with his wife, Irène, had been a prominent 'fellow traveller' in the 1930s. Like virtually all French intellectuals, the Joliot-Curies were stunned by the Nazi-Soviet Pact, and signed the statement issued by the Union des intellectuels français condemning this diplomatic volte-face. In

October 1940, Frédéric Joliot-Curie was recruited to a group of intellectual resisters convened by the writer Vercors. When the Resistance became a physical force, he used his position in the Collège de France to manufacture incendiary bombs for the *franc tireurs*, and learned at first hand that the Communists were the bravest of the brave. Because of their sacrifices, and those of the Soviet Union, Communism glowed with a new 'aura' at the Liberation, when Frédéric Joliot-Curie and other renowned figures (such as Picasso) joined the Party. His pre-eminence as a nuclear physicist, and his appointment as Head of France's Atomic Energy Commission in 1946, probably made Frédéric Joliot-Curie the most prized 'catch'. It is testimony to the PCF's integration into the national community at the time that an avowed Communist should have been placed in such a sensitive post. (Joliot-Curie was dismissed in 1950, at the height of the Cold War, and became the public face of the Communist-inspired Peace Movement discussed in Unit 11.)

The PCF operated a double standard with respect to affiliated intellectuals. Picasso, Joliot-Curie and a handful of others were recognized as 'autonomous' intellectuals whose illustrious names were sufficient service to the Party. The leadership quietly tolerated any non-conformity on their part with Communist cultural policy or with the supposedly scientific principles of dialectical materialism as long as their political convictions were in line with the Party's. But ideological conformity was expected of so-called proletarian intellectuals, that is ordinary party members in the teaching and scientific professions or engaged in the creative arts. The sociology of the PCF makes this entirely understandable. The apparatus was staffed by working-class men who had left school in their teens and acquired a command of Marxist-Leninism through the Party's correspondence courses, monthly educational classes and its network of schools. This was not an education that encouraged respect for critical, abstract thought, and the leadership did not feel it had much to learn from intellectuals. Thorez's views were faithfully conveyed in a party report, *Le Parti Communists, Les Intellectuels et la Nation* (1949), by Laurent Casanova. It put firmly in their place 'those Communist intellectuals [who] had not yet fully accepted the political and ideological position of the working-class'. The Party had 'a complete doctrine of scientific socialism', and therefore no need for intellectuals to serve as 'the Prince's Counsellor'. Intellectuals coming to the proletariat would 'often have to submit to a painful process of seeing certain previously accepted values criticized' (quoted in Werth, *France 1940–1955*, pp.521–2).

Exercise The report was written after the 'great schism' of 1947, so we must be careful about projecting its dogmatism back into the immediate post-war years. Now read Gildea, pages 147 to 150, and say what you would regard as the main source of tension between Communism and the intellectual generation that came to the fore with the Liberation.

Specimen answer Gildea regards existentialism (which you will study in some detail in Unit 4) as the core doctrine of the post-war intellectual community, and indicates why it coexisted so uneasily with Communism. Briefly, existentialism is an extreme form of *voluntarism*: men and women are condemned, according to this philosophy, to be free. Communism entailed 'historical determinism, [a] denial of subjectivity and individual choice' (Gildea, p.149).

Discussion Though the Party itself made relatively few intellectual converts, Communism attracted a huge camp following of sympathizers in the 1940s: people prepared to write for PCF journals, co-operate on action committees and front organizations with party members, and act as apologists for the Soviet Union. In some ways, such fellow travellers were of greater service to the Party than card-carrying intellectuals because they were better able to integrate communism with other elements of the national culture. For example, the progressive Catholics associated with the philosopher Emmanuel Mounier (1905–50) and the journal *L'Esprit,* helped bridge the chasm between communism (a form of atheistic materialism) and Christianity. The philosophical divide was narrowed partly because scholars were rediscovering the humanism of the young Marx and the extent of his debt to Hegel. Marx's early writings – which became widely known in France only after 1945 – focused on the concept of human 'alienation' and the stunting of people's many-sided creativity under capitalism. There were similar ethical concerns with realizing human potential in Mounier's philosophy of 'personalism', and he persuaded himself that communism would be a better community in which to nourish 'personhood' than capitalism. At a more mundane level, Catholics of Mounier's stamp recognized a Puritanism in Communist militants that was part of their own faith. The ascetic lifestyle of PCF deputies, and the fact that their wives often took humble jobs to balance the family budget, struck a cord with austere left-wing Catholics. The PCF was the most loyally Stalinist of all western Europe communist parties and, in their desire not to distance themselves from the party of the working class, French fellow travellers were extraordinarily indulgent towards the repression and terror in the Soviet Union, and the brutally undemocratic way the Soviet system was exported to central Europe after 1945. Maurice Merleau-Ponty, a close friend of Sartre and a colleague on the editorial board of *Les Temps modernes*, argued in its November 1946 issue that communist political practice was above judgements of right or wrong. The notorious 'show trials' of 1938 were – he argued – justifiable because, whatever the intentions of Stalin's opponents, the reality of their acts had endangered socialism and were 'objectively' treasonable. Such apologetics for Stalinism were quite commonplace on the 'fellow-travelling' left. Mounier, for example, gave a guarded welcome to the communist coup in Prague in February 1948. ❑

5 The end of tripartism and the split in the working-class movement

Tripartism was, from the start, a shaky political arrangement because of the ideological and political divisions between the three partners (see Unit 2, pp.54–5). When Félix Gouin formed a government after de Gaulle's departure, the Communists were again denied the three 'key' ministries of Defence, Interior and Foreign Affairs because of their susceptibility to Soviet influence, and there were open differences between the parties over the type of constitution they wished to see installed. Memories of the Communist betrayal of the Third Republic in mid September 1939 were scarcely concealed by the 'Tripartite Charter' under which the parties pledged to avoid polemics, and in the June 1946 elections a furious row erupted between Communists and Socialists after the Socialist Minister of the Interior denounced Thorez as a 'deserter'.

Exercise What, then, kept tripartism together until May 1947?

Specimen answer and discussion There was a shared illusion that France could act as a bridge between East and West, which is discussed further in Unit 6. But you should have thought principally of the parties' common identification with national economic reconstruction. The PCF was admirably placed to assist economic reconstruction at a popular level because of the control it had won, through its leadership of industrial resistance, of the CGT. Until the war, the CGT had been syndicalist in outlook and unaffiliated to any political party, but in 1945 Communists became a majority on its Bureau fédéral – the executive organ – and secured a dominance of the main labour federation which it retained throughout the Fourth and Fifth Republics. From 1945 to early 1947, the CGT was a model of respectability, restraining workers' wage demands, urging them on in the battle for production and channelling their grievances into 'pressure group' action on the government. ❑

Exercise

1. What do you think would be the best measure of the success with which the CGT restrained working-class militancy?
2. What dangers did the PCF-inspired policy of industrial moderation hold for the Party?

Specimen answers

1. The number of days lost through strikes. Consult Table 14 in *Documents and Texts 1* and you will see how few were lost in 1946 compared with subsequent years.
2. The danger that non-Communists would take the lead in industrial action to further working-class economic grievances and split the labour movement; there was even the danger that the industrial policy of the CGT would threaten the party's political leadership of the proletariat.

Discussion Non-Communists did indeed put themselves at the head of industrial militancy in wild-cat strikes, which became ever more frequent in late 1946. The most significant for our purposes was the strike, led by Trotskyist shop stewards, which broke out at the Renault works at Billancourt in April 1947. We will return to this incident in discussing the break-up of the tripartite government. In addition to this threat to the Communist-led unity of the labour movement coming from the far left, there was a threat coming from the right: civil servants and other white-collar workers resented Communist political control of the CGT and themselves had grievances which the anti-strike policy did nothing to settle. By late 1946, this anti-Communist minority had organized into the Force Ouvrière (FO) faction, which was to secede from the CGT and form an independent confederation a year later. ❑

A further source of strain on tripartism stemmed from attempts to restore French colonial rule. Between December and January 1947, the Blum government blundered into war with the Vietnamese, and in March serious riots broke out in Madagascar, which led French forces to massacre many thousands of the native population. French foreign and colonial policies were in the hands of Georges Bidault, the MRP Foreign Minister, and Marius Moutet, Socialist Minister for Overseas France. Understandably, Communist ministers felt little responsibility for policies they opposed in principle and over which they had no influence. When, on 17 April, five Malagasy members of the French parliament were arrested (in violation of their parliamentary immunity) for fomenting rebellion, the Communist ministers declared that they would leave the government rather than support its colonial policies. Next day they revoked this decision but released Communist deputies from the party discipline which had hitherto bound them to vote for the government.

This rift in tripartism would not have been so deep had it not been for the worsening conflict between East and West and the 'internalization' of the Cold War in French politics and society. In March 1947 Truman announced his doctrine of containment and, shortly afterwards, the great power conference in Moscow broke up without any resolution of the German problem and with the evident bankruptcy of French policy towards Germany. At the end of March, de Gaulle came out of political retirement and put himself at the head of an anti-Communist crusade, the RPF. Conservative French commentators had for some time been warning that economically and imperially France depended on American goodwill, and that the price of this goodwill was the expulsion of Communists from the French government. Truman had not called for this, but French anti-Communists acted as if he had.

The occasion for the expulsion of the Communists was provided by the industrial conflict at Billancourt and the refusal of the PCF to stomach any longer the government's policy of wage restraint. Blum's interim government had attempted to cut prices and freeze wages; it was a policy continued by its successor, the Ramadier administration. Official price control made little impression on the rampant inflation, apart from driving the necessities of life on to the black market. Wage restraint was more effective and, as a consequence, workers' real incomes fell precipitously in 1947. Discontent broke out at the Renault works in February and March, and then recurred on

30 April, when 20,000 came out in protest against the rising cost of living. The strikers were being supported by the Socialist and MRP press while the CGT was still trying to cajole them into line, so – for fear of being outflanked in the struggle for popular support and already alienated from the government's colonial policy – the Communist Party, press and *ministers* came out in favour of the strikers and dissociated themselves from official wages policy. Prime Minister Ramadier seized his opportunity and sacked the ministers on 4 May.

This was the decisive event in the history of both the post-war left and the Fourth Republic. The Communists had to decide whether they should continue to see themselves as within the party political 'game', still, that is, candidates for a patched-up coalition; or whether they should go into total opposition to the 'game' and present themselves as a revolutionary party waiting its revolutionary moment. There is much to suggest that the Party hierarchy was divided on this, with Thorez and Jacques Duclos still perceiving the PCF as a party of government within the system, and hardliners like Tillon, the former partisan leader, insisting on a stance of revolutionary purity.

The expulsion of the Communists also placed their former Socialist partners in government in a dilemma: the SFIO had been committed to tripartism since 1945 and its left wing wanted to maintain fraternal relations with the Communists. At the Socialist National Council on 6 May, a large minority, led by Guy Mollet, voted in favour of the resignation of the Ramadier government on the grounds that the PCF had acted under popular 'left-wing pressure' to which the Socialists should themselves be responsive. Blum and Ramadier secured a majority for the maintenance of the government 'under Socialist leadership' only by invoking the growing threat of the Gaullist RPF, a movement reminiscent in style and social base of pre-war fascist organizations. The Gaullist threat was real enough, but the strengthening commitment of the Socialist leadership to the USA, from whom further economic aid was needed and expected, was probably a still weightier consideration.

The worsening international situation determined that this rupture between Communism and the rest of the polity would be a permanent feature of the Fourth Republic. In late June, the Soviet Union decided to reject the offer of Marshall Aid both for itself and for all countries under its influence, and began to tighten its control over western Communist parties. They were now expected to foment popular opposition to American 'imperialism' – as Marshall Aid was painted – and take up an attitude of complete intransigence towards 'bourgeois' governments. During the PCF's late June congress, Thorez asserted that the Party remained 'a government party' and reiterated the sentiments of his famous London *Times* interview which you have already read (item 4 in *Documents and Texts 1*). He quickly changed his tune. In September, representatives of the major Communist parties of East and West were summoned to Poland to set up the Cominform, and here the French delegates were lambasted for the 'collaborationist' policy and 'bourgeois parliamentarianism' they had pursued under tripartism. The tasks of combating the Truman Doctrine and Marshall Plan were drummed into them, and the hardline sectarian attitude which the PCF was to adopt for more than a decade was defined.

During the summer and autumn of 1947, international and internal pressures strengthened anti-Communism in France. The western European economy appeared to be in a critical state because of trading deficits and dollar shortages. All but the Communist parties believed that only American aid could prevent economic ruin. The PCF's anti-Marshall stance was unpopular and helped drive the wedge between itself and the Socialists still deeper. Anti-Communism was a keynote of the SFIO congress in August, for the Socialists wished publicly to distance themselves from the PCF and win back the working-class support they had lost to it. Eastern European socialist refugees who attended the congress as fraternal delegates were witness to the 'Stalinization' of states within Soviet control. Meanwhile, de Gaulle was denouncing the PCF as a potential fifth column during the anticipated third world war; he mobilized anti-Communist sentiment with such success that the RPF enjoyed a sweeping victory during the municipal elections of October 1947. Furthermore, the end of tripartism had been the signal for a general revival of industrial militancy – usually Communist-led – which focused on the PCF, the class resentment of the petite bourgeoisie, who had fared least well in post-war France.

The massive series of strikes during November and December completed the process of internalization of the Cold War and the isolation of the PCF which had begun early in the year. They originated in Marseilles, where the local CGT and PCF organized demonstrations and strikes against the newly elected RPF-dominated municipal council, and rapidly spread to the railways, north-eastern coalfields and Parisian engineering industries.

Exercise In October 1948 strikes recurred in the French coal mines; these were similar in their violence and political motivation to those of 1947. Items 3.1–3.3 in the 'Archive film' compilation on Video-cassette 1 consist of film of the strikes in 1947 and 1948. View these and then write down what the film evidence tells you about the character and effectiveness of the strikes and the response of the authorities. You will be viewing British newsreels (probably using material shot by a French camera crew) so the commentaries were intended for UK consumption.

Specimen answer The strikes were frequently violent and involved sabotage (including the derailment of an express train which killed twenty). In certain areas they brought civil life to a virtual standstill. Key institutions were occupied by strikers and forcibly cleared by the police; the film shows what we think is a power station being broken into. The government responded with considerable force, using both the paramilitary police (the CRS) and the army. The film provides vivid evidence of a national political crisis.

Discussion The commentary describes the strikes as Communist-controlled and motivated with the political purpose of thwarting American aid and bringing down the government. It faithfully echoes the French newsreels, the non-Communist French press and just about every political figure outside the PCF. Communist direction and political motivation are, in fact, indisputable (although they were not the only causes of the strikes). What is much less clear is the PCF's precise political purpose: was it expecting the strikes to escalate into a general insurrection which would enable it to seize power? The question cannot be categorically answered, but given the caution Thorez and others had displayed since 1944, it seems scarcely credible that they had insurrection in mind. Was the PCF trying to demonstrate to the other parties that France was ungovernable without it, and thus force itself back into the political game from which it was excluded in May? This is more likely, but the anti-Marshall Aid keynote of the strikes appears (from the present perspective at least) to advertise the PCF's unfitness for government: what *modus vivendi* could there be with a party seemingly determined to jeopardize economic recovery? ❑

The strikes in November 1947 failed because rank-and-file hostility to Communist tactics led to a partial return to work, and poverty and undernourishment made the government's offer of a lump sum to all in the nationalized industries who went back by 10 December virtually irresistible. The collapse of the strikes brought the incipient division within the CGT (which we have already noted) to a head and the Force Ouvrière left the federation on 19 December. As was by no means unusual during the Cold War, American money (coming in this instance from the American Federation of Labor) was used to encourage the split and to set up the CGT-Force Ouvrière in April 1948.

With the Communists entering their 'ice age', this is a suitable point to terminate our discussion of the post-war French left. The 'ghettoization' of the Communist counter-community in France is a chief theme of Unit 11.

PART 2 THE LEFT IN ITALY, 1943–48

1 Introduction

This part of Unit 3 is concerned with the role of the Communist Party (PCI) and the Socialist Party for Proletarian Unity (PSIUP) in the period from 1944–48 when left-wing parties dominated the Resistance, contributed decisively to the re-establishment of a democratic-pluralist political system and participated actively in the first post-war governments. Throughout these years the two parties worked in relatively close association, and in 1948 they went to the country on a joint electoral platform. Not even the Cold War, which otherwise had an extremely divisive impact on Italian politics, undid the bonds of unity between Socialists and Communists. Rather the division of Europe into two distinct and hostile camps caused a split in the ranks of the Socialist Party, as a significant pro-American minority broke away from the PSIUP to form a separate force. As a result of this split, the Communists were able to reverse the narrow lead the PSIUP secured in the Constituent Assembly elections of 1946 and establish the position of primacy within the Italian left that they held until the end of the first Republic. Yet, even before its pre-eminence was formally established at the polls, the PCI demonstrated an ability to outclass its Socialist allies at almost every level. Its leaders were more astute, its organization was more extensive and its intellectual appeal was greater. Indeed, as far as the cultural field was concerned, the Communists were able to act as if it was virtually their exclusive domain. For these reasons, the PCI will be analysed in somewhat greater detail than the PSIUP in the text that follows.

Aims

1. To explore how it came to pass that the left, which in 1944–45 re-entered the Italian political arena full of hope and sure of the role it would play in forging a new national destiny, found itself out of power and marginalized by 1948.
2. To analyse the organization, ideologies and political perspectives of the left-wing parties.
3. To examine the social and geographical bases of their support.
4. To discuss the role of the PCI in relation to the intellectual and cultural movements that identified with it after the fall of Fascism.
5. To illustrate the position of organized labour in the immediate post-war period.

2 Liberation and the strategies of the left

In the course of the war of Liberation the forces of the left acquired new influence and prestige, such that they became central to the process of political transition. Of all the parties the PCI stood to gain the most from its participation in the re-establishment of national dignity and independence. Before the war it had been a small force which, following its foundation in 1921, had scarcely had time to win a following before Mussolini imposed a one-party state in Italy. To most Italians, Communists were little more than a figment of the Fascist propaganda which portrayed them as the subversive representatives of a remote, foreign-based international movement. Through its leading role in the Resistance, the PCI was able to broaden its appeal considerably, establishing itself as a champion of liberty and national sovereignty as well as re-establishing its credentials as the keenest promoter of the interests of the poor and the oppressed. At the close of the conflict it emerged as a major force in the country, a political party that aspired to interpret politically the general concerns of the Italian people.

Prior to the consolidation of the Fascist regime the Italian Socialist Party had been by far the largest party on the left, with a considerable following among the industrial working class and the peasant population of Italy's central regions. Unlike the Communists, however, it had not maintained any sort of internal underground network under Fascism and its leadership had dispersed under the pressures of exile. By the early 1930s the party had ceased to provide any real reference point for the anti-Fascist opposition. Thus the PCI, whose contribution to the Resistance was very much greater from the outset, was able to recruit widely in areas of previous Socialist strength. Yet although the PSIUP was organizationally weak and often politically divided, it did contribute forcefully to the pressure for change in the Liberation period. Under the leadership of Pietro Nenni, head of the party's dominant left-wing faction, it proclaimed the conquest of power by the workers as its goal. 'The Constituent Assembly or chaos' was the choice facing the nation, he declared, adding, with a taste for fiery rhetoric that recalled an earlier generation of leftist orators, that 'the Republic will be socialist or it will not be'.

The PCI and PSIUP were linked by a unity of action pact forged first in Paris in 1934 and confirmed in September 1943, following the Italian government's armistice with the Allies. Although co-operation between the two parties was rarely easy, it was based on a common view of the need to proceed with the struggle against Fascism even after its collapse as a political regime. Both Socialists and Communists thought that the old ruling class which had fostered Mussolini's rise to power in 1922 had to be replaced and radical changes brought about in the distribution of resources and power in the country. Economic reconstruction and the shaping of a new constitutional framework were seen as moments of a battle to bring about major modifications to the old social order. These views were not shared by the small Action Party which, although it would secure a mere 1.5 per cent of votes in the elections to the Constituent Assembly in June 1946 and dissolve shortly afterwards, was influential on the left before and during the Liberation period as a consequence of its prominent Resistance role and high intellectual profile. Some members of the party were attracted to Marxism and subsequently joined the PCI or the PSIUP, but most were of a liberal schooling. Yet although they had no vision of a new class order, Actionists none the less strongly pressed for institutional reform, a radical purge of the public administration and a break-up of the stranglehold which a few powerful monopolies had established over the national economy.

Throughout the war of Liberation the Communists insisted on the importance of national unity. In his talk on the Italian Resistance (Audio-cassette 1, side A), Paul Ginsborg argues that this led them to postpone the resolution of vital social and political questions until the end of hostilities. As a result, the Liberation of the north of Italy in April 1945 was a politically crucial moment. With the war finally over, the time for clear-cut decisions had arrived.

One option for the left which Paul Ginsborg stresses was to attempt political revolution using the armed force of the Resistance movement and capitalizing on the great popular mobilization of the Liberation period. But, although some left-wing historians and critics have since argued that the left parties, and in particular the PCI, let pass what was a potentially revolutionary moment in 1944–45, it is generally accepted that this was not a feasible option. The presence on Italian soil of the Allies, to whom, as Ginsborg shows, the Resistance had formally surrendered its autonomy, was a powerful obstacle to any successful revolutionary design. But it should also be kept in mind that the Resistance, as well as the whole post-war trend to the left, was a phenomenon that was broadly restricted to the north and centre of the country. Despite some agitation for land reform, an old set of social relations was still very much in place in the south of Italy. Poor, backward and almost devoid of the class consciousness which marked the more modern regions of the north, it offered little prospect for political revolution. Any very radical break in political arrangements may therefore have split the country.

Let us examine now the strategies pursued in practice by the two main parties of the left.

The PCI

On 27 March 1944 the Communist leader Palmiro Togliatti set foot on Italian soil for the first time in eighteen years. In a sensational move that perplexed many senior party members and infuriated the other left-wing parties, he immediately announced the PCI's willingness to collaborate with Marshal Badoglio, the veteran leader of Mussolini's colonial expedition to North Africa who had been appointed prime minister by the king following the downfall of the Duce in a palace *coup d'état* in July 1943. The *svolta di Salerno*, or Salerno turning point, as this shift of policy became known (after the small port just south of Naples where Togliatti landed), was a vitally important moment in the politics of the whole of the transition period. On the one hand, it set the stage for the formation of a government of national unity in which Communists and Socialists co-operated with Christian Democrats, Liberals and Monarchists in the struggle to free the north and centre of the country from Fascism and German Occupation. In this way it signalled the PCI's transformation from a conspiratorial force on the margins of political life to a leading party of government. On the other hand, it profoundly compromised hopes for a radical solution to the crisis of power resulting from the collapse of Fascism, invasion and war in that it accorded legitimacy to an old and discredited institutional order and made any far-reaching innovation in the structures of the state impossible. This was not clear in 1944 of course; but over time the negative consequences of the *svolta di Salerno* would become apparent.

Togliatti's strategy was very much a long-term one which counted on the growing influence of the left within the government coalition. His immediate aim in 1944 had been to insert the PCI in the process of political transition at the earliest opportunity and guarantee a role for the Party at a time when Italy's destiny was still largely in the hands of the Allies. This was something that could most easily be secured within the framework of a policy of national unity and collaboration. But unity was also important to Togliatti's conception of the political goals of the left. In his view the task before the PCI was not the creation of a socialist state but rather a 'progressive democracy' that would see the enactment of major reforms, bringing the industrial monopolies into public ownership and distributing land to the peasants while preserving the market system and respecting political pluralism. In putting forward this proposal, Togliatti drew on some of the ideas contained in the prison notebooks of Antonio Gramsci, his predecessor as leader of the PCI and the most prominent Communist martyr to the anti-Fascist cause. In particular he adopted the Gramscian idea that it was the job of the left to perform the historic function of the national bourgeoisie in Italy and carry through the democratic revolution which the Risorgimento in 1860 had failed to produce. To this end it was necessary for the working class to forge a new ruling 'social bloc' by winning the peasantry and wide sections of the middle class to its side. Translated into the political context of the post-war transition, this meant that the maintenance of the alliance with the Socialists and the Christian Democrats was seen as fundamental.

For many Communist militants the line of conduct which flowed from this policy was too cautious by half; but it was none the less pursued resolutely, and repeatedly justified by Togliatti and the leadership, even though the preservation of national unity proved to require continuous compromises on issues of substance. In Unit 2, Part One, Clive Emsley described how the impulse towards radical change in Italian society ran aground in the course of 1945. There were clearly a variety of reasons for this. But no analysis of the recuperation of power by the social and political forces the Resistance hoped to destroy can ignore the way the PCI failed to defend the gains of the Liberation period, or insist on radical reforms and a thorough purge of former Fascists when these issues threatened to divide the coalition. In this way the PCI did not strengthen the hand of the left, but offered conservative forces an opportunity to reassert the influence they appeared to have lost in the Liberation period. Even after the left failed to win the expected overall majority in the 1946 elections to the constituent assembly, the PCI continued to compromise to save the coalition, to the point of voting in favour of the inclusion of the 1929 Lateran Pacts in the Republican Constitution in the belief that this would enhance the Party's legitimacy and secure the eternal gratitude of the Christian Democrats and Catholics generally.

Exercise Turn to *Documents and Texts 1* and read the extracts from Togliatti's speech 'The tasks of the Party in the current situation' (item 6). In it you will notice that Togliatti stresses the new national role of the working class and its political representative. What importance do you think the Soviet Union had for the PCI at the end of the war?

Specimen answer On the basis of this document alone, it might be supposed that the USSR had little impact on the PCI and its policies. Indeed, judging by Togliatti's repeated references to rebuilding the Party, to 'creating a Communist party in completely new conditions', and to a new style of mass-supported activity, it would seem that the PCI was actually breaking with Leninism.

Discussion In other speeches made in 1944–45, Togliatti placed more emphasis on the Soviet Union and its role in resisting the advance of Nazism and barbarism in Europe. Yet at no point did he suggest that the Soviet model of society should be imported into Italy, and on the whole references to the USSR and to Marxism-Leninism were limited. It would be mistaken to deduce from this that the PCI was acting independently in the mid 1940s, however. The *svolta di Salerno* itself was to some extent made possible by prior diplomatic activity between Badoglio and the USSR, which formally recognized the royal government only two weeks before Togliatti proclaimed his Party's willingness to join it. Moreover, the promotion of national unity in the war effort, while it was clearly patriotic, also dovetailed with Moscow's requirements in so far as it intensified pressure on the Germans at a time when the Soviet Union was desperately trying to repel the Nazis from its soil. The PCI's accession to government also enabled Stalin to achieve a proxy presence in an area that had been designated as part of the western sphere of influence. Yet Togliatti was no puppet. He was the only Communist leader in Europe not to owe his position to Stalin, and the PCI was the only party to escape total subordination to the directives of the Soviet leadership in the thirties. Far from being a tool of Stalin's policy in Europe, Togliatti may actually have played an important part in formulating Moscow's strategy before his departure from the USSR in January 1944. In any event it would not be correct to view his political decisions as serving purely external interests. The stress he placed on political alliances clearly owed much to the popular front policies he developed, in conjunction with the Bulgarian Dimitrov, at the Seventh Congress of the Communist International in 1935. The unitary approach also fitted in neatly with Togliatti's own assessment of the tasks facing the Party in a complex situation that was by no means wholly favourable to the left.

The Socialists

Unlike the PCI, the PSIUP's priority to see the practical enactment of a range of radical reforms. But although the party made many principled stands it invariably failed to resolve issues in its favour at the level of government. The PSIUP's subsequent loss of influence on the left was in this sense preceded by a decline in its weight and leverage within the national unity coalition. Socialist leaders adopted what in practice was an 'all or nothing' posture on a variety of issues which led them – once it was clear that the Christian Democrat leader De Gasperi and not Pietro Nenni, the Socialist leader, would assume the helm of government in late 1945 – to resign themselves to a subaltern role. While the PCI's arguably excessive concessions were at least made with the aim of serving longer term interests, the Socialists' lack of combativeness seemed to find its only explanation in sour grapes. In order to ensure that the working class continued to be represented at the table of power the PSIUP remained a member of the government until May 1947, but it never recovered the sense of purpose that marked its conduct in 1944–45.

For some Socialists the root cause of their party's failure to establish itself as the dominant force lay in the unity of action pact which bound it closely to the PCI. This prevented the party from winning credibility as a force of government in its own right and undermined the distinctiveness of its positions, which on many issues were more markedly left-wing than those of the PCI. (Nenni, for example, wrote in his diary that Togliatti's support for the inclusion of the Lateran Pacts in the new constitution was 'cynicism applied to politics', and was premised on 'a calculus mistaken from top to bottom'.) The pact, it is alleged, also impeded the PSIUP in fighting off the expansion of Communist influence in institutions such as the trade unions and the co-operative movement, which before Fascism had been exclusively Socialist bastions. The sufferance of right-wing socialists in particular began to evaporate as they realized that the Communists aimed at a refoundation of the left on bases that would extinguish Socialist autonomy altogether. For Giuseppe Saragat the final straw came when Nenni announced, towards the end of 1946, that unity of action with the PCI could only be meaningful if it had unification as its ultimate goal. At an extraordinary congress called in 1947 Saragat led his supporters out of the PSIUP and founded a breakaway social democratic party, the PSLI, which would eventually embrace a marked anti-Communism as its main political credo. The consequences of this split were disastrous for the PSIUP (which, to avoid any hijack of the party's historic name, reverted to calling itself the PSI). At one stroke it lost its numerical primacy on the left and saw its effective political weight slashed by half.

Despite enormous pressure from its sister parties in western Europe, the PSI maintained a policy of unity of action with the PCI throughout the worst of the Cold War, and even formed a common front with the Communists to fight the elections of 1948. Yet this continuing example of left unity brought little joy to the Socialists. It not only allowed the right to tar the party with the same pro-Soviet brush as the PCI; it also put in jeopardy the PSI's survival as a major national force, for the party emerged from what was arguably the most bitter and polarized election in the whole of post-war Europe with fewer than half the deputies of its partner (52 as compared to the PCI's total of 131), and a credibility problem from which it would never fully recover.

Given this sequence of events, it is worth considering why Italian Socialists stuck so resolutely to left unity. Certainly there was very strong pressure from the base in favour of co-operation on the left, but similar pressure in France and elsewhere did not prevent Socialist parties from carefully guarding their autonomy. The difference lay in the strongly radical, and even revolutionary, background of many of the leading left-wing Socialists in Italy; men such as Nenni, Lelio Basso and Rodolfo Morandi were anything but social democrats (in the sense of the term today) and were passionately committed to working-class unity.

3 The geographic and social bases of left-wing support

Between 1944 and 1946 the PCI underwent a remarkable transformation from a small nucleus of 5,000 members to a mass party of very considerable dimensions. On his return to Italy, Togliatti stressed that the Party could not perform the tasks before it if it were to remain an élite group of professional revolutionaries. To be a truly national party able to influence all spheres of society, the PCI had to forge links with the mass of the people, and draw workers, peasants, professional people, small businessmen and intellectuals into its ranks. In one celebrated slogan of the period it was said that there should be a party section for every church spire in the land. It is doubtful if this goal was ever reached, but there can be no disputing the extended presence the PCI achieved in Italian life. From 502,000 members in 1944, it grew to 2,068,000 in 1946 and remained over the two million mark up until 1957. In contrast the PSIUP never exceeded 800,000 members.

The PCI owed its success to the prestige enjoyed by the Soviet Union at the end of the war, to its role in the Resistance and to the fact that it offered a vision of political activism which keyed in with a general view of national reconstruction. Yet the integration and socialization of a vast new membership of these dimensions was clearly no easy task. Few recruits had any notion of the Party's history or ideology and many were not even accustomed to using Italian. As you will recall from Unit 1, most people still used dialect for everyday communication in the 1940s, and popular culture was shot through with a myriad of local and regional differences. Consequently the process of internal education and consolidation was a long and complex one that would continue well into the 1950s. The leadership was greatly aided in this task by its Leninist tradition of democratic centralism. Party members were granted no real opportunities to voice dissent and were expected not only to accept the directives they received but to master the thinking behind them. In this way the PCI was gradually moulded into a relatively homogeneous political force.

Despite the great expansion of membership and the attempt the Party made to expand its influence even into the remote areas of the country, there remained a great regional imbalance in the distribution of its organization. In the north, in Lombardy, Liguria and the Veneto, membership increased by over 1,000 per cent between 1944 and 1946, while of the southern regions, only in Lazio, Puglia and Sicily was there any very significant increase. In some areas of the south, such as Basilicata and Sardinia, membership was sporadic in the extreme. In contrast a very solid belt of support was established in the central regions of Emilia-Romagna and Tuscany, which by themselves accounted for around one third of total Communist membership.

This regional imbalance was common to both the major left-wing parties and was reflected in the composition of the electorate. In 1946 the left's weakness in the south was particularly marked, as the table below illustrates.

Table 3.2 Regional distribution of votes in the 1946 election (in %)

	North	*Centre*	*South*	*Islands*
DC	37.3	30.0	34.9	35.2
PSIUP	28.5	17.7	10.0	11.5
PCI	22.4	24.7	10.9	8.8

For all the political and organizational successes of the PCI, it was the PSIUP which emerged as the largest party on the left in the elections to the constituent assembly in 1946. To the surprise of many, and to the dismay of the Communists, it won 20.7 per cent to the PCI's 18.9 per cent. The Socialists did particularly well in the northern cities, emerging as the largest party in centres such as Milan and Turin, while the Communists won ground in the countryside and small towns of the centre of Italy. But in most important respects the parties shared a similar electorate composed of industrial workers, agricultural labourers and a small, politicized section of the middle class. In 1948 the Communists in particular made a greater impact in the south, but these gains paled in the context of the general defeat of the left. In 1946 the PSIUP had won 4.76 million votes and the PCI 4.36 million; in 1948 the two parties together only won 8.14 million – a net loss of almost one million votes. The left alliance – the Democratic Popular Front – won just 31 per cent of votes, a result so poor as to provoke its dissolution immediately after the election.

The areas of the country where the left did well were by and large those that had lived through the experience of the Resistance. The PCI in particular drew enormous strength from the unique organizing role it had played in the partisan struggle. In the north and centre the left was also aided by the existence of a long tradition of collective organization and solidarity. The rapid growth of political parties in these areas was part of a wider process in which an organic working-class culture endowed with autonomous institutions took shape once more. Labour halls and social centres (*case del popolo*) were repossessed or new ones built from scratch by means of volunteer labour. Alongside party sections and cells, new mass associations were formed which drew in women, young people and children. In the interstices of these networks of solidarity a new style of activity was born: one in which politics meshed with community life. Parties and popular organizations represented the interests of ordinary people but they also organized dances, festivals, trips to the mountains or the seaside, as well as a range of educational activities and discussion groups. In the south all of this was missing, as Paul Ginsborg makes clear in his talk 'Agrarian struggles and reform in Italy, 1943–50' (Audio-cassette 5, side A).

To a great extent the PCI was a workers' party: 53 per cent of its members were industrial workers and a further 23 per cent were agricultural labourers or small peasant farmers. Although it welcomed people of all classes into its ranks, the core of its membership was drawn from the industrial proletariat. For ideological reasons the Party itself also privileged this aspect of its identity. It prided itself on maintaining a high degree of organization in the nerve centres of Italian industry, and its strong presence at Fiat and in other large engineering factories represented a symbol of immense importance. 44 per cent of central committee members were workers, while a mere 6 per cent were peasants. However, the PCI also drew on other classes in society. Some 31 per cent of its parliamentary representatives were professional middle-class people (journalists, doctors, lawyers, and so on) and a further 15 per cent were white-collar workers. Many middle-ranking cadres and some senior officials were auto-didacts who had come from very humble backgrounds, but most of the top-level leaders had been to university and some, including Togliatti himself, like Gramsci before him, were men of considerable intellectual distinction.

4 Marxism, communism and the intellectuals

Between 1944 and 1946 intellectual life in Italy was dominated by the new theme of 'engagement'. Stirred by the war, the collapse of the Fascist regime and the hopes for change engendered by the Resistance, artists, writers and critics sought to overcome the barriers that separated them from social and political life. As the party that emerged with most prestige from the Resistance, and as the one force to hold out a vision of reconstruction in which the desire of artists and intellectuals for social involvement might be realized and even institutionalized, the PCI stood to gain most from this sudden change of mood. Thanks to Togliatti's 'open door' membership policy, which permitted the enrolment of anyone, including non-Marxists, who accepted the Party's general aims, the PCI succeeded in attracting the support of a very significant section of the country's cultural élite. Even before the final defeat of Fascism, the Party had won the allegiance of important intellectuals such as the Latin scholar Concetto Marchesi and the philosopher Antonio Banfi, and of artists of the calibre of Luchino Visconti; after the Liberation writers including Cesare Pavese, Elio Vittorini and the distinguished poet Umberto Saba, as well as men such as Italo Calvino and Pier Paolo Pasolini, who would win recognition in subsequent years, flocked to its side. To a very real extent the PCI was the party of the intellectuals and of culture in the post-war years.

For the Communist leadership the Party's overtures towards artists, writers and academics were but one part of a general political design which aimed at the constitution of a new ruling bloc in Italian society. The best way for the left to reinforce the new standing of the working classes in society and extend its influence among the middle class, it was felt, was by encouraging the political involvement of the country's intellectuals and arguing for a new conception of art and thought which was profoundly immersed in the concerns of ordinary people. In this sense the Communists utterly rejected the view championed by the influential idealist philosopher and historian Benedetto Croce (see Unit 1, p.14), to the effect that culture was a special sphere standing above and separate from other realms of human endeavour. The programmatic declaration which Togliatti wrote for the first issue of the Communist ideological weekly *Rinascita* (*Documents and Texts 1*, item 7) contained a stern refutation of the idea that barriers could be erected between economics and politics, politics and culture, or individual creativity and society. The strength of the Marxist doctrine, he said, lay in its 'unitary and realistic conception of the whole world'.

Exercise Read Togliatti's 'Programme'. What were the major objectives of Communist cultural policy in the immediate post-war period?

Specimen answers

1 To reintroduce Marxism into Italian culture.

2 To equip party militants and newly recruited intellectuals with a theoretical grounding in Marxism.

3 To engage in polemic with those who denied the cultural legitimacy of Marxist thought. (Here Togliatti had in mind Croce above all.)

4 To draw on the resources of Italian intellectuals in reintegrating Marxism with the national intellectual tradition.

5 To extend the influence of the workers' movements into the field of culture for the first time.

Discussion The way Togliatti conceived the cultural policy of the PCI dovetailed with the cautious strategy of institutional penetration he imposed on the Party in the post-war political situation. At no point were intellectuals or artists who identified with the PCI expected to come to terms with any radically redefined notion of culture itself. As a group or category that justified and legitimated a given social order they were considered, as Gramsci had considered them, a necessary arm in the struggle to form a new ruling bloc in society. But whereas Gramsci discussed the role of the intellectual in the struggle for a revolutionary dislocation in Italian society, Togliatti's concern with the intellectual took as its starting point the need to win a secure place for the PCI in national life. Hence his focus was not on the organic intellectual, schooled and formed in the working-class movement itself, but on the traditional, or established, intellectual who could better assist the legitimation of Communism as a national phenomenon. The whole cultural policy of the Party, it may be said, was geared to such men, who were encouraged to patronize party festivals and events, write for specialized magazines and Communist newspapers and lend their names to party initiatives. In this way the Party offered intellectuals a prestigious role, more prestigious perhaps than that offered by bourgeois society itself, which, even in a country as 'backward' as Italy in the 1940s, increasingly resorted to modern means of mass communication to ensure social integration and consensus. The result was a cultural policy that was largely imprisoned within the world of high culture, that was divorced from potentially useful technical means, and that was extremely weak at the level of popular culture. ❑

Between 1944 and 1946 Communist cultural policy was tentative and open. Togliatti edited *Rinascita* personally and, although his position of authority was never in doubt, he did so in a flexible and enlightened way. His closest collaborators were not other senior figures in the Party or even men of his own generation, but handpicked young intellectuals whose job it was to propagate, interpret and apply the general policy lines he had set down. Many of these, including Antonello Trombadori, Mario Alicata and Carlo Salinari, belonged to a Roman group of critics and historians who, from the very early 1940s, had prefigured the notion of a tradition of ideas in the national culture different from the prevailing liberal and idealist ones. To their link with the nineteenth-century democratic literary critic Francesco De Sanctis, Togliatti added the names of Antonio Labriola (the founder of Italian Marxism), and Gramsci as developers of this progressive current.

The PCI's lack of success in the elections to the constituent assembly and its failure to consolidate its influence among the middle classes produced a series of tangible, and generally negative, effects on the PCI's cultural policy after 1946. Intellectuals and artists who had taken seriously the project of creating a new participatory and progressive democracy, and who had identified with the Party more or less on their own terms, found themselves faced for the first time with demands for conformity and discipline. The onset of the Cold War reinforced this tendency. As an example of the ensuing crisis in relations between the PCI and its intellectual supporters, let us consider the case of *Il Politecnico*, a magazine founded with the support and encouragement of the party leadership in 1945, but which, following sharp criticisms of its approach, was compelled to close down in 1947.

From the beginning of its brief existence *Il Politecnico* was the most independent, not to say maverick, of the publications associated with the PCI. Edited by Elio Vittorini, a writer and translator who, like many others, had joined the Party more out of general sympathy than ideological conviction, the magazine represented a unique vehicle for the cause of cultural regeneration. Whereas *Rinascita*, in line with Togliatti's aim of reintroducing Marxism and Communism into national life, devoted much effort to the elaboration of a new national tradition, *Il Politecnico* focused on developments within contemporary European and American culture at the expense of the purely national. Articles were published on existentialism, surrealism, psychoanalysis, anthropology and linguistics. Unconventional foreign writers including Hemingway were translated into Italian for the first time, and new cultural forms such as the cinema, jazz and comic art were given serious treatment. At first the PCI tolerated Vittorini's electicism. But in 1946 he was subjected to repeated criticisms by leading Communists including Alicata and Togliatti himself, who intervened to lament the fact that the magazine's original aims had been gradually replaced by 'an abstract pursuit of the new, the different and the surprising' which left little space for 'coherent choices and meaningful inquiry'.

In the dispute over *Il Politecnico* the PCI revealed a strain of cultural conservatism that in the furore of the Liberation had temporarily been set aside, but which would hold sway over much of the successive period. Its intervention, moreover, heralded the beginning of a phase in which the intellectuals and cultural movements that identified with the left were increasingly subject to political control. But it would be unduly simplistic to deduce from this that Vittorini's own position was unambiguous or in some way beyond criticism.

Exercise Examine Vittorini's letter to Togliatti, published in *Il Politecnico*, January–March 1947 (*Documents and Texts 1*, item 8) and then consider the following questions.

1 What do you think the PCI most objected to in Vittorini's conception of the relationship between politics and culture?

2 How does Vittorini see his own relationship with the Party?

3 What is the basis of the special claim he makes for culture?

Discussion Put in very simple terms, Vittorini's reply may be seen as a statement for autonomous as opposed to politicized culture. Culture, in his view, stands above politics and is therefore invested with separate values and tasks which it is the intellectual's duty to safeguard and perform. In this way Vittorini both rejected the Togliattian doctrine of the indivisibility of politics and culture and denied the mediating role of the Party in fixing the forms and priorities of cultural activity. In principle we may prefer this sense of distinction and concern for intellectual and creative freedom to Togliatti's emphasis on homogeneity and discipline, but the particular context of the argument should not be overlooked. Vittorini was not a free agent; he was a member of the PCI, and editor of a journal set up with the goodwill of the Party, which drew mainly on a Communist audience for its readership. Furthermore, his vision of cultural renewal rested on an idea of mass involvement in the discussion and resolution of cultural problems that, to stand even a hypothetical chance of success, had to rely on the channels of organization and communication of the PCI itself. It could be legitimately argued, therefore, that he quite simply expected too much from the Party.

To the modern reader Vittorini's concern with the role of the intellectual and the autonomy of culture may sound somewhat outdated. Even in Italy in the 1940s, it could be argued, the intellectual as such was no longer as socially or politically decisive as was widely believed. But Vittorini's statement came towards the end of a season in which artists and intellectuals had been assiduously courted by the left and in which, as a result, their status had been considerably enhanced. In this sense, it might be asserted that Vittorini's rather excessive estimation of the social role of culture owed something to the way in which Togliatti not merely accepted the figure of the traditional intellectual but actually confirmed his privileged position. The formal imposition of political direction eroded this in some way and provoked what, in effect, was a defensive reaction to safeguard established privileges. ❑

The Socialists advanced no cultural policy as such in the immediate post-war period. Lacking a strategic view of the need to forge the hegemony of the working classes on the cultural terrain, they made no special overture to artists and writers and paid no particular attention to the demands of the national culture. An ideological journal of the PSIUP, *Socialismo*, was published under Rodolfo Morandi's editorship between 1945 and 1947, but it was not an official mouthpiece. Overall the Party's appeal to the cultural élite of the country was minimal, but at the level of popular culture its contribution was considerable. Left-wing Socialist intellectuals devoted detailed attention to folklore and the cultures of Italy's subaltern classes in a way that found no real correspondence in the PCI.

5 The left and the labour movement

If we have not mentioned the trade unions before now it is because the single confederation in which they were drawn together, the CGIL, exercised no autonomous role in the period following the Liberation. Although the left predominated, the presence of Catholics meant that the same sort of compromises made at government level to preserve unity were reproduced within the trade union movement. At the first congress of the CGIL in May–June 1947, held immediately after the expulsion of the PCI and PSIUP from government, the Communists accounted for 55 per cent of the confederation's 5.4 million members. The Socialist component was the next largest at 22 per cent, while the Catholics stood at 13 per cent. But even though the Communist-dominated leadership showed a willingness to continue to make concessions, hopes that unity could be maintained despite the divorce in the national coalition proved to be short lived.

To all intents and purposes trade union unity ceased to exist in the period before the divisive elections of April 1948. Although they remained part of the same organization, trade unionists belonging to the parties of government and opposition took radically different stands on the issues of the day. While the former declared their support for the Marshall Plan and participated in the international meetings associated with it, the latter mobilized openly in favour of the Democratic Popular Front. Yet it was only in the wake of the dramatic events of July 1948 that the breach was formalized. Following the action of a lone student who fired three shots at Togliatti on the morning of 14 July as he walked from the Parliament building in Rome, wounding him seriously, an enormous wave of protest was unleashed. You can judge the scale of this from the newsreel reports of the incident contained in the 'Archive film' compilation (items 10.2 and 10.3 on Video-cassette 1, part 1). Following the dashing of hopes for reform and a crushing electoral defeat, workers took to the streets to express their anger and frustration. The involvement of the CGIL in the quasi-insurrectionary reaction to an act that was seen on the left as a possible prelude to the establishment of an authoritarian regime in Italy, was deemed unacceptable by trade unionists belonging to the parties of government. By failing to curb the extraordinary mobilization of workers in the industrial triangle of the north of Italy, which even Communist leaders were unsure whether to check or promote, despite Togliatti's whispered injunction not to let things get out of hand, Catholics argued that the CGIL majority had by their actions broken the pact of unity which linked the various factions of the confederation. Within weeks the split had hardened and an independent Catholic union was established.

With the left's definitive confinement to opposition, the CGIL began to adopt a different role. Whereas in the preceding period it had acted to restrain protest and increase production, it now adopted a more aggressive stance in defence of the structures of joint management established during the Liberation and against a government economic policy that produced contraction and recession. Clearly there were political factors in this. The close involvement of the parties in union affairs ensured that the influence of the PCI was preponderant on the CGIL after the split. Yet although many of its leading cadres and much of its financial resources came directly from the PCI, the union none the less maintained a distinct identity. Under the leadership of Giuseppe Di Vittorio, a former agricultural labourer from Puglia and a man of considerable personal magnetism, the CGIL rigorously promoted a policy of economic expansion in contrast to what it saw as the 'productive immobility' of the policy of Confindustria (the industrialists' confederation). To this extent it not merely took up problems connected with salaries and employment but also sought to address the whole question of national economic development. In itself this policy was positive. What rather undermined it was a belief, shared with the PCI, that Italian capitalism was incapable of expansion without the stimulus and involvement of the working-class movement. In this way the CGIL perpetuated the fiction of its own centrality at a time when it was being more or less completely ignored by the government and big business.

Bibliography

RIOUX, J.-P., *The Fourth Republic, 1944–1958*, trans. Godfrey Rogers, Cambridge, Cambridge University Press, and Paris, La Maison des Sciences de l'Homme, 1987 (first published in French in two volumes, 1980 and 1983).

AJELLO, N., *Intellettuali e PCI 1944–58*, Bari, Laterza, 1979.

BERTELLI, S., *Il Gruppo: la formazione del gruppo dirigente del PCI 1936–48*, Milan, Rizzoli, 1980.

GALLI, G., *La sinistra italiana nel dopoguerra*, Bari, Laterza, 1962.

GALLI, G., *Storia del socialismo italiano*, Bari, Laterza, 1978.

ILARDI, M., and ACCORNERO, A., *Il Partito communista italiano: struttura e storia dell'organizzazione, 1921–1979*, Milan, Feltrinelli, 1982.

SASSOON, D., *Togliatti e la via italiana al socialismo*, Turin, Einaudi, 1980.

SASSOON, D., *One Hundred Years of Socialism: the West European Left in the Twentieth Century*, London, Fontana Press, 1996.
WERTH, A., *France 1940–1955*, London, Robert Hale, 1956.

UNIT 4 Jean-Paul Sartre and *Crime passionnel*

Prepared for the course team by Stuart Sim

Study materials

For your work on this unit you will need to refer to the following materials:

Jean-Paul Sartre, *Crime passionnel*

Documents and Texts 1

Audio-cassette 2, 'Sartre: *Les Mains sales*'

Audio-cassette 3, side A, 'Sartre: *Les Mains sales*'

Audio-cassette 3, side B, 'Camus: *Les Justes*'

1 Introduction

This unit is concerned with the work of Jean-Paul Sartre, concentrating on his play *Crime passionnel* (1948). Sartre was one of the key figures of post-war European culture and the play will be examined in the context of his philosophical ideas (as expressed in three works of this period, *Being and Nothingness*, *What is Literature?* and *Existentialism and Humanism*). But the play is also relevant to the contemporary political situation in France; *Crime passionnel* is a very revealing source about the moral dilemmas facing French left-wing intellectuals in those politically turbulent years.

Before proceeding, I would like to clear up any possible confusion about the title of the play. Sartre's title for it is *Les Mains sales*. The literal translation of the French is *Dirty Hands*, and this is the title of the published American edition. The translator of your set book has decided to use the title *Crime passionnel*, which is how I refer to the play throughout this unit.

In this unit, we shall also be looking briefly at Albert Camus' play of the same period, *The Just* (*Les Justes*), and comparing the author's views with Sartre's on several issues. There are significant similarities in the themes of these plays, and both have considerable relevance to the political events of the time. Sartre and Camus reach very different conclusions, however, regarding the nature of human existence in general, and political commitment in particular, leading eventually to the rupture between them which is discussed in Unit 12.

The second section of this unit will introduce you to some of Sartre's philosophical ideas in order to help you undertake a reading of *Crime passionnel*. Please read this section and then the play before proceeding to section 3 of the unit, where you will be asked to do a series of exercises using specially recorded extracts from the play (to be found on Audio-cassettes 2 and 3).

Aims

The aims of the unit are as follows:

1. to outline the notion of commitment (*engagement*) and its role in Sartre's philosophical and literary practice;
2. to communicate the basic principles of Sartre's existentialist philosophy and to demonstrate how these inform the argument of *Crime passionnel*;
3. to contextualize *Crime passionnel* within the ideological struggles on the French left in the immediate post-war years;
4. to compare the political and metaphysical outlooks of Sartre and Camus through a study of *Crime passionnel* and *The Just*.

Why *Crime passionnel*?

Crime passionnel has been chosen for study because it exemplifies some of the key concerns of Sartre's philosophy of existentialism. It is also one of Sartre's most successful pieces of dramatic writing, and he shows considerable skill in synthesizing various dramatic genres and manipulating the audience's emotions while still managing to put across complex philosophical ideas. Sartre wrote *Crime passionnel* at a point in his career when he was deliberately seeking out a wider audience, and in formal terms it is a fairly traditional, realistic play the basic concerns of which are relatively easy to grasp.

Exercise In *What is Literature?* (1947) Sartre outlined the creed of the 'committed' (*engagé*) writer. Please turn to *Documents and Texts 1*, item 9, and read extract (a) from this text. How does Sartre view the writer's role, and what sort of literature would you expect such an approach to yield?

Specimen answer Sartre considers the writer to be some kind of teacher. If the writer follows the lead established here ('to act in such a way that nobody can be ignorant of the world') it is likely that the result will be a didactic and committed literature, which draws attention to contemporary social and political problems. ❑

As you will see, *Crime passionnel* displays commitment in the sense outlined above, dealing as it does with themes drawn from the contemporary political situation in France, where left and right were jockeying for power. Its interdisciplinary potential is quite considerable, therefore, being simultaneously a very dramatic piece of theatre, an exemplification of the author's philosophical doctrines, and a comment on the role and behaviour of the left in French political life.

2 Sartre in the 1940s: political and philosophical concerns

Intellectuals and politics

Jean-Paul Sartre (1905–80), philosopher, novelist, playwright and literary critic, was one of the major intellectual figures of the twentieth century. His most important philosophical work, *Being and Nothingness* (1943), expounded the doctrine known as existentialism and has had a profound impact on modern thought. Sartre's fiction, if not rated quite so highly as his philosophical endeavours, is still well regarded; the novel *Nausea* (1938) is probably his best known work. In our period of study Sartre held a dominant position in French cultural life, not just through his philosophy, novels and plays, but also through his editorship of the influential journal *Les Temps modernes*. The major philosophical text of his later career was the Marxist *Critique of Dialectical Reason* (1960). Sartre seems the very model of the French idea of 'the intellectual' as discussed in Unit 1: that is, someone whose life is devoted to intellectual pursuits and who can be regarded as a member of a distinct 'class'. He was a prodigiously active writer and disseminator of ideas throughout his life.

Exercise Can you think of any problem that the intellectual life would pose for a figure with pronounced left-wing views?

Specimen answer There are various things you might have noted. Intellectuals may have an over-theoretical view of the world; they may be more prone to defending pet theses than working out compromises with opponents (one of the prime political skills); they may lack experience of the concerns of the ordinary man and woman. They also may have a romantic view of working-class life. ❑

Left-wing political theory lays great store by the working class. The lifestyle and day-to-day concerns of the working class and the intellectual class are likely to differ quite considerably, and the left-wing intellectual can easily feel cut off from the class of people his political beliefs most dispose him to support. Then too, left-wing politics, especially in a period of reconstruction, is very much about action: action to correct social abuses and to reform the political structure of the state. Intellectual activity, on the other hand, is an essentially sedentary, and often solitary, experience, far removed from the world of action. In this connection the American critic Frederic Jameson has spoken of 'that malaise of continental intellectuals with their own specialized work which prevents it from ever seeming real work, real action' (Sartre, *The Origins of a Style*, p.8). This 'malaise' lies at the centre of *Crime passionnel*.

Sartre was well aware of the need to avoid being an 'ivory tower' intellectual, and he involved himself in political activities both during and after the war. He was a member of various clandestine wartime committees, such as the writers' group *Comité national des écrivains*, and had some connections through Camus with the Combat Resistance group. After the war Sartre became a prominent member of *Rassemblement démocratique et révolutionnaire*, a broad-front grouping on the non-Communist left, although one with little practical success in hard political terms.

Sartre as dramatist

But Sartre found other ways of involving himself with the fate of his fellow-men than political action and debate. During the 1940s he turned to playwriting and became an international name in this medium (having earlier used fiction as a vehicle for philosophical ideas in his novels). Sartre is known to have been very struck by the response to *Bariona*, a play he wrote while a prisoner-of-war of the Germans in 1940. The sense of community its performance created among his fellow prisoners made a deep impression on him. Drama henceforth became for Sartre a means of making contact with a wider audience than philosophical texts generally allowed, and for several years from *The Flies* (1943) onwards he cultivated the theatre – with considerable success.

Sartre adapted well to dramatic writing. Germaine Brée has suggested that drama appealed to him as 'the most immediately effective form of social literature, the one most immediately involving other human beings' (*Camus and Sartre: Crisis and Commitment*, p.251). We might also say that drama was well suited to Sartre's philosophical ideas and concerns, which often have a dramatic cast to them. In Brée's telling phrase, drama fitted 'Sartre's vision of commitment as crisis'. His plays are full of moments of crisis when characters must choose between opposing systems or ideals, and there is an inherently dramatic quality to such 'moments'.

The point I wish to make is that Sartre's fiction and philosophy are interrelated. No matter what the genre, he is, as David Caute has observed, 'always expressing and developing a total and related world view' ('Introduction' to *What is Literature?*, p.vii). We turn now to the philosophy that underpinned this world view.

Sartre as philosopher

Although we shall be dealing with his early existentialist philosophy here, it is well to remember that Sartre was to become increasingly sympathetic towards Marxism over the course of his career. One of the aspects of his work we are going to be most interested in is the tension between his existentialist beliefs and his sympathy for communism. Existentialism and communism have very different ideals and require different things from the individual. Just what these different things are we shall discover when we consider Hugo's plight in *Crime passionnel*: a plight in some sense representative of that of the French left-wing intellectual caught up in the political struggles of the 1940s.

Being and Nothingness (1943) is a long and complex work of philosophy and we can do no more in this particular context than sketch out its main lines of argument, preparatory to seeing how they inform the dramatic debate of *Crime passionnel*. We shall then examine *What is Literature?* for Sartre's views on commitment. Passing reference will also be made to *Existentialism and Humanism* (1946), a shorter and more accessible work of Sartre's but one he had reservations about in later years. (I will quote from the latter only where it makes a specific point more briefly than *Being and Nothingness*.)

Sartre was heavily influenced by the German philosopher Martin Heidegger, whose philosophy was particularly concerned with the nature of being and what it meant to be-in-the-world (his best-known book is *Being and Time*, 1927). Heidegger (and Sartre after him) held that there is no logical reason for being-in-the-world. We are 'thrown' or 'abandoned' there, and the human condition is consequently one of absurdity – there is no external reason for our existence. To be thrown arbitrarily into existence and to have to create the value of that existence through one's daily actions and relations with others is to force individuals back on to their own resources. The individual is left very exposed by such a state of affairs, having no external power (such as God) to appeal to for help or guidance. Such a philosophy has little concern with the essence of human being (a traditional philosophical concern – for René Descartes, for example, it was the 'mind'), and in technical terms it bases itself on the assumption that *existence* precedes *essence*. In Sartre's words, 'we must begin from the subjective' (*Existentialism and Humanism*, p.26), that is, from the brute fact of our daily experience of the world as individuals.

Exercise What might be the psychological effect of believing that there is no reason for your existence; that it is pure chance you are alive; that there is no God; and that you are an isolated figure in the world?

Specimen answer It might feed your sense of egotism, producing a range of feelings from elation through insecurity to fear. Many individuals would find it a liberating state of affairs to be freed from religion and conventional morality, and might regard it as a licence to act however they wanted. In others it would be just as likely to create feelings of unease or even outright anguish.

Discussion 'Anguish' is a key concept in existentialism. In Sartre's bleak words, 'In anguish I apprehend myself at once as totally free and as not being able to derive the meaning of the world except as coming from myself' (*Being and Nothingness*, p.40). This sums up the existential outlook: we are alone in the world and forced to discover the meaning of life through our daily actions: 'man is nothing else but that which he makes of himself' (*Existentialism and Humanism*, p.28). You may well find this a depressing picture of the human condition, but in the circumstances of the German Occupation and the subsequent reconstruction of France it exerted a powerful appeal, which was as much emotional as intellectual. If 'man is nothing but that which he makes of himself' then no one is bound by fate or forces outside his or her control. The individual can, in conjunction with other like-minded individuals, challenge authority and tradition and *change* things. He or she can choose to oppose the Germans or to create a more just society than had existed before the war. ❑

Sartre's existentialism is founded on a group of controlling concepts which we shall now briefly consider. Beginning with the argument that existence provides a better starting point for philosophical enquiry than essence, Sartre proceeds to examine the implications of such a position. His initial concern is to outline the nature of being and nothingness. Being has two varieties, being-in-itself and being-for-itself. The human person is both a being-in-itself (a thing) and a being-for-itself (a consciousness). We experience the world through consciousness, which is crucially aware of its separation from the world of things out there by a gap, or nothingness. Consciousness confronts 'the permanent possibility of non-being, outside us and within' (*Being and Nothingness*, p.5). That is to say, we are conscious not just of the gap between us and things (which exist at the level of being-in-itself only), but of our inward experience of non-being as each present moment fades away to become the dead past: 'consciousness continually experiences itself as the nihilation of its past being' (*Being and Nothingness*, p.28). In typically melodramatic fashion Sartre notes that 'nothingness lies coiled in the heart of being – like a worm' (*Being and Nothingness*, p.21). It is such dramatic potential that he exploits in his plays, where he considers the implications for the individual of the realization that we carry non-being within us, like an ever-present enemy.

We are, in Sartre's view, free at each point in our life to make choices, but freedom has its drawbacks. It is a condition of basic insecurity (the passage of time relentlessly presenting new and difficult situations to be dealt with) and as such it provokes an acute sense of anguish in us. To be free is to experience the anguish that comes from having to face up to the never-ending series of choices unfolding before us – 'I am condemned to be free ... we are not free to cease being free' (*Being and Nothingness*, p.439) – and from the knowledge that all our choices are in fact groundless, that is, made on the basis of nothing. Existential anguish is the product of that double realization of the necessity and the absurdity of choice, and to accept and live with that realization is to be in good faith.

Not everyone can cope with being in a state of anguish, and there are those who attempt to hide the truth of their existence from themselves. Such people are guilty of what Sartre terms 'bad faith' (*mauvaise foi*, sometimes glossed as 'self-deception'). 'In bad faith, it is from myself that I am hiding the truth' (*Being and Nothingness*, p.49). The consequences of such a mode of behaviour figure prominently in Sartre's drama.

The reality of the human condition, however, is that we cannot flee indefinitely from the tyranny of choice. Events catch up with us and there are periodic moments of crisis which force choice upon us. Sartre is adamant that all actions presuppose choice, and that the choice is always freely made, even if this has some awkward implications: 'even torture does not dispossess us of our freedom; when we give in, we do so freely' (*Being and Nothingness*, p.524).

Exercise Can you think of a counter-argument here?

Specimen answer You might well have observed that to talk of freedom of action when *physical* freedom is denied us seems rather absurd, and that coercion cannot generate a 'free' response. If we did not choose to be in that particular situation (and it is unlikely that we would *choose* to be tortured), then we can hardly be said to be free agents, or to have the means to make a rational choice.

Discussion Sartre's point, however, is that we are inevitably in *some situation or other*, and that we must accept responsibility for that situation even if it is not one of our own making. Neither do we ask to be born (we are 'abandoned' into the world), yet we have no alternative but to accept responsibility for our actions from that point onwards. It may seem a very restricted form of freedom that only allows a choice between being tortured and giving in to the torturer's demands, but that was precisely the situation that so often faced members of the Resistance, and in this sense Sartre's theories are pertinent to the wartime political situation. ❑

Sartre also insists that when we choose we must accept full responsibility for our choices and for the effect they have on others: 'man being condemned to be free carries the weight of the whole world on his shoulders; he is responsible for the world and for himself as a way of being' (*Being and Nothingness*, p.553). The world presents itself to the individual as a set of 'opportunities and chances' to be acted upon, and actions taken in response alter future opportunities and chances not just for the individual but for others as well. Each choice a person makes therefore acquires a profound sense of significance that 'extends to the entire world as a peopled-world' (*Being and*

Nothingness, p.556). Sartre further argues that individual actions take on a universal significance, because the choices made by an individual assume an 'image of man as he believes he ought to be' (*Existentialism and Humanism*, p.29). There is a distinct tendency on Sartre's part to pick extreme examples of choice and his plays further illustrate this trait. This is deliberate policy on his part: 'we have undertaken to create a literature of extreme situations' (*What is Literature?*, p.164). Extreme situations not only fit Sartre's philosophy but also make for inherently dramatic theatre. The emotional upheaval which accompanies extreme states translates well to the stage, which comes into its own in such larger-than-life situations. (Sartre was following a trend in this respect. Since the 1930s several French dramatists had shown an interest in dramatic situations in which the lead character was forced to make a critical choice; as in the work of Anouilh.)

Being 'responsible for the world' means that we are inescapably implicated in its daily workings. To refuse to face this brute fact of existence and the anguish that accompanies it is to lapse into bad faith, and as Sartre notes, 'most of the time we flee anguish in bad faith' (*Being and Nothingness*, p.556). It becomes the duty of the writer to force us to acknowledge our responsibilities, the need to accept and live with the necessity as well as the absurdity of our choices, and so to avoid bad faith. This is the problem Sartre tackles in *What is Literature?*, a work of literary theory written just prior to *Crime passionnel*.

Sartre as literary theorist

Sartre locates himself firmly in the problems of the present day in *What is Literature?*: 'the only question which is urgent for us: what is the situation of the writer in 1947 [...]?' (p.119). Sartre saw this situation as one of political crisis in which 'every day we must take sides' (p.206) – whether to support Russia or America, for example. It followed that the writer's task was to encourage readers to reflect on the problems of the time rather than to feed them escapist literature.

As a literary theorist Sartre is unashamedly polemical and it is likely that his wartime experience exercised an influence in this respect. Sartre's argument was that the Occupation of France had taught him that the author had a duty to steer his audience away from bad faith: 'We did not want to delight our public with its superiority to a dead world – we wanted to take it by the throat' (p.167).

Exercise Turn to *Documents and Texts 1* and read extract (b) from *What is Literature?* What points are being made here?

Specimen answer Writers can no longer hide from their social responsibilities in times of economic hardship, nor regard themselves as being beyond political problems. Writers now have a duty to place themselves at the service of their public; the problems facing that public are too pressing to be ignored. It would, in effect, be 'bad faith' for the writer to remain aloof from those problems. ❑

For Sartre, the problems of reconstruction led to a dramatic literature that was didactic, realistic, and fairly traditional in style. In an era when playwrights such as Brecht and Genet were challenging theatrical conventions (realistic portrayal of character, audience identification with character, drama as an essentially mimetic medium), Sartre generally eschewed experimentation. He presented well-made plays, stocked with credible characters and believable, if somewhat melodramatic, situations. Sartre's political and philosophical radicalism seems to stop short of his literary endeavours, which are much more conventional in form. His desire to appeal to an audience wider than the artistic avant-garde has to be taken into account in this context.

Writing in 1947, Sartre was facing the breakdown of what we might call the 'Liberation consensus', and political allegiances were fragmenting (four governments over the course of the year indicate the volatility of the political situation). Not only was there division between right and left but also on the left itself (as discussed in Unit 3). By 1947 the Cold War was well under way and the French Communists did not see eye-to-eye on the international situation with other groups on the left. There was much disagreement, for example, over the Marshall Plan and French colonial policy.

Although not a Communist, Sartre often expressed sympathy with communism's general aims in this period. Raymond Aron, a prominent critic of Sartre, described Sartre in 1969 as being 'a para-Marxist since 1945' (*Marxism and the Existentialists*, p.167), which quite neatly sums up his position in the later 1940s: almost, but *not quite*, a Communist. Being para-Marxist was not enough for the Communists, however, who savagely denounced Sartre's literary efforts. Soviet critics dubbed him an agent of Wall Street, and to the Communist newspaper *L'Humanité* the author of *Crime passionnel* was a 'nauseous writer' and a demagogue. Sartre replied in kind.

Exercise Turn to *Documents and Texts 1* and read extract (c) from *What is Literature?* What is the basis of Sartre's complaint against the Communist Party?

Specimen answer The main complaint is that the Communist Party, under Russian influence, has become increasingly authoritarian, and thus poses a severe threat to intellectual freedom. Sartre argues that the Party stifles debate by demanding uncritical acceptance of its political line ('the opponent is never answered; he is discredited'), and the political radical in him is dismayed by the Party's growing conservatism in the post-war period. ❑

Sartre's criticism indicates the problems that were building up on the left as the Cold War gathered momentum, as well as the ambivalent nature of his attitude to communism. He admires the *doctrine* of communism, but not its *practice* in the post-war period. Those tensions in Sartre's outlook are reflected in *Crime passionnel* and it is perhaps not surprising that Communist critics reacted adversely to the play, given the PCF's commitment to Zhdanovism in cultural matters (you will recall the discussion of this issue in Unit 1). Sartre may not be an experimental writer, but neither is he a socialist realist in the approved Zhdanovist manner.

The overall impression we gain in *What is Literature?* is of an author determined to make the act of writing relevant to his time. Writing becomes a weapon in the political struggle: 'literature throws you into battle' in Sartre's dramatic phrase (*What is Literature?*, p.47). So much for Sartre's theory of literary commitment; now we turn to the practice.

3 Crime passionnel

Crime passionnel was premiered in Paris in 1948 and was soon followed by London and New York productions (the former a success, the latter a flop). It found favour with the French bourgeois press but not with the Communist critics. In Simone de Beauvoir's graphic phrase, 'The Communists spat it out like tainted meat' (*Force of Circumstance*, p.161).

The play deals with the tensions experienced within the Proletarian Party (a communist type of organization) in an imaginary central European country, Illythia, during the Second World War. The Party is divided on matters of policy, and Hugo, a young intellectual and recent recruit, is assigned by a dissident faction to assassinate the Party's leader, Hoederer. *Crime passionnel* is an examination of communist tactics as well as an analysis of the conflicting demands of personal and political life, and how such conflicts can lead one into bad faith. Its ultimate message is deeply ambiguous, which is perhaps unsurprising given Sartre's ambivalent attitude to communism at this time. The atmosphere of *Crime passionnel* draws on the experience of the Resistance, with characters being confronted by desperate choices between revolutionary action or collaboration, life or death. It is one of Sartre's 'extreme situations', where 'the heroes are freedoms caught in a trap like all of us' (*What is Literature?*, p.217).

You should now read the play through.

The argument of the play

In this section we shall look at selected scenes from the play in order to trace how the argument unfolds. This exercise will be undertaken in conjunction with the recorded extracts, which you should listen to before proceeding to the discussion of each scene. You will find the recordings on Audio-cassettes 2 and 3. It will quickly become apparent that your set text and the recording do not correspond. In fact, different translations are involved: Kitty Black (1949) for the Methuen edition, Frank Hauser (1982) for the recording. The Hauser version was originally for radio performance and does not exist in published form. It is, however, the version currently favoured by the Sartre estate, and for copyright reasons we are obliged to use it.

At first sight this may seem very confusing, but with just a little effort on your part we are confident you can adapt to the situation (if nothing else, the exercise will prove a salutary reminder that translation is not a straightforward business). The course team feels that the benefits to be derived from hearing the play being brought to life by actors far outweigh the disadvantages of having to contend with two translations. The recording is designed to demonstrate how relationships develop between the characters, and also how those characters respond to extreme situations. No amount of reading can give you the emotional nuances that performance does, and since I want to claim that *Crime passionnel* is more than just an intellectual exercise, this factor of emotional impact becomes crucial. The recorded scenes are as follows: Prologue, pp.7–17 in your set book; Scene Two, pp.27–51; Scene Three, pp.60–71; Scene Four, pp.90–7; Scene Five, pp.108–11; Epilogue, pp.112–20. Please note that all quotations from the play in this section will be from the Hauser translation.

We shall also be paying close attention to the philosophical and political implications of the play's argument. Sartre constructs a series of dilemmas concerning bad faith, freedom and choice, and we shall be focusing on scenes where these dilemmas come to a head. Let us start with the Prologue to see what themes are established there. Please listen to the recording of the extract from the Prologue which is at the beginning of Audio-cassette 2.

Exercise In what sense could we be said to be in one of Sartre's 'extreme situations' in the Prologue?

Specimen answer Hugo is clearly in grave danger at the hands of the Party – and knows it: 'when he comes out, as a reward he'll be put down like a dog'. Olga manages to obtain a stay of execution, but for three hours only. Hugo is in effect being asked to plead his case while under sentence of death, one of the most extreme situations imaginable for an individual. ❑

Exercise Faced with imminent death, Hugo seems apathetic. Is Sartre suggesting that in this case the character has no freedom of action or choice?

Specimen answer and discussion I do not think so, because Hugo has already made several choices before the scene ends: to come to Olga's flat; to remain there even when advised to leave; to co-operate, even if only implicitly, in his own projected rehabilitation. Like the man being tortured, Hugo has the freedom to choose, even if it is only a case of the freedom to choose where to die.

Hugo's plight represents a more extreme version of the general human condition as described by Sartre in *Being and Nothingness*, where we are held to be 'abandoned' in the world to make what we can of the situation. With his protagonist's life in the balance at the end of the opening scene, Sartre has fulfilled his intention of taking his public 'by the throat'. ❑

Exercise What vision of the Party have you formed by the end of the Prologue?

Specimen answer and discussion It is clearly a monolithic entity which demands, and receives, total obedience on the part of its members: 'I received no orders about you. But if I did, I'd do as I'm told.'

Self-effacement becomes a primary requirement of political effectiveness in this world, and it is precisely this state that intellectuals find so difficult to achieve: 'I talk too much', as Hugo candidly admits. Personal life becomes subservient to political life, as even Olga's attempt at Hugo's rehabilitation proclaims. This downgrading of private life was, to Camus, one of the most distasteful aspects of membership of the Communist Party. ❑

By the end of the Prologue it has been established that this is a world where decisiveness in choice and action are vital. It is not possible to remain neutral, sides must be taken, and instances of bad faith will be ruthlessly punished. The argument will proceed to follow Hugo's career in the Party to show how he has exercised his freedom within the various traps life has set him. Various philosophical themes have been introduced, but they arise in a very natural and starkly dramatic way from the concrete social and political circumstances of individuals' lives. Sartre has constructed a site of debate for existentialist issues which forces us to see them in very human terms – bad faith being a matter of life and death for Hugo – and we shall now look at some other scenes from the play to examine how that debate is conducted.

The next extract on your cassette is from Scene Two (pp.27–51). Listen to it carefully, taking particular note of any changes of mood and tone of voice as the characters come to terms with each other. Personal and political concerns keep coming into conflict and generate a considerable amount of psychological tension. In this claustrophobic setting 'freedoms caught in a trap' is a very apt description of the characters' positions.

Exercise The bantering exchanges between Hugo and Jessica introduce a farcical note into the proceedings. What do you think Sartre is trying to reveal about their respective characters?

Specimen answer Jessica seems much more interested in people than Hugo does. As a Party member Hugo is required to subordinate personal considerations to political ones. His inability to describe Hoederer's appearance indicates how far this trait has been developed, and may represent an implicit criticism of communism's dehumanizing tendencies (as well as of the other-worldliness of the intellectual). Jessica's curiosity about others ('I want to have everyone') implies a character who is perhaps imbalanced in the other direction, and who is not giving enough weight to political matters. In each case bad faith is a possible accusation.

Discussion The tone adopted by Hugo and Jessica helps to place them firmly in the upper layer of the class structure (what with their flippant exchanges and Jessica's coyness, they sound as if they have strayed in from a drawing-room comedy). Their dialogue and manner jar in this setting, particularly when compared to the matter-of-fact directness of the party members in Scene One. There is more than a hint that they are merely playing at being revolutionary. To fool around with a gun hardly denotes maturity or a proper appreciation of the realities of their situation.

Observe too how frequent an image a gun has already become, as if symbolizing the ever-present threat of nothingness in human affairs. The absurdity of human existence, which can be terminated in a split second of sudden violence, is called to mind in this recurrent image. ❑

When Hoederer's bodyguards enter the mood alters to resemble that of a gangster film. Sartre shows himself to be very adept at switching styles throughout the play and such sudden changes in mood help to illustrate the basic insecurity of the human condition as an existentialist sees it. The characters are never allowed to settle in any one situation. They are forced instead to adapt to a constantly changing stream of events, some farcical, some serious, all potentially disorienting. Sartre's sudden shifts of style serve to signal this unsettled quality of existence to the audience.

Exercise The reaction of the bodyguards to Hugo foregrounds the latent hostility of the working class to intellectuals, and forces Hugo into admitting his past: a past he now wishes to eradicate in the service of the Party. What significance do you suppose the photographs in Hugo's suitcase have?

Specimen answer and discussion They suggest that he has not really jettisoned his past (bad faith under the circumstances) and is not free of it in the way that a communist revolutionary ideally should be. The locked suitcase carries unmistakable psychological overtones of bad conscience, and we get a sense of someone who is refusing to reveal himself fully to others. Hugo seems unwilling to expose himself to the anguish and risk that are necessary parts of living in the present. The photographs symbolize an investment in the past that is an act of bad faith, both as a human being dealing with others and as a communist engaged in revolutionary action.

Hugo is beginning to appear something of an egotist, which contravenes Sartre's belief that our actions should always be directed at others: 'What I constantly aim at *across* my experiences are the Other's feelings' (*Being and Nothingness*, p.228). ❑

Exercise What impression do you form of Hoederer? Play through Hoederer's sequence once again, paying close attention to his tone of voice if you are unsure how to answer.

Specimen answer He is a very authoritative figure who commands respect and obedience from those around him. There is an air of calm assurance about him which comes over unmistakably in the performance. Hoederer registers as someone who has overcome the 'continental malaise' (see p.6): he is both a man of ideas and a man of action. His ability to put trust in others is a mark of someone who is willing to experience the element of risk inseparable from living in the present (in this sense he is a model existentialist). ❑

Now move on to the extract from Scene Three (pp.60–71).

Hoederer's fatherly attitude towards Hugo emphasizes the latter's bad faith towards him. Hugo is neither Hoederer's secretary nor party colleague; he is simply *pretending* to be those things. In reality he is an assassin, but he is not sure of himself in this role either, hence his indecision. Contrast this with Hoederer's boldness in taking risks in this scene. Hugo is still trapped in an intellectual frame of reference, and cannot will himself into the state of mind of a man of action. The 'continental malaise' maintains its hold on him.

Exercise Might we see Hugo's reluctance to go through with a violent act as a redeeming feature of his character? Support your answer.

Specimen answer It could be argued that Hugo's reluctance suggests the promptings of conscience and is thus potentially redemptive, and a war-weary, anti-communist audience might well have reacted that way. But I suspect that this was not Sartre's desired effect. Hugo is not so much displaying a guilty conscience and humanitarian leanings as the bad faith of a failure of nerve, and he lacks the singularity of purpose the extreme situation of wartime requires. ❑

Crime passionnel now shifts more self-consciously into a play-of-ideas mode (another change of style) where the conflicting claims of the monarchist, bourgeois and proletarian parties are debated. The argument rages back and forth until Hoederer manoeuvres Karsky into an awkward position, where he must either choose to compromise his principles or be cut out of the anti-German coalition. It may seem to be an impossible choice to make, but Sartre's point holds that it is a choice, and that the one thing it is impossible to do is not to make a choice.

Exercise What does Hugo's intervention in the debate reveal about his character?

Specimen answer I would say the manner of it reveals his class background yet again. He seems *personally* incensed that a deal is being done with people of his father's class ('now they've followed me here'), and allows his feelings to cloud his political judgement. His outburst suggests that he is trying to deny the realities of the political situation.

Hugo and Karsky prove to have a lot in common. Both retain too much of a commitment to the past, and deceive themselves by refusing to make the choice the situation manifestly demands if progress is to be achieved. ❑

Exercise What effect is Sartre seeking to create with the explosion?

Specimen answer It adds an element of sheer theatricality to the scene, which makes the point that war is more than just talk. But it also has a deeper significance. It shows just how misplaced Hugo's outburst is. Politics (especially in wartime) is about hard choices, not about the purity of individual principles, and you cannot keep the present at bay. At *any* instant reality can intrude (often abruptly and dramatically so, as here) thus scattering personal principles. Holding on to the past is no help at such points. Such *coups de théâtre* neatly make Sartre's point that we can be suddenly faced with a life-and-death situation at any moment. ❑

Please go on to the next extract, from Scene Four (pp.90–7).

I have argued that there is considerable tension between Sartre's existentialist beliefs and his communist sympathies, and I feel that it comes to a head in this debate between Hugo and Hoederer.

Exercise How would you describe the respective approaches to politics sketched out by Hugo and Hoederer? And what could be said in favour of each?

Specimen answer Hugo's is an intensely personal approach, whereas Hoederer's is that of a thorough-going pragmatist. The personal approach has much to commend it (particularly with the hindsight we now have from our later vantage point, having observed the excesses so often committed in the name of ideology in the intervening decades); but so does pragmatism in the extreme situation that is wartime. Hoederer's clinical pronouncements – 'A Party is never an end but a means and there is only one end: power' – seem significantly more attuned to the realities of wartime than Hugo's passionately voiced idealism, attractive though the latter may be in an abstract sense.

Discussion I would argue that in this exchange communism begins to look unattractive. Hoederer freely admits that power is the Party's sole end, and although that may be the case with almost *all* political parties, it is rarely stated quite so baldly. His realism could well have been found offensive in the jittery political climate of 1948, with fears of Russian invasion in the air. So might his curt dismissal of wartime heroes ('Look, I don't give a damn about the dead') and his defence of lying. Hoederer's pragmatism about such matters begins to verge on a rather unpleasant ruthlessness.

There are grounds for saying that Sartre is both attracted and repelled by Hoederer's ruthlessness of purpose. While it certainly provides a corrective to the 'continental malaise', it also has overtones of inhumanity. The tensions in Sartre's political outlook are very much foregrounded in his treatment of Hoederer in this scene. ❑

Now play through the assassination, Scene Five (pp.108–11).

The assassination when it does come has a farcical quality, and it is difficult to know whether to regard Hugo's act as a crime of passion or a political assassination. It very much depends on how we choose to read that line of Hugo's, 'And you've set me free.'

Exercise What possible meanings can you suggest for this line?

Specimen answer Perhaps it means that he has been set free from Hoederer's influence – which could be seen as a regressive step, since it implies a reversion to romantic anarchism (and with it, bad faith). Alternatively, it could mean that the duplicity, as Hugo interprets it, of Jessica and Hoederer, has shocked Hugo into an awareness of the folly of permitting personal considerations to influence his actions. Hugo has either been set free *from* communism, or set free *for* communism. Either way, he has made a choice. What is difficult to determine – and this is part of the play's continuing fascination – is whether it is an act performed in bad faith or not. ❑

Now play through the Epilogue (pp.112–20).

Hugo cannot seem to unscramble his motives in killing Hoederer, and almost regards the act as self-generated: 'I didn't kill him, chance did.' This suggests that Hugo has not yet come to terms with his past. He cannot define himself as a man of action if he cannot claim responsibility for the act of murder. Until he can negotiate a new role for himself (which he cannot do until he clarifies why he killed Hoederer) Hugo will remain captive to the past. It has become a case of death or a break with the past: another one of Sartre's critical choices on which an entire existence hangs.

Olga offers Hugo the chance of rejoining the Party, but there proves to be a barrier. Hugo cannot accept the Party's change of policy: a change that incorporates Hoederer's old policy of co-operation with the Party's political enemies.

Exercise Why do you think Hugo reacts in this way to the Party's tactical shift?

Specimen answer Hugo has to confront what is for him a massive irony, having assassinated Hoederer as requested only to find the latter's policy surviving him. To claim responsibility for the act of murder is apparently to claim responsibility for a pointless act. Hugo cannot bring himself to ignore the irony or its implications, and he chooses death instead: 'Not fit for salvage.' ❑

Exercise Would you describe Hugo's death as a courageous act? Support your answer.

Specimen answer On one level it seems so. He dies for his ideals and because he refuses to lie to himself, or to collude with the lies of others. It could be described as the act of a man of integrity. An anti-communist audience could see Hugo as the victim of an inhuman system, and his death as a denial of communism and its devious political practices.

Discussion Whether the above reading would be consistent with Sartre's philosophical views is very debatable. It might be consistent with the anti-Communist Party views expressed in *What is Literature?* ('Progressive and revolutionary in its doctrine and its avowed ends, it has become conservative in its means'), but I would argue that it clashes with Sartre's general line of argument in *Being and Nothingness*. Death may represent a denial of communism, but it also represents a denial of the future and of choice. Hugo turns his back on freedom, commitment, responsibility, and others: all the things that make individual existence worthwhile, for all that they are attended by anguish. He opts instead for one last romantic gesture. Perhaps he is after all, as Brée argues, not a hero but an anti-hero. ❑

Exercise Do you see him as hero or anti-hero?

Specimen answer I would regard him as a Sartrean anti-hero on the grounds of his egocentricity, anarchistic leanings, and general inability to act in a decisive way. He displays exactly those traits that render an intellectual politically ineffective. But an argument is certainly possible either way, and your choice (pro-individual or pro-system) probably reveals a lot about your own political leanings! ❑

It is difficult not to take sides on this issue after going through the play, which is precisely what Sartre wants us to do, to become involved in its many crises.

The play validates Sartre's theory of the 'engaged' writer if we find ourselves being drawn into its concerns and dilemmas in this way.

Sides were certainly taken in 1948, and much of the support the play enjoyed was in fact in the nature of a bourgeois backlash to the Communist criticism of the play. Simone de Beauvoir argued that 'the play seemed anti-Communist because the audience was on Hugo's side' (*Force of Circumstance*, p.161), which was not Sartre's intention – although it might well suggest deep ambiguities in Sartre's own position which he could not quite resolve nor hide from his audience.

Summarizing the play

Let us now draw together what we have learned so far about the play's themes, their philosophical implications and their historical significance.

Crime passionnel constitutes a sustained exploration of the nature of bad faith, with Hugo as the major focus of attention. He is an egotist more concerned with self-image than his responsibility towards others. In existentialist terms he never does succeed in aiming across his own experiences to 'the Other's feelings'. He fails in his duty towards others, therefore, and reprehensible though this is at *any* time, in wartime it becomes positively dangerous and can cost lives. The wartime setting intensifies the implications of an egocentric style of life.

We might sum up Hugo's career as an illustration of John Donne's maxim that 'no man is an island'. To ignore this truth is to alienate oneself from the human race with predictably drastic consequences. Hugo's death amounts to suicide (since he chooses *not* to be salvaged) and is in itself the ultimate act of bad faith in that it robs his career of any possible meaning: 'Suicide cannot be considered as an end of life for which I should be the unique foundation. Since it is an act of my life, indeed, it itself requires a meaning which only the future can give to it; but as it is the *last* act of my life, it is denied this future [...] Suicide is an absurdity which causes my life to be submerged in the absurd' (*Being and Nothingness*, p.540). One has, in effect, lived for nothing.

The play is also crucially concerned with demonstrating the centrality of choice and action in human affairs. To be human is to be in a position where one must incessantly make choices, and to vacillate about choice amounts to a wilful disregarding of the human condition. This is the case no matter how unpromising the circumstances of choice prove to be. Both Hugo and Jessica are guilty of evasion of choice, and neither can be said to realize their potential as a result. If 'to be is to act', then they can hardly be said to achieve full humanity. They are certainly not fully human *for others*. If there is an ideal of behaviour in the play it is probably Hoederer, one to whom choice and action come naturally.

Sartre is very much exercised with the nature of freedom in *Crime passionnel*. The choice of an extreme situation (where alternatives are starkly outlined) enables him to extract the maximum dramatic impact from this aspect of his philosophy. Man is condemned to be free. We do not bring ourselves into being, and we are continually placed in situations not of our own creating, but freedom always carries the possibility of change and there is thus a positive element in Sartre's philosophy – limited though it is in extreme situations. Hugo's rejection of this possibility points up the perils of refusing to be committed: one *dies to others* in such a case; becomes a non-person; becomes nothingness.

The overall style of the play is carefully tailored to the notion of the extreme situation. There is little in the way of elaborate figures of speech, and there is a terse, urgent quality to much of the dialogue.

Exercise What is Sartre trying to convey by such directness of address?

Specimen answer That in an extreme situation all extraneous considerations are pared away and characters concentrate on essentials. When it comes to life-and-death situations there is simply no room for flowery language, or emotionally indulgent rhetorical flights of fancy.

Verbal economy is practised by most of the characters in *Crime passionnel*, most notably the more experienced party members (note the laconic tone they adopt in Scene One, for example). Time is clearly of the essence in this world, and it concentrates minds wonderfully to realize this. ❑

Exercise *Crime passionnel* is full of violent imagery which reinforces Sartre's view that we are constantly threatened by non-being. I have already mentioned the gun as a recurrent image carrying fairly obvious connotations of violence and danger: can you think of any other examples of recurrent imagery that fit in with this pattern?

Specimen answer We have explosions in Scenes One and Four. Blood also features prominently in the play. Injuries are sustained in the Scene Four explosion ('You're bleeding rather a lot', p.72) and Hoederer is shot in Scene Five. Hugo reminisces about his youth and how 'they made me drink fresh blood from the slaughter-house because I had no colour' (p.42). Violence and its consequences are never far from the surface of events, and infect the participants' language. Hoederer invites Karsky to 'squeal like a stuck pig' (p.69); Hugo complains that 'Here death is a job to be done. Like in a slaughter-house' (p.83).

Discussion The characters are clearly obsessed by images of blood and gore and a distinct air of menace pervades much of the play. Non-being constitutes an ever-present threat, and *Crime passionnel*'s characters seem permanently on the verge of crisis. The images that express this insecurity are basic, brutal and unambiguous. (You might also note a repeated use of animal imagery in the play; characters being variously described as pigs, whales, dogs, as if to suggest the difficulty of retaining one's humanity in an extreme situation.) Philosophical dilemmas in *Crime passionnel* are not mere intellectual abstractions, but matters of life and death. Metaphysics is successfully transformed into human drama. ❑

Sartre also makes extensive use of irony to communicate his existentialist vision. Hugo has to face the irony of having killed Hoederer, and of then discovering that the latter's policy has been adopted by the Party. Hoederer's death seems utterly pointless in that history has vindicated his reading of the political situation. The sheer absurdity of human existence is brought home to us very forcefully at such moments. All our actions are directed towards a future which can be taken from us suddenly and violently at any point. Whether politically or personally motivated, Hoederer's murder seems unnecessary and deeply ironical. Sartre's use of irony helps to underscore the basic insecurity of human existence, and here his literary and philosophical objectives can be seen to converge. It is all very well arguing that we are free to change, but a pointless death robs us of this possibility and draws attention to life's sheer contingency and absurdity. Irony seems to be implicit in the human condition: at which point literary figure and metaphysical attitude fit together like hand and glove.

This stress on contingency may be another reason why the play failed to appeal to Communists. To their way of thinking, to claim that life is absurd is to cast doubt on the ultimate value of the class struggle. For all its essentially sympathetic handling of Hoederer, the play seems to question the certainties of communist doctrine. Sartre leaves us stranded somewhere between existentialism and communism, which might well be an accurate reflection of his own philosophical position in the 1940s. Forced to choose between existentialism and communism, Sartre, ironically enough, ends up in no-man's land.

Crime passionnel is therefore very revealing about the dilemmas facing the French left-wing intellectual in the reconstruction period. The certainties of wartime and the Resistance are no longer there, and the potentially dehumanizing tendencies of communism are becoming ever more worrying. The ambiguities to be noted in the play effectively mirror the confusion on the left in the breakdown of the Liberation consensus.

4 Albert Camus: *The Just*

We turn now to Camus' play *The Just*, which deals with similar moral dilemmas to *Crime passionnel* but to very different effect. By analysing the respective handling of the dilemmas we should be able to establish the political and philosophical differences between Sartre and Camus in this period. The differences will provide further evidence for divisions on the left concerning the nature and scope of political commitment.

Albert Camus (1913–60) was one of the leading authors of the twentieth century and was awarded the Nobel Prize for Literature in 1957. Born and brought up in French Algeria, he had a varied career as a journalist (including editorship of the Resistance newspaper *Combat*), actor and theatre director as well as writer of novels, plays, essays and short stories. His career was tragically cut short by his death in a car crash.

First performed in Paris in 1949, *The Just* had a fair amount of success and ran for several months despite mixed reviews. As with *Crime passionnel*, the Communist critics were disapproving. You will find selected extracts from *The Just* in *Documents and Texts 1*, item 10. Performances of these extracts are recorded on Audio-cassette 3, side B. You should read each extract and listen to its recorded performance (either simultaneously or separately) before going on to the accompanying discussion. Once again I would stress the importance of listening for the emotional nuances that performance adds to the text. A brief exposition of the play follows first.

The Just concerns a group of terrorists in Czarist Russia who are planning to assassinate the Grand Duke Sergei as a gesture against the state and its authoritarian policies. Their first attempt is a failure because the bomb-thrower, Kaliayev (also called Yanek) cannot bring himself to throw the bomb at a coach containing children. A second attempt succeeds and Kaliayev is arrested. While in prison awaiting execution, he is visited by the Grand Duke's widow, who tries to make him repent of his crime and beg God's forgiveness. He refuses and is eventually hanged. Despite their grief at his death the group is already planning a new assassination attempt as the play ends. Between the assassination attempts there is much heart-searching on the part of the terrorists about the ethics of their activities as well as the personal sacrifices they must make, and Camus seems particularly interested in the psychology of revolutionary terrorism.

The Just has many surface similarities with *Crime passionnel*, as audiences noted at the time. Simone de Beauvoir tells an amusing story about an admirer rushing up to Camus after the first-night performance and declaiming, 'I like it better than *Les Mains sales*', unaware that Sartre was standing nearby (*Force of Circumstance*, p.207). The terrorists are required to give unquestioned obedience to their organization, and are often placed in life-or-death situations which stretch them to the limit psychologically as well as testing the depth of their revolutionary commitment. Death is an omnipresent threat in this world too, and the characters similarly exist under conditions of extreme crisis.

Reading the play

Now turn to *Documents and Texts 1*, item 10, for extract (a) from *The Just*, Act One. The recorded performance of this extract follows the final extract from *Les Mains sales* on side B of cassette 3. Three of the terrorists, Stepan, Annenkov (also called Boria) and Kaliayev, are arguing over which of their number is to throw the bomb in the coming assassination attempt.

Exercise The mood of the scene is tense. What lies behind this tension?

Specimen answer There are conflicts within the group as to motives, with Kaliayev retaining a humanitarian bias despite his terrorist activities ('We must love each other if we can'). Kaliayev's idealism confronts Stepan's cynicism in a debate about the legitimate aims of revolution and what ethics it should entail. Kaliayev requires justification to kill his fellow men, whereas Stepan appears to have moved beyond this stage into indiscriminate hatred. Annenkov's position is somewhere between the two. Camus clearly wants to explore a variety of attitudes to the ethics of terrorism, hence the range of views expressed by these psychologically very different characters. ❑

Exercise How would you describe the language in this extract, and how does it compare with *Crime passionnel*?

Specimen answer It is fairly impassioned and full of rhetorical flourish. Although there are, as you have heard, several impassioned exchanges in *Crime passionnel*, Sartre's language is in general plainer and less self-consciously 'poetic'. Camus' approach denotes a greater interest in the psychology of his characters, and a willingness to let them reveal their deeper emotions to the audience.

Now turn to extract (b), from Act Two. This is another debate about the legitimate aims of revolutionary activity, this time between Stepan, Annenkov, Kaliayev and Dora.

Exercise What is the main issue of this debate?

Specimen answer I would say it was an argument over whether the end justifies the means. For Stepan it does ('Nothing is barred that can further our cause'). For the others it cannot ('Hundreds of our brothers have died to prove that everything is not allowed').

Discussion Brée has argued that Stepan's defence of indiscriminate violence in this scene 'discloses the real though unconscious intent beneath the revolutionary rhetoric: ideological tyranny' (*Camus and Sartre*, p.222), and Camus does seem to be engaged in isolating Stepan here, as if to point out that even within terrorism there are limits. Perhaps Camus is also giving out a warning of what can happen when the individual becomes obsessed with abstract concepts such as 'justice' (note how self-conscious the characters sound when using this word). Underneath it all is a plea that we never lose sight of the human dimension in our political calculations. Camus' concern is invariably with the individual, not with abstractions. In this sense he is less explicitly philosophical a writer than Sartre, but perhaps more humanitarian. ❑

Exercise How would you describe the language in this extract? And what effect does it suggest Camus was striving for?

Specimen answer Again, I would tend to call it impassioned and rhetorical in style, with lots of ringing sentiments that sound as if they could be shouted from the barricades. There is also a 'stagey' quality about the speeches which suggests characters who are perhaps taking themselves too seriously. Camus may be implying that when commitment is taken this far it becomes artificial. Their hothouse environment means that these characters have lost touch with everyday reality, its concerns and language. ❑

Now turn to extract (c), from Act Three. Dora and Kaliayev are discussing the recent departure of one of their number, Voinov, who has lost his nerve. It is their last meeting before Kaliayev leaves to assassinate the Grand Duke.

Exercise What is Dora trying to communicate?

Specimen answer I would say that she is arguing the case for feeling over reason and political calculation ('once at least I must let my heart speak'), and insisting that there must be a space set aside for private life as well as public. It is yet another plea for the human dimension to be recognized in any political scheme.

Discussion Camus' concern for the individual emerges very strongly in this episode. Note how Dora tries to lead Kaliayev away from the abstract to the human and the individual: 'And me? Do you love me with tenderness?' It is a dramatic appeal that cuts across revolutionary rhetoric and radically undermines Kaliayev's position, as the manner of his exit suggests. His rhetorical confidence has evaporated after exposure to Dora's all-too-human vulnerability.

I suspect that Sartre would have regarded Dora's argument as an example of bad faith. Jessica's argument against violence in Scene Four (p.86) of *Crime passionnel* has the same kind of underlying appeal to the emotions, and Jessica is almost certainly intended to be an illustration of bad faith. ❑

Exercise What would constitute evidence for an accusation of bad faith on Dora's part? And how do you think Camus would defend his practice?

Specimen answer We could argue that she is allowing her emotion to get the better of her reason, thus disguising from herself the reality of the political situation within which the terrorists are obliged to operate. In this extreme situation there would appear to be a choice between condoning tyranny (by remaining passive) or protesting against it (by means of terrorist activity). That is the kind of stark choice we are given in Sartre's world. Camus seems to suggest that the situation is more complex; that basic human needs, such as the need to love and be loved, must be taken into account too. He is probably arguing that the choice outlined above – tyranny or terrorism – is an over-simplified opposition.

Once again the characters are permitted to disclose much more about themselves and their emotional states than in Sartre, and Camus probes into their psychologies to explore the cost exacted by the suppression of personal feelings in a revolutionary cause. ❑

Exercise How does the language signal this cost?

Specimen answer The speeches become quite disjointed as the scene progresses, and the rhetorical flourish of the earlier sequences is largely missing. There are gaps between many of Dora's utterances, suggestive of someone who is in emotional turmoil and having difficulty in articulating her confused thoughts. Kaliayev's broken speech at his exit is further evidence of the emotional cost of revolutionary obsession. ❑

I would imagine that Camus is trying to elicit our sympathy for the emotional deprivation his characters must suffer, which amounts to an argument against the inhumanity of revolutionary politics. In Camus we are witnessing a *personal* tragedy, whereas in Sartre we witnessed a *political* and *philosophical* one. If Sartre aims for the audience's throat, Camus aims for its heart. Now turn to the last extract, from Act Five. Dora and Annenkov are awaiting confirmation of Kaliayev's execution. Once again the ethics of terrorism are under review.

Exercise What is the gist of Dora's argument?

Specimen answer She is reiterating her earlier point that individuals matter more than abstract principles. Her doubts about those abstract principles come strongly to the fore: 'Ah Boria, what if the others do not live? And he has died for nothing?' This might be seen as a defence of the value of mundane, everyday existence as against grandiose revolutionary plans for the future. There is a horror developing in Dora's mind about the human cost of terrorist action, and also doubts about the organization's motives ('sometimes I think this is an arrogance that will be punished'). ❑

Dora's conduct once again seems designed to register differences between our two authors. Sartre would be unlikely to accept that sentiments such as 'It's easy, it's infinitely easier to die with one's contradictions than to live with them' were in any way justifiable or defensible.

Exercise Can you suggest why Sartre might react adversely at such a point?

Specimen answer To opt for death rather than life would amount to a denial of freedom, since freedom equals the freedom-to-change and death negates that possibility. Conflict is simply man's lot in Sartre's view, and it is in effect cowardice to choose (or even idealize) the 'easier' route of death. That is Hugo's solution and it is to be deplored: it is the wrong choice – the 'bad faith' choice – as far as existentialism is concerned. ❑

As usual, Camus' sympathy seems to go out to the individual caught in an impossible situation. Dora's broken speech rhythms provide further evidence of the stress she is under in coping with the contradictions of the terrorist position. Her speeches in this scene seem calculated to win audience sympathy rather than to promote philosophical speculation in the Sartrean manner.

Comparing *The Just* and *Crime passionnel*

Now that we have looked at both plays we are in a position to make direct comparisons between them.

Exercise How would you sum up the differences in approach between the two authors to similar moral dilemmas?

Specimen answer I would argue that Camus is less overtly philosophical a writer than Sartre, and that he displays a deeper concern for the individual. *The Just* is more of a psychological study than a political or philosophical drama, whereas with *Crime passionnel* the reverse is the case. Germaine Brée has argued that Camus 'was a man who essentially dealt in people', while Sartre 'dealt mainly in abstractions', although he was also 'deeply preoccupied by people' (*Camus* *and Sartre*, p.12), and I think this pinpoints an important distinction between these authors. We might say that Camus is preoccupied with the individual's *emotional* turmoil, Sartre with his *intellectual* turmoil. ❑

What this means is that Sartre tends to intellectualize emotional states, and to strive to reveal their philosophical implications (as illustrations of bad faith, anguish, and so on). Camus is less conceptually oriented and more interested in the suffering of the individual. We might even claim an anti-intellectual bias in *The Just.* Camus is at least implicitly critical of characters who perform actions on the basis of what their revolutionary theory (quite possibly the result of philosophical speculation) tells them to do, rather than following their gut feeling.

Camus can be seen to be moving towards a position of doubt regarding the validity of terrorist activity in general, because of its inhuman connotations; as he once remarked in a letter, 'even when it succeeds, revolution shows us a horrible face' (quoted in Olivier Todd, *Albert Camus*, p.300). Sartre, on the other hand, is more likely to judge the value of any given instance of terrorist activity against a concept like bad faith than against human suffering. It depends on the nature of the choice offered to the individual, and the degree of honesty he or she brings to it. The ethics of terrorist activity depend upon the situation for Sartre. Camus suggests a more absolute view of ethics: it is simply wrong to kill children, no matter what justification you feel you may have for your action. In this sense Camus is more self-consciously a moralist than Sartre, engaged in disclosing what Brée has called the 'irrefutable logic of unreason' connected with terrorism (*Camus and Sartre*, p.200).

There are also marked differences of approach with regard to private life. Camus clearly feels that totalitarian political parties do not allow enough scope for this, whereas Sartre would seem to be more willing to countenance a subordination of the personal to the political. We might sum up by saying that Camus' primary concern lies with the private individual and Sartre's with the political one, and that each author perhaps has a tendency to downgrade the other's concern. In the context of late 1940s France, with the reconstruction of political life a pressing issue (and one that was straining loyalties and alliances dating back to the Resistance), these respective positions indicate the wide scope for division on the left. It seems to shape up as a division between those who believe in the individual and those who believe in the system, with different notions of commitment being involved. By the early 1950s the positions had crystallized more fully in the work of Camus and Sartre, and can be treated as symbolic of what is happening generally on the left. But the warning signs for what became *The Rebel* controversy were there to be seen in earlier years.

5 Conclusion

The significance of *Crime passionnel*

It should have become apparent by now that, given its philosophical and political implications and historical significance, *Crime passionnel* is a text particularly suited to an interdisciplinary approach. It is permeated by philosophical ideas and provides a very telling illustration of some of the key concepts of existentialism. *Crime passionnel* offers a notably more accessible entry to Sartre's philosophical concerns than *Being and Nothingness* – the nature of bad faith, for example, registers with far greater clarity when we are given a demonstration of how it works out in terms of individual conduct. Indeed, existentialism becomes drama in a very natural way; Brée's point that Sartre is 'a born dramatist' (*Camus and Sartre*, p.252) is well made.

But *Crime passionnel* is more than just an illustration of Sartre's philosophical system. It is also a significant literary work in its own right: tautly constructed, intellectually and emotionally challenging, and theatrical in the best sense of the word. The quality of performance it has generated from our actors is surely proof that we are dealing with a substantial piece of dramatic writing. Sartre manages to invest the play with a sense of dramatic urgency – an urgency brilliantly captured in our performance I feel – and its main themes still have considerable relevance several decades on. How much freedom for manoeuvre does the individual really have in dealings with others? Does the individual matter more than the system? Should one be prepared to kill for an idea? Do ends justify means? These are questions of no less import nowadays, whether or not we are caught up in extreme situations.

Crime passionnel also benefits from being considered within its actual historical situation, and it is a very interesting source about the effect of that situation on the sensibilities of left-wing intellectuals. The competing claims of various ideologies were taxing intellectuals on the left in the aftermath of the war, and *Crime passionnel* is a significant contribution to the debate that was raging. The ambiguity of the play captures the sense of ideological confusion at the time, and Sartre's ambivalent attitude to the Communist Party articulates many of the fears felt by his left-wing contemporaries. At the very least Sartre communicates a sense of wariness about communism, and the collective reaction of Communist critics to even the hint of criticism about communist methods is evidence of a hardening of political attitudes as the Cold War developed. The broad consensus that had marked the early days of Liberation had collapsed and nothing less than total, unqualified support was being demanded by groups like the Communist Party. Sartre's unease about what this involved was certainly shared by many other intellectuals on the left.

Crime passionnel is significant for us, therefore, because it works on various levels and enables us to reach a greater understanding of French culture in the 1940s. It enables us, for example, to appreciate the political implications of Sartre's existentialist philosophy, with its appeal to a generation confronted by a series of large-scale social crises – from Occupation through economic reconstruction to Cold War. It also helps us to understand something about the moral dilemmas facing the intellectual in this troubled period, when commitment was not an abstract notion but a practical necessity. 'Every day we must take sides' as Sartre put it, neatly expressing the urgency of the situation confronting the individual.

Sartre's turn to the theatre in itself demonstrates the degree of urgency he felt, theatre being a more immediate medium than philosophical discourse and with correspondingly greater public impact. *Crime passionnel* works on a philosophical, political and literary level, therefore, and constitutes a site where interdisciplinary concerns quite naturally meet. That is why it is such a rich work for study on a course such as this.

Sartre versus Camus

The Just also encourages interdisciplinary study, and we have seen how it represents a different strand of thinking on the left from Sartre's. Camus is moving steadily towards a liberal humanist position in his work, as *The Just* with its concern for the individual suggests, whereas Sartre eventually shelved most of his doubts about communism and adopted an increasingly pro-Marxist line in his political and philosophical writing. Relations between the two figures (at one time very cordial) progressively deteriorate as we move into the 1950s, and Sartre versus Camus becomes a highly symbolic debate for French culture.

While we must not reduce a complex cultural phenomenon such as the breakdown of the Liberation consensus to the specifics of the relations between two individuals, Sartre and Camus can be considered to represent distinct currents of thought in post-war French intellectual life, and their break over *The Rebel* thereby takes on wider significance. We shall consider this wider significance in Unit 12.

References

ARON, R., *Marxism and the Existentialists*, translated by Helen Weaver, Robert Addis and John Weightman, New York, Harper and Row, 1969.

BEAUVOIR, S. DE, *Force of Circumstance*, translated by Richard Howard, Harmondsworth, Penguin, 1968.

BRÉE, G., *Camus and Sartre: Crisis and Commitment*, New York, Dell, 1972.

JAMESON, F., *Sartre: the Origins of a Style*, New York and Guildford, Columbia University Press, 1984.

SARTRE, J.-P., *Being and Nothingness*, translated by Hazel E. Barnes, London, Methuen, 1957.

SARTRE, J.-P., *Existentialism and Humanism*, translated by Philip Mairet, London, Methuen, 1948.

SARTRE, J.-P., *What is Literature?*, translated by Bernard Frechtman with an introduction by David Caute, London, Methuen, 1967.

TODD, O., *Albert Camus: a Life*, translated by Benjamin Ivry, London, Chatto and Windus, 1997.

UNIT 5 The Roman Catholic Church, 1943–58

Prepared for the course team by Geoffrey Warner

Study materials

For your work on this unit you will need to refer to the following materials:

Documents and Texts 1

1 Introduction and aims

You will recall from Unit 1 that Roman Catholicism is one of the unifying themes of the first part of this course. This unit is given over entirely to an examination of the Roman Catholic Church in France and Italy during the period of Liberation and reconstruction, c.1944 – c.1954. It is intended that when you have completed it you should:

1 be able to assess the extent of Catholic belief and practice in France and Italy;

2 be able to describe how the Church was organized, both centrally and locally;

3 have an understanding of how the Church mobilized support and be able to assess how successful it was in doing so;

4 be able to discuss the relationship between the Church and society – in particular, to describe its attitude to the principal political developments in France and Italy in the post-war decade.

Although, as indicated above, we are going to look at 'the extent of Catholic belief' in the two countries, you will find that there is not much reference to the strictly religious content of that belief except in so far as it relates to the other issues being discussed. The body of Roman Catholic belief is large, complex and continually evolving. For example, there were important developments in this period in beliefs about the Bible and in the organization of the liturgy (the form of church services). Several commentators have argued that these developments foreshadowed some of the enormous changes in the Church resulting from the Second Vatican Council (1962–65) which is discussed in Unit 29. Be that as it may, we shall be saying little if anything about them here.

Belief and practice

Like many statistics, those relating to religious belief need to be interpreted with care. When the Fascist census of 1931, for example, was used to show that 99.6 per cent of the Italian population was Catholic, it was rarely pointed out that the relevant question on the census form did not actually ask respondents what (if any) religion they currently believed in, but to which one they had been registered as belonging at birth. It is much more illuminating to look at religious practice, for all the great religions expect their adherents to participate in various forms of religious activity. The most obvious measure in the case of Roman Catholics is attendance at mass. This is the service that contains the Eucharist – the commemoration of the last supper which Jesus took with his disciples before his crucifixion, as recorded in all four Gospels of the New Testament. Catholics are expected to attend mass every Sunday, as well as on certain other major holy days, such as Christmas Day and All Saints' Day (1 November). We are fortunate in having two public opinion polls which give us a good idea of the extent of this practice during the period of our course.

In November/December 1947 the French Institute of Public Opinion (IFOP) asked respondents whether they had been to mass on either of the last two Sundays. The answers are shown in Table 5.1.

Table 5.1 Attendance at mass in France, 1947

	All %	*Men %*	*Women %*
Yes	37	27	47
No	58	68	48
Other	5	5	5

(Source: Sutter, *La Vie réligieuse des Français*, vol.2, p.815)

A poll carried out by the Italian public opinion polling agency DOXA, which asked respondents in February 1954 what they had done on the previous Sunday, provides a rough comparison. It showed that 51 per cent of men had been to mass, and 73 per cent of women.

Another IFOP poll, conducted in August/September 1952, revealed that 33 per cent of men and 22 per cent of women said that they attended mass very rarely. (This same poll brought out the difference between belief and practice very clearly, for it also showed that 77 per cent of men and no fewer than 92 per cent of women considered themselves to be Catholics.) In Italy, a DOXA poll of April 1953 recorded 14 per cent of men and 6 per cent of women as saying that they did not attend mass.

Exercise What conclusions would you draw from this public opinion poll data?

Discussion There are two clear conclusions:

1 If we use attendance at mass as an indicator, Italians were consistently more 'devout' than the French. A higher proportion of both men and women attended mass than their French counterparts, and a lower proportion said they never or rarely attended. Moreover, these differences are quite considerable: nearly twice as many Italian men as French attended mass, and almost four times as many French as Italian women said they did not go to mass or went rarely.

2 By the same token, women in both countries were consistently more 'devout' than men. Almost half as many again of Italian women attended mass compared with Italian men, and the difference between French women and French men was even greater. ❑

Of course, attendance at mass does not tell us everything about the strength of a person's Catholic convictions. It could simply be a matter of habit and/or social conformity and does not necessarily mean that he or she pays any more than token allegiance to the Church's teachings. The 1952 IFOP poll, however, put some rather more searching questions which provided correspondingly more interesting answers. Respondents were asked whether they took any notice of the Church's instructions with regard to reading matter, plays and films, and whether they took its position into account when they voted. Table 5.2 summarizes the answers.

Table 5.2 Effect of the Church's instructions on political and cultural behaviour in France, 1952

		All %	*Men %*	*Women %*
Reading matter	Yes	24	15	32
	No	67	75	59
	No reply	9	10	9
Plays and films	Yes	19	12	27
	No	68	76	60
	No reply	13	12	13
Voting	A lot	16	12	20
	A little	2	21	27
	Not at all	55	63	47
	No reply	5	4	6

(Source: Sutter, *La Vie réligieuse des Français*, vol.2, p.673)

These figures show that the Church's influence over the everyday behaviour of French men and women was less than their attendance at mass might have indicated, although once again women were more likely to pay attention to the Church's views than men. Unfortunately, there are no comparable data for Italy.

A final point worth making in this connection is that, by and large, religious belief and practice in both countries was stronger in the countryside than in the towns. Indeed, the larger the town, the weaker the hold of religion on the inhabitants. This phenomenon is undoubtedly linked with that of the 'de-Christianization' of the urban working class which we will discuss in more detail in connection with the French worker-priest movement later on in this unit.

2 The nature and structure of the Church

Exercise Turn now to *Documents and Texts 1* and look at item 11. This consists of extracts from a papal encyclical on 'The Mystical Body of Christ and our Union in it with Christ' (*Mystici Corporis*) of June 1943. Encyclicals are letters sent by the pope to all bishops in communion with the Roman Catholic Church and are an authoritative statement of his views on the issue(s) with which they deal. Opinions differ as to the extent to which individual Catholics are bound by their contents, but they are certainly supposed to pay them the closest attention. Encyclicals are normally written in Latin, the official language of the Church, and are referred to by their first few words.

Before reading it, you should bear in mind the following points:

1 *Mystici Corporis* is a very long document, consisting of 113 numbered paragraphs. You will note that we have reprinted a mere eleven, and not even all those in full, so you will only be reading about one-tenth of the original. Our extracts have been chosen deliberately to illustrate a

particular aspect of the encyclical's teaching; they should not be taken as representing all that it has to say.

2 Note the style of the document. Although ecclesiastical Latin is not as ornate as the language of the great Roman authors, it still possesses a certain grandeur which comes over in the translation. The text, as in most papal pronouncements, is peppered with references to the Bible and other writings. The sources of the direct quotations have been indicated in square brackets. 'The Fathers of the Church' referred to in paragraph 17 are writers of the early centuries of the Christian era whose works elucidate and build on the beliefs of the early Church. Taken together with subsequent pronouncements of the Church itself (and statements of Pope Gregory the Great (590–604) and Pope Leo XIII (1878–1903) are specifically cited), the writings of the Fathers constitute one of the twin foundations on which Catholic doctrine rests: namely, tradition. The other foundation, of course, is scripture. Incidentally, the 'Venerable Brethren' who are mentioned are the bishops, and so on, of the Church to whom the encyclical is formally addressed.

Now read the document and summarize what it says about the nature, structure and membership of the Church.

Discussion Your answer should read something like this:

1 The Church is compared to a human body, with all the parts connected to and dependent on one another.

2 This body is organized in a hierarchical fashion. Just as every functioning body must have a head, so must the Church. In the case of the Church, it is Jesus Christ, but he works through his 'Vicar on earth', i.e. the pope. Beneath the pope are the bishops. They exercise considerable power in their own right – 'the ordinary power of jurisdiction' mentioned in paragraph 42 is power belonging to the office of bishop – but they are nevertheless subordinate to the pope (who, indeed, appoints them in the first place).

3 Membership of the church is defined quite narrowly and people can be either separated or excluded from it (paragraph 22). Those Christians who do not subscribe to the tenets of the Catholic faith and who do not submit to its organizational hierarchy (e.g. Anglicans) have 'separated themselves' from the Mystical Body of Christ, the one true Church. Even if you are a member of the latter, however, you can be excluded 'for grave faults committed', and as we shall see (below, pp.166–7) these are not necessarily confined to what we would normally call religious matters.

4 All members of the Church are expected to work very hard in its interests. There is no room for passengers in this organization. (What is meant by Catholic Action will be explained below, p.160) ❑

We shall now look in more detail at some of the aspects of the Church's structure and organization raised by *Mystici Corporis*, beginning with the papacy, which for many is the institution that they most associate with the Roman Catholic Church.

According to Catholic doctrine, the pope's position in the Church is based on Jesus Christ's delegation of his authority to his disciple Peter, recorded in Matthew 16:18–19: 'And I tell you, you are Peter, and on this rock [the original Greek text involves a pun on the words 'Petros' (Peter) and 'Petra' (rock)] I will build my church.' Catholics trace this 'apostolic succession' in a direct, unbroken line from Peter (the first Bishop of Rome), through his successors to present-day popes. Most non-Catholic Christians do not accept this reasoning.

They are even more unhappy about the dogma of 'papal infallibility', which was pronounced at the first Vatican Council of 1870. We must beware of interpreting this dogma in the same way as the American schoolchild, who allegedly wrote that 'since the pope is infallible, he has to be very careful what he says'. The pope is indeed careful in what he says, but his infallibility is only exercised in matters of faith and morals and even then only in very special circumstances. Since 1870, in fact, only one infallible papal pronouncement has been made, and we shall be considering it later in this unit (see p.158).

An Ecumenical Council, which was composed of all the cardinals, bishops, and heads of religious orders, together with certain theologians acting in an advisory capacity, was the most powerful counterweight to papal power, but even such a Council had to be summoned by the pope and its conclusions endorsed by him to be valid. In any case, there had only been one since the Council of Trent in the sixteenth century: the Vatican Council of 1870. We know that Pius XII (1939–58) contemplated convening another in 1950, to coincide with the celebration of the 'holy year' (see p.154), but this was dropped for fear of possible disagreements among the assembled dignitaries. It was left to his successor John XXIII (1958–63) to summon the Second Vatican Council, which did so much to transform the Church (see Unit 29).

Despite reportedly finding it difficult to make up his mind on difficult issues, Pius XII did not hesitate to make his views known and to compel obedience to them once he had done so. Not only did he proclaim the only infallible dogma to be uttered by a pope since 1870 (although he, of course, would have argued that this represented God's truth and not his own personal opinion), he also staked out a maximalist claim for papal pronouncements in general in the encyclical *Humani Generis* of 12 August 1950, arguing that papal encyclicals either expressed already existing (and therefore binding) Catholic doctrine, or defined it where it was still unclear. Finally, Pius XII exercised his authority in a peculiarly autocratic style. 'I don't want collaborators,' he is once reported to have said; 'I want executors.'

In order to exercise his authority Pius XII deliberately adopted a high profile. A passage in *Mystici Corporis* not reproduced in your extracts states that 'it is absolutely necessary that [the pope] be visible to the eyes of all, since it is he who gives effective direction to the work which all do in common'. If the present pope, John Paul II, is regarded by many as a 'media pope' par

Figure 5.1 *Pope Pius XII in 1949 on the fiftieth anniversary of his priesthood.*
(Photo: Dena Süddeutscher Verlag Bilderdienst, Munich.)

excellence, it was undoubtedly Pius XII who launched the trend. He strengthened Vatican Radio, which had been founded by his predecessor Pius XI in 1931, and pioneered the use of television. He made countless speeches, many of them broadcast, on all manner of subjects, from the Virgin Mary to the gas industry.

Media coverage of the papacy reached a peak in 1950, on the occasion of the celebration of the 'holy year'. The first 'holy year' had been proclaimed by Pope Boniface VIII for 1300 and it was originally intended that there should only be one every hundred years. By the end of the fifteenth century, however, the interval had been reduced to twenty-five. In 'holy years' Roman Catholics who make a pilgrimage to Rome and fulfil certain conditions when they get there are granted a special 'indulgence', that is, a remission of the temporal penalty which they would otherwise have to undergo in respect of sins for which they have confessed and been forgiven.

Assisting and advising the pope is the equivalent of a civil service known as the Curia. It is divided into Congregations, Courts and Offices. The second category, which deals as its name implies with matters of ecclesiastical law, need not concern us here, and it would only be confusing to describe the others in detail. It is important, however, to say something about one Congregation – the Congregation of the Holy Office – and one Office – the Secretariat of State. The Congregation of the Holy Office (from 1965 called the Congregation of the Faith) was the direct descendant of the Inquisition and was responsible for questions of faith and morals. Presided over by the pope himself, as are the more important of the Congregations, it is run on a day-to-day basis by a Cardinal Secretary.

The Vatican is an independent state and the Secretariat of State is, in fact, the equivalent of a foreign office, dealing with relations between the papacy and other governments. Until 1944 it was presided over by the Cardinal Secretary of State, Luigi Maglione, but after his death Pius XII broke with tradition and acted as his own Secretary of State. It is said that he did this because he could not make up his mind between the two rival candidates for the post, Domenico Tardini and Giovanni-Battista Montini, who was later to become Pope Paul VI (1963–78).

In theory, and usually in practice, all Congregations, Courts and Offices are run by cardinals. The title of cardinal, symbolized by the famous red hat, is an honorific one bestowed on senior members of the clergy by the pope. There are two main classes of cardinal: residential bishops who continue to live in and administer their dioceses, and cardinals resident in Rome, who are expected to take part in the Curia. The collectivity of cardinals, known as the College, has of course one vital role to play: it elects a new pope from among its number. Until the reign of Pius XII the majority of the College of Cardinals had always been Italian, which is one reason why popes were almost invariably Italian too. His own nominations, however, deliberately produced a non-Italian majority for the first time.

As indicated in *Mystici Corporis*, the key element in the structure of the Church below the papacy and the Curia is constituted by the bishops. The pope appoints bishops, and he can remove them, but as John L. McKenzie has written, while a bishop is in office, he 'alone possesses all ecclesiastical power in his diocese. [...] No one does anything as a Catholic in the diocese which is not ultimately, if not immediately and directly, authorized by the [bishop]. [...] The [bishops] stand at the head of the action of the Roman Catholic Church on the local level, and they have no ecclesiastical superior other than the Pope' (*The Roman Catholic Church*, p.51). A diocese is the name for the administrative area subject to a bishop. (It is also often known as a see.) Dioceses are often grouped into provinces, and the most important diocese of a province is headed by an archbishop. The latter, however, does not have any jurisdiction over the other bishops in his province.

Below the diocese the administrative unit of the Church is the parish. This, of course, is the 'sharp end' of the Church as far as most of its members are concerned. The parish priest is the representative of the Church with whom they are most often in contact and through whom they receive the most authoritative exposition of its teaching. Priests could and did exercise enormous influence, particularly in the more backward areas where they were a traditional source of advice and support for the inhabitants. Priests, however, were not autonomous agents. They were responsible to their bishop and could be disciplined or even removed by him.

One final point should be made about the nature of the ecclesiastical organization described in this part of the unit, although you are probably aware of it already. It was exclusively male, which is why the use of masculine pronouns to describe its members does not constitute sexist language. There were of course religious communities of women, which were run by women, but these were outside the principal chain of command presented here. A woman could not, and still cannot, become a priest, a bishop, or a pope in the Roman Catholic Church.

3 Mobilization

As we saw in Units 1 and 2, Resistance and Liberation resulted in the destruction of both the Fascist regime in Italy and the Vichy regime in France. Although, at the time of their collapse, the Church was not sorry to see them go, its attitude had not always been hostile. Indeed, both these regimes had been, to a varying extent, supported by the Church and had received important favours in return.

In the case of Italy, as we noted in Unit 1 (p.20), relations between the Church and the pre-Fascist state had not been good. The political turmoil that followed the end of the First World War, and which carried the threat of a repetition of the Bolshevik revolution in Italy, did not make things any better. From Rome's point of view, Mussolini and his Fascists seemed a better bet than red revolutionaries or ineffective liberals, even if this did mean pulling the rug from beneath the feet of the Catholic, but democratic, Partito Popolare Italiano (Italian People's Party). The Church, moreover, benefited considerably from Fascist rule. Under the terms of the Concordat of 1929, for example, the Church's jurisdiction in matrimonial affairs was accepted and Roman Catholic religion was taught in all state schools. In addition, of course, the Church's traditional enemies – freemasons, Socialists and Communists – were persecuted by the government. There were quarrels, notably over the regime's attempts to monopolize youth organizations, but relations between church and state were far better than they had been under any pre-Fascist government.

In France, the collapse of the Third Republic in 1940 was seen by many devout Catholics as just retribution visited on an atheistic regime. Alluding to the legislation of 1882, which instituted secular state education in France, the French commander-in-chief, General Weygand, was reported to have told the cabinet in June 1940: 'France deserved its defeat. It was beaten because, for fifty years, its governments have driven God from the schools.' By contrast, Vichy seemed a welcome deliverance, especially when it restored compulsory religious instruction in schools and paid out state subsidies to Church schools. It also banned freemasonry, passed laws against abortion and alcoholism, and made divorce more difficult. It was small wonder, therefore, that Cardinal Gerlier, the Archbishop of Lyons and France's leading prelate, could proclaim that 'Pétain is France and France is Pétain', or that, in 1941, the archbishops and bishops in both the occupied and unoccupied zones of the country could subscribe to a joint declaration pledging their support to the regime and urging their flocks to follow their example.

The Church's growing disillusionment with Fascism and Vichy was not simply the result of a cynical calculation that they were increasingly likely to end up on the losing side in the Second World War, but of a mounting opposition to the war itself. Although it had enthusiastically backed Italy's imperialist invasion of Ethiopia in 1935–36 and its participation in General Franco's 'anti-Communist crusade' in the Spanish Civil War from 1936–39, the Church's support for Italy's entry into the Second World War had been distinctly muted. This was no doubt a result of its hearty dislike of Italy's ally, Nazi Germany, which was rightly regarded as scarcely less anti-Christian than the Soviet Union and which had similarly indulged in the persecution of the Church. As both Fascist Italy and Vichy France became increasingly subordinate to, and identified with, Nazi Germany, so the Church's coolness towards them became more and more pronounced.

A number of commentators have criticized the Church for its acquiescence in the horrors perpetrated by the Axis powers during the Second World War, but while it may be argued that it could and should have done more to resist them, there is really no doubt where it stood. Although the Vatican undoubtedly hoped that the German armies would defeat the Soviet Union in 1941, it refused specifically to endorse the invasion. On 5 September 1941, Mgr Tardini of the Secretariat of State told the Italian ambassador, who had come to request such an endorsement, that while Communism was the Church's worst enemy, it was not the only one. 'Nazism has carried out and is still carrying out a thoroughgoing persecution of the Church', he explained. 'The swastika is therefore hardly the appropriate device for a crusade.' Ten days later, in some notes for an audience with the American ambassador, Tardini wrote that he hoped Communism would be defeated and destroyed in the current campaign, but also that 'Nazism will come out of it weakened and be defeated'. The SS's intelligence service described Pius XII's 1942 Christmas message as 'one long attack on everything we stand for', while *Mystici Corporis* roundly condemned Nazi killings of the physically handicapped, the insane and the chronically sick.

In turning against Fascism and Vichy, however, the Church was well aware that it was providing hostages to fortune in that the political forces which looked increasingly likely to take over from these discredited regimes included powerful Communist parties. How would the Church cope with this situation, which must have looked equally menacing from its point of view? Apart from continually and emphatically warning the Allies of the dangers of Communism, it sought to strengthen its own position by mobilizing the faithful and by extending its own influence. In the rest of this unit we shall be looking at four case studies of this process.

Marian devotion

I wrote at the beginning of this unit that we would not be looking very much at the strictly religious content of Roman Catholic belief during the period covered by this course. What follows may seem at first sight to contradict this assertion. After all, what could be more strictly religious than the veneration of the woman whom Christians believe to be the mother of God? If you bear with me, however, I think you will soon see that such veneration also carried with it distinctly secular implications.

The Virgin Mary has always occupied an important place in Roman Catholic belief and worship. One of the most famous Catholic prayers, the Ave Maria, or

Figure 5.2 *Procession at Bareggio, Milan, during the return of the Madonna Pilgrimage, 1950. (Photo: From* Italia moderna, *V. 3, Banca Nazionale del Lavaro, 1984.)*

Hail Mary, is directed specifically to her. She became even more prominent during the hundred years following the middle of the nineteenth century. First of all, there was a series of alleged visions of Mary by children or adolescents, the most famous of which took place at Lourdes in France in 1858, and at Fatima in Portugal in 1917. These two sites became important shrines for pilgrimages of the faithful. Secondly, in 1854 Pope Pius IX (1846–78) proclaimed the dogma of the Immaculate Conception. This stated that Mary, unlike the rest of the human race, had been conceived free from the taint of original sin.

Why this sudden flowering of Marian devotion during this period? One explanation, surely, is that during the nineteenth century the Church was under increasing attack from all manner of secular movements and that one form of defence was to return to the roots of the faith, especially those that were popular with the great bulk of ordinary believers, which Marian devotion certainly was. It was no coincidence that (in 1864) Pius IX had also issued a Syllabus of Errors, a long list of liberal and rationalist propositions which were roundly condemned by the pope in the name of the Church.

As a Catholic commentator, the Revd Donal Flanagan, has pointed out, it is, however,

> [...] the pontificate of Pius XII, particularly in its latter years (1950–58), [which] represents the high point of the Marian movement of the nineteenth and early twentieth century. The recorded statements of this pope on the Blessed Virgin outbulk the combined contributions of his five predecessors.

> Pope Pius XII engaged himself with discretion, it is true, but heavily on the side of the Marian movement. And while he took occasion to point out the dangers, and the need for a solid theological approach, there is no doubt that without his support and encouragement the ever greater manifestations of Marian piety simply could not have taken place. In the years 1950 to 1958 we find a mounting crescendo of Marian enthusiasm.
>
> (Flanagan, 'An ecumenical future for Roman Catholic theology', p.8)

On All Saints' Day (1 November) of the 'holy year' 1950, Pius XII made use for the first, and so far only, time of the doctrine of papal infallibility, which had been proclaimed at the First Vatican Council of 1870. The pope made the Assumption of the Blessed Virgin Mary an article of faith for all Roman Catholics. The Assumption, which refers to the taking up of both the body and soul of Mary into heaven at her death, had been celebrated by Catholics for centuries (remember Calvino's 'Adam, One Afternoon', pp.11–12) but it had not been the subject of a formal dogmatic definition by the Church. In the 1953 encyclical *Fulgens Corona*, issued on 8 September (the date chosen by the Church to celebrate Mary's birth), Pius XII announced a Marian Year to run from December 1953 to December 1954, the centenary of Pius IX's proclamation of the dogma of the Immaculate Conception.

Exercise Turn now to item 12 in *Documents and Texts 1*. This consists of two short extracts from speeches by Pius XII. Read them and then state briefly how the pope uses the examples of Mary to make a point in each extract.

Discussion In the first extract the pope uses the example of Mary to stress the importance of motherhood for women; in the second he uses her as an inspiration in the struggle against the 'enemy' of the Church. As you will see in more detail in Unit 13, the Church had strong opinions about the role of women in society. It would perhaps be going too far to say that it subscribed simply to the view that 'a woman's place is in the home', for it did urge women to play an active part in politics and other extra-domiciliary activities, but there is no doubt that it believed in the primacy of the family unit and the crucial importance of the wife and mother in maintaining it. It also firmly maintained, in the words of another sentence from the same address to midwives, that 'marriage [...] is not ordered by the will of the Creator towards personal perfection of the husband and wife as its primary end, but to the procreation and education of a new life'. It followed from this that abortion, sterilization and artificial methods of birth control were wrong, and, indeed, much of the document in question is devoted to their condemnation.

Advocates of these practices were doubtless numbered among the 'enemy' referred to in the second extract, but you would almost certainly be right if you thought that the principal target here was the Soviet Union and the forces of 'atheistic Communism'. This will become clearer when we look at the nature and role of 'Catholic Action' in the next section. What both extracts show, of course, is the way in which Mary could be used to mobilize the faithful in support of the Church's policies. Verse 38 of Chapter 1 of St Luke's Gospel, which is cited in the first extract you read, has a much wider implication than the particular context in which it was used. Mary unquestioningly accepted God's will as conveyed to her by the angel Gabriel; good Catholics must similarly accept God's will as conveyed to them by the Church. A figure of great veneration, particularly by the masses, and, at the same time, a symbol of total obedience, Mary was indeed a powerful weapon in the armoury of the Church. ❑

Catholic Action

You will have seen that the second extract in the last exercise was addressed to Italian Catholic Action and you will also have noticed that *Mystici Corporis* referred to this organization (see p.152). What was Catholic Action? An American scholar, William Bosworth, gave as good a short definition as you are likely to find in his book, *Catholicism and Crisis in Modern France*, in 1962. 'Catholic Action', he wrote, 'comprises all laymen's groups which are formally mandated by the Hierarchy to aid it in its apostolic function' (p.97). It should be added straightaway that if Bosworth were to write that sentence today, he would almost certainly use 'laypersons' instead of 'laymen's', since women played an important part in Catholic Action, as we shall see. The important point is that the members of Catholic Action were not members of the clergy; they were ordinary, if often highly committed, Roman Catholics. Bosworth goes on to point out that not all Catholic groups were part of Catholic Action because the latter was 'formally mandated by the Hierarchy'. He explains 'apostolic function' in terms of two different notions. The first is that of bringing non-Catholics into the Church through conversion; the second is to stimulate existing Catholics to become, through their attitudes and action, 'Christian witnesses' to the society around them.

Laypersons' groups had existed in the Church for some time – certainly since the second half of the nineteenth century – but Catholic Action in its present form really got under way in the inter-war period as a response to de-Christianization and other threats to the Church. Pius XI was a particularly keen supporter and is indeed sometimes referred to as 'the pope of Catholic Action'.

Italy

There is no doubt that throughout the period covered by AA304, Catholic Action was both more numerous and influential in Italy than in France. During the Fascist period its organizations had been the only ones not controlled by the Party or the state, although relations between Church and government over the issue were often strained. Azione Cattolica Italiana (ACI – Italian Catholic Action) was a federation consisting of seven branches, the most important of which were Gioventù Italiana di Azione Cattolica (GIAC – Italian Youth of Catholic Action (for males), Gioventù Femminile di Azione Cattolica (GF – Female Youth of Catholic Action); Unione Uomini (Men's Union); and Unione Donne di Azione Cattolica Italiana (UDACI – Women's Union of Italian Catholic Action). Table 5.3 shows the membership of these four branches from 1946 to 1954.

Table 5.3 Membership of branches of Italian Catholic Action, 1946–54

	GIAC	*GF*	*Unione Uomini*	*UDACI*
1946	367,392	884,992	150,866	369,015
1947	377,632	826,900	170,392	393,776
1948	411,780	968,179	187,338	417,870
1949	413,924	893,776	202,998	429,980
1950	454,302	1,008,301	231,579	473,748
1951	503,979	1,104,831	239,360	515,491
1952	507,733	1,118,211	253,288	533,884
1953	549,932	1,185,929	271,773	570,654
1954	556,752	1,215,977	285,455	597,394

(Source: Carlo Falconi, *La chiesa e le organizzazioni Cattoliche in Italia*, p.399)

Exercise What are the three main conclusions which strike you from a study of Table 5.3?

Discussion

1 Apart from one or two minor hiccoughs, there was a steady and impressive expansion in all branches over the period in question. Membership of the GIAC in 1954 was 52 per cent up over 1946; that of the GF 37 per cent; that of the Unione Uomini by 89 per cent; and that of the UDACI by 62 per cent.

2 The women's organizations had many more members than the corresponding men's organizations. This is perhaps not surprising in view of what we know about the greater devotion of women (see above, p.150).

3 The youth organizations had more members than their adult counterparts. (Interestingly enough, this decline in involvement with age can be traced in more detail within the two youth organizations themselves, for they were divided into sections according to age, and there is a steady decline in membership with age.) This phenomenon is no doubt a result of the firmer grip which the Church had on young children as opposed to adolescents and young adults. ❑

All four groups were organized at national, diocesan and parish levels. The Church was in control throughout. ACI was in fact responsible to the local bishops and priests in whose dioceses and parishes it operated. In addition, ecclesiastical assistants (i.e. chaplains with supervisory powers) were attached to individual branches of each organization, and all key leadership posts were filled by the Church.

Mass membership did mean that not all members were as committed as they might have been, but Gianfranco Poggi has described the profile of an ideal ACI member as follows (for 'he', read 'he/she' throughout):

> This person wears his [ACI] lapel button at all times, receives communion every time he attends Mass (two to five times a week), has a 'spiritual director' in the person of a priest, besides going to weekly confession. He

> does not dance, even if he is in his late teens or early twenties, nor does he attend films judged unbecoming by ecclesiastical authorities. He reads the Catholic newspaper, and at election time is an active propagandist for the Catholic party. At work (or in class, if he is a student) he does not tolerate blasphemy and promptly reacts to any criticism of the Church, priests, or the Catholic party. He is very keen on apologetics, especially on such themes as the existence of God. Most of his leisure time is spent within the framework of the parish and the ACI local. Besides attending the weekly meetings, he goes to the parish house to watch TV, to play cards, or to help the priest with the youngsters. He thinks of himself primarily as a Catholic.
>
> (Poggi, *Catholic Action in Italy*, pp.41–2)

Poggi also describes some typical activities of the ACI parish branch:

> Local ACI branch headquarters are generally in the parish house. In the afternoon they are play areas for the children [Italian schoolchildren only go to school in the mornings, although they start at 8 am], and at night they become meeting places for the older members. The adult meetings generally have a spiritual part, when the ecclesiastical Assistant speaks, and a cultural part, when the weekly instalment of the 'annual campaign' theme (the Christian family, the social doctrines of the Church, etc.) is expounded by one of the lay leaders and discussed by the members. It is also during the weekly meeting or in special meetings that the members discuss the apostolic needs of the parish, such as contacting a family of newcomers or counteracting the bad influence that a new high school instructor with leftist leanings is having on his pupils. Election time generally brings an increase of activity directed to getting votes for the Christian Democratic Party.
>
> (Poggi, *Catholic Action in Italy*, p.42)

On the electoral front the most remarkable achievement of Catholic Action was undoubtedly the work of the so-called civic committees at the time of the 1948 elections. The brainchild of Luigi Gedda, the national president of the Unione Uomini, they were launched in February 1948. According to an American CIA report in May, there were some 300 regional and more than 18,000 local (i.e. parochial) committees. These performed the tasks that would normally have been done by a well-oiled party machine – which the Christian Democrats did not possess. They distributed leaflets, organized a lottery, hired and put to work more than 2,800 speakers and organizers for the two-month campaign, and gave others lifts to the polling stations. They had spies in the enemy camp, which enabled them to anticipate their opponents' propaganda and respond to it immediately. They even set up a clandestine radio transmitter, which they did not have to use, to broadcast the election results in case the Communists seized control of the state radio stations. Gedda himself put the total membership of the civic committees at 300,000. Although they were in theory separate from Catholic Action, their membership, especially at local level, was identical. And, of course, they were successful. Even Togliatti could not refrain from sending a letter of congratulation to Gedda after the elections.

France

There were no similar triumphs that could be attributed to Action Catholique Générale (ACG – General Catholic Action). Since there are no readily available series of membership figures for the various affiliated organizations, we cannot even be sure how successful they were in attracting support. Organizationally, the major difference between French and Italian Catholic Action was that the former had a strong tradition of functional organizations relating to members' employment, whereas Italian Catholic Action possessed only a few which were grafted on to the main body after the war. The two most powerful were the Jeunesse Ouvrière Chrétienne (JOC – Christian Workers' Youth) and the Jeunesse Agricole Chrétienne (JAC – Christian Farming Youth), which were both paralleled by corresponding organizations for young women, the JOCF and the JACF, the 'F' in both cases standing for 'féminine'. There were also male and female organizations for students and middle-class youth. These youth groups had adult continuations, which were not divided according to sex. JOC/JOCF membership, for example, led on first of all to that of the Mouvement Populaire des Familles (MPF – Popular Family Movement), which was in fact excluded from Catholic Action in the late 1940s as too left wing. This was then replaced in 1950 with Action Catholique Ouvrière (ACO – Working-Class Catholic Action). The corresponding adult organization for the JAC/JACF was the Mouvement Familial Rural (MFR – Rural Family Movement).

Of these, the rural movements were much stronger than those that represented the urban working class. Thus, the JAC/JACF probably had about 300,000 members in the 1950s, whereas the JOC/JOCF, which had had 65,000 members in 1937, had only about 10,000 in 1959. Only founded in 1950, the ACO did well to reach around 25,000 members nine years later. It also evidently succeeded in dissuading the Church from banning Catholics from membership of the Communist-dominated CGT in 1954 on the grounds that this would deprive it of any influence in what was the most powerful, and in some areas the only, trade union organization.

Alongside the functional Catholic Action groups were two 'general' organizations, again divided by gender: the Fédération Nationale d'Action Catholique (FNAC – National Catholic Action Federation), and the Ligue Féminine d'Action Catholique Française (LFACF – French Women's Catholic Action League). These were much bigger affairs. Writing in 1957, the French commentator Adrien Dansette cited 2,100,000 as the membership of the LFACF and 600,000 as that of the FNAC. He went on to wonder, however, to what extent these figures represented more than the simple payment of an annual subscription. Moreover, William Bosworth states that soon after it was founded in 1924 the ancestor of the FNAC was said to have had three million members, so that 600,000 represented a sharp decline.

Bosworth also gives a description of 'general' Catholic Action activities at parish level in France which can be set alongside that of Gianfranco Poggi with respect to Italy.

> Local ACG activities can be put under three headings. First, the active ACG members usually organize a propaganda and information team in the parish

> which distributes tracts, puts up posters, and even goes door-to-door working for 'Catholic' causes. One of its chief jobs is disseminating information on Catholic schools. [...] Tracts are always distributed before all elections, local or national, recalling to the general public that they should vote only for candidates inspired by the Catholic social doctrine, that a Catholic cannot vote for a Communist, etc.
>
> The second local ACG activity occurs only in parishes where there are particularly dynamic members. In such parishes, an information center is established, whose main task is distributing publications of Catholic inspiration. [...]
>
> The third activity is a general effort towards civic education. This is carried on primarily by the [LFACF], while the information centers are usually staffed by [FNAC] members. [LFACF] members themselves are a prime audience for material from various Catholic agencies specializing in political and social information. Complete dossiers of civic material are sent from these agencies and from the [LFACF] national office to members in all parts of France, with the hope that this material will filter down to the mass of [LFACF] women and will influence parishes where the Church has remained strong.
>
> (Bosworth, *Catholicism and Crisis in Modern France*, pp.141–2)

Like its Italian counterpart, French Catholic Action was closely supervised by the Church. The French hierarchy had a special Secretary for Catholic Action charged with directing and co-ordinating all groups. In addition, each group was watched over by a bishop, and local bishops had to approve the groups functioning in their dioceses. Chaplains were appointed at all levels, and the national officers of each organization were vetted by the Church.

French Catholic Action, although widespread and active, did not play such an interventionist role in national politics as Italian Catholic Action did in Italy. Bosworth, for example, describes the intervention of the head of the LFACF in 1951 in favour of the Barangé law, which gave state subsidies to Church schools, as 'truly exceptional'. Why was this? It is hard to say, but it may have had something to do with the fact that Roman Catholicism itself was not as strong in France as it was in Italy, that the lay tradition was more powerful in France than in Italy, and even that French Catholics were less subservient to the Vatican than their Italian counterparts, because of their so-called 'Gallican tradition' of independence. Finally, there was no one in French Catholic Action to compare with Luigi Gedda in Italy.

Before taking leave of Catholic Action, it must not be forgotten that it represented only one set of Catholic organizations: that directly dependent on the Church. There was a whole series of other groups of more or less directly Catholic inspiration. In France, for example, the scout movement was predominantly Catholic. There were also trade unions and various groups of professional people and intellectuals. In Italy the ACI claimed that all other Catholic groups were 'dependent' on, 'co-ordinated' with, or actually 'adhered' to it. They ranged from sporting organizations for young people (rigorously segregated according to sex so as to preserve their members' purity) to the Associazione Cattolica Esercenti Cinematografici (ACEC –

Catholic Association of Cinema Managers), set up by the ACI in 1945 to co-ordinate the managers of the parish cinemas, which accounted for about a third of all the cinemas in Italy.

If you also bear in mind that there was a flourishing Catholic press and publishing industry in both France and Italy, you can see how the total complex created a kind of social system in miniature in which faithful Catholics could at one and the same time be protected from pernicious influences and be prepared to go over to the offensive. The anti-clerical left, of course, was organized in a very similar fashion (see Unit 11).

The Catholic political parties

From your study of Unit 2, you will already be aware that there were two powerful Catholic political parties in France and Italy at the time of the Liberation: the MRP and the DC respectively. We will now explore the connections between these parties and the Church, and the extent to which the latter was able to use them for its own ends.

The first point to emphasize is that the Church was not responsible for the creation of either the MRP or the DC. When, in the spring of 1943, the Vatican was asked by the Americans what sort of regime it thought should replace Fascism, its internal deliberations and its reply indicated that it favoured a return to something like the pre-Fascist liberal state. There was certainly no suggestion that it envisaged the emergence of a new mass Catholic party which would be in a position to take over the reins of government. Much has been made of the fact that the DC's future leader, Alcide De Gasperi, worked in the Vatican library during the war, but this did not mean that he was particularly close to the pope. The DC emerged, not as a result of Vatican intrigues, but out of the political situation that followed the fall of Mussolini and which was described in Units 1 and 2. The Church had no option but to deal with it.

Similarly, in the case of France, the MRP grew out of Catholic elements in the Resistance. There was even some doubt as to whether it should be an explicitly Catholic party at all, but two reasons probably ensured that it was. In the first place, the party's future leader, Georges Bidault, who had replaced Jean Moulin as chairperson of the CNR, reminded his Catholic Resistance colleagues that women would soon be given the vote and that they could be more easily mobilized behind Catholic candidates. You will remember (see p.151) that French women were more likely to heed the advice of the Church when it came to voting than were French men. This was the main reason why the Third Republic's anti-clerical politicians had opposed giving them the vote! In response to the suggestion that women's innate conservatism might sidetrack the party from its revolutionary objectives, Bidault optimistically replied: 'We shall carry out a left-wing policy with a right-wing electorate.' The second reason was that, in view of the Church hierarchy's open support for Vichy (see p.156), it was felt important to demonstrate that there was a body of Catholic opinion opposed to the regime, for otherwise the Liberation might produce a new surge of anti-clerical feeling. For the same reason, however, the hierarchy's relations with the new party were not very intimate to begin with, and there was of course no specific reference to Christianity or Catholicism in its title.

It is also true that not all French Catholics voted for the MRP. If just over half of regular churchgoers told IFOP (French Institute for Public Opinion) in 1952 that they would vote for the MRP, one-fifth said they would vote for the right-wing independents, and about the same proportion expressed a preference for the Gaullist RPF. Although many priests no doubt advised their flocks to support the MRP, many did not, and indeed an article in the Vatican's daily newspaper during the 1951 election campaign which urged French Catholics not to abandon the party for the RPF was so untypical as to cause a mild sensation in France and earn the author a tart rebuke from General de Gaulle, who was of course a devout Catholic.

Relations between the Church and the DC were much closer. We have already seen how Italian Catholic Action, in the shape of Luigi Gedda's civic committees, intervened decisively in favour of the party in the 1948 elections. The ecclesiastical hierarchy, from Pius XII downwards, also left no doubt as to which way it thought Italian Catholics should vote. Just over fifteen months after the election, on 1 July 1949, a decree of the Holy Office imposed the penalty of excommunication (i.e. exclusion from the Eucharist) not only on all Communists, but even on those who read their publications.

Nevertheless, the Church and the DC did not always see eye to eye. After the referendum on the monarchy and the elections to the constituent assembly in June 1946 (see Unit 2, p.59), one of the DC's leaders, Mario Scelba, wrote indignantly:

> As far as the general aspect of the struggle was concerned, there was an extremely active propaganda campaign on the part of the clergy and Catholic Action in favour of everyone voting and in the preparation of 'pre-constituent' weeks organized by the bishops, days of prayer, etc. Nothing wrong with that. We were dealing with the constituent assembly and important moral, religious and ecclesiastical issues were at stake. What was intolerable was the direct and large-scale action for the monarchy and for monarchist candidates on the DC lists. There were detailed and peremptory instructions, and just as detailed and peremptory exclusions. [...] Men with no talent were pushed to the front simply because they were monarchists and first-class men were fought, slandered and brought down. [...] Opting for the republic meant being social-communists and friends of the devil, because the republic had become the synonym of social-communism.

(Scoppola, *La proposta politica di De Gasperi*, pp.252–3)

Scelba was admittedly one of the more enthusiastic republicans in the DC, but most of the party's leadership was opposed to the monarchy. The Church clearly did not approve.

It did not approve either of the DC's national coalition with the left-wing parties. On 12 November 1946, just after local elections in Rome had witnessed the triumph of the joint PSI–PCI list, Mgr Montini bluntly told De Gasperi: 'Any collaboration with the anti-clerical parties, not only for the commune of Rome, but also for the government, is unacceptable. If the DC persists in this

CURIA VESCOVILE DI PIACENZA

DOPO IL DECRETO DEL SANTO UFFIZIO

AVVISO

E' peccato grave:

1° Iscriversi al Partito Comunista.
2° Favorirlo in qualsiasi modo, **specie col voto.**
3° Leggere la stampa comunista.
4° Propagare la stampa comunista.

Quindi non si può ricevere l'assoluzione se non si è pentiti e fermamente disposti a non commetterlo più.

●

Chi, iscritto o no al Partito Comunista, ne ammette la dottrina marxista, atea ed anticristiana e ne fa propaganda, è

APOSTATA DALLA FEDE E SCOMUNICATO

e non può essere assolto che dalla Santa Sede.

●

Quanto si è detto per il Partito Comunista deve estendersi agli altri Partiti che fanno causa comune con esso.

Il Signore illumini e conceda ai colpevoli in materia tanto grave, il pieno ravvedimento, poichè è in pericolo la stessa salvezza dell'eternità.

UNIONE TIPOGRAFICA PIACENTINA

Figure 5.3 *Notice posted by the diocesan authorities of Piacenza after the Vatican decree of 1 July 1949. It warns Catholics of the ecclesiastical penalties for joining, supporting and especially for voting for the Communist Party. (Photo: Curia Vescovile di Piacenza.)*

collaboration, it will be considered a "pro-enemy" party. The DC would no longer have our support or our sympathy' (Scoppola, p. 310). De Gasperi, who was as anxious to dispense with Socialist and Communist support as anyone, was nevertheless a realist. 'What about the constituent assembly?' he asked. Montini took the point. The Church's principal short-term objective in Italy was to ensure that the post-Liberation regime incorporated the 1929 agreements with Mussolini into its new constitution. Thanks to the efforts of the DC, and the support of Togliatti (who even then was dreaming of a 'historic compromise' between Communists and Catholics), this was achieved at the end of March 1947. Two months later, the PCI was dropped from the government (see Unit 2, p.61).

Despite its clear victory in 1948, by 1952 the Vatican was beginning to have doubts as to whether the DC was strong enough to keep the Communists out of power. The pope was particularly alarmed that they might gain control of Rome in the municipal elections. The proposed solution, eagerly espoused by Luigi Gedda of Catholic Action, was to extend the DC electoral list to the right, to include not only the monarchists, but even the neo-Fascists of the Movimento Sociale Italiano (MSI – Italian Social Movement). The manoeuvre failed, but De Gasperi was aghast. On 9 June 1952 he wrote to Scelba:

> They are insisting in the Vatican on the tactical manoeuvre floated during the local elections. [...] I fear the worst, namely that they are considering an initiative for a new party. Unfortunately the omens are clear and unmistakable. Every real or assumed deficiency on our part will be used as a pretext. The truth is that all our arguments in favour of the democratic regime have not succeeded in persuading them because it is felt that democracy is too feeble to resist extremism.
>
> (*De Gasperi scrive*, vol.1, p.209)

Some historians have suggested that one objective of the special electoral law, which De Gasperi brought in before the 1953 elections and which was designed to make it virtually impossible for the left to win, was to reassure the doubting Thomases in the Vatican. Unfortunately for De Gasperi, the law was not successful enough and the DC did very badly in the elections. He lost control of both the government and the party, and although the Church did not withdraw its support from the DC, it was not particularly sorry to see him go. (These events are discussed in more detail in Unit 10.)

Despite the occasional disagreement, however, the Church could derive considerable satisfaction from the actions of the Catholic parties in post-war France and Italy. They both played a vital role in the political life of their respective countries. They were instrumental in limiting the influence of the Communists before 1947 and in excluding them from power altogether thereafter. In addition, they helped to secure many concrete advantages for the Church. The maintenance of the 1929 agreements in Italy has already been mentioned. In France there was the Barangé law of 1951, which provided for subsidies for Church schools.

The worker-priest movement

Our final case study differs from the others in two important respects. Firstly, it concerns an initiative in which the Vatican not only played no part, but to which it became steadily more hostile. This hostility derived from the second difference – that, unlike the other developments we have studied, this was regarded by the Church as a dismal and dangerous failure.

According to Gianfranco Poggi, 'Catholic Action is a structure promoted by the Church in an effort to establish and maintain a viable contact with an estranged world.' No part of this world was more estranged than the urban masses. As Pius XI put it in 1929, 'The greatest scandal of the nineteenth century is that the Church in fact lost the working class.' One of the most imaginative attempts to deal with this problem took place in France precisely in the period of Liberation and reconstruction. It was the worker-priest movement.

On 26 April 1943 the Archbishop of Paris, Cardinal Emmanuel Suhard, was having lunch with his private secretary. The latter told him excitedly of a duplicated document he had just been reading, written by two JOC chaplains, Abbot Henri Godin and Abbot Yvan Daniel. When Suhard read it, he was as impressed as his secretary and ordered it to be circulated to leading figures in the French hierarchy. 'I have received a manuscript from Paris', one of them declared; 'A bomb is going to explode in the Church of France.' The 'bomb', when commercially published later in the year (it sold more than 80,000 copies), was called: *La France, pays de mission?* ('France, a Missionary Land?').

Exercise We have printed some extracts from *France, a Missionary Land?* as item 13 in *Documents and Texts 1*. Please read this item now and then try to answer the following questions.

1 Are Godin and Daniel concerned with the whole problem of de-Christianization in France?

2 What was the extent of the problem?

3 Why was the existing parochial system unable to solve it?

4 What is Godin's and Daniel's proposed solution?

5 What did Godin and Daniel believe would happen if nothing was done?

Discussion

1 No. Godin and Daniel recognize that there are large areas of rural France that are de-Christianized, but they are only concerned with the towns, and particularly with the working class.

2 According to their calculations, no fewer than 8 million members of the working class were 'pagans'. This represented some 20 per cent of the total French population. One chapter of Godin's and Daniel's book goes into these calculations in some detail. They were able to rely on a flourishing school of religious sociology in France, which had arisen during the inter-war period and which had pioneered various techniques for measuring the extent of religious observance.

3 The existing parochial system was essentially 'bourgeois' (i.e. middle class) and this put off the working class.

4 'A small picked group' of missionaries would have to leave the existing parochial system and move into the working-class environment. The ultimate aim of the Church should be not merely the conversion, but

also the extinction of the proletariat. However, this would require the assistance of 'human society [...] as a whole'.

5 Godin and Daniel feared that if the working class was not reclaimed for Christianity, it would fall prey to a rival *mystique*. The nature of this *mystique* is not spelled out, and it is not entirely clear what they had in mind. One possibility, of course, is Communism, but can they really have believed that this might 'not be too unlike the religion of Christ'? Another possibility, which gains credibility from the date of the book, is that they were referring to some form of fascism, perhaps even Vichy's own so-called 'National Revolution'. The trouble with this interpretation, however, is that a statement such as 'liberal capitalism and the exclusive reign of profit have deeply corrupted morals and institutions' could have been lifted straight out of Vichy's own propaganda. Of course, they may have meant no more than secular materialism, which had always been condemned by the Church, and still is. ❑

Cardinal Suhard organized a retreat at Lisieux over the Christmas/New Year of 1943–44 to discuss the ideas of Godin and Daniel. There emerged from this the establishment of the Mission de Paris ('Paris Mission'). Godin was appointed to run it, but he was killed soon afterwards in a domestic accident and his place was taken by Jacques Hollande.

Although Godin and Daniel had urged that priests must get out of the existing parochial structure in order to convert the working class, they had not specified that priests should actually work alongside those they were seeking to influence. This idea, however, gained impetus as a result of the clandestine chaplaincy which the French hierarchy authorized in April 1943 to minister to those thousands of Frenchmen who were deported to Germany by the Nazis in order to work in German war industries. By the end of the war, there were no fewer than 275 of these chaplains. Since they were clandestine, they had of necessity to pose as workers themselves and to work with their flock.

The point about the worker-priest movement after the war was that it adapted this wartime expedient and turned it into the key element of the strategy for the conversion of the working class. If you wanted to minister to the workers, it was argued, you should become one. As one of the worker-priests, Jacques Loew, put it: 'Dungarees, manual labour – prerequisites for the rediscovery and rescue of man.'

By the end of 1947 there were 25 worker-priests. Between 1952 and 1954 their number hovered around 100. Half of them worked in Paris and the other half in provincial industrial centres. Oscar Arnal, the author of the best book in English on the subject, has written:

> The type of work that they undertook varied greatly. Most, however, toiled in heavy industry, especially in the metallurgical trades. There they served as common laborers, though some, with the passage of time, learned a trade and became specialized workers such as turners, adjusters, machinists and electricians. A number of others remained at the more difficult chores, such as firemen at the large furnaces which produced molten steel. Some worker-

> priests found employment on the docks of France's major ports [...] while others toiled to construct large hydro-electric dams in the French hinterland. Francis Laval was a miner; Lucien Lacour became the chaplain of the Parisian firemen; Auguste Rosi ministered to prostitutes (though not for a salary); Jean Volot was a sailor; and Jacques Riosse labored as a technician in the movie industry. Finally, a number of worker-priests either performed artisanal work or toiled as sweated labor in small non-union workshops.
>
> (Arnal, *Priests in Working-Class Blue*, p.80)

Not surprisingly, most (though not all) of the worker-priests were young men, born in the early 1920s.

Sharing not only the labour of the working class, but also in many cases its living conditions and leisure pursuits, the worker-priests gradually built up a considerable degree of empathy with those they had come to convert. More significantly, perhaps, they began to understand and sympathize with much of the working class's alienation from 'the system'. Several worker-priests joined trade unions, including the Communist-dominated CGT. Some even became officials and were involved in industrial disputes. Jo Gouttebarge, for example, was elected as a CGT shop steward at his steel works in Saint Étienne at the end of 1952. In August 1953 he organized an eight-day stoppage at the plant in support of striking railwaymen and hid over 200 strikers in a local church crypt when they were chased by the police. The most notorious incident of all, however, occurred when two worker-priests were arrested at the Communist-sponsored demonstration of 28 May 1952 against the appointment of General Matthew Ridgeway as the new NATO Supreme Commander. They were thoroughly roughed up by unsympathetic policemen and published a detailed account of their experiences.

As may well be imagined, this involvement in left-wing causes did not go down well with the Church authorities. In May 1951 the French bishops drew up a draft manual for the guidance of worker-priests. This reminded them, among other things, that they must remain obedient to their bishops and that spiritual activities must have priority over temporal ones. They had been 'sent into the proletariat to evangelize it,' the manual pointed out, 'and not to direct its terrestrial liberation.' Two years later, the Bishop of Marseilles went even further and announced his intention of winding up the worker-priest team working in his diocese because of their temporal activity and adoption of Marxist values.

By this time, moreover, Rome was becoming anxious. The worker-priest movement had received a cautious endorsement from Pius XII in November 1946, when a delegation from the Mission de Paris and the parallel Mission de France had visited him in the Vatican. 'Be careful,' he had warned, however, 'their [i.e. the priests'] vocation is at stake'. Just under seven years later, on 23 September 1953, the new papal nuncio (diplomatic representative) to France summoned twenty-six members of the French hierarchy to tell them that the Vatican had decided that the experiment must be brought to an end. What was more, he added, 'the measures should be taken as if they come from you'.

Despite the friction between the hierarchy and the worker-priests, the former was still by and large very much in favour of the movement. Cardinal Maurice Feltin, the Archbishop of Paris since Suhard's death in 1949, complained to his fellow bishops: 'Rome must take into account that after this the church will appear definitely linked to capitalism. [...] We must go to Rome to explain that to the Holy Father.' On 4 November 1953 Feltin, accompanied by Cardinals Achille Liénart of Lille and Pierre-Marie Gerlier of Lyons, saw Pius XII. But, as Arnal writes, 'there was no room for negotiations; they were there to receive instructions'.

Pius XII was prepared to let priests continue some type of 'apostolate in the midst of the workers' milieu', but it was abundantly clear that the old idea of worker-priest would not be tolerated. The Pope insisted on five major changes in their ministry:

1. these missionary priests had to 'be chosen especially by their bishop';
2. they would be required to receive a specialized doctrinal and spiritual formation;
3. the extent of their manual labour would be limited to safeguard 'all the exigencies of their priestly state';
4. they were to abandon all 'temporal *engagement*' which included 'trade union and other responsibilities';
5. finally, they were to have clearly defined links with other priests and the parish.

As the Pope is reported to have said, 'If it's a choice between apostolic effectiveness and priestly integrity, I choose priestly integrity' (Arnal, *Priests in Working-Class Blue*, p.149). There must be no dilution of the pure milk of the Church's doctrine. Loyal and obedient Catholics that they were, the French bishops accepted the Pope's decision and called on the worker-priests to do likewise.

Exercise You should now read the extracts from the French bishops' letter of 19 January 1954 to the worker-priests and the latter's reply, which took the form of a communiqué issued on 2 February. These are printed as items 14(a) and (b) in *Documents and Texts 1*. What do you think is the essence of the bishops' argument and of the worker-priests' reply?

Discussion The bishops do not really address the substance of the issues at stake in their letter. 'Your suffering is too deep,' they write, 'for us to hope to allay it by putting arguments before you.' Instead, they appeal to the priests' faith, not so much in their beliefs as in the structure of the Church. The whole emphasis of the letter, indeed, is on the chain of command, stretching from Rome, through the bishops, down to the individual priest, a concept to which considerable attention was devoted at the beginning of this unit. Even if the priests believe that the pope and the bishops are mistaken, they should submit, for 'there is no mistake in obedience'.

As for the worker-priests, their position is one of defiance. They do not accept that there are genuine religious reasons for the action taken against them, and point instead to the pressure exerted by those responsible for the oppression of the workers whom the priests were seeking to convert, represent and defend. They conclude: 'The respect and confidence they [i.e. the workers] continue to show towards us make it impossible for us to accept any compromise. [...] Consequently we declare that our decisions will be taken in a spirit of total respect for the working-class state and for the struggle waged by the workers for their liberation.'

In the light of this, it is not surprising that about two-thirds of the worker-priests refused to accept the Church's directives and endured whatever penalties the authorities chose to impose on them. They were to have the last word, moreover, for the Second Vatican Council lifted the ban on worker-priests in 1965. ❑

What is lacking in all the accounts of the worker-priest movement is any detailed evidence of how effective it was in converting those who had hitherto been unbelievers, 'pagans' in Godin's and Daniel's term. There were some concessions made in the liturgical field involving the use of the vernacular instead of Latin, and the extension of evening masses which were easier for workers to attend, but we simply do not know what impact these had on observance. What clearly worried the papacy was that instead of worker-priests converting the workers to Catholicism, the workers seemed to be converting the worker-priests to Communism. Given that Communism was seen as the Church's arch-enemy in the post-war period, this was intolerable. Nevertheless, the worker-priest movement did focus attention on the relationship between the Church and contemporary capitalism, a debate that is still very much alive today, and not least in Latin America where the 'liberation theologians' are in many ways spiritual descendants of the French worker-priests.

4 Conclusion

The Roman Catholic Church was clearly a most powerful institution in both France and Italy in the post-war years, although the evidence suggests that its influence was greater in Italy than it was in France. Centrally and hierarchically organized, it was able to exercise control over its members in a way that bears some comparison with totalitarian political organizations. Like them it engaged in mass mobilization and employed tough discipline against dissidents and opponents. Through a network of social organizations, more or less closely subordinated to it, the Church spun a cocoon around the faithful, seeking to protect them against pernicious influences. Communism was undoubtedly the most pernicious influence, as well as the most imminent threat, as far as the Church was concerned. Much of its own mobilization was directed towards the defeat of Communism and certainly its relations with external organizations (political parties and governments) are incomprehensible without taking this factor into account. The Church, however, was extremely flexible in its choice of both tactics, and allies, and woe betide anyone who took its support for granted.

References

ARNAL, O., *Priests in Working-Class Blue: the History of the Worker-Priests (1943–1954),* New York/Mahwah, Paulist Press, 1986.

BOSWORTH, W., *Catholicism and Crisis in Modern France: French Catholic Groups at the Threshold of the Fifth Republic*, Princeton, Princeton University Press, 1962.

DE GASPERI, M.R. (ed.), *De Gasperi scrive*, vol.1, Brescia, Morcelliana, 1981.

FALCONI, C., *La chiesa e le organizzazioni Cattoliche in Italia*, Turin, Einaudi, 1956.

FLANAGAN, D., 'An ecumenical future for Roman Catholic theology' in Alberic Stacpoole (ed.), *Mary's Place in Christian Dialogue*, Slough, St Paul's Publications, 1982.

GODIN, H. and DANIEL, Y., *La France, pays de mission?*, Paris, 1943.

MCKENZIE, J.L., *The Roman Catholic Church*, London, Weidenfeld and Nicolson, 1969.

POGGI, G., *Catholic Action in Italy: the Sociology of a Sponsored Organization*, Stanford, Stanford University Press, 1967.

SCOPPOLA, P., *La proposta politica di De Gasperi*, Bologna, Il Mulino, 1977.

SUTTER, J. (ed.), *La Vie réligieuse des Français à travers les sondages d'opinion (1944–1976)*, vol.2, Paris, Éditions du CNRS, 1984.

UNIT 6 The United States and France and Italy, 1943–56

Prepared for the course team by Geoffrey Warner

Study materials

For your work on this unit you will need to refer to the following materials:

Documents and Texts 1

Audio-cassette 1, side B, 'The United States, France and the war in Indo-China'

1 Introduction and aims

In April 1945 the Soviet leader, Joseph Stalin, remarked to Milovan Djilas: 'This war is not like those in the past; whoever occupies a territory also imposes on it his own social system. Everyone imposes his own social system as far as his army can reach. It cannot be otherwise.' In one sense this unit is an extended commentary on the relevance of Stalin's comment to what happened in France and Italy after the war. Since both countries were liberated by British and American armies, and since the United States enjoyed a position of overwhelming military and economic preponderance at the end of the war, it would be reasonable to assume that, if Stalin's hypothesis was correct, the American social system would have been 'imposed' on France and Italy. The hypothesis can only be tested, of course, by means of an examination of the relations between the United States on the one hand and France and Italy on the other during the war and post-war periods. Such an examination forms the content of the present unit. After working through the unit, you should be able to:

1. summarize American policy towards France and Italy between 1943 and 1956, explaining how and why it changed over time;
2. explain the principal foreign policy objectives of French and Italian governments during the same period, and the extent to which they clashed with those of the United States;
3. analyse how far American policy and power restricted the choices open to French and Italian governments, both at home and abroad;
4. consider how the relationship between the United States and France and Italy was perceived by public opinion in the two European countries;
5. analyse how successful French and Italian governments were at manipulating the relationship between their countries and the United States.

Before embarking on this task, however, it would be as well to emphasize one important point about the nature of the unit, even though it is probably obvious enough from the above list of aims. This unit is exclusively concerned with *politics*. The equally important question of the nature and extent of American influence in intellectual and cultural life is dealt with in other units – especially Unit 15.

2 From war to peace, 1943–45

On the face of it, American policy towards the political future of both France and Italy during the later stages of the Second World War was straightforward and identical. 'The future French government', President Franklin D. Roosevelt told a press conference on 17 November 1942, 'will be established not by any individual in metropolitan France or overseas, but by the French people themselves, after they have been set free by the United

Nations'. On 28 July 1943, just three days after the overthrow of Mussolini, he told a radio audience: 'Eventually Italy will reconstitute herself. It will be the people of Italy who will do that, choosing their own government in accordance with the basic democratic principles of liberty and equality.'

Things were not, however, as simple as these bald statements implied. Even if the French and Italian peoples were to be given the right to choose their own governments, they would not be able to exercise that right in a political vacuum. Not only were there governments already in existence in both countries, but there were also rival contenders for power. Moreover, the United States, like the other Allies, had a view as to the most desirable outcome from its own standpoint. Any 'choice' would undoubtedly be influenced, if not determined, by these factors.

France

Let us begin by looking at the situation in respect of France. Largely in the hope of preventing it from becoming too closely aligned with the Axis powers, the United States had continued to maintain diplomatic relations with Marshal Pétain's Vichy regime, even after American entry into the Second World War in December 1941. Britain, on the other hand, had no formal relations with Vichy and supported General de Gaulle's Free French movement, although it did not officially recognize it as the legitimate government of France.

When General de Gaulle came to Britain in the summer of 1940 to raise the standard of continued resistance to the Axis, he was a relatively unknown army officer, and one, moreover, who was in open defiance of the orders of his superiors. He was the first to realize that, in these circumstances, he faced an uphill task with precious few resources.

> But this very destitution [he wrote after the war] showed me my line of conduct. It was by adopting without compromise the cause of national recovery that I could acquire authority. It was by acting as the inflexible champion of the nation and of the State that it would be possible for me to gather the consent, even the enthusiasm, of the French and to win from foreigners respect and consideration. Those who, all through the drama, were offended by this intransigence were unwilling to see that for me, intent as I was on beating back innumerable conflicting pressures, the slightest wavering would have brought collapse. In short, limited and alone though I was, and precisely because I was so, I had to climb to the heights and never then to come down.
>
> (De Gaulle, *War Memoirs*, vol.I, *The Call to Honour*, pp.88–9)

The trouble with this approach was that it frequently antagonized the very allies whose support de Gaulle so desperately needed. The British prime minister, Winston Churchill, was once moved to complain that the Cross of Lorraine (the Gaullist emblem) was the heaviest cross he had to bear, while one of Roosevelt's advisers expressed similar sentiments in rather more pungent terms when he described the Free French leader, to the president's delighted approval, as 'one of the biggest sons of bitches who ever straddled a pot' (Bohlen, *Witness to History*, p.205).

It was indeed Roosevelt who insisted that de Gaulle and the Free French be deliberately excluded from any knowledge of or participation in the Anglo-American landings in French North Africa in November 1942 (Operation TORCH). De Gaulle was furious, and so were many others when the Allies negotiated a ceasefire with Admiral François Darlan (a leading member of the Vichy regime who was in Algiers at the time of the Allied landings) and seemed to accord him a considerable degree of recognition. Vichy broke off relations with the United States and disowned Darlan, but the question remained whether he was less representative of the fascism the Allies had pledged themselves to destroy than his erstwhile superior, Marshal Pétain.

Darlan's assassination by a young royalist on Christmas Eve 1942 removed him from the scene, but this did not solve the problem of which French authority, if any, was to administer North Africa under the aegis of the Allies. The British government – or, to be more accurate, the Foreign Office, since Churchill did not always share its enthusiasm – pressed the claims of General de Gaulle and the Free French. However, although Free French involvement was conceded at the 'summit' conference between the president and the prime minister at Casablanca in January 1943, de Gaulle was forced to share power with General Henri Giraud, a somewhat colourless American protégé. Moreover, when Churchill visited Washington in May 1943, Roosevelt succeeded in persuading him that the time had come for Britain and the United States to abandon de Gaulle altogether. However, the British prime minister was subsequently overruled by his cabinet colleagues in London.

Roosevelt's profound antagonism towards de Gaulle was not simply because of the latter's stiff-necked intransigence. Roosevelt believed that the general was essentially a British stooge who enjoyed little support inside France. He also felt that he was a would-be dictator, who spent too much time on political intrigue to the detriment of the Allied war effort. Even if the president was wrong on these points, there were at least legitimate grounds for concern. But was there, perhaps, a more fundamental objection to de Gaulle which was less creditable to the president? Anthony Eden, the British foreign secretary, thought so, and set it out in a draft memorandum for the cabinet on 13 July 1943: 'There are grounds [...] for believing that some at any rate of the governing authorities in Washington have little belief in France's future and do not wish to see France again restored as a great imperial power' (PRO, PREM3/181/8). Eden went on to argue that, in view of Britain's need for a strong France to strengthen its own post-war security, this was not a policy which any British government could endorse.

Exercise Read item 15 in *Documents and Texts 1*. This is an extract from the American record of a conversation between President Roosevelt and Joseph Stalin at the Teheran conference in November 1943. In the light of this document, how accurate would you say Eden's suspicions were?

Discussion The answer is, surely, very accurate indeed. In his discussion with Stalin, Roosevelt was openly contemptuous of General Giraud, who, as stated above, was an American protégé. He said that he did not believe that France could be restored as a strong nation for 'many years', and this did not seem to worry him in the least. Finally, he was extremely critical of French colonial policy and was strongly of the opinion that Indo-China should be taken away from France. All this confirms what Eden wrote in his draft cabinet memorandum. ❑

For Roosevelt, France was a symbol of European decadence. Its corrupt political and social system had not only collapsed in the face of the Nazi onslaught, thereby exposing others to even greater danger, but its exploitative imperialism had also contributed to the breakdown of the international system and the descent into war. The American president was determined that the post-war world should be reconstructed – under the aegis of the United States naturally – along lines that would prevent any recurrence of the developments which, in his view, had brought about the Second World War. (Many of Roosevelt's strictures on France applied, of course, with equal force to Britain, but that is another story.)

Despite Roosevelt's opposition, by the end of 1943 de Gaulle had not only succeeded in outmanoeuvring his political rivals in North Africa, including the hapless General Giraud, but also in gaining the allegiance of the organized Resistance inside France. As the D-day landings approached, President Roosevelt came under increasing pressure, not only from the British, but also from a growing number of his own advisers, to recognize de Gaulle's French National Committee as the provisional government of France. Despite the pressure, Roosevelt refused to budge until events forced his hand. On 11 July 1944, just over a month after D-day, the United States extended *de facto* recognition to de Gaulle's provisional government. Full *de jure* recognition was not accorded, however, until 23 October, by which time it had become overwhelmingly clear, even to Roosevelt, that there was no acceptable alternative to the General.

Italy

Turning to developments in Italy, we find that after the Allied invasion of Sicily in July 1943 and the subsequent overthrow of Mussolini, Britain and the United States found themselves in an almost identical situation to that which had confronted them in French North Africa some eight months earlier: namely whether or not to deal with a government – that of King Victor Emmanuel III and Marshal Badoglio – which, although tainted with fascism, could nevertheless 'deliver the goods' in the shape of an armistice agreement and future co-operation with the Allied forces. As with Admiral Darlan, the Allies subordinated their principles to military expediency, and met with similar vociferous condemnation from anti-fascists at home and abroad. The main difference between Allied policy in France and Italy was that whereas, in the former, the British had taken the lead in urging the claims of the anti-fascist de Gaulle on the reluctant Americans, in the latter it was the Americans who exerted similar pressure in favour of anti-fascist Italians on the unwilling British.

Interestingly enough, Churchill levelled the same accusation against the Italian anti-fascists as Roosevelt levelled against de Gaulle: that they were unrepresentative. Moreover, just as Roosevelt's policy towards de Gaulle was influenced by his hostility towards France, so Churchill's towards the Italian anti-fascists was influenced by his hostility towards Italy. Ever since Mussolini's invasion of Ethiopia in 1935, Italy had posed a serious threat to Britain's position in the Mediterranean, in Africa, and in the Middle East. The British prime minister and his colleagues were determined that it should not be permitted to pose such a threat again.

President Roosevelt, on the other hand, was much more favourably disposed towards Italy than he was towards France. There were probably two main reasons for this. The first was the existence in the USA of some six million citizens of Italian descent, most of whom voted for Roosevelt's Democratic Party. The second was that Italy simply did not represent the threat to Roosevelt's vision of the post-war world in the way that France, and especially a strongly nationalist France under de Gaulle, undoubtedly did. Despite Mussolini's pretensions, there is no evidence that Roosevelt ever took Italy seriously as a world power. Its colonial empire was small and never concerned him in the way that the French empire did, while Italian expansionism had not directly threatened American interests, in the way that it had those of the British.

If de Gaulle succeeded in outmanoeuvring the Americans, the Italian anti-fascist parties did the same with Churchill. When, in June 1944, they engineered the resignation of Marshal Badoglio and his replacement by one of their representatives, Ivanoe Bonomi, the British prime minister was furious, but Roosevelt refused to support him in his demand that Badoglio be reinstated.

Despite these parallels between developments in France and Italy, however, there remained one crucial difference between the two countries. France was an ally, while Italy, its 'cobelligerency' notwithstanding, remained an ex-enemy and subject to strict controls imposed under the terms of the armistice agreements. As the Italian historian, Ennio di Nolfo, has written:

> [...] from the moment that Italy was accepted as a 'cobelligerent', all of the efforts of the Badoglio government and of those which followed it were aimed at obtaining 'Allied' status for Italy, or the recognition of a position of equality which defeat had made impossible but which diplomatic adroitness might manage to recover.
>
> (Becker and Knipping (eds), *Power in Europe?*, p.489)

It is in this context that we must assess the agreement, announced on 14 March 1944, for the exchange of diplomatic representatives between Italy and the Soviet Union. The latter had been excluded by the western Allies from any effective say in the running of liberated Italy, and by going behind their backs to forge a direct link with the Russians, the Italian government was at one and the same time seeking to demonstrate that it still had some room for manoeuvre and to put pressure on the British and Americans to treat Italy more leniently.

This development was followed, more or less immediately, by the so-called *svolta di Salerno* ('Salerno turning point'), when the Italian Communist leader, Palmiro Togliatti, on his return from the Soviet Union, cut the ground from under the feet of the other anti-fascist parties by announcing the PCI's willingness to co-operate with the Badoglio government (see Ginsborg, p.43).

Both these events came as unexpected and unpleasant surprises to the British and Americans. They did not produce much in the way of concessions to the Italians, but they did elevate the fear of a Communist takeover in Italy to a position of prominence in the minds of Allied decision makers which it was rarely to lose in the years that followed. According to a report of the political section of the Allied control commission of 19 April 1944, these events illustrated

> [...] two things with remarkable clarity: the strength of the Communist Party in influencing politics in Allied-occupied Italy and the influence of the Soviet Union in determining the policy of the party [...] [The] country [is] already ripe for that swing towards extremes which is the inevitable corollary of a shattered economy and the threat of inflation. More than twenty years ago a similar situation provoked the March on Rome [i.e. Mussolini's takeover in October 1922] and gave birth to Fascism. We must make up our minds – and that quickly – whether or not we wish to see this second march developing into another 'ism'.
>
> (*FRUS, 1944*, vol.III. pp.1112, 1114)

The concern, which was also voiced in the report, that the Communists dominated the northern Resistance was reflected in various developments that took place at the end of 1944 and the beginning of 1945, notably the Allied agreement of 7 December 1944 with the National Committee for the Liberation of Upper Italy (CLNAI) which pledged the latter to hand over power to the Allied military government, and the parallel agreement between the CLNAI and the Bonomi government in which the northern Resistance recognized the latter's authority (see Unit 2, pp.48–9).

The Communist 'threat' in France and Italy

The perceived threat from the Communist Resistance in France was not as great as it was in Italy. It was correctly predicted that the French Communists would co-operate with the Allies and not attempt to seize power. Nevertheless, General de Gaulle asked for and received a demonstration of American military strength in Paris in order to reinforce his position after the capital was liberated in August 1944. In the course of the following month, one of his military commanders requested and obtained the release of two Free French divisions currently fighting the Germans so that they could be sent to help restore order in Toulouse and Limoges, where, he claimed, the Communists were doing exactly as they pleased. Moreover, the supreme Allied commander, General Eisenhower, used the threat of disorder in France as an argument in favour of according *de jure* recognition to de Gaulle's provisional government in October 1944.

Growing American anxiety about Soviet and Communist intentions was undoubtedly an important factor in the evolution of United States policy towards France and Italy in the concluding months of the war. This evolution was particularly marked in the case of France. President Roosevelt was no more enamoured of General de Gaulle than he had been previously, but he supported, or at any rate failed to oppose, various measures that had the effect of recognizing France's position as a great power. Thus, he accepted French participation in the occupation of Germany and agreed to France acting as one of the sponsors of the San Francisco conference on April–June 1945, which set up the new United Nations Organization. De Gaulle petulantly refused to accept the invitation, but France emerged from the conference as one of the five permanent members of the Security Council, along with the United States, the Soviet Union, Britain and China. Roosevelt even began to soften his hitherto adamant opposition to the restoration of French rule over Indo-China and, after his death on 12 April 1945, his successor, Harry S. Truman, did nothing to stop it from happening once the war in East Asia had ended. As a State Department document stated in June 1945:

> Since the liberation of France and our recognition of the de Gaulle government, it has been our policy to make every effort to assist France, morally as well as physically, to regain her strength and her influence, not only with the view towards increasing the French contribution to the war effort but also with a view towards enabling the French to assume larger responsibilities in connection with the maintenance of peace.
>
> (*FRUS*, *Conference at Berlin*, vol.I, p.252)

A similar document on Italy, which was dated 30 June 1945, and which received President Truman's specific endorsement, was more open in its expression of concern about the threat from Communism. '[O]ur objective', it stated, 'is to strengthen Italy economically and politically so that the truly democratic elements of the country can withstand the forces that threaten to sweep them into a new totalitarianism' (*FRUS*, *1945*, vol.IV, pp.1009–10).

Exercise Now read items 16 (a) and (b) in *Documents and Texts 1*, which consist of extracts from the American records of conversation between General de Gaulle and the US ambassador in Paris, Jefferson Caffery, and between the Italian ambassador in Washington, Alberto Tarchiani, and a State Department official. Both conversations took place in May 1945, which was the month in which the Second World War ended in Europe. What do these extracts tell you about the preoccupations of the French and Italian governments at the time?

Discussion This is not quite such a simple question as it might look. At first glance, the preoccupations of the French and Italian governments seem both obvious and identical: considerable anxiety about the Russian threat to Europe. But wait a minute. In both cases, the alleged threat is brandished in an effort to secure concessions from the United States. In the case of France, these were 'coal, raw materials [...] various other supplies' and armaments for the French army. In the case of Italy, it was the ending of the restrictions of the armistice regime under which the country was still treated as a former enemy. Perhaps it was these issues that were the real preoccupations of the French and Italian governments, and invoking the Russian threat merely a tactic which they employed to put pressure on the United States.

I would argue that the French and Italian governments (or, at least, their non-Communist members) were concerned about the Russian threat, and even more about the threat to their position from their own Communist parties, but not quite so much as the Americans were thought to be, and probably were. What we have here, in fact, is a good example of an attempt by the French and Italian governments to manipulate their relationship with the United States (see aim 5 on p.177 above). We shall encounter further examples in the rest of this unit. ❑

3 Building the barricades, 1945–49

From the point of view of international relations, the years following the end of the Second World War were dominated by the emergence of the antagonism between the United States and the Soviet Union, the so-called Cold War. We do not have the space to go into the vexed question of which of the two superpowers was more 'to blame' for the antagonism; all that we can do here is to show how the evolving situation influenced and was influenced by developments in France and Italy.

Both the French and Italian governments were alarmed by the growing conflict and sought to preserve a position of benevolent neutrality between the antagonists. The French foreign minister, Georges Bidault, told his cabinet colleagues on 9 May 1947 that 'the international situation was becoming more difficult. We were being confronted [...] by people who say: Are you for or against us? If we don't succeed in making an attempt at conciliation, we run the risk of being caught up in a system of hostile blocs' (Auriol, *Journal, 1947*, p.224). At about the same time, the Italian foreign ministry was hoping for an Anglo-Franco-Italian agreement, which would act as the 'framework for a European system which does not form a bloc directed against anyone, but rather an element of balance between the two superpowers capable of carrying out that task of mediation which no country could effect on its own' (Morozzo della Rocca, *La politica estera italiana e l'Unione Sovietica*, p.222).

Such attitudes undoubtedly commanded a great deal of popular support. As late as August/September 1948, 40 per cent of French adults and 37 per cent of Italians questioned in a parallel poll seemed to be saying 'a plague on both your houses' when they expressed the view that both the Soviet Union and the United States were aiming at world domination, a far higher proportion than in any other West European country and one that cannot be attributed solely to the presence of large Communist parties. An interesting point of comparison is that whereas 91 per cent of Britons believed that the Soviet Union wished to dominate the world, only 38 per cent of Italians and 30 per cent of French people shared their opinion.

For two main reasons, however, a policy of neutrality was simply not feasible. The first was the economic dependence of both France and Italy on the United States. This was particularly acute in the case of Italy. A brief for talks between the Italian prime minister, De Gasperi, and the Russian foreign minister, Vyacheslav Molotov, in August 1946 bluntly stated: 'Italy depends on

America for its day-to-day existence' (Morozzo della Rocca, *La politica estera italiana e l'Unione Sovietica*, p.152). The Italians tried to diversify their sources of supply by asking the Russians for help, but the latter were in no position to offer any. A Russian diplomat had told the Italian ambassador in Moscow a couple of months previously that coal, iron, fuel, timber and wheat were all needed for the Soviet Union's own post-war reconstruction.

Secondly, it became increasingly doubtful whether the United States would tolerate such a policy. The Americans feared that if a country did not support their objectives, it was in danger of falling under the influence of the Soviet Union. Thus, a secret State Department policy paper on France of 15 September 1946 roundly declared:

> Today [...] France is the scene of an internal political battle, the outcome of which is of the greatest importance to the United States, and whose ramifications will extend to all the countries of Western Europe. The world drama of Russian expansion is being played in miniature on the stage of France. [...] The United States wishes to see a France which is friendly and strong, serving as a bulwark to our security, our concept of democracy and our material interests on the continent of Europe [...] Conversely we should strive to prevent the development of a France which might eventually become the western bastion of an inherently hostile 'continental system'.
>
> (Byrnes Papers, policy and information statements)

The Russians, of course, behaved in a similar fashion in East Europe, progressively extinguishing the vestiges of pluralism in countries such as Hungary and Czechoslovakia.

To judge from their policy towards Italy and France, it seemed as if the Soviet Union had virtually abandoned western Europe to the Americans. The Italian ambassador in Moscow had informed Rome as early as April 1945 that the Russians regarded Italy as being in the American sphere of influence, while Molotov told him on Christmas Eve of the same year that countries in eastern Europe, such as Romania, were far more important to the Soviet Union than Italy. And French foreign minister Bidault's pretensions as a mediator were dented at the four-power Moscow conference in March–April 1947, when Stalin lumped him together with his British and American counterparts as 'You ... westerners'.

The Russian attitude in the negotiations leading up to the conclusion of the Italian peace treaty on 10 February 1947, for example, was markedly unsympathetic towards Italy. Among other things, the latter lost all its pre-war colonies and suffered an amputation of part of the province of Venezia-Giulia around Trieste. In 1945 Tito's Communist partisans had tried to annex the whole area to Yugoslavia, but had been thwarted by the threat of force on the part of Britain and the United States. Under the terms of the peace treaty, the pre-war frontier was shifted slightly in Yugoslavia's favour, while Trieste itself was provisionally declared a 'free territory' under the ultimate supervision of the United Nations, although the city and its hinterland were further divided into two zones of military occupation (Zone A under the Yugoslavs and Zone B under the British and Americans) according to the

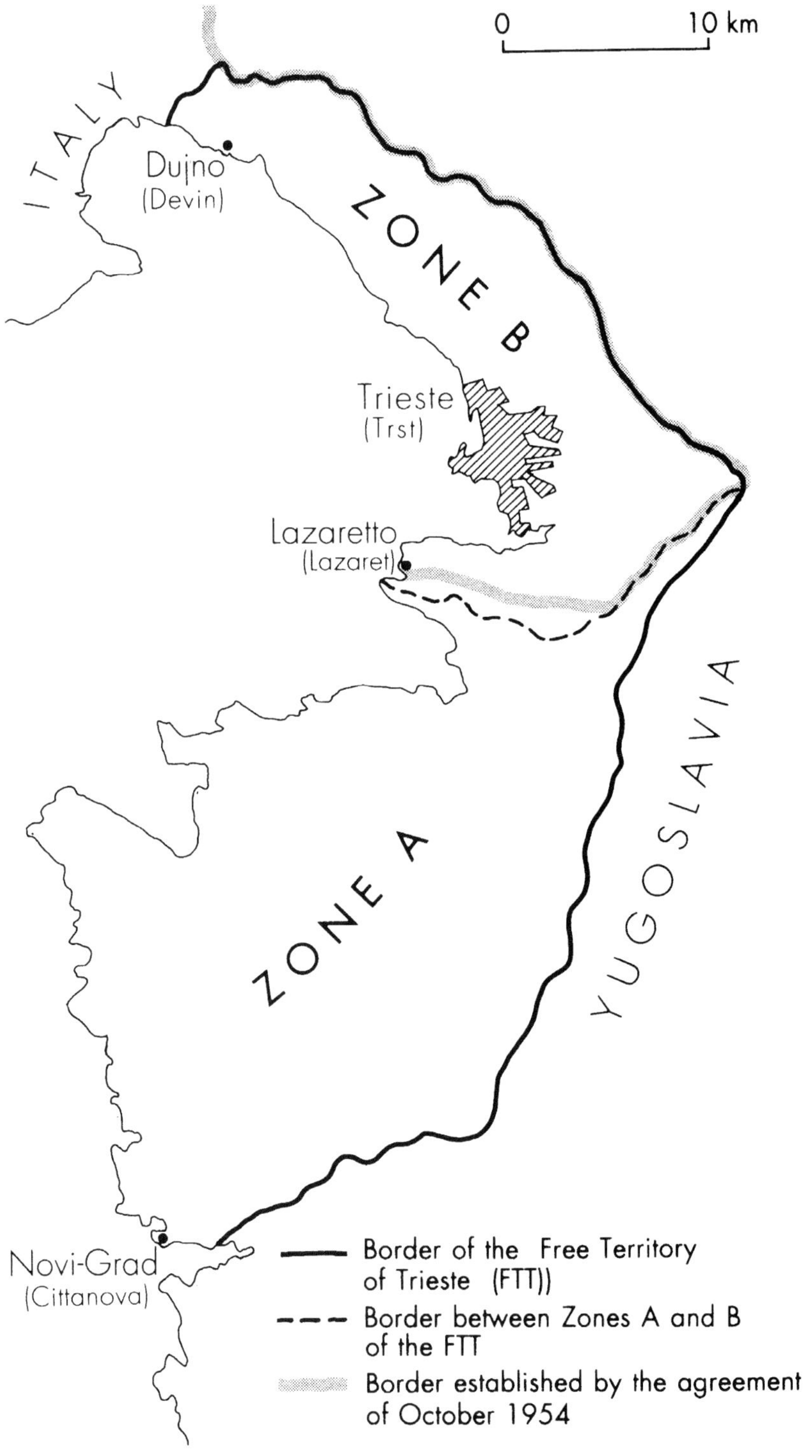

Figure 6.1 *The free territory of Trieste, 1945–54. (Redrawn from John C. Campbell (ed.),* Successful Negotiation: Trieste 1954, *Princeton, New Jersey and Guildford, Princeton University Press, 1976, p.x.)*

provisional demarcation line agreed in June 1945 (see Figure 6.1). This was a compromise in a dispute in which the Soviet Union had supported the Yugoslav claims, much to the irritation of the Italian government.

The French also found themselves at odds with the Russians over French plans for Germany, a country that had invaded France three times in less than a century (1870, 1914 and 1940). Both the de Gaulle government and its successors wanted to dismember Germany and shift the French frontier to the Rhine, but they gained no support from the Russians, who seemed more anxious to win over the Germans than the French.

In 1947 the United States began to formulate an overall strategy for the preservation of western Europe from Communism. The process began on 21 February when the British government, which was in the throes of economic difficulties, informed Washington that it could no longer provide military assistance to Greece and Turkey. This was a serious development because both countries were thought to be under threat from the Soviet Union and its allies. But the longer term dangers were perceived to be even greater. If the Soviet Union was aiming at the control of the eastern Mediterranean through its pressure on Greece and Turkey, the under-secretary of state, Dean Acheson, told congressional leaders on 27 February 1947, in Western Europe

> [...] it was [also] clear that [...] employing the instruments of Communist infiltration and subversion, [it] was trying to complete the encirclement of Germany. In France, with four Communists in the Cabinet, one of them Minister of Defense, with Communists controlling the largest trade union and infiltrating government offices, factories and the armed services, with nearly a third of the electorate voting Communist, and with economic conditions worsening, the Russians could pull the plug any time they chose. In Italy a similar if less dangerous situation existed, but it was growing worse.
>
> (Jones, *The Fifteen Weeks*, p.140)

France and Italy clearly occupied an important place in American thinking. Indeed, when the civilian and military bureaucracies were asked what other countries, apart from Greece and Turkey, needed urgent assistance, they appeared well up on the list, and in the case of the military, above the two eastern Mediterranean states. Moreover, when President Truman went before Congress on 12 March 1947 to appeal for funds for Greece and Turkey, he generalized his message by declaring that 'it must be the policy of the United States to support free people who are resisting attempted subjugation by armed minorities or by outside pressures' (Jones, *The Fifteen Weeks*, p.272). Thus was born the so-called 'Truman Doctrine'.

The Marshall Plan

The threat to France and Italy did not take the form of civil war (as in Greece) or a possible Russian invasion (as in Turkey). The problem, as Acheson had pointed out to his audience of congressional leaders, was internal subversion growing out of an economic crisis. In a speech at Harvard University on 5 June 1947 Acheson's superior, General George C. Marshall, launched an initiative for the economic recovery of western Europe. Hard on the heels of the 'Truman Doctrine' came the 'Marshall Plan'.

Exercise Most of Marshall's Harvard speech is printed as item 17 in *Documents and Texts 1*. You should read it now and then answer the following questions.

1. What did Marshall see as Europe's principal economic problem?
2. What would happen if nothing were done about it?
3. How could it be solved?

Discussion

1. Marshall argued that there had been a 'dislocation of the entire fabric of the European economy'. In particular, there was a danger of the breakdown of the division of labour, on which a modern economy is based. Because the agriculture sector was falling back towards self-sufficiency, people in the towns were short of food and governments were having to purchase such necessities from abroad, thereby using up funds that were needed for reconstruction.
2. If nothing were done about the problem, Europe would 'face economic, social and political deterioration of a very grave character'. This would have, moreover, serious consequences for the American economy. Marshall did not spell out what these consequences were in his speech, but one of the documents on which it was based pointed out that the United States would be deprived of an important market for its goods and thus slide into a depression.
3. The only answer to the problem, in Marshall's opinion, was to break the vicious circle by a substantial injection of aid from the United States. 'Such assistance [...] must not be on a piecemeal basis', and 'should provide a cure rather than a mere palliative'. Once again, he did not specify the details, but the document referred to in the previous paragraph spoke of $6 or $7 billion worth of goods over three years. An important feature of the proposal was that the United States should not draw up the details of the programme: 'The initiative must come, I think, from Europe.' ❑

France and Italy were not specifically mentioned in Marshall's speech. Nor was any other European country. Their needs, however, were very much in American minds. The background document to which reference has already been made emphasized that France could only finance its balance of payments deficit until the end of 1947, while Italy could not last even that long.

Marshall's speech was purposely couched in the broadest terms. There was no direct criticism of the Soviet Union or Communists, although the warning that 'governments, political parties or groups which seek to perpetuate human misery in order to profit therefrom politically or otherwise' would meet with American opposition, was clearly aimed at them. Indeed, it was deliberately left open to the Russians to take part in the Plan, on the assumption that, if they did so, this would effectively destroy their economic stranglehold over eastern

Europe, and that, if they did not, this would render them responsible in the eyes of European public opinion for the division of the continent.

The details of the Marshall Plan, together with its organizational structure, were thrashed out during the rest of 1947 and early 1948. Both the French and Italian governments eagerly embraced the plan, and in so doing were supported by public opinion. In a French poll in September 1947, 64 per cent of respondents said that France was right to have taken part in the Marshall Plan discussions, and only 8 per cent that it was wrong. In a similar Italian poll in January 1948, 65 per cent said that they were favourable to the plan, and only 14 per cent were opposed.

Acceptance of Marshall Aid did of course entail a degree of American interference in the economies of the recipient countries. In the case of France, for example, the French government had to agree to import such relatively useless American goods as cigarettes and chewing gum, while simultaneously allowing access by the United States to strategic raw materials from France's overseas territories. On the other hand, some of the American conditions – such as the taking of steps towards the balancing of the budget – were also favoured by many French politicians and could now be more easily 'sold' to parliament and public opinion as part of the 'price' for Marshall Aid. Moreover, the French did succeed in extracting an important concession from the Americans: namely, that the so-called 'counterpart funds' (i.e. the franc equivalent of the dollar aid) could be used, not solely for financially conservative purposes, as the United States wished, but for productive investment under the Monnet Plan (see Unit 2, pp.69–72).

More important than the economic consequences of Marshall Aid, perhaps, were the consequences for international affairs. The French government, as we have seen above, had favoured the dismemberment of Germany. In early 1948 the British and Americans were bent on creating a West German state.

> There isn't the ghost of a chance [Bidault told the French cabinet on 26 May 1948] of combining the benefits of Marshall Aid with the obstruction of a Germany which would, moreover, be 50 per cent compatible with our views. There are times when one must know how to stop. If we want to act on our own, we shall lose everything. In our present unfortunate situation, we must pursue only the logic of our national interest.
>
> (Auriol, *Journal, 1948*, p.241)

The French government and parliament reluctantly accepted the London treaties of June 1948 which laid the foundations for the Federal Republic of Germany. The new state came into being on 24 May 1949. Only the Saar territory, which had been incorporated into the French customs area in 1946, remained as a monument to the former policy, and, after prolonged negotiation and bad feeling on both sides, this was eventually returned to West Germany at the beginning of 1957.

Other political consequences of the Marshall Plan were triggered off by the Soviet reaction to it. You will recall from Unit 3 (pp.100, 116) that the Communist ministers had been dropped from the French and Italian governments in May 1947. At the time the Soviet Union and the Communist parties themselves blamed this on American pressure, but no hard evidence has come to light to support this accusation. It seems that Ramadier and De Gasperi acted either in anticipation of what they thought the Americans wanted, or else – and this is much more likely – did what they wanted to do anyway, secure in the knowledge that they could count on the approval and support of the United States. As one historian remarks:

> French politicians hardly needed outside prodding to expel the Communists from the coalition [...] In 1947 anti-communism was developing in France with fervour equal to if not greater than in Washington, and French politicians intended to eliminate the Communists just as soon as they felt strong enough to do so.
>
> (Irwin M.Wall, *The United States and the Making of Postwar France*, p.67)

The episode, of course, merely reinforced the Russian belief that France and Italy were American satellites.

The Marshall Plan made matters even worse. Not surprisingly, the Soviet Union regarded it as an attempt by the Americans to extend their domination over the whole of Europe. Not only did it refuse to take part in the plan itself, but it also prevented its eastern European satellites from doing so and treated those countries which did as co-conspirators in the American plot. In September 1947 a new international Communist organization was set up, the Cominform ('Newspeak' for Communist Information Bureau), and at its foundation meeting, the then number two in the Soviet hierarchy, Andrei Zhdanov, declared that the world was now divided into two camps: the imperialist and anti-democratic camp led by the United States, and the anti-imperialist and democratic camp led by the Soviet Union. The French and Italian Communist parties were bitterly criticized at the meeting for having been too concerned with playing the bourgeois parliamentary game, even after their expulsion from the government, and Zhdanov made it clear that their main task henceforth was to take the lead in resisting what he called 'the American plan for the enthralment of Europe'. This barely disguised call for a new, more militant approach led to a sharp deterioration in the political and economic climate in western Europe as the Communist parties and their trade union allies launched an all-out attack on the Marshall Plan (see Unit 3, p.101). This policy may have served the interests of the Russian state, but it drove the French and Italian Communist parties into a political ghetto from which they did not emerge for more than twenty years.

If there was no American intervention in the French and Italian political process when the Communists were expelled from the government, there certainly was such intervention to counter the effects of the Cominform's anti-Marshall Plan offensive. In the case of France, it was felt that the most urgent task was to do something about the Communist stranglehold over the trade union movement, and when the US ambassador in Paris pointed out that the main problem of the anti-Communist labour leaders was lack of funds, money began to flow into their coffers, first of all from American trade unions, and subsequently from the Central Intelligence Agency (CIA). In December 1947 the anti-Communists broke away from the CGT to form their own union, the

Force Ouvrière (see Unit 3, p.100). The US ambassador in Paris described this step as 'the most important event that has occurred in France since the liberation' (*FRUS, 1947*, vol.III, p.819).

In Italy, the priority of the US was to prevent the Communist–Socialist alliance from winning the elections which were due to take place in April 1948 (discussed in Unit 10 and in Ginsborg, pp.115–18). The importance of this policy is illustrated by the fact that it was the first item on the agenda of the newly formed National Security Council (NSC), a body that co-ordinated American foreign and defence policy at the highest level. American intervention in the election campaign took various forms. One was direct financial subsidy to sympathetic political parties, and the US House of Representatives Select Committee on Intelligence disclosed in 1976 that the CIA alone gave $1 million to help the Italian centre parties, the bulk of it going to the Christian Democrats. There was also an immense propaganda effort. Italy was saturated with pamphlets, flooded with films and bombarded with broadcasts which extolled the American way of life and American aid, and warned of the dire consequences of voting for the Communists or their allies. Indeed, the State Department announced publicly that all American aid would cease if the Communists won the election. Finally, in response to a Soviet suggestion – itself clearly designed to influence the outcome of the elections – that Italy's pre-fascist colonies should be restored to its control, Britain, France and the United States formally proposed on 20 March 1948 that the Free Territory of Trieste (see above, pp.185–7) should be returned to Italy.

As you will see in Unit 10, the Christian Democrats won the 1948 elections outright, the only time such a feat has so far been achieved by any Italian political party since the end of the Second World War. How far the American campaign – or, indeed, that run by the Vatican (see Unit 5, p.162) – was responsible for this result is impossible to tell, but it surely had some influence.

However undesirable you may think this American intervention in the political processes of France and Italy was, you must bear two things in mind: first, it was not unique (the Soviet Union was also intervening on behalf of its supporters, albeit probably not to the same extent as the United States); secondly the intervention was welcomed, and indeed solicited, by its beneficiaries. It was French anti-Communist trade union leaders who told the US embassy in Paris that shortage of money was the main obstacle to their organizing resistance to the CGT's plans, and it was Italian politicians and diplomats who implored the Americans for aid and other concessions to prevent their country from 'going Communist'. In these circumstances, you may ask yourself, 'Who was manipulating whom?'

The North Atlantic Treaty

Spiking the guns of the PCF and the PCI inside France and Italy was all very well as far as it went, but what would the United States do in the event of a Russian invasion of western Europe? In retrospect this appears to have been an extremely remote contingency, but things did not look quite so simple at the time. In February 1948 Czechoslovakia's democratic system succumbed to a well-organized Communist coup from within. Early the following month strong rumours began to circulate that the Soviet Union was about to apply diplomatic pressure to Norway as a first step in bringing that country into the Russian orbit. This cable was followed by the first Russian moves to restrict access between the western zones of Germany and the western sectors of Berlin, moves that developed into a total blockade of rail, road and canal traffic in June. These various developments induced a state of considerable anxiety on the part of many in western Europe and the United States.

Since western Europe's armed forces were so weak, it was obvious, as some wit remarked at the time, that all the Red Army needed to reach the English Channel was a good supply of boots – unless, that is, the United States came forward with a guarantee that it would intervene with its own military forces in the event of a Soviet invasion. In March 1948 the US administration indicated that it was prepared secretly to examine the possibility of such a guarantee. The subsequent negotiations eventually culminated, on 4 April 1949, in the signature of the North Atlantic Treaty, the first peacetime alliance in the history of the United States.

France and Italy were both founder-members of the North Atlantic Alliance, but their paths to this position had been very different. There was never any doubt that France would take part. At the end of 1947 the French cabinet agreed on the need for a military agreement with the United States and repeatedly appealed to the Americans for their assistance, without which the defence of western Europe was impossible. Public opinion was also favourable, although much less overwhelmingly. Thirty-nine per cent of a sample questioned in April 1949 thought France should sign the North Atlantic Treaty and only 18 per cent were opposed. The latter figure was probably not too different from the proportion of Communists in the country, and their leader, Maurice Thorez, caused a sensation in February 1949 when he suggested that, in the event of a Soviet invasion of France, the French people would greet the Red Army as liberators. Just as important as the polarization between Communists and anti-Communists, however, was the extent of apathy and ignorance: 20 per cent of those polled had no opinion about the desirability of signing the treaty, and no less that 23 per cent had never even heard of it.

In Italy, neutralist pressure from the left wing of the Christian Democrats and even from the Vatican (which feared the consequences of a Russian invasion), led to a more cautious attitude on the part of the government. The latter soon discovered, moreover, that some of its prospective partners, especially Britain, were not at all enthusiastic about Italy's participation, arguing that it could contribute little but would demand much. The Italians therefore toyed briefly with the idea of some sort of armed neutrality, albeit one backed by an American guarantee, but eventually concluded at the turn of 1948–49 that there was no alternative to membership of the emerging Atlantic pact. Paradoxically, Italian public opinion seems to have been more favourably disposed than that in France. Forty-six per cent of those asked in November 1948 were in favour of Italy joining the pact and only 15 per cent against. There was still, however, a large proportion (37 per cent) of 'don't knows'.

Italy found the strongest external support for its membership from the French government, which was anxious to extend the scope of the forthcoming treaty southwards in order to protect France's North African territories. American opinion was divided. Some sections of the bureaucracy shared Britain's reservations, but Italophiles in the State Department argued strongly in favour of the need to strengthen further the position of the De Gasperi government, and the military, although mindful of Italy's weakness, attached considerable importance to its strategic position in the Mediterranean. The pro-Italian faction eventually won out and the United States government threw its weight behind Italian adherence to the treaty, which meant that the other countries had little option but to concede the point. With the signature of the North Atlantic Treaty, it can be argued that the process of integrating France and Italy into the American sphere of influence was complete.

4 Trials and tribulations of a relationship, 1949–56

A federal Europe?

A key ingredient of American policy towards western Europe in the period covered by this course was support for a political and economic federation. Just as there was a United States of America, it was argued, so there should be a United States of Europe, which would be, at one and the same time, easier to deal with, and a more effective bulwark against Communism, than a collection of individual nation-states.

There was also much sympathy for this idea in western Europe itself. It grew out of the experience of the Second World War, which had once again demonstrated the folly of unrestrained nationalism, and it figured in the programmes of many of the anti-fascist resistance organizations. By 1949–50, the three personalities most closely associated with the movement towards western European unity at the governmental level were De Gasperi, Robert Schuman (who succeeded Georges Bidault as French foreign minister in July 1948), and Konrad Adenauer, who became the first Chancellor of the Federal Republic of Germany in September 1949. All three came from border areas – De Gasperi from Trento in northern Italy, Schuman from Lorraine in eastern France, and Adenauer from the Rhineland in western Germany. Indeed, De Gasperi had originally been an Austrian citizen and Schuman a German. All three, moreover, were leading figures in their respective countries' Catholic political parties. This similarity in their backgrounds may have encouraged the internationalism of the three men, but there is little doubt that national interest also played a major part in their Europeanism. For De Gasperi (as for Adenauer), European unity was a means whereby his country could finally bury its Fascist past and play a constructive role in international politics on a basis of equality; for Schuman, it was a way in which France could ensure that the new, and potentially powerful, West German state could be harnessed to French interests and not threaten them.

The main obstacle to European unity was seen by many, both in western Europe and in the United States, to be Britain. Under its Labour government Britain had many reasons, ranging from its Commonwealth connections to its attachment to socialist planning, for not wishing to mesh its economy too closely with that of a predominantly conservative continental Europe. It was not altogether surprising, therefore, that when Schuman called on 9 May 1950 for the integration of western Europe's coal and steel industries under a supranational authority, his proposal should be welcomed by Italy, West Germany and the United States, but rejected by Britain.

Exercise A long extract from Schuman's proposal is printed as item 18 in *Documents and Texts 1*. You should read it now. What would you say was Schuman's main objective and why did he choose this particular approach to achieve it?

Discussion At various points in his statement Schuman refers to the desirability of a united European federation, the formation of which, he argues, is essential to prevent a future war. He realizes, however, that such a federation cannot be created in one fell swoop: 'It will be built through concrete achievements which first create a *de facto* solidarity.' The proposed coal–steel pool is such a measure, which 'will lead to the realization of the first concrete foundation of a European federation'. This much was clear enough, but perhaps it struck you that the future war Schuman is seeking to avoid is not, as you might think in view of the contents of this unit so far, one between the Soviet Union and the western European countries, but one between France and Germany. Indeed, the whole proposal has to be seen in the context of Franco–German relations. ❑

When France was compelled to go along with the Anglo-American plans for a West German state in 1948 (see above, p.189), the French foreign ministry began almost immediately to think in terms of solutions other than dismemberment which would protect France from the threat of another German invasion. The integration of the new West German state into a united Europe soon emerged as the front-runner. By January 1949 France was advocating a steel pool. By 'Europeanizing' this basic commodity, which was of course essential to a war-making capacity, French security would be much more effectively guaranteed than by attempting to impose international controls from outside.

Jean Monnet, the head of the French planning office, was independently reaching similar conclusions, and it was he who persuaded Schuman to launch his initiative. In his view, the whole position of France as a great power was at stake. If it failed to act, he wrote in the spring of 1950,

> [a] group will form round the United States, but in order to wage the cold war with greater zeal. The obvious reason is that the countries of Europe are afraid and are seeking help. Britain will draw ever closer to the United States; Germany will develop rapidly, and we shall not be able to prevent her being armed. France will be trapped once more in her old Malthusianism, and this will inevitably lead to her eclipse.
>
> (Monnet, *Memoirs*, p.294)

The French, it seems, were more concerned about Germany than the Soviet Union.

Why, in these circumstances, was the United States so keen on the Schuman plan? The answer is that the Americans knew that a solid defence of western Europe could not be established unless and until the old antagonism between France and Germany had been healed, and the Schuman plan seemed the most effective way of bringing this about. Although the principle had been welcomed by a number of western European countries, the negotiations to turn it into a reality were not easy and the United States often intervened discreetly to nudge them along. On 18 April 1951 the treaty establishing the European Coal and Steel Community (ECSC) was signed by France, West Germany, Italy, Belgium, Luxembourg and the Netherlands.

The defence of western Europe

On 25 June 1950 the Russian client state of North Korea invaded the American client state of South Korea. The background to this event was highly complex, but the issue seemed perfectly straightforward to the United States government at the time. As President Truman told the American people, the attack on South Korea 'makes it plain beyond all doubt that Communism has passed beyond the use of subversion [...] and will use armed invasion and war' (Truman, *Memoirs*, vol.II, p.339).

The outbreak of the Korean war threw the recently formed North Atlantic Alliance into a turmoil. After all, if the Russians could instigate a war in East Asia, might not they do the same thing in Europe, where a divided Germany paralleled a divided Korea? And if they did, would the alliance be able to hold them? The trouble with the North Atlantic Treaty was that it was based on a colossal bluff. Its members, including the United States, could not put into the field anything like the number of troops which the Soviet Union and its eastern European allies were capable of deploying. This problem was not so serious when the treaty was signed, since at that time the United States possessed a monopoly of the atomic bomb, but in September 1949 the Russians had exploded their first nuclear device. Even before Korea, the military in a number of alliance countries (including France) had come to the conclusion that the only effective way to strengthen western Europe's defences was to rearm the West Germans. Politically, however, this was unacceptable; memories of Germans in uniform were still too recent and unpleasant. This was true in the United States as well as in Europe, but the Korean war changed the administration's view almost overnight. After having secured promises of vastly increased rearmament programmes, the United States government confronted its allies in September 1950 with a virtual ultimatum: either accept the principle of German rearmament or forgo the commitment of additional American troops to Europe and the appointment of a supreme commander for the alliance.

Italy was willing to accept the American demand. The Italian government took the view that a disarmed Germany was more likely to be attacked than one that was in a position to defend itself. Moreover, the further east the alliance's line of defence was drawn, the better for Italy. France, on the other hand, was adamantly opposed. The aim of French policy, as we saw in our discussion of the Schuman plan, was to contain Germany, not to rearm it. At the same time, the French wanted American troops and a supreme commander in Europe as much, if not more, than anyone else. It was up to them, therefore, to come up with a solution to the dilemma. On 24 October 1950 the French prime minister, René Pleven, unveiled a counter-proposal, suggested to him by the ubiquitous Jean Monnet, for the formation of a European army, integrated at the level of the smallest possible unit, with a common budget and a political superstructure consisting of a European defence minister responsible to a European parliament. All West Germany's forces – but not all those of France – would form part of this European army. Like the Schuman plan, the scheme was intended to spin a cocoon of supra-national restraints around West Germany from which it could never escape. It was doubtful whether even this suggestion would prove acceptable to French public opinion. When asked in October 1950 whether Germany should be included in a European army, only 29 per cent of the sample replied in the affirmative compared with 51 per cent in the negative.

It was certainly unacceptable to the Americans. 'To me', Secretary of State Dean Acheson wrote later, 'the plan was hopeless, a view confirmed by General Marshall [now Secretary of Defense] and concurred in by the President, and protracted discussion of it dangerous' (Acheson, *Present at the Creation*, p.459). Nevertheless, 'protracted discussion' was precisely what took place and by July 1951 the US administration had reluctantly been forced to the conclusion that, if it wanted German rearmament, it was going to have to have it within the framework of the French proposal for a European army.

The treaty establishing the European Defence Community (EDC), within which the European army would be set up, was signed on 27 May 1952 by the same six countries that had established the ECSC. Whereas the ECSC treaty was ratified fairly quickly, however, this was not the case with the EDC treaty. The French government was particularly fertile in excuses for delay: there had to be some form of British association with the EDC (Britain had refused to join for the same reason it had refused to join the ECSC: namely, opposition to its supra-national features); the United States had to promise to keep its troops in Europe; the French role in Indo-China (see Audio-cassette 1, side B and p.200 below) had to be recognized and supported by the North Atlantic Treaty allies, especially the United States; finally, additional protocols to the treaty, some of which undoubtedly diluted it, had to be accepted. All these proposals were justified on the grounds that France was too weak by itself to confront and contain West Germany within the EDC.

There was growing exasperation at the French attitude on the part of the United States, especially after Truman's Democratic administration was replaced by that of the Republican, General Eisenhower, in January 1953. After all, it was pointed out, the EDC was a French idea. At the Anglo-Franco-American 'summit' meeting in Bermuda in December 1953, the new president bluntly asked Georges Bidault, who had returned as French foreign minister the previous January, 'Just what nation does France now regard as a potential enemy, Germany or Russia?' (Eisenhower, *Mandate for Change*, p.245). It was a good question, but if the answer was 'obvious' to Eisenhower, it was not to Bidault. The French had never wanted to rearm the Germans and had only accepted the idea with extreme reluctance after the American ultimatum of September 1950.

French caution was deeply rooted in political and parliamentary realities. Table 6.1 shows the evolution of public opinion towards the European army as shown in successive polls.

Although the proportion of opponents had fallen, so had that of supporters, and the increase in those expressing no view showed that opinion was still quite volatile. As for parliamentary opinion, it is doubtful whether there was ever a majority for the EDC after the elections of June 1951 (see Unit 10). This saw, among other things, the return of a large number of Gaullist deputies, who regarded the idea that France should merge any part of its armed forces into a European army as a betrayal of the nation's heritage. Finally, the death of Stalin in March 1953 seemed to bring signs of some relaxation in international tension, which could be interpreted as meaning that German rearmament was no longer necessary.

Table 6.1 French public opinion towards the European army

	September 1952	*June 1953*
In favour	48%	43%
Against	30%	23%
No view	22%	34%

(Aron and Lerner, *La Querelle de la CED*, p.139)

What may perhaps be particularly surprising in these circumstances is the extent to which the United States was not only prepared itself to make concessions to the French, but also to cajole others into doing so. For the Americans, the unpalatable truth was that there was a limit beyond which they felt they could not go in putting pressure on France. When a member of the NSC argued on 5 March 1954 that 'the time was now at hand to warn the French to get ahead and ratify EDC or else we would pull out our forces from Europe', President Eisenhower reminded him that 'we must never allow ourselves to forget that in stationing US forces abroad we are defending ourselves and not merely the French' (*FRUS, 1952–1954*, vol.V, part 1, p.888).

As if the French were not causing enough problems, the Italians now began to create difficulties as well. Their anxieties stemmed from the situation in Trieste. You will recall that, in March 1948, the British, French and Americans had proposed that the whole of the Free Territory should be handed over to Italy (see above, p.185). This was an empty gesture to a large extent because the Soviet Union predictably refused and it would have meant driving the Yugoslavs out of Zone A by armed force. The logical solution would have been to have agreed on partition along the existing line between the two zones, but nationalist feeling in both Italy and Yugoslavia made this difficult, if not impossible. The situation had also changed in one other important respect. Marshal Tito's regime and the Soviet Union had fallen out in a blaze of publicity in June 1948 and the former began to move closer to the western powers.

'Wanting to keep Tito split from the Soviet Union,' President Eisenhower subsequently recalled in his memoirs, 'the United States could no longer [...] back Italy to the hilt in its claim to everything' (*Mandate for Change*, p.412).

The failure to obtain a satisfactory settlement of the Trieste question was probably a factor in the Christian Democrats' relative failure in the June 1953 elections (see Unit 10), but not a very important one. Almost immediately afterwards, however, Trieste was to move into the forefront of Italian politics. In August 1953 the new Italian prime minister, Giuseppe Pella, sent troops to the frontier as a result of rumours to the effect that Yugoslavia was about to proclaim the formal annexation of Zone A. On 13 September Pella proposed a plebiscite in both zones and simultaneously made it clear that Italy's ratification of the EDC treaty depended on a satisfactory solution to the problem. The British and Americans reacted to the crisis by unilaterally offering to hand Zone B over to Italy, but this only made matters worse, for the Yugoslavs declared that they would regard the entry of Italian troops into Zone B as a *casus belli*.

A public opinion poll in November 1953 showed that 61 per cent of Italians questioned approved of Pella's policies and that only 10 per cent opposed them. Over half could think of no acceptable alternative to giving Italy both Zones A and B, although only around 7 per cent advocated a solution by force. It must have been about this time that the American ambassador to Italy, Clare Booth Luce, penned her version of 'For want of a nail' as follows:

> For the want of Trieste, an Issue was lost.
> For the want of an Issue, the Election was lost.
> For the want of De Gasperi, his NATO policies were lost.
> For the want of his NATO policies, Italy was lost.
> For the want of Italy, Europe was lost.
> For the want of Europe, America [...]
>
> (Eisenhower, *Mandate for Change*, p.409)

If the non-Communist opposition did not take strong action, she warned President Eisenhower on 3 November 1953, within two years Italy would be the first western democratic country to go Communist by legal means, and the most effective step the United States could take to strengthen this opposition was to implement the proposal to hand over Zone B to the Italians.

This advice was clearly unacceptable if the result was to be a war between Italy and Yugoslavia. Fortunately, wiser counsels prevailed on all sides and, in February 1954, negotiations began between the British, the Americans and the Yugoslavs for a peaceful settlement. A provisional agreement was reached at the end of May and it was communicated to the Italians at the beginning of June. After further negotiations, a final agreement was concluded on 9 October 1954. The territorial solution is shown in Figure 6.1 and, as can be seen, was very close to a straight partition along the line of the zonal boundary. In addition, Trieste itself was to remain a free port and both the Italian and Yugoslav governments promised to respect minority rights on their sides of the boundary.

The solution to the Trieste problem came too late to save the EDC, if indeed Italian ratification would have made much difference. Pierre Mendès France, who became French prime minister on 19 June 1954, finally brought the treaty before the National Assembly, where it was voted down on 30 August by 319 votes to 264. An unholy alliance of Communists and Gaullists voted more or less solidly against, while the pro-European MRP was equally solidly in favour. What was revealing was the way in which pro-government parties such as the Socialists and the Radicals were split down the middle. The prime minister himself was no enthusiast for the treaty and, having failed to secure further amendments to it from the other signatories, announced that, since the issue was so divisive, he and his cabinet colleagues would abstain. For the same reason he refused to make the issue one of confidence in his government.

After almost four years of fruitless discussion, it was little short of astonishing that the problem of West Germany's rearmament was, to all intents and purposes, solved within the following two months, together with that of the country's assumption of full international sovereignty, negotiations on which had been proceeding in parallel with those concerning the EDC. The *deus ex machina* was the British foreign secretary, Anthony Eden, who came up with the idea of reviving the Brussels treaty of 1948, which had included Britain, France and the Benelux countries, and inviting West Germany (and Italy) to join it. Unlike the EDC, the Brussels treaty organization was not supranational and the British were already full members. In addition, Eden made the unprecedented pledge that Britain would keep its forces on the continent of Europe for as long as its treaty partners wanted, thereby giving the French the assurance against German preponderance for which they had so long sought in vain. The West Germans also helped by making a unilateral renunciation of the right to manufacture nuclear, chemical and biological weapons and by accepting restrictions in respect of the manufacture of certain other armaments. International conferences in London and Paris in September–October 1954 reached agreement on these questions. On 5 May 1955 the Federal Republic of Germany became a fully sovereign state and four days later it was welcomed as the fifteenth member of the North Atlantic Alliance.

After the collapse of the EDC, there was probably little that France could have done to delay German rearmament any further. Its allies were so angry at what had happened that, if there had been any further obstruction, they might well have rearmed the Germans without any safeguards. If this is true, Mendès France succeeded in obtaining the best possible deal for his country. To judge from a public opinion poll taken in October 1954, however, the French people would still have preferred a position of neutrality in the Cold War. Fifty-three per cent of those asked said that France should not take sides in a war between the United States and the Soviet Union, with only 22 per cent favouring siding with the Americans. The only consolation that supporters of the North Atlantic Alliance could draw from this poll was that a mere 2 per cent believed France should line up with the Russians!

The war in Indo-China

French enthusiasm for neutrality probably owed much to the fact that France had just emerged from a real war and, moreover, one that had lasted the best part of eight years. This was the conflict in Indo-China. We saw earlier in this unit how President Roosevelt had originally opposed the return of Indo-China to France after the Second World War, but how both he and President Truman had eventually relented (see above, pp.180 and 183). In retrospect it might have been better for France if they had not, for the French found themselves confronted by an increasingly powerful indigenous nationalist movement in Vietnam, led by the Moscow-trained Communist, Ho Chi Minh. Negotiations between the French and Ho's movement, the Viet Minh, finally broke down at the end of 1946 and the long guerrilla war began.

Exercise The Indo-China war had considerable repercussions on relations between France and the United States. Audio-cassette 1, side B, 'The United States, France and the war in Indo-China', goes into this question in some detail. You should listen to it now, read the associated notes, and then try to sum up how successful you think the United States was in influencing French policy in Indo-China. I know this is a big question, but I do not want you to write an enormous amount on it. Keep your answer to a paragraph.

Discussion I think it is fairly clear from the cassette that the United States had very little influence on French policy. The French did fight the Viet Minh for nearly seven years, and this was what the Americans wanted. The French then decided, however, that they wanted a negotiated settlement of the war, and although the United States was unhappy about this, it felt compelled to go along with it for the reasons explained on the cassette. Moreover, the United States did not like the terms of the Geneva settlement, but was unable to prevent it. Finally, the United States appears to have had relatively little success in persuading the French to grant full independence to the Associated States. All this, it should be noted, occurred in the context of a war that was increasingly financed by the Americans. The old adage, 'He who pays the piper calls the tune', definitely does not seem to have applied in this case.

The reason for this relative lack of American influence is also fairly clear: the United States felt that the disadvantages of extra pressure on the French outweighed the advantages, not only in Indo-China, but also in Europe. Ultimately, they were more enthusiastic about both the French presence in Indo-China and in the EDC than the French were themselves. ❑

5 Hungary and Suez, 1956

In Unit 1, it was noted that 1956 formed a watershed year in international relations because of Khrushchev's denunciation of Stalin at the 20th Soviet Communist Party Congress in February and the Hungarian and Suez crises that simultaneously erupted in early November. In this penultimate section, these events will be considered from the perspective of the United States' relations with western Europe, and more particularly with France. Hitherto this unit has emphasized the autonomy politicians in Paris were able to exercise *vis-à-vis* Washington. The Suez debacle was to prove a humiliating demonstration of the limits of French (and British) power, just as the Hungarian crisis brutally manifested the realities of Soviet power.

The immediate origins of the Suez crisis lay in the nationalization of the Suez Canal Company announced by the Egyptian leader, Colonel Nasser, on 26 July 1956. The shareholders (who were mostly British and French nationals) were promised compensation and Egypt could plausibly claim it was acting within its sovereign rights. In Britain and France, government ministers regarded the nationalization of the Suez Canal as the final provocation of a dangerous demagogue whom they were now determined to topple. Both the Conservative prime minister, Sir Anthony Eden, and the French Socialist premier, Guy Mollet, saw Nasser as a latter-day Hitler who should not be appeased. More than half of western Europe's oil came through the canal, so it was of vital strategic and commercial interest to both countries.

Nasser had been stung into action when John Foster Dulles, the American Secretary of State, peremptorily withdrew the offer of financial assistance for the Aswan dam project. Dulles had hoped thereby to 'punish' Nasser for his friendly relations with the Soviet Union which had been supplying arms to Egypt since May 1955. In the event, Egypt and the Soviet Union became even closer: Russia stepped in as the dam's financier and provided the engineering skills. Though perturbed by Nasser's decision, the USA was not greatly affected. There were no American citizens among the canal shareholders and very little of the oil coming through the canal from the Persian Gulf was destined for America. Washington had generally tried to extend its influence in the 'Third World' by supporting nationalist regimes and distancing itself from the European colonial (or former colonial) powers. The Eisenhower administration sympathized with Britain, its closest ally, but was unambiguously opposed to the use of force against Egypt. At the end of July, Eisenhower sent a personal representative to London to urge restraint on the Eden government. Dulles arrived a few days later with a letter from the President reiterating this message. The USA wanted to impress the international community with its impartiality and escape all taint of colonialism. It consequently sought a diplomatic solution to the crisis by proposing an international conference that met in London between 1–23 August. Nothing was achieved except delay.

Beneath their common purpose, Paris and London had different reasons for overthrowing Nasser's regime. While British ministers were fixated with reversing imperial decline, the French were primarily concerned with ending the Algerian insurrection that had broken out in November 1954. The politicians in Paris deluded themselves that violent nationalism had little popular support among Algerian Muslims, and believed the insurrection would be crushed if denied Egypt's military, political and moral support. They may have been right: the ALN (National Liberation Army) was poorly equipped until Nasser made an arms agreement with Czechoslovakia in September 1955, and Cairo became the assembly point for its munitions. The city was a sanctuary for Algerian exiles and Nasser never disguised his political support for their struggle. During an official visit to Cairo in March 1956, he told the French Foreign Minister, Christian Pineau, that it was Egypt's duty 'to assist our Arab brothers everywhere'. Robert Lacoste, who was appointed Minister Resident for Algeria in February 1956, summed up the argument for military intervention: 'One French division in Egypt is worth four divisions in Algeria'. This rationale was very widely accepted in France where all the major newspapers – except those aligned with the Communists – denounced Nasser's move and demanded firm action.

Members of the French government had a further reason for intervention. Pineau, Maurice Bourgès-Maunory, the Defence Minister, and Mollet were strong supporters of Israel, a state that seemed to embody their own socialist values. They were shamefully conscious of how little had been done to save European Jewry in the 1940s, and were determined not to acquiesce in the destruction of Israel by its Arab neighbours. This was not an 'unreal' fear: some ex-Nazis had sought refuge in Egypt and contributed to the viciously anti-Jewish propaganda broadcast by Radio Cairo. Allowing Nasser to retain control of the canal would, the French believed, give him a stranglehold on the Israeli economy. Britain still subsidized and armed the conservative Arab monarchies, Jordan and Iraq, and British ministers were markedly less sympathetic towards Israel than their French counterparts. The Franco–Israeli axis was to prove highly significant in the unfolding of the crisis. Although Eden and Mollet had instructed their service chiefs to plan a joint military operation after the canal's seizure, Eden drew back from the projected invasion when the Americans made their opposition clear. The French and Israelis took the lead in planning military intervention. Shimon Peres and Moshe Dayan drew up the plan of attack with Pineau and the French Generals Ely and Challe at the beginning of October. What they proposed was the now notorious collusion whereby Israel would launch an attack across the Sinai desert, after which France and Britain would intervene to protect the Canal Zone by 'separating' the belligerents. Britain rejoined the conspiracy at the request of Guy Mollet after British ministers had persuaded themselves the Americans would condone the use of force. On a visit to the United States, Harold Macmillan, one of the most bellicose British ministers, completely misread American attitudes. The tripartite protocol of agreement was signed by Pineau, Ben Gurion, the Israeli premier, and Selwyn Lloyd, the British Foreign Secretary, at a meeting in Sèvres on the 22–24 October. Coincidentally, on the 22nd the Algerian nationalist leader, Ahmed Ben Bella, was captured after the Moroccan plane he was travelling on was forced down over Algeria. The French, at least, had a jubilant expectation that they were about to achieve their goals.

Israeli forces attacked on 29 October, and were within twenty kilometres of the canal by the following day. Paris and London then sent an ultimatum requiring the belligerents to withdraw their troops from a strip sixteen kilometres on either side of the canal. Israel agreed, but Egypt – as hoped – refused, and so provided the pretext for Franco–British intervention. While Egyptian bases were being bombarded, the United Nations General Assembly voted by an overwhelming majority (which included the USSR and the USA) for a ceasefire, and later adopted a Canadian resolution proposing the dispatch of an international force. Despite virtually unanimous condemnation in the UN, Franco–British forces occupied Port Fouad and Port Said while the Israelis captured Sharm-el-Sheikh. On the evening of 5 November, the Soviet ambassador was withdrawn from Israel, and Bulganin and Khrushchev wrote to Ben Gurion, Mollet and Eden with a crude threat of nuclear intervention. (At the same time, they proposed to the Americans joint military action to re-establish peace in the Middle East.) The Soviet threat was not taken seriously in London and Paris. What condemned the military adventure to fiasco was Washington's attitude. It was patently obvious France and Britain had conspired with Israel, and Eisenhower – who was seeking re-election on the 6 November – was outraged at his allies' duplicity. Having begun the adventure to secure their oil supplies, they should – a furious president commented – be left to 'boil in their own oil'. Eisenhower took two decisive steps to impose a ceasefire: on 5 November he announced that the Europeans could not count on American oil to replace supplies from the Gulf – a serious threat when petrol restrictions were already necessary and panic food-buying had begun – and he allowed a run on sterling to develop. Though the British economy was stronger than the French at this time, it was more exposed to such financial pressure. The franc could only be exchanged on international markets under strict conditions while the pound was more easily convertible. A forced devaluation of the pound would have sent Britain's import bill soaring. Eden gave way before the double pressure on 6 November, and telephoned Mollet to say Britain was accepting a UN supervised ceasefire. The disgruntled French could only follow suit a few hours later. The British and French stopped fighting on 7 November without achieving their military and political objectives. The invasion troops were slowly withdrawn and a UN peacekeeping force was imposed between the Egyptians and Israelis.

France and Britain both emerged discredited and weakened from the episode: every Arab country except the Lebanon had severed diplomatic relations; their humiliation was a political and diplomatic triumph for Nasser; the nationalization of the canal was an accepted fact. The USA displaced Britain as the dominant western power in the Middle East, where the Soviet Union's influence was also greatly boosted. Yet governmental and public reactions to the Suez setback were rather different in France and Britain. Politically (and physically) Eden was a broken man, and compelled to resign in the New Year; Mollet's government won a vote of confidence by 325 to 210 on 20 December, and survived until late May 1957. (It was the longest-serving ministry during the Fourth Republic.) A clear majority of the Assembly 'seemed ready to believe that the shame of Munich had indeed been redeemed, that the future of Algeria had been preserved, and that Israel was now safe' (Rioux, *The Fourth Republic*, p.275). By contrast with Britain, there was little public rancour over Suez in France where most acquiesced in the expedition and a large minority actively supported it. According to IFOP polls conducted in Paris on 3 November, 37 per cent approved of the invasion while the majority favoured a diplomatic solution.

Why were French political passions not mobilized as they were in Britain? A press campaign highly favourable to the government, and the latter's tight control of news broadcasting on public service radio, were two reasons. Another was that French Algeria was still a popular cause. But a further factor was that the 'natural' community of opposition to the Suez adventure – the Communist Party and its electorate – found itself very embattled in early November. On the 7th, thousands of Parisians demonstrated violently outside the PCF headquarters, attempted to ransack the offices of *L'Humanité*, the party newspaper, and clashed with the police and Communist counter-demonstrators.

What prompted their anger was the crushing by Soviet troops of the reformist government of Imre Nagy and its supporters in Budapest. The course of the Hungarian tragedy can be traced only in outline here.

Following the Soviet Communist Party's twentieth congress, the Hungarian Communist Party splintered between hardline Stalinists led by Mátyás Rákosi (First Party Secretary during the brutal sovietization) and reformist elements that clustered around Nagy, a former political prisoner of the regime. Rákosi was forced to resign on 17 July by a visiting Soviet delegation for not heeding the wind of change blowing from Moscow, but his replacement was ineptly chosen and the Hungarian party lost all cohesion. By late October, student activists – inspired partly by a reform movement that brought Wladyslaw Gomulka to power in Poland – were demanding the evacuation of Soviet troops, general elections with several parties participating, and a revision of the entire economic system. On the 23rd, after a massive demonstration in Budapest, Nagy was appointed prime minister by the panicking Central Committee, which simultaneously appealed to the Soviet garrison to restore order. Nagy found himself the reluctant leader of a national, democratic rebellion against foreign domination and the single party dictatorship. Violent clashes took place between revolutionaries and the secret police. Under popular pressure, Nagy restored a multi-party system, and announced Hungary's withdrawal from the Warsaw Pact. A neutral, democratic Hungary was intolerable not just to the Soviet leadership, but to communist rulers in Czechoslovakia, East Germany, Romania and Bulgaria. They (and the Chinese) urged that the rebellion be suppressed without delay. Red Army tanks moved into the city on 4 November, a date presumably chosen to capitalize on the disarray in the western alliance.

The prestige of the Soviet Union sank abysmally in western Europe, where 'fellow travellers' repudiated their links with communist-front organizations, such as the Peace Movement, and many party intellectuals tore up their cards. None was more tainted than the PCF. Thorez had staked too much on fidelity to Stalin (even moulding himself in Stalin's image) to contemplate de-Stalinization. Though he and other French delegates to Moscow had been shown an advance copy of Khrushchev's speech, they denied its authenticity for months (unlike Togliatti who promptly made its contents known to the PCI). To Thorez, Hungary was a fearful demonstration of where de-Stalinization would lead. The PCF hastened to applaud the Soviet intervention which, its newspapers claimed, had averted a fascist restoration of capitalism. Not even the Party's electorate believed this rubbish: commercial radio stations had kept the French well informed about the drama, and polls showed Communist electors shared the general public hostility to the Soviet move. Although the PCF weathered the crisis in terms of retaining voter loyalty, it was never so isolated in the political landscape, nor so detested by non-Communists.

Ostensibly, the events in central Europe in the autumn of 1956 were a golden opportunity for the Americans to divide their communist adversaries and fracture the Soviet bloc. However, the evidence shows they exercised great caution in the belief that a direct revolt against Soviet power could not succeed without American and NATO military assistance, which would have led to war. Contrary to legend, neither of the radio stations supported by the Central Intelligence Agency – Radio Liberty nor Radio Free Europe – called directly for an anti-Soviet uprising. Nor did the CIA activate its networks of trained agents among central European refugees to exploit the situation. The balance of terror, and the accepted division of Europe into 'spheres of influence', meant that the USA could do no more than protest verbally. To put it bluntly, the Americans could coerce their allies out of Egypt, but had to tolerate Soviet tanks in Budapest. The French political analyst, Raymond Aron (who opposed the Suez adventure) put the point with some acerbity:

> It was only in 1956, with the two simultaneous crises in central Europe and the Middle East, that Europeans became fully aware of their subordination to their own Big Brother and the price to be paid for the security ensured them by a power more powerful than themselves. Reduced, not to essentials, but to the Europeans' realisation of them, the combined events – Hungary and Suez – entailed two inevitable and incompatible alignments: while all the members of the Atlantic alliance were denouncing the Red Army's suppression of the Hungarian revolt, the United States in coalition with the Soviet Union was mobilising the United Nations and the world's conscience in condemnation of the British and French. The action by the united Western powers remained purely verbal; the Soviet-American action against the British and French achieved what it set out to do.

(Aron, *The Imperial Republic*, pp.54–5)

6 Conclusion

You may recall that we described this unit as a commentary on Stalin's dictum that occupation and liberation 'imposed' a particular social system on the countries involved. Was this true in the case of France and Italy?

Up to a point, the answer is 'Yes'. Unlike the countries in eastern Europe liberated by the Soviet Union, France and Italy retained capitalist economies and pluralist political systems. The United States worked to ensure this through such policies as the Marshall Plan, the financing of the French non-Communist trade unions, and large-scale intervention in the Italian elections of 1948. And what the Italian ambassador in Paris wrote about his country in June of that same year – 'the reality is that [...] we have ceased to be independent [...] We are as free to make a *rapprochement* with Russia as Poland is to make one with America' (Tarchiani, *Dieci Anni*, p.154) – was probably equally true, as he also believed, of France as well. Even neutrality, was probably not an option.

At the same time, it is important to make two important qualifications. The first is that the influence was not all one way. If France and Italy had to accommodate their policies to American needs, so the United States had to modify its policies to take account of French and Italian requirements, sometimes against its better judgement. We saw this most clearly in the case of Indo-China, but you can doubtless find other examples in the unit.

Secondly, the word 'imposed' does imply that what was done was done *against* the wishes of those involved. Was this really so? It is true that the French and Italian Communist parties were strongly opposed to American policies, but they were never in a majority and were in any case not always able to command the support of their own voters. This was particularly true as regards the Marshall Plan, which was tremendously popular with French and Italians alike. Elections, moreover, were free in France and Italy, which was more than could be said of eastern Europe, especially after 1947. It would, be difficult to maintain that all, or even a majority, of those who voted against the Communists did so as a result of American influence, and if the United States did do all it could to prevent the Communist opposition from coming to power, at least that opposition existed and one was free to vote for it. We may therefore observe in conclusion that, while it is true that the process of Liberation did indeed ensure that France and Italy fell into and remained in the American sphere of influence, this had less all-embracing consequences than those that followed in countries liberated by the Soviet Union. Paradoxically the real limitations on French (and British) power in the international system did not become fully evident until they tried to act independently of the USA in 1956.

References

ACHESON, D., *Present at the Creation: My Years in the State Department*, New York, Norton, 1969.

ARON, R., *The Imperial Republic: the United States and the World, 1945–1973*, London, Weidenfeld and Nicolson, 1975.

ARON, R., and LERNER, D. (eds), *La Querelle de la CED*, Paris, Armand Colin, 1956.

AURIOL, V., *Journal du Septennat, 1947–1954*, vol. I, *1947*, vol. II, *1948*, Paris, Armand Colin, 1970, 1974.

BECKER, J. and KNIPPING, F. (eds), *Power in Europe? Great Britain, France, Italy and Germany in a Postwar World, 1945–1950*, Berlin/New York, Walter de Gruyter, 1986.

BOHLEN, C.E., *Witness to History, 1929–1969*, London, Weidenfeld and Nicolson, 1973.

BYRNES, J.F., unpublished papers deposited in the Robert Muldrow Cooper Library, Clemson University, Clemson, South Carolina, USA.

EISENHOWER, D.D., *The White House Years,* vol. I, *Mandate for Change, 1953–1956*, Garden City, New York, Doubleday, 1963.

FRUS: see under United States.

DE GAULLE, C., *War Memoirs*, vol. I, *The Call to Honour, 1940–1942,* London, Collins, 1955.

JONES, J.M., *The Fifteen Weeks,* New York, Viking Press, 1953.

MONNET, J., *Memoirs*, Garden City, New York, Doubleday, 1978.

MOROZZO DELLA ROCCA, R., *La politica estera italiana e l'Unione Sovietica, 1944–1948*, Rome, La Goliardica, 1985.

PRO: see under United Kingdom.

RIOUX, J.-P., *The Fourth Republic, 1944–1958*, Cambridge, Cambridge University Press, 1987.

TARCHIANI, A., *Dieci Anni tra Roma e Washington,* Milan, Mondadori, 1955.

TRUMAN, H.S., *Memoirs,* vol. 2, *Years of Trial and Hope, 1946–1953,* London, Hodder and Stoughton, 1955.

UNITED KINGDOM, unpublished government records deposited in the Public Record Office, Kew, London.

UNITED STATES, DEPARTMENT OF STATE, *Foreign Relations of the United States, 1944*, vol.III; *Conference at Berlin (Potsdam) 1945*, vol.I; *1945*, vol.IV; *1947,* vol.III; *1952–1954*, vol.V, part 1; Washington, US Government Printing Office, 1965, 1960, 1972, 1983.

WALL, I.M., *The United States and the Making of Postwar France, 1945–1954*, Cambridge, Cambridge University Press, 1991.

UNIT 7 Art and politics in post-war France

Prepared for the course team
by Francis Frascina and Charles Harrison

Study materials

For your work on this unit you will need to refer to the following materials:

Documents and Texts 1

Plates for Unit 7

Audio-cassette 4, side A, 'Picasso and Taslitzky'

Video-cassette 1, part 2, 'Art and political engagement, 1947–53'

1 Introduction and aims

The relationship between artistic forms of expression on the one hand and political beliefs and actions on the other was a subject of concern and debate throughout the twentieth century. During the Second World War and the post-war years this relationship was called into question in particularly dramatic ways. In this unit we are concerned both with the various alternatives and problems facing artists at the time, and with the problems of interpretation and analysis which their works present in the context of a historical study. Our aim is thus twofold:

1 to introduce you to a range of art and of art-historical issues relevant to the course as a whole;

2 to raise questions relevant to the more general issue of the role of art history in interdisciplinary study of the modern period.

In this unit we concentrate on art in France because Paris was widely regarded as the metropolitan centre of modern art throughout the first half of the century, and because the problems of the relationship of art and politics were historically vivid in post-war French culture and society.

In the second section of the unit we provide some art-historical background, firstly to explain how modern artists conceived the alternative forms of practice open to them at the outset of the war, and secondly to sketch out the conditions of art under the German Occupation of France. This preliminary discussion is necessary since what was largely at stake in the artistic debates of the post-war years was the nature of precedent and the measure of continuity in a national and international tradition.

Section 3 contains a guided comparison of two paintings, one by Pablo Picasso and one by Boris Taslitzky, for which you will need Audio-cassette 4. The object of this exercise is both to acquaint you with two relevant and contrasting works of the period and to take you through some general problems of interpretation and evaluation. This leads in to a discussion of 'Forms of resistance', and of the various ways in which 'resistance' was interpreted.

The fourth section of the unit is concerned with the artistic culture of the 'Aftermath', including discussion of the question of 'realism' and its interpretation, and the various representations of post-war 'man' and post-war society offered by artists working in France around 1950. Towards the end of the unit you will need to watch Video-cassette 1, part 2, 'Art and political engagement, 1947–53', which discusses issues raised by examining characteristics of some paintings in the exhibition *Art in Europe: the Decisive Years 1945–1953,* held in the Museum of Modern Art, St Etienne, in 1988.

The reproductions

You will find reproductions of the works of art referred to in this unit and in its associated cassettes in a separate binding, *Plates for Unit 7.* This booklet is bound as a loose-leaf pad so that you can extract pictures for comparison. You should remember that these are *reproductions* of the original works of art. Their quality is inevitably variable in terms of colour, legibility of detail, and so on. You should read carefully the captions to the reproductions. They contain essential information about the work of art which will not be repeated in the unit. They indicate artist, title, date, medium, dimensions and present whereabouts (unless the information is not available). It is particularly important to note the dimensions of a work (always given as height x width). Size and scale are important factors which are rarely apparent in reproduction.

2 The politics of modernism in the visual arts

The artistic culture of modernism was an outcome and a part of the social and political changes that took place in Europe during the nineteenth century and in the first four decades of the twentieth. Specifically, the terms of reference for debate about the nature and function of the visual arts during the period under review were established in the light of early twentieth-century political history and of varying interpretations of that history. The very idea of a 'modern' – as opposed to merely contemporary – art suggests that some distinctive quality of the age is to be represented and expressed. How is this representing to be done? What are its telling images and symbols and with what techniques particularly is it associated? Answers to such questions will clearly be influenced both by fundamental beliefs about meaning in history and in political and social life and by the significance attached to certain types of artistic practice.

Speaking in very broad terms, we can say that theories of modernism in the visual arts have tended towards one or other of two apparently polar positions. According to the first, art is its own justification. It is assumed that works of art are intrinsically important and that the works of art that are most important historically are those that are most interesting, or 'best', aesthetically. The analysis of some work of art is not primarily a matter of deciding what it depicts or refers to, or what story it tells or what moral it points; rather it is a matter of response to its formal and technical qualities – its own shape, colour, form, surface texture, and so on – and not simply to what these may happen to look like or to symbolize. The value of art is seen to lie in its independence from specific historical concerns; that is to say in its relative disinterestedness. Someone committed to such a view might point to the examples of Henri Matisse and Pierre Bonnard (see Colour plates 1 and 2 in *Plates for Unit 7*), who appear to have worked in France throughout two world wars without the least shadow of either conflict having fallen perceptibly on their art. Those who accept the absolute priority of art and of aesthetic values might find something heroic in such concentration against the odds.

According to the second viewpoint, art is seen as a contingent aspect of culture, and culture as the product of social and historical existence. Art is inextricably related to social and political life and is not to be measured independently. Rather it is understood and assessed in the context of its time and according to the historical conditions and alternatives of political life. Questions of value or quality are necessarily implicated in the meanings and divisions of social and political life. Indeed, art has a special potential to represent or to express these meanings and divisions, and has thus an important role to play in assisting people to grasp the true nature of social reality. In such a view the autonomy of art is relative. This is to say that, while the practice of art has its own rules, conventions and traditions, specific social and economic relations are the factors that ultimately decide its significance.

From the later nineteenth century until at least the 1960s, and especially in France, the dominant tendency of modern art seemed to be towards the abstract and away from the illustrative and narrative. Though realist aspirations were not lost in this tendency, they were not easily recognized or represented as such. Realism was often (mistakenly) identified with *descriptiveness* and narrative in pictures, and the very possibility of modernism in painting was regularly associated with a kind of freedom from the requirement of likeness to things in the world and from the idea of art as a kind of story-telling. In the first three decades of the century, and particularly in the wake of the Russian Revolution, artistic modernism was often, though not always, associated with a challenge to the status quo, and thus with the political and indeed revolutionary left. The (modernist) idea of art as importantly *divorced* from the functions of description and narrative was associated with a critique of traditional and, especially, academic values (such as adherence to conventions of likeness and to conservative techniques and forms of subject matter). Particularly in the early years of the Russian Revolution, modernist art served to express an imaginative engagement with the possibility of new forms of expression in a transformed social world. However, this was not the view of the function of art which was transmitted from Moscow as Communist Party policy under Stalin. In the 1930s those artists and intellectuals who identified both with the Russian Revolution and with modernism thus found themselves working against the grain of the Party.

As you have already seen from earlier units, the problem of the accessibility or comprehensibility of art – debates about 'popularity and realism', 'art and the people', 'art and society', and so on – concerned the artists and intellectuals of the left throughout the period between the wars. Though the issues are complex, the problem can be put in very simple terms: modernist art was not popular with the working class and in this sense not evidently 'democratic' or 'progressive'; on the other hand, popular art was technically regressive from the standpoint of modernist interests. 'Modernist' art may have been 'oppositional', but not in the terms of the proletariat.

Three dominant tendencies in the modern art of the pre-war decade may be identified with different interpretations of the artist's position and function *vis-à-vis* the problems of art and politics. Each may in turn be connected to a different perception of the political history and direction of modern Europe, and each helped to form a distinct view of the nature and function of art during the 1940s.

1 The abstract artists

For the abstract artists – many of them already refugees either from Stalin's Russia or from Hitler's Germany and most of them associated with the Paris-based group Abstraction-Création – the artist's role was to be either a kind of philosopher without words, or a designer of ideal forms and visual prototypes for some coming democratic society, or a combination of the two (see works by the Frenchman, Hélion, and the Belgian, Vantongerloo, Plates 1–2). For them, modern art's popularity was a future prospect. The position of the abstractionists was largely underwritten by that strain of transcendental and utopian socialism which was more a cultural than a political force in early twentieth-century Europe. Their belief that social change is initiated by philosophical or 'spiritual' change continued a strain of Hegelian idealism which had long been overthrown in the minds of others by the materialist critique of Marx.

2 The Realists

The Realists' view of the function of art followed Communist Party policy. For them the business of art was to represent the proletariat, its history and its destiny, and to serve its interests; it followed that form and content must be comprehensible and vivid (see Plate 3, Taslitzky, and Plate 4, Gruber). For the Realists, post-revolutionary Russia represented the achievement of that Communist state which Marx had foreseen as the goal of socialism. For those concerned to demonstrate their solidarity with the achievements of the Revolution and their commitment to the work of expanding it to all countries, the cultural policy of Stalin's Russian state was the model for progressive activity in the arts. As you know from Units 1 and 3, Socialist Realism was promoted as official Party policy towards the arts from 1934 onwards. The works of Gerasimov (Plate 5) and Ioganson (Plate 6) provide two examples of Soviet painting consistent with this policy.

The attraction and authority of Socialist Realism should not surprise us. The aspiration to Realism had an impressive critical pedigree in the art and literature of the nineteenth century – Courbet's paintings being prime examples (Plate 7). And in the political climate of Europe during the later thirties and early forties, it was not easy for committed socialists to entertain the idea that Stalinist 'Socialism' was a *betrayal* rather than a fulfilment of the ideas of Marx and the achievements of the Russian Revolution. Even for those who continued to identify with Russia as the source and centre of European socialism, however, the interpretation of realism was to remain a contentious matter. We shall return to the problems of realism in art in section 4.

3 The Surrealists

For the Surrealists, art was a weapon to be used against its own consumers. In the words of André Breton, principal theorist of the group, painting was a 'lamentable expedient' in the service of revolution, a means to haunt the bourgeoisie with its own repressed fears, fantasies and desires, a constant demonstration of the irrationality of its concept of reason, an assertion of the power of the 'Surreal' over the real. A typical example is Masson's *In the Tower of Sleep*, 1938 (Plate 9). In Surrealist theory, an analysis of the technical implications and possibilities of modern art was joined to a critique of the repressive nature of bourgeois society, the latter informed by the social theories of Marx and the psychoanalytical theories of Freud. Among the collective strategies adopted by the Surrealists were forms of exhibition and installation designed to frustrate the normal expectations of the bourgeois public and to undermine traditional concepts of the 'art object'. See, for instance, the installation views of the International Exhibition of Surrealism in 1938 (Plates 10 and 11). For Breton, the Cubism of Picasso (as in Plate12) represented an open break with the 'treacherous nature of tangible entities'. It followed that 'The plastic work of art, in order to respond to the undisputed necessity of thoroughly revising all real values, will either refer to a *purely interior model* or cease to exist' (*Le Surréalisme et la peinture*, 1928; translated in *What is Surrealism?*). In other words, if art was to provide any pictorial content, this would be drawn not from the ordinary appearance of the external world, but from the materials of imagination, fantasy and dreaming. This material was to be released by means of 'automatist' techniques designed to frustrate the conventional controls of taste and orderly composition. Popularity was not an issue for the Surrealists. Rather the *un*popularity of modern art was a guarantee of critical virtue in the face of the repressive tastes and protocols of bourgeois society.

The Surrealist group divided in the later twenties over the issue of membership of the PCF and of acceptance of its directives. André Breton and Louis Aragon were among leading members of the group who joined the PCF in 1927, only to meet accusations from within the Party that Surrealism was a romantic, idealist and counter-revolutionary movement. Aragon's commitment to a notion of Party solidarity was to cause a complete breach with his former Surrealist associates in 1932 and to lead him to support the cause of Socialist Realism from 1934 onwards. (He was present at the Soviet Writers Congress in 1934 when the official policy of Socialist Realism was first publicly promulgated.) For Breton and the remaining majority of the group, however, resistance to the requirement of programmatic realism was also resistance to what they saw as a dogmatic tendency within the Party. Breton was one of that relatively small number of western intellectuals who correctly perceived Stalinism as a counter-revolutionary misrepresentation of communism. He was expelled from the Party in 1933 along with other Surrealists and in 1938 co-authored with the exiled Leon Trotsky a document calling for a 'Free Revolutionary Art'. This proclaimed a cultural policy along the lines of Trotsky's perpetual revolution and made clear that the doctrinaire aspects of both fascist and Stalinist regimes were hostile not only to socialism but also to the integrity and freedom of cultural forms. During the war the Surrealists were regarded as beyond the pale by conservatives and Communists alike.

3 Wartime practices

Art in the Occupation

The official German attitude towards modern art was made clear shortly before the outbreak of war. In 1937 the Nazi party staged an exhibition of 'Degenerate Art' in Munich, including under that title the works of many of the principal contributors to the modern movement, alongside paintings by the mentally ill. The productions of 'degenerates, Bolsheviks and Jews' were contrasted with the academic and neo-classical styles of 'true German art' shown in another exhibition in Munich during the same year. For many conservatives and even liberals in France, the fall of the Republic was an opportunity to re-establish those 'basic truths' with which they felt at home, and there were those in France (as there were in England) who assented willingly enough to the spirit and the substance of the attacks by Hitler and Goebbels on modern art and modern artists. The apologists for Pétain's Révolution Nationale drew very similar contrasts between the 'degenerate', 'decadent' and 'anarchistic' art of the pre-war avant-gardes, and those forms of culture by which traditional values and 'la gloire française' were to be reasserted.

This tended to mean the restoration of classical styles and academic competences and the uncritical celebration of public authorities. Although France had become known abroad before the war as the centre of development of modern art, the administrative structures of the state concerned with the production and evaluation of art had remained virtually unchanged since the early nineteenth century. The reigning aesthetic was academic; that is to say its paradigm of practice was a figurative art in a classical style, such as Rohner's *The Drowned Man* (Plate 8). The modern tradition had developed alongside this structure and in relative independence from it, constituting not simply an alternative resource of artistic style and technique, but an alternative resource of meaning and value – a virtual alternative culture. Reassertion of the 'authority' of the academic tradition under the conditions of the Occupation was an inevitable aspect of the attempt to reimpose order, authority and unity on the national culture as a whole. It should not surprise us that the chosen stylistic form of artistic 'order' coincided closely with the official German model.

You should now turn to *Documents and Texts 1* and read the extract from 'Marshal Art' and from 'A general policy for the fine arts' (items 19 and 20), which exemplify Vichy cultural policy as discussed above. The style approved by Hitler and by the Nazis was forcefully demonstrated in an exhibition of sculpture by the German artist Arno Breker held at the Orangerie in Paris in 1942 (see Plates 14 and 15). Pétain wrote to congratulate the artist on the exhibition and received a work from him as a gift. An enthusiastic catalogue introduction was provided by Jean-Marc Campagne, a critic and official of the Beaux-Arts (Office of Fine Arts) who had written in a collaborationist journal in the previous year that Paris had no reason to envy Berlin if it could match the effort evident 'everywhere else'. On the occasion of the exhibition a supporting 'Committee of Honour' was composed of members of the Vichy administration, writers, architects and artists. The artist-members, with the addition of the sculptor Aristide Maillol (see Plate 16), had all travelled to Germany the previous year on a 'study voyage' organized on the initiative of Goebbels. Among them were several painters who would have been counted among the moderns, and who might thus have been seen as contributors to the 'decadence' of French culture at the time of the fall of Paris: André Derain (Plate 17), André Dunoyer de Segonzac (Plate 18), Cornelius van Dongen (Plate 19), Othon Friesz (Plate 20) and Maurice de Vlaminck (Plate 21).

We should beware of reading the above as simple evidence of collaboration. Breker had lived and worked in Paris from 1927 to 1934 and had made many acquaintances among French artists during this time. The 1920s had seen a revival of classical styles in the hands of many French artists who were far from conservative figures – Picasso (Plate 13), Derain and Maillol among them. And it had been an item of faith among the community of modern artists in France before the war that art was a cosmopolitan practice and that the presence of artists from abroad (Picasso notable among them) was both a cause and a measure of the cultural ascendancy of Paris. The maintenance of contact on the level of art was likely to have been seen by some – perhaps naively – as an alternative rather than a form of submission to the ethos of collaboration, and also, perhaps, as a means of assisting the release of French artists interned in both France and Germany.

We should also beware of perceiving a preoccupation with order and with the national tradition as the concern of academicians and conservative administrators alone. Rather, both collaborators and those who identified with the political combat of the Resistance claimed authorization from national values and from 'l'esprit français'. Both claimed to be defending a true national tradition against the false and foreign. The idea that the French tradition was a classical tradition had been advanced by modern architects and artists associated with the Purist movement between the wars. Now the most vocal defences of modern art were those that drew attention to a distinctively 'French' orderliness, rationality, clarity and objectivity. Bernard Dorival, curator of the Museum of Modern Art, Paris, described the 'French genius' in terms of 'reason united with intuition to render a serene account of the world', and defended the notion of a 'pure painting' based on logic rather than chance (in *Les Problèmes de la peinture française contemporaine*, 1946; a collection of essays written 1940–44). A similar view was presented by the painter and theorist André Lhote, who was to be Fine Arts correspondent of the post-war publication, *Les Lettres françaises* (see Plate 23). A former Cubist and member of Abstraction-Création, Lhote treated both the legacy of Cubism and the status of Picasso with circumspection, referring rather to an 'authentic' French tradition as continued and exemplified in the works of Matisse (Colour plate 1), Bonnard (Colour plate 2) and Braque (Plate 24) (*Peinture d'abord*, 1942). These latter painters were generally singled out during the war by those like Lhote who stressed the independence of art from political considerations and who identified a quintessentially French art as one in which 'feeling', 'order' and 'craftsmanship' were the paramount virtues. Such terms were not so different from those employed by Pétain's cultural officials, and it was under such an interpretation of the 'French tradition' that the academic and the modern – or an edited version of the modern – were brought to coexistence during the years of the Occupation. So long as it could be contained within a concept of national and racial virtue and orderliness, the business of modern art could be allowed to continue in Salons, dealers' galleries and auction houses. Indeed, the Parisian art market flourished during the Occupation.

In August 1942 the Museum of Modern Art in Paris was reopened by Louis Hautecoeur, Pétain's nominee as Secretary General of Fine Arts, in the presence of German representatives. The display included works by many of the principal French modernists – Matisse, Bonnard and Braque notable among them – alongside examples of academic classicism. For the most part the conservative critique of modernism proceeded on relatively simplistic terms. Still lifes, landscapes and portrait busts in the 'modern manner' continued to be exhibited and sold throughout the Occupation. The works that attracted unfavourable attention were generally those whose subjects were deemed either objectionable or incomprehensible, or both. According to the critical framework elaborated both by conservatives and by liberal defenders of the modern, such works were not properly French. Those who exhibited them took a certain risk. Thus an exhibition of gouaches and paintings by Wassily Kandinsky at the Galerie Jeanne Bucher was suspended on the grounds of its degeneracy in July 1942. But then Kandinsky, besides being a founding figure of abstract art, was a Russian emigré, and an artist whose work had already been banned in Germany (see Plates 25 and 26).

Picasso was a conspicuous omission from the Museum of Modern Art exhibition in 1942, though he remained in Paris from August 1940 throughout the Occupation. His status was equivocal. A foreigner by birth, he was also the most prestigious of modern artists in France before the war. In June of 1942 he and his work were virulently attacked by the painter Vlaminck, one of those who had been on the artists' journey to Germany the previous year. Vlaminck accused Picasso of having dragged French painting into indescribable confusion, and of bearing the responsibility for suffocating the spirit of creation, faith and sincerity in work and life. For Vlaminck, Cubism, the development in art for which Picasso (Plate 12) and Braque were largely responsible and by which Vlaminck himself had been affected some thirty years before, was 'a perversity of the mind, incompetent, amoral, loved by pederasts' (*Comoedia*, 6 June 1942). In 1943 a commentator noted with approval that 'Vlaminck triumphs everywhere – there is hardly a picture dealer in Paris who has not one of his works [...] in the window. We are availed of a kind of permanent Vlaminck exhibition throughout Paris' (Pierre Jeannet, *Je suis partout*, 3 October 1943, quoted in Dorléac, *Histoire de l'art*, p.126) (see Plate 21). It seems that Vlaminck's work was found rich in those qualities of 'feeling', 'eloquence' and 'virility' which were dwelt on in the art criticism of the Occupation. If there is a lesson to be learned from this episode it concerns the critical price that is paid when a defensive national pride is allowed to set the terms of reference for culture. In the first four decades of the century, it could be argued, no one had done more than Picasso to secure the continued vitality of modern French art. As Bertrand Dorléac has written, 'It is in the anti-modern discourse of this period that we rediscover the traditional grounds of exclusion: xenophobia, anti-semitism, anti-communism [...] which is not to say that there exists no discourse against modernity which is exempt from these notions' (Dorléac, p.105).

One further exhibition deserves mention. In May 1941 the Galerie Braun staged a show under the title 'Twenty young painters in the French tradition'. Though this exhibition was staged with the backing of the official association Jeune France, and was passed by the German representatives of the Propaganda Staffel (the effective bureau of censorship of the occupying power), it was to be represented after the Liberation as an act of resistance against the German presence. This was perhaps in part because the post-war School of Paris was to be identified with artists associated with this exhibition and its aftermath, such as Bazaine (Colour plate 3) and Lapicque (Colour plate 4). The painter Jean Bazaine, co-organizer of the exhibition, wrote in the *Nouvelle Revue française* ('Guerres et Evasions', Paris, April 1941) to remind his readers that 'French painting has for thirty years been our sole act of presence in the world, and one of the rare living ferments of our epoch'. The military defeat of France, he urged, 'should not be allowed to lead by extension to a general rout of all that our civilization has given of the best'. What was required, he believed, was the continuation of that tradition of modernist experiment which was the 'French tradition'. A year later the critic Gaston Diehl identified this group of young artists, then aged between 30 and 45, as a distinct generation. Among those he mentioned were Bazaine, Maurice Estève (Plate 22), Alfred Manessier (Plate 27), Charles Lapicque (Plate 28), Édouard Pignon (Plate 29) and André Fougeron (Colour plate 5). Generally speaking, what these artists shared at the time was a recognition of the importance of the formal lessons of the Cubism of Braque and Picasso and of the supposed 'liberation' of colour in the painting of Matisse and the so-called Fauves (an avant-garde group in Paris at the beginning of the century). Within this loose principle of aesthetic association some artists, such as Bazaine and Manessier, were developing in the direction of extreme abstraction, while others, the Communists Pignon and Fougeron notable among them, were to become committed 'realists'.

Wartime themes: a study of two paintings

For this section you should work through Audio-cassette 4, side A, 'Picasso and Taslitzky'. The cassette consists of a discussion and exercises concentrating on two paintings, Pablo Picasso's *The Charnel House*, 1944–48, and Boris Taslitzky's *The Little Camp at Buchenwald*, 1945 (Colour plates 6 and 7). You should have these plates available so that you can refer to them while you listen to the cassette. You will also need the following plates for background information and for comparison:

photographs of stages of Picasso, *The Charnel House*, 1945 (Plates 31(A) and (B))

Picasso, *The Aficionado*, 1912 (Plate 12)

Picasso, *Guernica*, 1937 (Plate 32)
Picasso, *The Milliner's Workshop*, 1927 (Plate 33)
Taslitzky, *Buchenwald*, 1944 (Plate 34)
Gerasimov, *Collective-Farm Holiday*, 1937 (Plate 5)
Ioganson, *The Interrogation of Communists*, 1933 (Plate 6)

Forms of resistance

For those artists in France whose production could be contained within an orderly image of Race, Country and Nation, it was at least possible to continue working and exhibiting during the Occupation. For the remainder, many of them of foreign origin and thus not eligible to contribute to the self-regeneration of French culture, there were three principal alternatives. The first was exile, with New York as the preferred venue. This was the alternative adopted by many of the most prominent writers and artists associated with the Surrealist group, among them André Masson (Plate 35), Yves Tanguy (Plate 36), Salvador Dali, André Breton and Max Ernst (German born, but a resident in Paris for most of the period between the wars; Plate 38). They could hardly have hoped for any form of shelter in France, either from the occupying forces or from the newly empowered representatives of that bourgeois culture they had so determinedly pilloried. (Breton was briefly arrested in Marseilles at the time of a visit there by Marshal Pétain.) The Surrealists were known in New York as a result of a large and successful exhibition of 'Fantastic Art, Dada and Surrealism' which had been held at the Museum of Modern Art, New York, in 1936, and after the fall of Paris the privately organized American Emergency Rescue Committee made contact with Breton among others. For the duration of the war the Surrealists formed a virtual colony in exile in New York, where they contributed to a receptive and rapidly developing modernist culture. This is not to say, however, that there was no Surrealist presence in France during the Occupation. Breton broadcast to the French through the Voice of America, while there were many members of the movement, including Paul Eluard, who remained in France. Through writings and illustrations in clandestine publications (notably the review *La Main à plume*, 'The Hand with a Pen', first published in 1941) and through occasional brief exhibitions of work such as Brauner's *The Ideal Man*, 1943 (Plate 37), in relatively unfrequented galleries, the Surrealists kept alive a determined form of resistance to the idea of a rational French tradition and a decorous and purified culture. They did so almost entirely without critical support.

The second alternative was to adopt the position taken by Wassily Kandinsky (Plates 25 and 26) who, in the words of another painter, Alberto Magnelli, was 'aware of the drama of man, but in silence', not wishing that this drama should find expression in his painting, but rather that he should 'give joy, serenity, and by his paintings touch the spirit in order to stimulate the rediscovery of hope, the immaterial, poetry and the sublimity of colours' (quoted in Dorléac, *Histoire de l'art*, p.127).

Figure 7.1 *Artists in exile; photograph taken by George Platt Lynes on the occasion of an exhibition at the Pierre Matisse Gallery, New York, March 1942. From left to right, first row: Matta Echaurren, Ossip Zadkine, Yves Tanguy, Max Ernst, Marc Chagall, Fernand Léger; second row: André Breton, Piet Mondrian, André Masson, Amédée Ozenfant, Jacques Lipchitz, Pavel Tchelitchew, Kurt Seligmann, Eugene Berman. (Photograph courtesy The Museum of Modern Art, New York)*

The third alternative was consciously and actively to give expression, through art, to the tragedy of Occupation and/or to the spirit of Resistance. The line to be drawn here is potentially a fine one. It is not clear that this alternative is wholly distinct from the second one. It might be that Kandinsky would have claimed that he was doing precisely the same thing by insisting that a free and autonomous art stands in opposition to all forms of repression – a familiar enough defence of artistic modernism during the rise of fascism in the 1930s. It does indeed seem that the exhibition of works by Kandinsky was offensive to the occupying authority. What we are referring to here, however, are those forms of art that are more explicitly engaged with historical themes, which appear to derive their imagery and their representational materials from contemporary conditions, and which mobilize these materials in such a way as to give them a morally unambiguous meaning and expression. (That said, we should also acknowledge that among the artists who did just this, some were working in exile. André Masson's *La Résistance*, Plate 35, is a case in point.)

Exercise Look now at:

Fautrier, *Hostage No. 3*, 1943–45 (Colour plate 11)

Gruber, *Job*, 1944 (Plate 39)

Fougeron, *Rue de Paris '43*, 1943 (Colour plate 5).

Consider the following questions. (The questions are related and may be best considered together rather than in turn.)

1. Does each of these works unambiguously express the (or a) meaning of Occupation and Resistance. Is any one more ambiguous than the others?
2. Does the title of each work – rather than its specific pictorial qualities and references – serve to give it a particular meaning and relevance?
3. To what extent might the apparent meaning of each work have depended on the context in which it was seen?

Discussion It is clearly virtually impossible to consider the meanings of these works in isolation from the context of their production and exhibition and from the associations made by their titles. The extent to which each may be said to refer unambiguously to themes of Occupation or Resistance is a matter of the relative specificity of the image and of the title. The Fautrier, for instance, might simply be seen as a somewhat crude painting of a head, or even as a semi-abstract work which merely resembles a head, were it not for the title. To ask how closely the work is connected to its title is perhaps to ask about the work's 'sincerity' – to inquire whether some experience of the Occupation or of Resistance featured at some level as a necessary cause of the painting (which is one of a long series of 'hostages', the majority of them even less descriptively head-like than the example reproduced). Certainly, on their first showing after the Liberation in 1944, Fautrier's wartime works were widely seen as testimonials to France's sufferings.

The symbols used by Fougeron are more detailed and more explicit. We do not need the legend 'Rue de Paris '43' to identify this as a scene of urban poverty. His forms of stylization, emphasis, lighting, and so on serve to endow the painting with a certain sense of attitude or message. Clearly, though, much of the painting's poignancy derives from its status as a representation of life under Occupation, which the legend serves to affirm. Fougeron painted two versions of the picture and both were publicly exhibited in Paris in 1943, one at the Salon des Tuileries and the other at the Salon d'Automne. Despite a visit to the former by officers of the Propaganda Staffel, the work attracted no more than one brief condemnatory review.

The Gruber might be said to lie somewhere between the other two images. Though the technique involves a more descriptively detailed treatment than Fougeron's, the solitary nude, despairing figure is a symbol open to a relatively wide range of interpretations – a range that the title 'Job' does little to narrow, since the name already stands as a token of solitary and undeserved suffering. To see the painting as historically vivid, we need to read it in the context of the Occupation. This reading is perhaps encouraged by the text lettered on the depicted piece of paper: '*Maintenant encore ma plainte est une revolte, et pourtant ma main supprime mes sanglots*' ('Now once more my cry is a revolt, and yet my hand suppresses my sobs'). ❑

The questions asked above are important for two reasons, one methodological and the other historical. From a methodological point of view we need to be able to distinguish, so far as possible, between the reading *out* of meaning from the observable formal properties, images and details of a work of art, and the reading *in* of meanings we expect or hope to find, but which the work does not actually carry. Of course, the two forms of reading are not wholly distinct or distinguishable. Works of art confront a world of expectations and interests and they have their existence largely as objects of interpretation. At some level, however, we want what we say to be testable against the observable properties of the thing we say it about, and the test will not be a real one unless our expectations, interests and cherished interpretations are at risk in the outcome. The question of the 'sincerity' of Fautrier's work is related to this issue. If he had actually called his paintings 'Hostages' in a spirit of opportunism, so that people would read into them a solidarity with Resistance martyrs which he had no actual right to claim, would his opportunism be in some way uncoverable as a quality, or rather a form of impairment, of his work? If we want to be able to talk about the (political) meaning and significance of works of art, we have to be able to confront the form of problem of which this is an example.

The historical point is related to the methodological one. Following the Liberation and the attendant 'épuration' (purging or cleansing) of French culture, retrospective distinctions between the arts of collaboration and of resistance respectively were matters of great significance to the national self-image. On the one hand it was seen as necessary to weed out those who had brought dishonour on the 'tradition' of French art; on the other hand, the greater the number of artists who could be seen as having practised some form of cultural resistance, the greater the pride to be attached to that tradition and the more morally secure the grounds of its continuation. Clearly any artist whose work could feasibly be interpreted as a form of resistance was now likely to be accepted as an honourable representative of the national culture. This category included not simply those like Taslitzky, Gruber and Fougeron whose anti-fascist credentials were impeccable and whose symbolism was more or less overt, but also the entire group of the 'Jeunes Peintres de Tradition Française' ('Young Painters in the French Tradition') and all those who had remained 'independent' either under the Occupation or in exile. Organized by the Veterans' Association of French Partisans and held at the Musée National d'Art Moderne in 1946, a large exhibition on the theme 'Art and Resistance' celebrated an unbowed artistic culture (Plates 40 (A)–(B) and 41). The Taslitzky and Picasso paintings discussed on the audio-cassette were both exhibited. Besides these and the forms of art discussed in this section, the exhibition included work by figures such as Pierre Bonnard, who had spent the years 1939–45 in isolation at Le Cannet, near the Mediterranean, painting nudes, flowers and views from his studio window (Colour plate 2).

In the light of the discussion of Fautrier's *Hostage* there is one more point to be made. It should be clear that it was not actually our intention to impugn his motives. It is important, however, to be aware – as artists themselves often are – of the ways in which myths and preconceptions tend to condition interpretation. The Romantic conception of the artist as a solitary and uncompromised medium for 'the truth' has continued to function during the modern period, and was absorbed into a modernist conception of the moral and political autonomy of art. In the wake of the Liberation, the concept of the artist as an 'independent' – as a morally autonomous, and therefore uncompromised, figure – was clearly one that served to enlarge the ranks of those who could be seen as having contributed *culturally* to the French Resistance, and thus to the honour of the nation.

4 The aftermath

The Occupation and Liberation had one all-important consequence for the visual arts in France. The authority of the academic was virtually destroyed, as it had been implicated with the collaborationist regime. Furthermore, the status of Paris as the centre of modern art was now affirmed not only by the aficionados of culture but also by the curious representatives of the victorious powers. For those for whom the fall of Paris had been first and foremost a *cultural* disaster, the survival of modern art in Paris was a measure of the survival of western civilization. An exhibition of the work of Picasso and Matisse was exported to the Victoria and Albert Museum, London, in December 1945, followed six months later by Braque and Georges Rouault at the Tate Gallery. Such shows were received as signs that all was well by those who supported the cause of modern art. A year later the American critic Clement Greenberg paid tribute to the continuing centrality of French art (albeit in a judgement he was to withdraw some eighteen months later):

> The School of Paris remains still the creative fountain-head of modern art, and its every move is decisive for advanced artists everywhere else – who are advanced precisely because they show the capacity to absorb and extend the preoccupations of that nerve-centre and farthest nerve-end of the modern consciousness which is French art.
>
> (*The Nation*, 29 June 1946)

In the early 1980s, the French modern art of the post-war years was surveyed in two major retrospective exhibitions, *Paris-Paris 1937–1957*, at the Pompidou Centre, Paris, in 1981, and Aftermath: France 1945–54; *New Images of Man*, at the Barbican Art Gallery, London, in 1982. Both exhibitions seem to have been intended in part to reclaim for the Paris of the forties and early fifties some of the status in modern art history which it lost to New York during the later fifties and the sixties. These exhibitions and their substantial accompanying catalogues have divided the art of the period into certain broad compartments or categories. For the sake of simplicity we have reduced these to three principal groupings.

1 The older generation of modernists whose reputations reached back well beyond the war – those referred to by Greenberg as the 'School of Paris'. Principal among these were those acknowledged during the Occupation as the masters of the modern French tradition, Matisse, Bonnard and Braque, together with Picasso, now reintegrated into the 'School of Paris', and Léger (Colour plate 8), disqualified from public recognition during the Occupation, perhaps on the grounds of his manifest sympathy with the industrial working class, but greeted on his return from exile in America as an uncompromised French master.

2 The proponents of various forms of 'realism'. This group may be divided into those, such as Taslitzky (Colour plate 7 and Plate 42) and Fougeron (Colour plates 9 and 10, and Plates 43 and 44) who were associated with a form of Socialist Realism consistent with Party policy; those such as Léger (Colour plate 8 and Plate 47), Pignon (Plate 30), and Picasso (Colour plates 12 and 13, and Plates 45 and 46), whose work at the time could wholly or in part be included under a definition of 'social realism' and who, while they were not bound by the cultural directives of the Party, were Party members during the later 1940s and 1950s; and a few others, identified in one way or another with the political left, who painted in a variety of figurative styles.

3 A wide range of artists practising in a variety of overlapping 'post-war' styles, some more and some less evidently continuous with the interests of the pre-war avant-gardes. The factor that united them was their rejection of the possibility of 'objectivity' in art, and their unwillingness or inability to submit to the conventions either of naturalism or of Social Realism. This category may be roughly subdivided into the following:

   (a) Painters interested in deliberately primitive and 'naive' styles and in the idea of 'Art Brut' ('raw' or 'crude art'). The leader and best known representative of this tendency was Jean Dubuffet (Colour plate 15 and Plate 48); others included Gaston Chaissac (Plate 50) and Roger Bissière (Plate 51).

   (b) Artists working with the legacy of Surrealism (Plate 52) and with the idea of fantasy and the unconscious as sources of pictorial imagery, among them Picasso, Masson and the South American Roberto Matta (Plate 49).

   (c) Painters seen as 'Existentialists', as 'without traditional roots', and as working at the 'frontiers of identity'. Art-critical jargon

> apart, these were generally painters who used relatively improvisory techniques to produce pictures which were both abstract and informal. Many of them were of foreign birth. Included within this tendency are Fautrier (Colour plate 11), Georges Mathieu (Plate 53), the American Sam Francis (Plate 54) and the German expatriates Hans Hartung (Plate 56) and Wols (Wolfgang Schulze) (Plate 58).

You may have noticed one feature common to all three of the major groupings: Picasso's name appears in each. With the Liberation it seems that his status was once again seen as 'heroic'. In October 1944, the same month that he joined the PCF, he was accorded a retrospective exhibition of seventy-four works at the Salon d'Automne, redesignated the 'Salon de la Libération' and held at the Grand Palais in Paris. In the same Salon there was also a section of work by the 'Jeunes Peintres de Tradition Française', many of whom owed a considerable debt to Picasso's example. The conjunction was significant. Both the strength of Picasso's own continuing presence – for nearly fifty years – within the Parisian art world and the manifest variety of his work helped to render complex, if not insecure, those conceptions of the 'modern French tradition' which had hardened into a virtual orthodoxy during the Occupation.

During the post-war years the nature of that tradition became once again a matter of open and public debate. The sides were drawn along lines related to those sketched out at the beginning of section 2, though again it needs to be stressed that many artists – Picasso notable and influential among them – found positions for themselves between the two extremes. In the next section we shall review those post-war debates on realism within which the authority of the 'School of Paris' was called into question, but first we want to look briefly at the post-war School of Paris and at 'Art Brut'.

The very designation 'School of Paris' implies the supposed authenticity of its representatives – their rightful inheritance of the 'tradition française'. As was suggested earlier, it was indeed from within the abstract or near-abstract tendency of the former Jeunes Peintres that the 'official avant-garde' was formed after the war. André Lhote (Plate 57) played the role of a senior liberal in helping to articulate critical policy. 'Both in his public lectures from 1946–1948, and in his role as teacher at his painting academy, André Lhote advocated a conciliatory form of modernism, capable of soothing contemporary neuroses' (Viatte, 'Aftermath: a new generation', in *Aftermath* catalogue, p.12).

The typical School of Paris painting after the war was vaguely figurative or wholly abstract, with a relatively shallow illusion of depth and a brightly coloured surface divided either by brushy strokes of paint or by a pattern of intersecting planes, as if the colour and brushwork of Matisse and Bonnard had been applied to the Cubist framework of Braque and Picasso. This is most evident in the work of artists such as Bazaine (Colour plate 3), and Lapicque (Colour plate 4). Such painting was indeed in an unbroken modern tradition, but it was hardly a speaking vessel for the history out of which it had emerged. In fact this very deficiency may have been what ensured its success with those for whom the 'tradition française' was a tradition of artistic *disengagement* from politics and morality. Practices that are pursued separately from historical conditions, however, tend rapidly towards the academic.

In the aftermath of the trauma of Occupation, one alternative to the pursuit of the 'tradition française' was to make a kind of moral virtue of the very lack of tradition; strategically to assume a state of primitivism, in which the only appropriate form of art is an 'Art Brut'; in the words of the dramatist Antonin Artaud, to assume that 'We are not yet in the world. [...] Things have not yet been created, the *raison d'être* has not yet been found' (Plate 55). Referring back to the moment of the mid forties, one of the supporters of Art Brut, Michel Tapié, wrote:

> One needed temperaments ready to break up everything, whose works were disturbing, stupefying, full of magic and violence to reroute the public. To reroute into a real future that mass of a so-called advanced public, hardened like a sclerosis around a cubism finished long ago (but much prolonged), a misplaced geometric abstraction, and a limited puritanism which above anything else blocks the way to any possible, authentically fertile future.
>
> (Tapié, 1953, quoted in Viatte, in *Aftermath* catalogue, p.13)

The notion of a lack of *raison d'être* in fact harks back to the anti-rationalism of the pre-war Surrealist movement, to which Artaud had been a contributor, while the idea of an art 'full of magic and violence to reroute the public' might well have been taken from the writings of André Breton. On his return from America in 1946, Breton was indeed to be influential in drawing attention to the primitivist tendency of post-war French art, in supporting 'naive' painters, and in connecting the mentally ill and the primitive in terms of the liberty of their imagination. In accordance with the precedents of Surrealist theory, the 'liberty' envisaged was a form of ideal freedom from the kinds of repression and self-censorship applied in the processes of civilization and socialization.

The term 'Art Brut' was used in 1947 for an exhibition of the artefacts which the painter Jean Dubuffet had been collecting since 1945, 'works of art' produced by those supposedly free from the constraints and preconceptions of culture, whether 'naives', 'primitives', psychotics, eccentrics or children (Plates 59 and 60). In 1948 a 'compagnie de l'Art Brut' was formed, with Dubuffet, Breton and Tapié among its founders. Its aims, in Dubuffet's words, were: 'To seek out the artistic productions of humble people which have a special quality of personal creation, spontaneity and liberty with regard to convention and received ideas. To draw the public's attention towards this sort of work, to create a taste for it and encourage it to flourish' ('Notice sur la Compagnie de l'Art Brut', in Dubuffet, *Prospectus*, p.489; quoted in *Aftermath*, p.18). Dubuffet was thus both following a pre-war precedent set by the Surrealists, in promoting 'uncultured' production as a critique of cultured aesthetics, and offering the idea of an art free from culture and from historical conscience as a kind of solution to the dilemmas of the post-war avant-garde in France. His own paintings of the time were sophisticated, thickly painted works in which naive and childlike styles of representation were used to give expressive force and character to portraits and figures (Colour plate 15 and Plate 61). It was a highly successful formula.

The problem of realism

In Unit 1 you considered competing definitions of 'realism' discussed by Marcus with reference to Italian neo-realist films (*Documents and Texts 1*, item 2). You may wish to re-read your notes on that text and recall the options for the left during 1943–48 which were outlined in Unit 3. Certainly the meaning of realism was fiercely contested among artists and critics from the mid 1930s onwards. With particular respect to developments in painting, we can isolate four different (though interconnected and overlapping) ways in which the concept of realism was and may be employed.

1. The normal 'on the streets' sense of the term is to mean 'lifelike' or 'referring to life'. We say 'that picture looks very realistic', meaning that we can easily recognize what it looks *like*. In this sense the term implies a judgement of competence. We are saying that the artist has done a good job of making the picture correspond to our view of the thing it depicts – a view for which the development of photography has often provided seeming confirmation. It might appear that this is a straightforward enough issue, but the history of modern art tells us that it is not. For example, when Gustave Courbet exhibited his 'Realist' paintings of peasants and country scenes in the nineteenth century (see, for example, *Burial at Ornans*, Plate 7), they were contemptuously dismissed by leading critics on the grounds firstly that they were incompetent and secondly that life was not like that. 'Life', presumably, was as it appeared in proper and 'tasteful' paintings. There are two lessons to be learned. The first is that we see in terms of certain conventions, assumptions and expectations and in terms of certain fixed measures of competence, and we tend to call art 'realistic' or 'true to life' when it confirms them. The second is that we tend to dismiss paintings as incompetent – as badly done – when we are unable to perceive *how* they are realistic, that is, when they don't confirm our assumptions. This suggests the need for a more sophisticated view of realism than one simply based on judgements of photographic 'lifelikeness'.
2. The second view of realism, therefore, acknowledges that our 'reality' is always relative, that it is built up out of a series of beliefs and ideas and representations, which may or may not correspond to 'the truth' or 'the real'. Our assumptions about reality are in constant need of correction. This process of correction is what we mean by learning. Art has its part to play in this process, not by affirming any fixed set of assumptions about what the world looks like, but rather the reverse, by offering a challenge to any system of representation which has become fixed, academic and dogmatic. According to this view, therefore, realism is a *critical* mode and one that is likely to involve constant changes in the terms of reference of style, technique and competence.

Within this concept of realism, a figurative painting or a photographic image is not necessarily any more realistic than an abstract painting. The former may simply enshrine a fixed and redundant set of assumptions about the natural or social world, while the latter may, as a thing in its own right, serve critically – and thus 'realistically' – to challenge established principles of order, harmony and good taste. The problem we are left with is that if reality is relative, what authority attaches to the critical revision of representation? Why should any one set of assumptions be abandoned for another? To answer this question we need some explanation of the means of generation of *false* views of reality. If we can show how false views are produced and acquired, we can explain why they should be abandoned.

3 This is where 'Social Realism' comes in. According to socialist theory the dominant representation of reality in any given society will be the one that favours and serves the interests of the ruling class. In this sense it will be partial and therefore inadequate or false. The aim of Social Realism is to correct and to overcome this partiality; that is, to achieve a representation of reality that engages with the diversity of human experience and human interests. No picture can lay claim to realism if it does not engage with these conditions. Claims by abstract artists to be dealing with 'a form of life more real than life itself' are seen as irredeemably *idealistic*. Talk of 'spiritual forms of expression', and so forth, simply covers up the kinds of abstraction of meaning from social life which are performed by those who don't want or don't know how to get their hands dirty. A 'French tradition' conceived in terms of such abstractions can only be a *bourgeois* tradition, and will thus be unrepresentative.

4 The notion of '*Social* Realism' is broadly compatible with both the critical spirit and the humanist tenor of Marxism. As you are aware from studying the Marcus text in Unit 1 and texts by Togliatti in Unit 3, in 1934 in Moscow the idea of *Social* Realism was codified, by Zhdanov, into the Stalinist doctrine of *Socialist* Realism. This was to remain official Communist Party policy, supposedly binding on Party members everywhere, until the dissolution of the Cominform (Communist Information Bureau) in 1956. Among the other speakers at the Soviet Writers Congress in 1934 were Louis Aragon and André Malraux. Zhdanov's doctrine involved a vulgarization of the theories of Marx and was not so much incompatible with as explicitly antagonistic to modernism in all its forms, including those that were informed by Marxism. Zhdanov started from the assumption that 'the present state of bourgeois literature [and by extension bourgeois art] is such that it is no longer able to create great works of art'; this was a consequence of 'the decadence and disintegration of bourgeois literature, resulting from the collapse and decay of the capitalist system'. He established the virtues of Socialist Realism by contrast:

> Comrade Stalin has called our writers engineers of human souls. What does this mean? What duties does the title confer on you? In the first place, it means knowing life so as to be able to depict it truthfully in works of art, not to depict it in a dead, scholastic way, not simply as 'objective reality', but to depict reality in its revolutionary development. In addition to this, the truthfulness and historical concreteness of the artistic portrayal should be combined with the ideological remoulding and education of the toiling people in the spirit of socialism.
>
> (*Soviet Writers' Congress*, 1934, p.21)

Exercise Compare the meanings of 'realism' presented in definitions 1, 2 and 4. As represented by Zhdanov, does Socialist Realism appear closer to the 'critical realism' discussed in 2 or to the 'on-the-streets realism' described in 1?

Discussion We'd say it's closer to the realism of definition 1. Zhdanov assumes the truth of a view of history – a highly Manichean view in which the bourgeoisie is all decadence and the 'toiling people' all revolutionary virtue – and then proceeds to identify truthful portrayal with whatever confirms that view. His view of what *ought* to be the case regulates over the portrayal of what *is* the case. But while it is one thing to assert that workers should be happy, it is quite another to claim that a picture of a smiling worker is 'realistic'. All too easily the doctrine of Socialist Realism reduces to the demand that pictures should look *like* the world as described in Party propaganda. From the point of view of the modernists, this requirement of likeness produced technical conservatism in Socialist Realist art just as surely as it did in the Academy and the Salon. And in their terms a technically conservative art could not be realistic (for the reasons suggested in 2 above). Those modernists who were also supporters of the revolution turned to another theorist whose revolutionary credentials were at least as good as Stalin's. In 1938 Leon Trotsky wrote:

> Art, like science, not only does not seek orders, but by its very essence, cannot tolerate them. Artistic creation has its own laws – even when it consciously serves a social movement. Truly intellectual creation is incompatible with lies, hypocrisy and the spirit of conformity. Art can become a strong ally of the revolution only in so far as it remains faithful to itself.
>
> ('Art and politics', p.10) ❑

But if the doctrine of Socialist Realism seems relatively easy to criticize in this way, we should recognize that the case for some form of Social Realism is a strong one, particularly in the face of modernist claims for the disinterestedness and autonomy of art. During the Occupation the latter claims must have rung very hollow in the ears of Communists such as Fougeron and Taslitzky, who joined the Resistance and who used their artistic skills in clandestine attacks on the Nazis (see Plates 63 and 64). The image of disinterestedness is one that modernists have been able to sustain only by allowing certain principles of exclusion to operate. At its best, the aspiration to Social Realism has at least served to represent in art the interests and position of the oppressed and the marginalized.

Post-war art and political engagement

Exercise Before continuing the discussion of the relationship between 'realism' and political engagement in post-war art practices, you should watch Video-cassette 1, part 2, 'Art and political engagement, 1947–53', in which there is an examination of paintings that represent a range of options taken by artists in the PCF, including Fougeron, Picasso, Léger, Singer and Taslitzky. Before watching the video you should read the accompanying notes. ❑

A form of realism had been practised by those French artists who followed the Communist Party line from the mid thirties onwards, and the PCF had initiated debates on the subject before the war. It was only with the post-war resurgence of the PCF, however, that Socialist Realism became a strong force in the world of French art, strengthened, no doubt, by the wartime credentials of such artists as Taslitzky and Fougeron. The work they were able to put on show following the Liberation, however technically conservative in modernist terms – see, for example, Taslitzky's *The Delegates* (Plate 42) – testified as clearly as anyone could wish to the spirit of opposition and resistance. Following the example of the pre-war Popular Front, a 'Front National des Arts' had been formed as part of the Resistance movement. Gruber, Pignon, Taslitzky and Fougeron were among those artists who were associated with both. With the Liberation, the Front National concerned itself with the business of the 'épuration' of the ranks of French artists. In early October 1944 a Steering Committee met under the presidency of Picasso and issued a demand that certain collaborating artists and critics should be arrested and tried (a demand subsequently moderated after study of individual cases). Among the other members of the committee were Lhote, Gruber, Pignon and Fougeron (who acted as executive secretary). At the same time a group of 'Jeunes Peintres du Front National des Étudiants' ('Young Painters of the National Front of Students') wrote to condemn those who had accepted the invitation to travel to Germany in 1941. In the event the one sanction applied was the exclusion of the latter from the Salon d'Automne de la Libération.

This was also a time of significant recruitment of artists to the Communist Party; foremost among these were Picasso, who joined in October 1944, and Léger, who joined the following year. An interview in which Picasso discussed his reasons was first published in part in the left-wing American journal *New Masses* (New York, 24 October 1944) and in full a few days later in *L'Humanité* (Paris, 29–30 October 1944).

Exercise Turn now to the extract from the interview published in *L'Humanité* in October 1944 (*Documents and Texts 1*, item 21) and to the excerpts from an interview with Jerome Seckler which took place during the following month and January 1945 (item 22). This was also published in condensed form in *New Masses*. Make notes on what you think these two texts tell us about Picasso's views on political choice, artistic expression and the relationship between them. (When reading the Seckler interview you will need to refer to Picasso's *Guernica*, Plate 32, and still life with *Bull's Head, Book, Palette and Candle*, Plate 65).

Discussion It is clear in the context both of his immediate community (Aragon, Eluard, Cassou, Fougeron) and of the wider political transformations after the Liberation of Paris in August 1944, that for Picasso membership of the PCF was an important demonstration of solidarity. It's also clear that he did not regard art as the pursuit of arbitrary or totally autonomous concerns. Though he refused suggestions that there was any automatic or transparent relationship between style or subject matter and possible social or political commitments, at the end of the Seckler interview he acknowledged a connection between art and politics. And, in his statement on joining the PCF he talks of 'drawing' and 'colour' as 'weapons' in attempts to bring an 'increase in liberation'; 'I am aware of having always struggled by means of my painting, like a genuine revolutionary'. What does he mean by 'weapons' and 'liberation': does he see himself, for instance, as an 'engineer of human souls'? ❑

Compare, now, Picasso's statements with those in the extracts from Zhdanov and Trotsky on page 230. To which does Picasso seem closest? In his implicit rejection of the doctrine of Socialist Realism, Picasso's views are more consistent with those expressed by Trotsky. This is unsurprising for two main reasons. First, as you are aware from the discussion of Picasso's work in the audio and video cassettes, his art practice demonstrates a critical engagement with what is problematical in artistic representation; it does not rely on sentiment or the 'certainties' of attitude. The second is that the artistic and intellectual community of which Picasso was part consisted mainly of Surrealists who, particularly in the 1930s, were largely pro-Trotskyist and anti-Stalinist.

Figure 7.2 *Demonstration at Pére-Lachaise in memory of the victims of Nazism, Paris, 16 October 1944; with Eluard (at the front), Picasso and the Front National Universitaire. (Photo: Lapi-Viollet)*

For Picasso, as for his close friend Paul Eluard, the Surrealist poet, the experience of the war diminished the contradictions which membership of the PCF had represented in the late 1930s. According to Françoise Gilot, when Breton returned from exile, where he had been broadcasting for Voice of America, he refused to shake Picasso's hand because he had joined the PCF. For Breton this was a betrayal of the Surrealist pro-Trotskyist critique of the PCF and of its Stalinist associations. Picasso replied that for him, as for Eluard, the experience of remaining in France during the Occupation had changed the nature of political choice.

For Picasso and for Léger there was still the possibility of artistic dissent and relative autonomy within the Communist Party and of renegotiation of the artist's role. While both of them engaged with contemporary social themes in their work (see Picasso's *Massacre in Korea*, 1951, Plate 45; *War* and *Peace*, 1952, Colour plates 12 and 13, and Plate 46; Léger's *The Constructors*, 1950, Colour plate 8; and *Homage to David*, 1948, Plate 47), neither painted works that followed any doctrinaire example of Soviet Socialist Realism. In fact, though Picasso often appeared at public functions in support of the PCF (see Figure 7.3) and painted portraits of Thorez, his work was criticized by some Party members as 'decadent' because of his pursuit of styles and themes regarded as incompatible with the Party. One vivid instance is the secretariat of the PCF's 'categorical disapproval' in *L'Humanité* of the publication in *Les Lettres françaises* of the portrait of Stalin by 'comrade Picasso' (see Plate 67). It didn't express the Party's view of 'official respect', nor follow an approved style (see also Plate 62).

Figure 7.3 *Picasso, Louis Aragon and Pozner at a demonstration in Parc des Princes, Paris, at the end of the Congress of Partisans of Peace, May 1949. (Photo: H. Roger Viollet)*

There was no doubt of the PCF's adoption of a particular view of 'realism'. On 29 November 1946 Aragon declared in *Les Lettres françaises*, 'I consider that the Party does hold an aesthetic doctrine and its name is realism'. This 'doctrine' became more narrowly defined in April 1947, when Maurice Thorez addressed the Party Congress at Strasbourg in terms that closely followed those of Zhdanov:

> To decadent works by bourgeois aesthetes, partisans of art for art's sake, to the pessimism without solution and the retrograde obscurantism of the existentialist 'philosophers' [...] we have opposed an art which should be inspired by socialist realism [...] an art which would aid the working class in its struggle for liberation.
>
> (quoted in Caute, *Communism and the French Intellectuals*, p.327)

The years after 1947 were characterized by fierce commitments to different views about the relationship between aesthetics and politics and the nature of 'realism'. Taslitzky recalls that the antagonism between Communist painters and the new school of abstractionists was so 'very violent' they had to avoid each other by crossing the street. And the strength of belief in the PCF as the only viable agency for achieving socialism and freedom led critics such as Aragon to attack those on the 'left' who, though committed to various forms of humanism, were not committed to the Party. For instance, in the first editorial of *La Nouvelle Critique*, December 1948, Aragon described Sartre, Mauriac, Léon Blum and Malraux as 'rummagers in dustbins'.

Equally vociferous were the critiques published by the Surrealists who continued to mount international group exhibitions (Plate 52). The Surréalistes Révolutionnaires published two tracts in 1947, the year of the Marshall Plan, the Cominform, the move to Zhdanovism in the PCF, and growing criticism of French colonialism in Indo-china. *Rupture Inaugurale* (dated 21 June 1947) reasserted their Trotskyism in the face of the PCF's adherence to the aesthetic doctrines of Moscow. The other tract was *Liberté est un mot vietnamien* (*Documents and Texts 1*, item 23), which you should now read.

In the style of Surrealist 'interventions' during the 1930s, this latter publication is highly critical of French colonialism and of its suppression of liberty and of demands for independence in an 'occupied' country: significantly, attention is drawn to the struggle by the French themselves with German Occupation in the preceding years. In many respects members of the PCF shared the anti-colonial views expressed in this critique, though they were highly critical of the Surrealists' Trotskyist tendency. As you saw in the video programme, Aragon's art criticism of Fougeron (Colour plate 10) and Singer (Plate 68) was also fiercely anti-capitalist and anti-colonialist, though his criteria of artistic competence were totally at odds with those of the Surrealists. While the war in Indo-china and particularly demonstrations of workers' dissent were major *issues* for the Surrealists, they became central artistic *subjects* for many artists committed to the Party, for example in Fougeron's *Atlantic Civilization* (Colour plate 10), which is discussed in the video. (See also Unit 6 and Audio-cassette 1, side B, for discussion of Indo-China.)

It is difficult to recover the sense of historical urgency and passion with which artists addressed such contemporary issues. Two related exhibitions from the early 1950s raised some of these issues with respect to the concept of the value and function of art for artists in the Party. The first of these was in 1951, when some forty paintings, drawings and related studies, produced by Fougeron in 1950 in support of the miners' recent political struggles, were exhibited at Bernheim-Jeune, one of the most prestigious galleries in Paris, with which Fougeron had a contract. Fifty thousand people visited the gallery before the exhibition travelled around France. Three of the paintings shown were *Terres Cruelles, National Defence* (Plate 44) and *The Judges* (Colour plate 9). The historical context for these images was the political confrontation between the miners, supported by the PCF, and the French government. At this time coal production was doubling, working conditions were deteriorating and miners' purchasing power was seriously diminishing. In 1947, a year of severe economic instability, thousands of miners went on strike. This was followed in October 1948 by an eight-week strike. While calling for 'Charbon à bas prix' ('coal at its lowest price') the government would not admit the realities of working conditions: in 1948 alone 348 miners were killed and thousands injured. Fougeron's *National Defence,* 1950, is supposed to depict the results of the action taken by Jules Moch, the SFIO Home Minister, to break the strike of 1948:

> [Moch] who had already used troops and police against the 1947 strikers, this time equipped them with war material, tanks, gas and machine guns. Four miners were killed and hundreds were wounded. [...] Nearly half the miners' delegates were arrested and jailed, and in some areas, miners were forced to go down the pits at machinegun-point.
>
> (Adereth, *The French Communist Party,* p.154)

The second of these exhibitions was the Salon d'Automne of 1951. On 6 November 1951, just before a presidential visit to the Salon, the government ordered the police to remove from the walls seven canvases which had associations with the PCF. These works were: Jean Milhau's *Maurice Thorez Is Improving* (he had been seriously ill); Marie-Anne Lansiaux's *The March of the First of May*; Berberian's *Political Demonstration*; Bauquier's *The Dockers,* in which dockers are depicted striking in protest against ships being loaded for Indo-china (Plate 66); Taslitzky's *The Strike at the Port de Bouc* (Colour plate 14 and Plate 69) depicting the CRS (Compagnies républicaines de securité; a paramilitary security force) and their dogs attacking dockers striking for the same reason; Singer's *10th February at Nice,* commemorating the day when, according to Aragon, 'the population of the city threw a launching ramp for a V2 rocket into the sea'; and a portrait of Henri Martin by 'Sorel' (an alias for Taslitzky).

Denunciations of government censorship were marshalled in leftist publications, such as *Les Lettres françaises, Arts, Le Parisien libéré* and *L'Humanité,* and protests were made by Matisse and Picasso. Only two paintings were reinstated – the *Thorez* portrait by Milhau and Lansiaux's *First of May.* The government, under pressure from several quarters concerning 'la sale guerre' in Indo-china, claimed to have acted in the interests of 'le sentiment national'.

In his review of the Salon d'Automne, published in *Les Lettres françaises*, 15 November 1951, Aragon claimed that 'Here is an instance where to paint ceases to be a game'. Under the heading, 'L'Art et le sentiment national', he attacked the intervention of government agencies and drew attention to the difference between the 'national sentiment' imposed by the state and the 'national sentiment' that sustained the Resistance under Vichy. Comparison between the official responses of the state to art during and after the war raises some major questions. As you will recall from page 218, works of art were removed from display during the Occupation while official discourse emphasized particular notions of the 'French tradition', the 'classical' and the 'anti-modern'. In 1951, when those paintings deemed to be not in the 'national interest' were removed from the Salon d'Automne, was this evidence of continuation of an ideology of repressive humanist nationalism from the years of Vichy? In the *context* of 1951, realist paintings such as these may have seemed challenging to the cultural authority of the state. It is certainly true that acts of censorship are often revealing of an unwillingness or inability to confront uncomfortable questions, particularly where the maintenance of order and security is supposed to be at stake.

'Images of Man'

During the years after the war the slogans of humanism were revived to serve the ends of national reconciliation. Believers in the continuity of (French) culture rallied around the central concept of Man – 'l'homme' – under which all (including women) were to be gathered. In the articulation of this concept artists played a crucial role. Were not such figures as Picasso, Matisse and Léger the very embodiments of continuity in French culture? And yet no representation of the human could easily escape being shaped either by the experience of recent history – which offered powerful demonstrations of what we choose to regard as *in*humanity – or by beliefs about the priorities of reconstruction and hopes for the future organization of society.

Exercise Look at Picasso, *War* and *Peace* (Colour plates 12 and 13, and Plate 46), Dubuffet, *Le Metafisyx* (Colour plate 15), Léger, *The Constructors* (Colour plate 8), and Fougeron, *The Judges* (Colour plate 9). As a conclusion to this unit we want you to consider these paintings in terms of the concepts of modernism and realism which we have discussed. In the light of the information given in the unit and in the accompanying audio and video material you should be able to make distinctions between them in terms of: (a) the kind of context within which each image is represented; (b) the various devices used to engage and to direct the interest and imagination of the viewer; and (c) the image of humanity which each appears to present.

Discussion There is no 'correct' set of conclusions to the process of inquiry suggested above. The following comments are offered more as a form of dialogue with your own findings – and in amplification of the information available – than as prescription regarding what you *ought* to have come up with.

The two large-scale Picasso panels were installed in 1952 in a deconsecrated chapel in the town of Vallauris, redesignated as a 'Temple of Peace'. Affixed to the facing walls of a long rectangular space, they follow the curve of the barrel vault to arch over the viewer's head from each side. The subjects are treated allegorically and symbolically. 'War' is a demon in a classical chariot, opposed by a heroic nude figure holding the scales of justice and shielded with the dove of peace (Colour Plate 12). The figures in *Peace* occupy a kind of golden age. The winged horse and piping faun are familiar both from classical mythology and from other phases of Picasso's own work. In both panels the form of pictorial space employed is one that appears dreamlike, unparticularized, timeless, mythological. Pictorial space and figures alike are relatively flat and shallow. This form of relatively 'abstract' presentation had by the mid century at least become a *conventional* means of signifying timelessness and universality of meaning. There are some grounds for scepticism about the actual universality of Picasso's imagery. The murals were painted during the Korean war, at a time when the exposure of alleged American germ warfare featured in French newspapers, and particularly in the Communist paper *L'Humanité*. In the early spring of 1952, while Picasso was working on the first designs for *War* and *Peace*, the execution of a group of Greek Communists drew protests from French artists and intellectuals. *L'Humanité* published a personal statement from Picasso in which he referred to the 'grain of horror sown in handfuls by the headlights on the open chest of Greece, by governments sweating in hate and fear'. It seems that the reports of germ warfare and the image of the 'grain of horror' somehow came together in Picasso's imagination to produce the image of the panful of malignant organisms and insects sown by the demon in *War*. The references to ancient Greek imagery and mythology may also have been suggested in part by current events, while the idealized soldier at the left of *War* surely at some level expresses Picasso's own idealization of the Communist Party, for which two years earlier he had designed the symbol of the dove of peace, and which he, like many others, identified with determined opposition to fascism. If the works appear 'universal' in meaning, we should still ask of what the universals are composed, and what particular views of human potential, human society and human conflict underlie the visions of *War* and *Peace* which the artist offers.

In Dubuffet's painting the image is barely contextualised at all. Rather than suggesting an imaginary space for it to inhabit, the artist organizes his representation of the human figure in such a way that it appears to occupy virtually the whole surface of the canvas. In fact the literal edges of the latter appear to define the very shape that the figure takes. The character of both the drawing and the paint surface are such as to confront the spectator directly with the image, rather than to create a field of associations around it. The style of the drawing is almost aggressively 'unaccomplished' and 'unartistic' – though of course, as we have suggested, interest in the idea of the naive, the primitive and the vulgar was an *artistic* interest in the later 1940s and 50s. If the painting conveys an image of the human, it is one as it were unformed and unmarked by civilization. The suggestion the painting may be taken to convey is that our common humanity is secured, if at all, only at the level of the pre-social. In such a suggestion there is a buried implication: that no specific and contingent form of social organization can be justified by reference to human nature.

Léger's painting offers a more clearly optimistic vision of the human, of the future and of the relationship between the two. That is to say it appears to propose a future that is constructed by men working in concert as social beings. The context is one that clearly signifies the modern and the industrial, and which does so in a way that seems approving of both. Léger has said of the series of *Constructors* of which ours is only an example: 'I saw the men balancing high up on the iron scaffolding. I saw man like a tiny gnat, seemingly lost in his own inventions, with the sky above him. I wanted to portray that: the contrast between man and his inventions, between the worker and all that architecture in metal.' It is arguable how much of this sense of contrast survives in the painting. Those observers who accord priority to the decorative achievements of modern art might claim that its components are resolved into a kind of formal harmony, which the figures occupy as apparently 'natural' denizens. They might say that the priority of the 'aesthetic resolution' – the need to have the painting succeed as a *painting* according to a certain modernist notion of what that entailed – ruled out expression of those kinds of conflict which the subject might have suggested to someone less optimistically disposed. On the other hand, Léger's painting might be regarded, by those sceptical of the notion of 'aesthetic resolution', as representing an engagement with a particular project of 'modernité': as an attempt to preserve and to extend the dialectical relationship between recognizably social imagery and self-consciously modern techniques.

Conflict of a relevant kind certainly seems to lie behind Fougeron's painting, which is one of his *Pays de mines* ('Mining country') series (see p.235). Though the figurative context of the painting is relatively vague in its physical characteristics, its dramatic and emotional character is inescapable, as is the directness of its address to the imaginary spectator. If it is not we who are notionally being judged, we are made to stand in the place of those who are. It is precisely this use of art to engage with the conditions of existence in the social world – and to say something about them – that distinguishes the Fougeron painting from the others, though, as we have seen, Picasso's murals may have had some similar intent, while some of Léger's work certainly demonstrates concern with a notion of the 'social'. It could be argued that the 'effectiveness' of Fougeron's painting is bought with the currency of technical conservatism. We are back with the problems with which we opened this unit – those concerning the contested values of modernism in the visual arts. ❑

Bibliography

ADERETH, M., *The French Communist Party: a Critical History (1920–84)*, Manchester University Press, 1984.

Aftermath: France 1945–54: New Images of Man, London, Barbican Art Gallery, 1982.

ARAGON, L., *Écrits sur l'art moderne*, Paris, Éditions Flammarion, 1981.

L'Art en Europe: les années décisives 1945–1953, Musée d'Art Moderne de Saint-Etienne, Éditions Skira, 1987.

Art et idéologies; l'art en Occident 1945–1949, Centre Interdisciplinaire d'Étude et de Recherche sur l'Expression Contemporaine, University of Saint-Étienne, 1976.

Art in Western Europe: the Post-War Years 1945–1955, Des Moines Art Centre, 1978.

BREKER, A., *Paris, Hitler et Moi*, Paris, Presses de la Cité, 1970.

BRETON, A., and TROTSKY, L., 'Manifesto: Towards a Free Revolutionary Art', *Partisan Review*, vol.iv, no.1, 1938, pp.49–53.

BRETON, A., *Le Surréalisme et la peinture*, 1928; translated in *What is Surrealism?*, trans. David Gascoyne, London, Faber, 1936.

CAUTE, D., *Communism and the French Intellectuals, 1914–1960*, London, Oxford University Press, 1964.

DORLÉAC, L.B., *Histoire de l'art, Paris 1940–1944; ordre national – traditions et modernités*, Paris, Publications de la Sorbonne, 1986.

DUBUFFET, J., *Prospectus et tous écrits suivants*, compiled and edited by Hubert Damisch, Paris, Gallimard, 1967.

Fautrier 1928–1958, introduction by Herbert Read, London, Institute of Contemporary Arts, 1958.

L'Art Brut Préféré aux Arts Culturels, Paris, Galerie Drouin, October 1948; translated in Harrison and Wood, 1992, as 'Crude Art Preferred to Cultural Art'.

FOUGERON, A., 'Le Peintre à son creneau', *La Nouvelle Critique*, Paris, December 1948; translated in Harrison and Wood, 1992, as 'The Painter on his Battlement'.

HARRISON, C. and WOOD, P. (eds), *Art in Theory 1900–1990*, Oxford, Blackwell, 1992.

KEEN, K.H., 'Picasso's Communist interlude: the murals of "War" and "Peace"', *Burlington Magazine*, vol.cxxii, no.928, July 1980.

LHOTE, A., *Peinture d'abord: essais*, Paris, Denoël, 1942.

Fernand Léger: the Later Years, London, Whitechapel Art Gallery, 1987.

MOULIN, R., *Le Marché de la peinture en France*, Paris, Les Éditions de Minuit, 1967.

Outsiders, Arts Council of Great Britain, London, Hayward Gallery, 1979.

Paris-Paris; créations en France 1937–1957, Paris, Musée National d'Art Moderne, Centre Georges Pompidou, 1981.

La Planète affolée: Surréalisme – dispersion et influences 1938–1947, Centre de la Vieille Charité, Marseilles, Éditions Flammarion, 1986.

Les Réalismes (1919–1939), Paris, Musée National d'Art Moderne, Centre Georges Pompidou, 1980.

ROSEMONT, F., *André Breton and the First Principles of Surrealism*, London, Pluto Press, 1978.

ROY, C., *Fernand Léger, Les Constructeurs*, Paris, Falaize, 1951.

Soviet Writers' Congress, 1934, London, Lawrence and Wishart, 1977.

TAPIÉ, M., *Un Art Autre*, Paris, 1952.

TASLITZKY, B., *Tu Parles*, Paris, Les Éditeurs Françaises Réunis, 1959. *Tracts Surréalistes et Déclarations Collectives*, Tome 2, *1940–1969*, Paris, Le Terrain Vague, 1982.

TROTSKY, L., 'Art and politics', *Partisan Review*, vol.v, no.3, 1938.

VIATTE, G., 'The So-called Demise of Paris', *Flash Art*, no. 119, November 1984. Westkunst; Zeitgenossische Kunst seit 1939, Cologne, Messehalle, 1981.

VIATTE, G., 'Aftermath: a new generation' in *Aftermath* catalogue, 1982.

WILSON, S., ' "La Beauté Révolutionnaire?", Réalisme Socialiste and French Painting 1935–1954', *Oxford Art Journal*, vol.2, no.3, 1980.

WILSON, S, 'Paris Post-War: in Search of the Absolute', *Paris Post-War: Art and Existentialism 1945–55*, London, Tate Gallery, 1993.

Les Années 50, Paris, Centre Pompidou, 1988.

UNITS 8–9 The Italian Neo-realist Cinema

Prepared for the course team by Tony Aldgate

Study materials

For your work on these units you will need to refer to the following materials:

Documents and Texts 1

Video-cassette 2, 'Neo-realist feature film compilation'

Video-cassette 3, 'Umberto D'

Audio-cassette 4, side B, 'Italian neo-realist cinema'

Cassette Notes 1

1 Introduction

Let me begin as I mean to go on – with reference to a film. There is a much-quoted scene in the 1949 film of *The Third Man* with which you may be familiar. The setting is, of course, occupied Vienna in 1945 and has nothing to do with Italy, let alone post-war Italy. But, at one point, Harry Lime departs from a meeting with his friend of long-standing, Holly Martins, and delivers the following short speech:

> In Italy for thirty years under the Borgias they had warfare, terror, murder, bloodshed – but they produced Michelangelo, Leonardo da Vinci and the Renaissance. In Switzerland they had brotherly love, five hundred years of democracy and peace, and what did they produce ...? The cuckoo clock.

Don't worry. I am not about to compare Italy during the Renaissance with several hundred years of Swiss history. Nor do I wish to become entangled in drawing ill-founded parallels between Italy under thirty years of Borgia rule and Italy in the period of the *ventennio* – the twenty years stretching from Mussolini's assumption of power to the overthrow of Fascism in 1943–45. Least of all do I want to argue that these two periods are immediately or easily comparable for their cultural legacy. How would one set about comparing the works of Michelangelo Buonarroti, the painter, with those of Michelangelo Antonioni, the film maker?

One might, however, observe simply in passing that periods of destruction and devastation, of profound political and social upheaval, are generally followed by a wave of *cultural* reconstruction and regeneration, as they are in other spheres of activity, and that these periods are more likely to give rise to such bursts of creativity than are those of relative calm and tranquillity. To that extent Harry Lime got it right, though historians may still debate the nature and degree of the consequent change. More relevant for my purposes, it is arguable that certain European cinemas in the twentieth century have enjoyed especially rich creative phases in the aftermath of substantial and widespread national ferment – witness, for example, the cinema in Russia after the civil war, the German Expressionist cinema in the 1920s, the British cinema during and after the Second World War.

Nowhere is this phenomenon more evident, perhaps, than in Italy in 1945, with the advent of the neo-realist cinema. The title alone – the Italian cinema of the 'new realism' – is sufficient, as it is broadly construed by standard film histories on the subject, readily to evoke much of its character, intent and purpose. These histories characterize it as a reaction to what had previously obtained and which consciously chose to break with that past. It sought faithfully to render the present, 'warts and all'. It advocated a more positive and purposeful role for the Italian cinema in the future. For Italians, then, as one account would have it, the neo-realist cinema fulfilled 'a political, social and cultural need to rediscover the "true" Italy' in the aftermath of twenty years of Fascist domination. More generally, it is argued that 'The emergence of neo-realism in Italy in 1945 is one of the most interesting cultural phenomena of the twentieth century'.

These are large claims, and compel pause for thought. Go beyond the sweeping generalizations on the nature of neo-realist cinema and the grandiose claims for its influence, and a host of questions immediately spring to mind. What was so 'new' about neo-realism? Where did it come from? What inspired it? Who were the proponents of the neo-realist movement, what interests did they stand for or represent, and did they really constitute a coherent movement, with unity of aim and purpose? What, precisely, were the neo-realists' ambitions and were they realized in their films? Did the films achieve their desired social and cultural effect and, if not, what factors militated against their success? What part, finally, did the neo-realist cinema play in the reconstruction of Italian culture after the fall of Fascism, and what was its legacy?

These are some of the questions that we shall be seeking to answer in the next four weeks. It's quite a long time for the topic, you might think. But you will certainly need that amount of time, I assure you. There's a lot to be got through, not least in the way of viewing and analysing film. But, there again, it is a subject that amply repays the time and effort spent on it. It is enjoyable, exciting, enlightening. And the films selected for detailed analysis constitute examples of some of the richest work ever produced for the cinema. They are 'classics' of their kind.

Aims

After working through these units you should:

1 have a broad knowledge of the origins of neo-realism, its position within the Italian film industry, and its main practitioners;

2 be able to describe the principle thematic and stylistic characteristics of neo-realist films, and to exemplify these with reference to the film material provided;

3 be able to assess the achievements and legacy of the neo-realist cinema.

Studying film may be a departure for you. It should be emphasized that you are doing this within the context of an interdisciplinary course. So, while you should develop your own reading of the film material on the video-cassettes, you will not be expected to present a sophisticated technical analysis of the way the films are made.

2 The neo-realist cinema: antecedents and characteristics

During your work on Unit 1, you read the introduction to Millicent Marcus's book for the light it sheds generally on the debate about realism. I should like you to turn to it once again, paying particular attention this time to her comments on neo-realist cinema (*Documents and Texts 1*, item 2, pp.18–19).

Exercise How does Marcus characterize the Italian neo-realist cinema and what does she identify as its distinguishing features? I suggest you list your responses under the headings (1) origins; (2) exponents; (3) style; (4) intent; (5) obstacles; (6) achievements. This is rather a wide-ranging question to start with, I know, but Marcus does succinctly highlight certain basic features, which you should be able to pick out. I have not provided you with a model answer to this exercise, but the following discussion is organized under these six headings. While I have based my discussion on Marcus, I have elaborated on her points and introduced new material as preparation for the next section, in which you will begin to view the films.

1 Origins

The neo-realist cinema did not just arise overnight, of course, nor was it a wholly new beginning, despite claims to the contrary. Like its literary equivalent, it was inspired, at least in part, by nineteenth-century writers such as Luigi Capuana and Giovanni Verga, exponents of Italian verismo. Verga, in particular, was an influential forerunner who provided a narrative model or prototype for the neo-realists. There was a crucial difference, however, in that the latter aimed for a more active and interventionist role for their art. This aim was born largely of the experience of the Resistance and the war of Liberation, and of sharing the ideals that were engendered in regard to post-war reconstruction.

However, in addition, Marcus argues that neo-realism owed something to a realist strain which had consistently been an element of Italian cinematic modes of depiction. In the period of the silent cinema this strain had been occasionally submerged in waves of melodramas and historical epics – *Quo Vadis* was as popular a screen subject in 1912 as it was in 1952, the only difference being that the Italian film makers cared a bit more than their Hollywood counterparts about historical veracity. Along with sentimental comedies, melodramas and historical epics were the predominant genres, making up the staple bill of film fare through into the sound era.

Although Marcus does not mention it, a variant of the comedy/melodrama became increasingly prevalent in the 1930s. This was pejoratively dubbed the 'white telephone' film (so called because this status symbol was associated with the affluent settings and characters typical of such films), a nickname that has been used to typify feature film production in Fascist Italy. These films played on apparently apolitical, innocent emotions, offering escapist entertainment and reportedly little else.

Of course, it was not as simple as that. During the Fascist era there were made a small number of films which may be said to have directly prefigured the neo-realist style. Marcus cites several by title and we shall shortly be looking at an extract from probably the best known of them, Luchino Visconti's *Ossessione*. Visconti's film was not well received by the Fascist authorities. But other films by, for example, Alessandro Blasetti and Mario Camerini were well received, and they too were of a realist nature.

Fascist officials in charge of the film industry wanted a high-quality film output and men such as Luigi Freddi, head of the reorganized and centralized *Direzione Generale per la Cinematografia* from 1934 to 1939, sought to achieve this. Despite generous state subsidies, the Fascist regime did not stir itself to formulate an artistic policy for the cinema and Freddi was left very much to his own devices. The first state film school (*Centro Sperimentale di Cinematografia*) opened its doors in 1936 – Rossellini and De Santis were among its students – the huge Cinecittà studio complex was built with state money in Rome and opened by Mussolini in 1937, and influential film periodicals were started up. The *Centro* launched probably the most important periodical, *Bianco e Nero*, in 1937, the year after the founding of the theoretical journal *Cinema*. Marcus cites Visconti as the standard bearer of the *Cinema* group of writers who sought an alternative to the clichés and falsehoods of the Fascist film industry, as indeed he was. But in 1938 it was the dictator's son, Vittorio Mussolini, who became editor-in-chief of *Cinema*.

In short, then, when looking for the origins of the neo-realist cinema, one has to take sufficient account of the influences carried over from the Fascist era. As Christopher Wagstaff rightly concludes:

> Historians generally say that the Fascist regime and Freddi never got their Fascist cinema, the one they wanted. But the facts, the films themselves, tell another story, one with a twist, however; the artistically sound cinema that they sought and achieved was anti-fascist, or at the least, non-fascist, and the full blossoming of the seeds planted by Freddi came after the collapse of Fascism with the neo-realist school, all of whose members had been nurtured and trained in Fascist institutions.
>
> ('The Italian cinema industry during the Fascist regime', p.173)

2 Exponents

This is easy, of course, since Marcus lists them, ranking them into masters and disciples. You will probably be familiar with some of the names. From the first category, we shall be looking at some films of De Sica and Zavattini, of Visconti, and Rossellini. From the second, we shall see examples of the work of De Santis.

The extent to which they formed a coherent movement or school is a trickier question. In fact, it is really only when one has seen a number of their films that it proves possible to appreciate why, for all the diversity among these film makers, there is still ample reason to group them together as upholders of a certain school, as Marcus and most commentators have done. So perhaps we should largely reserve judgment on that issue.

It is sufficient, for the moment, to observe that the neo-realist film makers certainly shared a moral commitment and used similar techniques in film making. But their stylistic differences varied enormously. There was no commonly agreed aesthetic code, no set of *a priori* rules for their cinematic practice and, indeed, the critical formulation of neo-realist rules only happened after the event, when the films had been made – again, a matter to which we shall return when discussing the scriptwriter, Cesare Zavattini, and his essay (reproduced as item 24 in *Documents and Texts 1*) in relation to the films he made with De Sica.

One further point that Marcus mentions, however, is that while the film makers maintained a resolutely anti-establishment stance, they were not of the same political persuasion and were reluctant for the most part, she argues, to embrace a Marxist perspective. She does not go much deeper into this aspect, other than to suggest that it might provide one explanation of why the neo-realists lacked unity of political purpose and ultimately waned in influence. We shall explore this issue later.

3 Style

Here, once again, Marcus is fairly explicit. Location shooting, lengthy takes, unobtrusive editing, natural lighting, a predominance of medium and long shots, respect for the continuity of time and space, use of contemporary, true-to-life subjects, an uncontrived, open-ended plot, working-class protagonists, a non-professional cast, dialogue in the vernacular, implied social criticism – these were the formal characteristics of the neo-realist style. Of course they did not constitute a fast set of rules and by no means did all the film makers fully adhere to them.

Furthermore, in the early days of neo-realism, straight after the end of the war, it was the case that a good many of these elements were thrust on the film makers as much as they were consciously chosen. With many of the studios in ruins, for instance, and the premises at Cinecittà largely appropriated by the occupying American forces for use as a refugee camp, film makers were forced out on to the streets and compelled to use natural locations if they wanted to continue their work. They used stolen cameras and such things as studio lights were considered luxuries, and were often unobtainable. Even the supply of electricity was intermittent.

Rossellini makes much of the enormous practical difficulties he experienced in the production of *Rome, Open City* (1945), not least in regard to the availability of vital film stock: 'I bought my negative from street photographers, who used 35mm negative in their Leicas. So I had one piece thirty metres long, another twenty, another fifty. I had one quality of negative for one piece, and a different quality for another.' Furthermore, because of the high cost of laboratory work he was unable to see the rushes (unedited film from a day's shooting) as his film progressed.

It would be foolish, though, to push the argument about contingency as a governing force too far. There was a distinct and discernible neo-realist style. For example, the film makers shot on location for the most part because they chose to do so. And they continued to do so after Cinecittà reopened its doors in 1948. Location shooting was essential to their purpose.

Having acknowledged that fact, however, it is important to put the neo-realist method in context. Too much is often made of the supposed 'truth' and 'veracity' of the neo-realist product – a 'truth' born of, for example, photography redolent of reportage, freedom of camera movement, naturalistic lighting, the use of non-professional actors. The real truth is that compromises were made in practice, as you would expect. Indeed, some of them were inherent in the Italian film making process, and they were very much taken for granted and were rarely challenged or confronted, even by the neo-realists.

An interesting example relates to the habit of using postsynchronized sound, of shooting the film 'silent' and then 'dubbing' the sound on afterwards. The Italian cinema had a long tradition of dubbing. It arose around 1930 with the advent of American sound films, which, of course, required dubbing into Italian for the dialogue to be understood. 'It soon proved to be the case that the dubbing of American films into Italian was not more difficult to achieve than the production of Italian dialogue films', one commentator has observed, and 'after a slight hesitation the Italian public reaccustomed itself to American films, in spite of the imperfect synchronization, and it has put up with dubbing ever since' (Geoffrey Nowell-Smith, 'The Italian cinema under Fascism', pp.147–8).

The neo-realists also resorted to dubbing, though obviously for different reasons. In part, once again, it was forced on them in the straitened circumstances following the war. Thus, to save money when making *Rome, Open City*, Rossellini shot without sound recording and only dubbed the dialogue later. In addition, however, the technique allowed for greater freedom of camera movement and proved less restricting overall. It had distinct advantages, in short. The habit persisted and most of the neo-realist films were shot silent and postsynchronized – this may not always be so obvious on the films you see since Italian studio technicians proved increasingly adept at recreating, in a studio, sounds and effects of high quality.

De Sica's *Bicycle Thieves* was also shot 'silent'. There is an oft-repeated anecdote, originated by the director himself, recounting how he was offered millions of dollars to fund his production by an American producer – later versions of the story suggest this was Darryl F. Zanuck or David O. Selznick – provided he was willing to cast Cary Grant, a guaranteed box-office success, in the leading role of the worker. De Sica desperately needed financial backing at the time to get his production off the ground and so he was compelled to be realistic. But he was also 'a realist', of course, and the prospect of having to use Grant in this particular film clearly defied his realist tenets. De Sica turned down the offer and the unknown Lamberto Maggiorani got the part. He was better suited to it, after all, being a steel worker from the Breda factory and plainly a non-professional actor. In fact, he was only spotted by De Sica in passing because he had brought his son along to audition for the part of the young boy in the film.

It's an evocative little story. In the event, however, for all that he used a genuine worker in the film, De Sica was not above engaging an actor to dub the voice of Maggiorani when it came to the postsynchronization process, so that his colloquial speech was more generally accessible. So much for the use of the vernacular. Clearly, even neo-realism had its limits.

4 Intent

We have already touched on 'intent'. Zavattini noted the view that 'the war was the keystone for neo-realism' (*Documents and Texts 1*, pp.68–9): 'This overwhelming event upset men's souls; film directors, each in his own way, tried to transpose this overwhelming emotion on to the screen.' De Sica echoed these sentiments:

> The experience of the war was decisive for us all. Each felt the mad desire to throw away all the old stories of the Italian cinema, to plant the camera in the midst of real life, in the midst of all that struck our astonished eyes. We sought to liberate ourselves from the weight of our sins, we wanted to look ourselves in the face and tell ourselves the truth, to discover what we really were, and to seek salvation.

Notice the language used, the hint of a moral imperative. Marcus is right to stress that there was a consensus among this generation of neo-realist film makers. They shared a common commitment which as well as uniting them gave them the confidence to believe, to use Marcus's words, that 'the ideal could impinge on the real and that man could forge his own destiny in accordance with his highest moral promptings'. Undoubtedly, neo-realist film makers shared an ethical impulse: they had aspirations 'to change the world', to mould it closer to their own desires and, to that end, they advocated social justice and social change in the post-war Italian state.

Were these any more than just noble declarations, however? In that they highlighted some social problems for scrutiny then plainly they fulfilled their interventionist purpose. But did they go further and identify possible political solutions which accorded with their moral ideas? This is a thorny question, and opinions differ strongly on it. Undoubtedly some would say so. Let us have a few comments to keep the debate going until we reach the films and can hopefully form a better judgment for ourselves.

The noted French film critic and theorist, André Bazin, for instance, clearly thought that *Bicycle Thieves* had political meaning above and beyond its social import. Indeed, he rated it a 'Communist film'. Simon Hartog briefly alludes to Bazin's comments in his useful introduction to the published script of the film, but he proceeds to take issue with Bazin's conclusions. The film is not partisan but descriptive and informational, Hartog replies, and 'If, as Bazin suggests, the film is overtly political, it is difficult to see any implied or stated political solution in the film.'

Hartog believes that *Bicycle Thieves* amounted to little more than a demonstration of 'simple protest' against unemployment. His conclusion is that the neo-realist film makers adopted an 'aesthetic posture' which had some 'political significance' in itself, but that they ultimately manifested 'only a preliminary and incomplete consciousness' of the problems inherent in both their position and Italian society at large. They therefore failed to question 'the larger formal and political structures'.

It is an interesting thesis and one that has often been advanced when discussing the political importance of neo-realism in general, especially in more recent years. We shall see whether it proves credible when looking at another film by De Sica and Zavattini, *Umberto D*, and when finally assessing neo-realism's significance. In turning to consider the obstacles which confronted the neo-realists, there thankfully seems to be greater unanimity among commentators.

5 Obstacles

The offensive of the Catholic Church, the increasingly stringent censorship, and the growing hold of the Christian Democrats on government – these are generally held to be the major factors which impeded the neo-realist film makers in their endeavours. Marcus concurs, and in regard to the first element, cites the case of the attack on *Bicycle Thieves* by the Vatican newspaper *L'Osservatore romano*. One could cite many other such examples of the Church warning against the influence of neo-realist films. The Church had long taken an interest in the cinema and in 1936, Pope Pius XI had instructed all priests to warn their congregations against attending films 'which offend Christian truth and morality'.

To offer guidance on such matters, the *Centro Cattolico Cinematografico* had been established in 1934. It published the weekly *Segnalazioni cinematografiche*, which was distributed to all parishes and listed critical judgements on individual films, and the monthly *Rivista del cinematografico*, which contained articles of a more general nature. The *Centro* also offered advice on those subjects, themes and scenes which it deemed suitable for treatment; this advice was available in advance of going into production to all film producers, directors and scriptwriters who sought it. In short, the Church ran its own pre-production and post-production censorship board and this was, of course, in addition to those methods employed by the state.

As you would expect, very few neo-realist film directors appear to have taken up this offer of pre-production advice. But their finished films still came up for scrutiny. The standards applied by the Church's reviewing authority were well known for being severe and, not surprisingly, the neo-realist films fared badly at its hands. Of the films you will see, *Rome, Open City* was classified on the list of 'Recommendations for believers' as 'Dangerous for children'; *La Terra Trema* and *Umberto D* were considered just about suitable 'For adults with restrictions'; but *Riso Amaro* was 'Forbidden to all believers'.

Of course, it is one thing to pontificate about what people should or should not see; it is another thing actually to stop them from going to the cinemas to see what they like. The Church had no such powers. Yet even here it managed to exert considerable influence. Pius XI, for instance, had cannily realized that by controlling the places of exhibition, the cinemas, you not only dictated what was shown on the screen, and thereby what people saw, but you were also likely to be able, in time, to apply pressure on what was produced for those outlets.

Thus, he advocated the building and ownership of a large circuit of parish cinemas in the belief that, 'through the organization of such halls, which often represent the best clients for the industry, it will be possible to require that the industry itself produce films corresponding fully to our principles, which will then be projected easily not only in Catholic cinemas, but also in the others'.

Very little was done along those lines in the 1930s and during the war, in large measure because it was felt that the censorship policies exercised by the state were enough to prevent the exhibition of films which the Church might find objectionable. But clerical pressure to increase the growth of parish cinemas revived after the advent of neo-realism. It found support among

Christian Democrat politicians who proved more than willing to push for an increase in the rate of ministerial licences granting permission for parish cinemas, sometimes at the expense of traditional cinemas.

It has been estimated, for example, that between 1945 and 1955, licences for the purposes of enlargement or renovation of existing premises were granted to 774 commercial cinemas and to 546 parish cinemas, and for the purpose of constructing new cinemas to 447 applicants from each quarter. Of the applications from commercial interests for permission to construct brand new cinemas in that time, some 34.8 per cent were rejected, but only 10.1 per cent of parish applications were turned down.

Estimates differ, though, on the total number of both sorts of cinemas in existence throughout the forties and early fifties. One source states that by 1953 there were 7,517 commercial cinemas in operation as against 3,000 parish cinemas. Another source suggests that commercial cinemas outnumbered parish cinemas by a ratio of seven to one. It seems likely, however, that one-third of all cinemas were Church-controlled by the mid 1950s.

Whatever thc exact nature of the figures for the period, one thing is clear: the Roman Catholic Church exerted considerable influence, by one means or another, over the Italian cinema. More specifically, it was a powerful force to be reckoned with by the neo-realist film makers. In addition, of course, they also had to contend with the pressures brought to bear by the state in the form of censorship and other controls, and the fact that post-war Italian governments were increasingly made up of Christian Democrat administrations which proved decidedly antagonistic to neo-realism and all it represented. State censorship of the Italian cinema was nothing new. It had evolved at much the same time that censorship had been established for other European cinemas – in the period immediately preceding the First World War. Antonio Salandra had formulated the legislation, and a royal decree of 31 May 1914 had laid down that the purpose of state censorship of the Italian cinema was to prevent the public exhibition of:

1. performances offensive to morality, *buon costume* (good moral standards), public decency, and to private citizens;
2. performances contrary to national dignity and reputation, or to public order, or which can disturb good international relations;
3. performances offensive to the decorum and prestige of public institutions and authorities or officials and agents of the police;
4. repugnant scenes of brutality and cruelty, including those directed towards animals; of frightful crimes or suicides; and in general perverse actions and acts which instruct in or incite to crime or disturb minds or stimulate ill results.

It was a simple and basic set of rules which was elaborated by Salandra's successor, Francesco Severio Nitti, in 1920. Consequently, when the Fascists came to power they found they really did not need to do much more, except by way of amendment and refinement, to add to the near complete and effective foundations that had already been laid for the control of film content.

The rules were codified into a general cinema law in September 1923 and a bit of tinkering followed thereafter. But from 1935 the Fascist regime enacted no further legislation on the subject of film censorship. It was simply not required.

One sure sign of how relatively untainted by Fascist influence the basic censorship code was thought to be (though the Fascists always rigorously enforced it, as, Marcus reminds us, Visconti found out to his cost) was made clear in October 1945. Inevitably, the first post-war administration, headed by Ferruccio Parri, set about repealing all the reviled Fascist laws and regulations covering, among other things, the film industry. However, an exception was made of those provisions in the 1923 act relating to state powers of censorship in banning the selection and treatment of controversial cinematic subject matter. It was thought that a censorship code of some sort was still urgently required. And, crucially, it was also felt that this bit of film legislation owed little to Fascist inspiration and more to the respected politicians of an earlier age. The 1923 Fascist code, in effect, merely served to bring together what had been enacted between 1914 and 1920. Thus it was allowed to stand and to serve again in October 1945. Interestingly, nobody was found to argue against the retention of film censorship powers, from either the left or the right. Pietro Nenni and Palmiro Togliatti appended their signatures to the 1945 decree, along with Parri and many others.

It was expected, however, that Alcide De Gasperi would seek abrogation of the 1923 code by the time his government came to formulate legislation for the 1949 film act, not least after the Christian Democrat Party's espousal of 'freedom of speech, writing and every other means of communication' during the drafting of the 1948 Constitution. In the event, his government refused to repeal the existing censorship legislation and, furthermore, enshrined it in Article 28 of the new film act. In the interval between the Constituent Assembly and the 1949 act there had, of course, been a general election in which De Gasperi's party had won an absolute majority. As Marcus mentions, the new film laws very much bore the imprint of the minister responsible for them, Giulio Andreotti, and in fact the principal law was dubbed 'la legge Andreotti'.

One purpose of the new laws was to protect the Italian film industry against American competition, for a huge number of American films had deluged the home market in the years following the end of the war. Imported films were taxed and compulsory programming of Italian films was imposed on domestic cinemas for eighty days in the year. This exhibition quota sought to triple the number of Italian films in distribution.

But it was no good calling for more Italian films if there were not enough Italian films to be shown. Andreotti wished to increase the number of 'good' films in production and to that end he was prepared to advance production loans. The price to be paid for this support to the industry, however, came in the form of increased ministerial control over film content. Andreotti wanted a big say in what constituted a good film and in advance of production. Pre-production censorship was introduced and all scripts were to be submitted to a special ministerial commission. Needless to say, loans were only advanced and cash prizes awarded to those films displaying 'particular artistic value', as officially construed. And producers were thereby discouraged from backing those projects which sought to deal with themes and subjects that were officially frowned on and unlikely to receive financial assistance.

While it would not be strictly correct, therefore, to say that this system actually prevented film makers from embarking on controversial subjects, nevertheless that is very much the way it was intended to work in practice. And finally, as Marcus reminds us once again, the minister reserved the right to deny an export licence to any film which managed to escape the net yet still 'presented Italy in an unflattering light' – remember the 1914 censorship stricture about 'national dignity and reputation' – thereby preventing it from possibly recouping costs or accruing profits in the potentially lucrative foreign markets.

Unfortunately for the neo-realist film makers, Andreotti did not much like their films. He was in office as Under-secretary with responsibility for the cinema from 31 May 1947 until the death of his mentor, De Gasperi, in August 1953. His term of office throughout was marked by a profound distrust and antagonism towards neo-realist films and their directors. His censors excised material they found objectionable, in at least one instance his ministry vetoed a film project because a neo-realist, Giuseppe De Santis, was the proposed director; he personally denounced the films in parliament and, as Marcus recounts, De Sica earned his opprobrium not least for *Umberto D*, which Andreotti described as a 'wretched service to his fatherland'.

Further detail of the running battle between Andreotti and De Sica, in particular, must await discussion in the context of the films themselves. Suffice to say for the moment that in the organizations of state censorship and the Christian Democrat Party, and among its politicians especially, the neo-realist movement faced opponents as formidable as it did in the Roman Catholic Church.

6 Achievements

In view of the power of the opposition, comprising almost the full force of the Italian establishment it must have seemed, it is perhaps surprising that the neo-realist movement achieved any success at all. But succeed it did and Marcus does well to sing its praises. The Italian cinema owes it 'a lasting debt', she concludes, and still shows signs of its stylistic influence, at the very least. It lent strength, nobility and dignity of purpose to a medium which had become somewhat debased, tarnished and moribund, elevated it to the rank of a genuine art form and contributed significantly thereby to the rebirth of the Italian cinema and, some would argue, the reconstruction of post-war Italian culture.

Having said that, however, it is important to remember that its moment was short, as Marcus sensibly acknowledges. In all it lasted for less than ten years, from 1945 to 1954, and thereafter many of its exponents moved off, perhaps not surprisingly, into the mainstream of Italian film making. In certain cases they were simply returning to the realms they knew so well (as with De Sica and Zavattini), and they prospered. Then the left found its voice, issuing accusations of 'betrayal' of neo-realist ideals – a charge that has been levelled

Figures 8/9.1–6

Roberto Rossellini

Giuseppe De Santis

Vittorio De Sica

Luchino Visconti

Cesare Zavattini

Giulio Andreotti

ever since and which we shall return to. Other neo-realist film makers didn't make the transition so easily and some never bothered to try.

During those years, furthermore, only a small number of neo-realist films was ever made. Sources vary on the exact score given the inevitable disputes on what precisely constituted a neo-realist film. But there does seem agreement that between forty and fifty films demonstrated what might broadly be construed as the neo-realist influence and of that number about twenty were strictly neo-realist (to be compared, for instance, with a figure of 313 feature films produced in Italy between 1945 and 1950).

Nor, indeed, can it be claimed that the neo-realist cinema commanded a grassroots popular support which compensated for the small number of films it produced. Far from it. In truth the international critical acclaim it undoubtedly received and the many film festival prizes it won often surpassed its appeal at the Italian box office, except for a few notable instances. Most Italians preferred the comedies of Erminio Macario and Totò, or the melodramas by Raffaele Matarazzo. Of that there is no doubt.

These films were often critically scorned and rarely exported to English-speaking countries, but they packed audiences into the Italian cinemas. (A rough British equivalent would be the films of George Formby, which were panned by the critics but made him the top British box-office draw of the late 1930s and early 1940s. His films were rarely exported, since it was thought they were very much a local product, even parochial, and consequently would not 'travel well'.)

Macario had the big film hit of 1947, Totò's prodigious output of films kept him in the top ten of box-office attractions between 1948 and 1957, and a trilogy of Matarazzo's films gave him first, second and third places among box-office successes in 1949, 1950 and 1951 respectively. If Italians wanted to look elsewhere for their film entertainment, then of course there was always the traditional American bill of fare to hand and American films were immensely popular. Christopher Wagstaff will provide a fuller explanation of where neo-realism fits into the wider context of the Italian film industry and box office when you listen to Audio-cassette 4, side B, towards the end of these units.

The fact of the matter is that in neo-realism we are dealing for the most part with an 'art house' cinema, so called, and with 'quality' film making, though in this instance, I would argue, that does not necessarily mean it was also 'élitist' and 'esoteric'. Far from it. Neo-realism had discernible roots. It was very much of the people and for the people, even if it did not always reach the people or prove popular. Does that mean it was all to very little avail? Before we try to settle that question and finally assess neo-realism's achievements, or attempt to write its epitaph, perhaps we should look at some of its films.

3 The films

After that rather protracted discussion it will doubtless come as a relief to turn to the initial film extract. You will find all the extracts from the films on Video-cassette 2, 'Neo-realist feature film compilation'.

Ossessione, 1942

As Marcus mentions, Visconti's first feature production is interesting in part because it turned out to be a harbinger of the movement that was to flower at the end of the war. When it came out in 1942, however, it was a revelation and an innovation. It is difficult for you fully to grasp that aspect, perhaps, when you have nothing else to compare it with from the Italian cinema of the period.

When contemplating the extract from *Ossessione* ('Obsession'), though, you might care to ponder initially how it compares with films that you have probably seen from the same year, 1942, but from different national cinemas. How does it look against, say, the American film, *Mrs Miniver*, or Noel Coward's British film, *In Which We Serve*, or anything else you can think of from the time? It's not a strictly fair comparison, I know, and would create profound problems if we were to push the point too far.

A more accurate comparison might be with the American cinema of the 1930s or with the French cinema of such directors as Marcel Carné and René Clair, and all those atmospheric vehicles for the talents of scriptwriter Jacques Prévert and actor Jean Gabin. Visconti had in fact worked in France as an assistant to Jean Renoir, greatly admired his work, and drew much inspiration from him. Indeed, it was Renoir who in 1940 gave Visconti a copy of the French translation of James M. Cain's novel *The Postman Always Rings Twice*, on which *Ossessione* is based. However, the simple comparison I am suggesting might help to build up a picture of how fundamentally different *Ossessione* was to other films of that year. Not that it was widely seen, of course, even in Italy, where the lightweight and insubstantial 'white telephone' films predominated.

As we know from Marcus, *Ossessione* was not what Visconti had intended for his first feature film. He had planned to use a short story by Verga, but that project was barred by the Fascist film censors who did not fancy the idea of a film 'about banditry and self-degradation'. In the event, Visconti and his scriptwriting team, made up of *Cinema* critics and graduates from the *Centro Sperimentale*, including De Santis, came up with their adaptation of Cain's best-selling American thriller. (The production credits for all these films can be found in the supplementary booklet, *Cassette Notes 1*.) This script was passed by the film censors or, to be more precise, it was granted approval to move into production. Little did they realize what they were in for.

Before viewing the extract from the film, please read the following synopsis.

Synopsis

Ossessione unfolds in the Delta Farrarese, in northern Italy. The events are very simple and revolve around the trio involved in almost every tragic love story: a dissatisfied wife (Giovanna), a complacent husband (Bragana), and a stranger (Gino). Gino, a wanderer without a stable occupation, finds work at Bragana's inn and soon becomes Giovanna's lover. It appears to be increasingly difficult to keep the affair hidden from Bragana and the tension reaches a breaking point. Gino decides to resume his wandering life; Giovanna follows him but, tired and dejected, she decides to turn back after having covered only a short distance.

Gino meets another wanderer, the homosexual Spagnuolo, and stays in his company until the day on which, by chance, he sees Giovanna again at a fair. Rediscovering their passion for each other, the two lovers decide to eliminate Bragana. On their way home from the fair they murder him, simulating an automobile accident which the police find very suspicious.

A period of guilt and hostility between Gino and Giovanna follows the murder, but the news of Giovanna's pregnancy brings a short-lived peace. The two lovers decide to leave the place that reminds them of their crime in order to start a new life, but their dream is shattered by a real automobile accident in which Giovanna loses her life. The last scene of the film shows Gino being arrested while Giovanna's body lies in the road.

Exercise Now watch the extract (Video-cassette 2, extract A), which is taken from the very beginning of the film. As you watch the film consider how it compares with any other film of the period with which you are familiar. You might also think about how the style of the film might be described and how, given what you know of Italy at this time, it might have been received. ❑

What strikes me straight away about *Ossessione*, and forcefully so, is just how different it is in comparison with other films I know from the period. We are not dealing with nice, refined genteel folk of the type to be found in *Mrs Miniver* or Noel Coward's film, folk who lead simple uncomplicated lives. Greer Garson and Walter Pidgeon would not be seen dead in Signor Bragana's trattoria. No, these are rough, crude, down-to-earth people with their emotions very much to the fore and the film is nothing if not, to use that word again, 'realistic'.

It is obviously a love story and even the brief opening extract we see hints darkly, with its dramatic build up and climatic musical crescendo, at the likely *ménage à trois* and dire events that will follow. But it is a tragic love story and a study in obsessive passion of a different order from something like *Brief Encounter*, which the British cinema might offer in comparison and which in any case did not come out until a few years later, in 1946. Even then, Trevor Howard and Celia Johnson would hardly do for Gino and Giovanna – can you imagine it? 'The characters are living through a genuine passion,' Roy Armes has rightly pointed out, 'which is looked at directly and honestly and portrayed without glamour' (*Patterns of Realism*, p.55). Little wonder that Visconti has gone down on record as saying: 'Above all it is the intimacy of relationship between Massimo Girotti and Clara Calamai that I sought to translate with most accuracy.'

The two leading characters are attracted to each other from the outset, drawn together thereafter, and soon inextricably linked, sometimes with a distinctly melodramatic touch. Witness her double take on first seeing the stranger; her compliment on observing his 'fine shoulders'; the query 'why don't you eat?' and, later, 'are you still hungry?'; the pocketing of the money he has paid for the meal and the deliberate deception of her husband into thinking he has not paid; the constant sensual caressing of her own arms and shoulders, the alert eyes, not least when she realizes her husband has brought Gino back into their midst, possibly to stay for a while longer.

Figures 8/9.7–12 *Ossessione*

Gino

Gino and Giovanna

Gino and Giovanna

Gino and Giovanna

Gino and Giovanna

Giovanna's death in the road accident

The stranger, for his part, starts off with a comment full of *double entendre* about Bragana being lucky for having 'a good wife. Such a cook'. He too engages in a conscious deceit at her husband's expense when he pockets the lorry's distributor and sends Bragana off to find a replacement. (Later, the other pocket is filled with the key to the trattoria as Gino locks up before he and Giovanna make love.) He also joins in with her meaningful banter: 'Yes', he's still hungry, but this time: 'I can't afford to pay.' No matter. There have been enough knowing looks between the two of them throughout. No payment is required.

Money is not unimportant, however. It brings comfort, guarantees security and wins a position and status, of sorts. Gino knows about the lack of the former – he is unemployed, compelled to get around by hitch-hiking uncomfortable lifts, and picks up odd jobs whenever he can. Giovanna has suffered from the pangs of not knowing where the next meal will come from, it transpires, and the travails of depending on men to supply it, with all that that usually entails. She married Bragana for security, despite the difference in their ages.

On leaving the Bersaglieri (mountain troops in the regular army), Bragana bought the trattoria and now is on friendly terms with the local priest. But he is petty minded about losing a few plates or a chicken, marvels at Gino's vagrant nature, and is bossy to all and sundry, not least his wife to whom he lays down the law about being 'master' in his own home and enjoying the freedom to go out, when and if he chooses.

The film is strong, then, on characterization and motivation, and the social context is carefully delineated. But it is also especially adept at creating a distinct sense of place, of location: it was originally planned to call the film *Palude* ('Marsh'). In this Visconti anticipates the neo-realists for whom the setting was always important and who were theoretically concerned with the problems of landscape and milieu. We are presented with an unflattering provincial background of endless dusty roads and a bleak landscape. The interiors are just as authentic, creating the dingy, well lived-in atmosphere of the trattoria.

The characters, furthermore, are firmly placed within the setting and linked to it by means of some expressive camera work. An initial shot from a crane brings together Gino, the lorry, the men at the petrol pump and the trattoria. There is a preponderance of lengthy takes which merge characters with their environment, and a reliance on middle-distance shots to emphasize the same. Close-ups are reserved for moments of great emotion and crisis when they are effectively reinforced by an evocative musical score.

In all, *Ossessione* was an artistic success and a creative *tour de force* of a sort that had rarely been evident in the Italian cinema. It was recognized as such and greeted with much enthusiasm by the younger critics on *Cinema* and elsewhere. It did not go down well, however, with the Fascist authorities. No film made during the Fascist era had ever shown unemployment (except in a highly sanitized way). And while adultery had been broached as a subject (even the matter of consummated adultery, for instance, in De Sica's film from the same year, *The Children Are Watching Us*), this was hardly a recommendation. Visconti's film, furthermore, not only showed a consummated adultery with all its murderous ramifications, but was also seen to challenge the institution of marriage, a cornerstone of both Fascist and Roman Catholic ideology. In this regard, the symbolic figure of the homosexual Spagnuolo was especially important. He represents, as Armes has noted, 'the essential male freedom'. And, as Visconti has commented: 'At the time, this character was the very symbol of revolution and freedom of thought.' I have not explored the character at all because, of course, he does not appear in the extract you see. But he is a key figure.

Ossessione predictably caused controversy. Vittorio Mussolini reportedly stormed out of the special premiere arranged by the *Cinema* critics, shouting: 'This is not Italy'. The Catholic Film Centre damned the film and priests attacked it. There were calls for its withdrawal as, for example, in the pages of the Bologna daily *Avvenire d'Italia* on 15 July 1943:

> We wish to direct the attention of the authorities towards a film which has already been forbidden or discontinued elsewhere and which has now surfaced in our town. We do not wish to apply to it any aesthetic criteria. The only conclusion to arrive at might be that the film is just imitating the French kind of realism that must not be transferred to Italy. The film is a concoction of repulsive passions, humiliation and decay. It is an offence to the Italian people, the life of which it pretends to portray on a thoroughly imaginary and impossible level.

The film was withdrawn and the original negative destroyed when the bulk of the official film industry moved north to Mussolini's republic of Salò, though Visconti managed to retain a copy.

Ossessione was not a film about wartime experiences. Nor did it employ non-professionals and a documentary style, though Visconti was attracted to the idea of working with the former, as we shall see, when it came to his next film some years later. What *Ossessione* did do, however, was provide a stunning example for other film makers to emulate. It was a precursor of neo-realism.

Rome, Open City, 1945

The fictional events depicted in *Rome, Open City* are confined within a relatively short period of time, barely seventy-two hours in the lives of its small group of leading characters. As both its principal scriptwriter and director have indicated, however, the film owed its inspiration to historical events which took place mainly in the period between the Nazi occupation of Rome, in September 1943, and the Allied liberation of the city, in June 1944. 'We made *Rome, Open City* under the impression, the suggestion, and the influence of what we had just lived through', wrote Sergio Amidei. 'You had to avoid being a poet and everything an artist usually is,' Roberto Rossellini elaborated, 'and force yourself to look around in a strictly realist fashion.'

Though the film did not start production until two months after the Liberation, in fact its genesis lay in the spring of 1944 when Rossellini received a commission from a wealthy Roman lady to make a short documentary about

Don Morosini, a Roman priest who had been shot by the Germans. Subsequently, she suggested a second documentary be made on the Resistance activities of the Roman children. The director then combined both themes into plans for a full-length feature film, drawing also on the stories of Don Papagallo, another murdered priest, and Celeste Negarville, a leading Communist figure in the Resistance. As a founding Christian Democrat member of the cinema workers' branch of the Committee of National Liberation, Rossellini had some knowledge and experience of the resistance (though his first three films were propaganda films sponsored by the Fascist regime). And, as Amidei recognized: 'We have all been the instrument of the will of the underground army that was anxious to write its page for the book of history.'

Synopsis

The Gestapo chief, Bergmann, is desperately looking for Giorgio Manfredi, a leader of the underground. Bergmann has discovered his whereabouts. As the Nazi patrol closes in on Manfredi's house, he escapes and seeks refuge at the home of Francesco, a printer and fellow Communist. He is met by Pina, who is set to marry Francesco the following day and is already carrying his child.

Money must be carried to a secret rendezvous by Father Don Pietro who is invaluable to the underground. Pina sends her present child, Marcello, to fetch the priest so Manfredi can tell him of the plans. Marcello is a member of a gang of young saboteurs and they blow up a Nazi installation. Meanwhile, the Gestapo has cultivated Marina, Manfredi's mistress, through a woman agent who has kept her supplied with narcotics and other luxuries. Don Pietro keeps the rendezvous with the partisans and delivers a million lire concealed in a book.

Next day, while preparations for Francesco's and Pina's wedding are being made, the apartment is raided. Francesco is taken away. Manfredi escapes. Pina runs after the truck that is carrying away her bridegroom and is shot down. The underground is notified of the arrest and lies in wait to ambush the lorries bearing the prisoners. They machine gun it. Most of the prisoners escape. Manfredi and Francesco take refuge in Marina's apartment. When Manfredi discovers Marina is a drug addict, however, an argument ensues. Their affair is ended.

Marina overhears Manfredi and Francesco plan to hide in a monastery. Out of revenge and desperation, she informs her Gestapo friend, Ingrid. As Manfredi, Francesco and Don Pietro are making ready to leave for the monastery they are captured and only Francesco escapes. The Gestapo's purpose is to obtain information and break the unity of the priest and the underground leader. But Manfredi has made a pact with Don Pietro in the prison cell not to reveal anything. Bergmann cannot break their bond, despite threats and torture.

Figures 8/9.13–18 *Rome, Open City*

Pina and Francesco

Pina and Marcello

Don Pietro

Manfredi

Bergmann

The children on the Via Trionfale

Don Pietro refuses to make Manfredi admit anything. Manfredi dies and the priest is declared a traitor and ordered shot by a firing squad. As he goes to his death another priest, there to administer the last rites, tells him to have courage. Don Pietro's last words are: 'It's not difficult to die well. The difficult thing is to live right.'

Exercise You should now watch Video-cassette 2, extracts B and C (two short sequences which follow one another closely in the first half of the film), and extract D (a longer sequence from the very end). Remember that the production credits to the film are in *Cassette Notes 1*.

1 What, essentially, does *Rome, Open City* celebrate, and what are the major contrasts being drawn by Rossellini?

2 What formal and stylistic methods are employed by Rossellini to achieve his purpose?

Discussion 1 With the onset of Liberation, Italo Calvino recounted, the Italians found themselves, 'face to face, equals, filled with stories to tell; each had a tale, each had lived an irregular, dramatic and adventurous life, and snatched the very words from their neighbour's mouth' ('Preface', p.v). This film was part of that general process. It was meant to be, in all, a chronicle of events as experienced in Rome during the Nazi Occupation.

In particular, as these extracts make very clear, the film highlights the nature of the Resistance to that occupation, embracing as it did both an underground partisan army, united in purpose despite differing political and ideological allegiances, and an increasingly widespread grass-roots movement, emanating directly from the people and including even the younger members of the population. The Resistance is imbued with ideals (witness Francesco's talk with Pina on the tenement stairs promising 'a better world'), it has strength of character (hence the capacity to withstand torture, the refusal to betray each other), and its adherents are heroic and willing to lay down their lives for the cause (as Manfredi and Don Pietro do in the end).

Though in this instance the Resistance activities are largely thwarted, the ideals it represents and the example it sets are taken to heart by the next generation and will undoubtedly come to fruition after the war is over. This is, to my mind, the intent of the final scene in which the children observe Don Pietro's death and then walk back to Rome along the Via Trionfale (Triumphal Way), with the dome of St Peter's in the background. Thus, a fusion of secular and religious influences is achieved – a fusion that invokes antiquity, but which avoids the rhetorical excesses with which antiquity was much overlaid during the Fascist era. History is reappropriated for use in the period after the fall of Mussolini.

To anticipate this finale, furthermore, there is an earlier deliberate transposition of the imagery you would expect to accompany the deaths of Manfredi and Don Pietro. The Communist is the one tortured and framed in a distinctly Christ-like fashion at the end, whereas the Catholic is granted a more mundane execution, astride a chair. But, to repeat, their sacrifice is not in vain, and here Rossellini's Christian humanist message, advocating a mix of secular activism and Christian spirituality, is most evident. The children's education is complete only after they have witnessed the priest's death. Then, the streetwise Romoletto ('little Romulus') – who is inclined, you will notice, to address his gang as 'Comrades' – is free to lead his band of saboteur urchins back into the city, the better equipped to deal with the future. While essentially a celebration of the Resistance in defeat, Rossellini concluded his film on an optimistic note, arguing that the unity that the Resistance had engendered should be continued into the post-war world.

To take his points further, Rossellini draws a simple contrast, at least initially, between the powers of good and evil. Obviously, the people of Rome and the forces of the Resistance, especially, comprise the former and the German occupiers and their collaborators the latter. Thus Bergmann is depicted as vicious and sadistic, displaying little regard for human life. He is cunning, however, recognizing that there have been 'enough martyrs', and so consigns Manfredi to an anonymous grave. His woman agent, Ingrid, casually discards Marina when she has served her purpose. She makes a point of retrieving the fur coat she gave her, for future use (though it is only hinted at in the extracts you see, Ingrid has exercised a measure of lesbian control in her relationship with Marina, as well as being the supplier of her drugs).

For the most part, then, the Germans are portrayed as cruel, ruthless, or sexually aberrant. They are hardly fully rounded characters and serve as mere cyphers – though cyphers, it must be remembered, that would not have been seen much, if at all, in the Italian cinema previously. Hence, the fact that they still made quite an impression (a matter to which we shall return when discussing the public reception afforded the film). By contrast, perhaps predictably, the Italian characters are presented as fully realized figures displaying great depth and subtlety. The two very different heroes, the Catholic and the Communist, are sympathetically rendered. So, also, are Francesco and Pina, the latter not least when she has to deal with a wayward son, her contentious sister, Lauretta, and a frenetic household, all on the eve of her wedding. Little wonder she is weary. Her chat on the stairs with Francesco, as you see, is warm and appealing. The fact that she was already pregnant with Francesco's child must have caused a few raised eyebrows among cinema audiences in Catholic Italy when the film was released in 1945. But, there again, her saving graces in comparison with the dissolute and weak collaborator, Marina, were plain for all to see. 'It is through these last two, both daughters of the working classes,' maintains Millicent Marcus, 'that Rossellini avoids sentimentalizing the proletariat, showing that for every Pina there is a Lauretta or a Marina, ready to exploit the situation for selfish or mercenary ends'. Such contrasts and careful touches added considerably to the film's rich store of credible human values and emotions.

2 Rossellini achieved his purpose through a variety of formal and stylistic methods, all of which have generally been held to help mark *Rome, Open City* as the first true film in the neo-realist canon. There is also an obvious use of comic elements to enhance the realism. This is particularly evident in the initial extract you see.

After the serious business of blowing up a German installation (and a stirring piece of musical accompaniment), the young boys return to their tenement basement. They are filled with pride at their daring and successful deed. But as they climb the stairs to enter their respective flats, they are picked off one-by-one by irate parents, worried at their being out after curfew. As the sounds of scolding increase in number, Rossellini cleverly uses his camera within the confines of the tenement location to show us Marcello's mounting fear of what awaits him in his flat at the top of the stairs. Clearly Pina's anger is worse than anything the Germans might throw at him, and his ego is suitably deflated.

There are several comic interjections of this kind throughout the film, sometimes capitalizing on the skills of actors Aldo Fabrizi (Don Pietro) and Anna Magnani (Pina), both of whom learned their craft in music halls. Comedy is intermingled with the serious aspects until Rossellini distinctly shifts the perspective, on the death of Pina, and the film moves wholly into a tragic mode of the sort we witness so graphically in the final scenes. But the mixture was established here and was to prove much in evidence in subsequent neo-realist films.

Similarly, *Rome, Open City* displayed many of the stylistic features that were to follow. The lighting is low key, deliberately so, and we have already noted the use of a tenement location and the Via Trionfale. The film is full of location shooting, including even Sergio Amidei's personal flat for the opening scene of Manfredi's escape. But, significantly, Rossellini did resort to a studio when he felt it was absolutely necessary to do so and he used the small Via degli Avignonesi studio belonging to Liborio Capitano. There he created Marina's flat, Don Pietro's room and, as must be clear from the final extract, the Gestapo headquarters (reportedly a reconstruction of the headquarters of Gestapo chief, Herbert Kappler, in the Via Tasso). By these means Rossellini managed to capture an authentic and uncontrived look for his finished film, so much so that critics have often commented on its newsreel quality. The newsreels, though, were already in existence and had been for a long time. By contrast,

Rossellini's film offered much that was new in the realms of feature film. Its contribution to neo-realism has been well summarized by Roy Armes:

> On all kinds of levels *Rome, Open City* set the pattern for the subsequent development of the neo-realist movement: in its techniques of location shooting and post-synchronization of dialogue; in being financed largely from outside the film industry and making its profits abroad; in its closeness to life as it is lived; in its use of children; in the discovery of Anna Magnani and Aldo Fabrizi and the accommodation of them to new roles; and in its overall pattern of a story of defeat ending with a sense of the problems being not fully resolved.
>
> (*Patterns of Realism*, p.74) ❑

Only in one respect, perhaps, does Armes somewhat overstate the case. The film was certainly a success abroad, not least in France and America after its 1946 premieres in both countries. It won the Grand Prix at the Cannes Film Festival in that year and went on to be the sensation of the Paris cinemas. In America, it was hailed as the best film of the year and took between one and three million dollars at the box office. But it was also a considerable success in its home country.

Rome, Open City received its Italian premiere in September 1945. The critical response was divided. The Church could hardly carp, given the heroic portrayal of one of its priests. But the film was classified as 'dangerous for children' on the basis of its graphic depiction of violence and the introduction of sordid themes involving sex and drugs. Among cinemagoers, however, the film was a definite hit. In the first few months of its release, until the end of 1945, it took 61 million lire at the Italian box office. For a film that had cost 11 million to produce, that was a sizeable profit – though little of it found its way into the pockets of the film makers since the film had been sold outright to a distributor for 13 million lire. Subsequently it continued to enjoy huge popular success and by the end of the 1945–46 season, *Rome, Open City* had achieved first place in box-office returns.

It is difficult to account for this success with any degree of certainty, of course, particularly in the light of the subsequent failure of so many neo-realist films. Perhaps it was the novel appeal of the subject matter and its treatment, all very new to Italian audiences in 1945 and doubtless seen as sensational. Perhaps it was because of the film's obvious message and its identification of Italians with the fight against Fascism. It did, after all, bear witness to 'the beliefs in the months immediately following the liberation', as Armes states, and it captured 'the note of hope with which the year 1945 ended'. In that regard, if no other, it was very much a film of and for the moment.

Paisà, 1946

For his next film, which he began shooting in the first months of 1946, Rossellini returned to the events of the war for his subject matter. Once more, though, what he produced was hardly what you would call an ordinary war film any more than, on this occasion, it followed the path of a conventional narrative. With the confidence born of his success with *Rome, Open City*, Rossellini adopted a different approach to the storyline for *Paisà*. (The title, incidentally, derives from the American soldiers' half-affectionate, half-contemptuous slang term for an Italian. Albeit strictly untranslatable, it is clearly a colloquial form of 'paesano' meaning countryman, neighbour, kinsman, even friend.) It is often argued that *Paisà* was even more distinguished than its predecessor. In demonstrating Rossellini's complete grasp of the medium and the full effectiveness of his stylistic method, *Paisà* is viewed by many as the director's most important film and, in the eyes of some, as the most impressive film of the entire neo-realist movement.

The script evolved from a series of personal reminiscences and anecdotes recounted to Rossellini by a band of his friends including Sergio Amidei, Marcello Pagliero (who had played Manfredi and was himself a film director), the author, Vasco Pratolini, and Klaus Mann (son of the author, Thomas Mann). Although the dialogue was to be much improvised when shooting began, Rossellini fashioned a script which would have a far wider canvas than his previous film. This time he intended to cover the whole of the period from July 1943 to the winter of 1944 and to traverse the length of Italy, following the Allied invasion forces from the beaches of Sicily to the marshlands of the Po River valley.

To this end, Rossellini organized his narrative into six discrete episodes: an American commando force landing in a tiny Sicilian port; the occupation of Naples, where a black American military policeman has his boots stolen in an encounter with a young boy; Rome, six months after its Liberation, when a GI picks up a prostitute he does not recognize from an earlier meeting; Florence, and the struggle for control of the city between partisans and Fascists; the visit of three US Army chaplains to a remote Franciscan monastery in the Apennines; and, finally, the marshes of the Po delta in the winter of 1944 where partisans and American OSS officers still fighting with the Germans are captured and executed. Clearly, Rossellini was not so concerned this time with establishing a conventional storyline. The individual episodes complemented each other, reinforced each other, and worked up in a cumulative fashion towards a coherent whole. But they remained separate and discrete little stories for all that, as you will shortly see, each a mini-feature film in its own right you might say. Though by no means unknown in the cinema, it was still a highly innovative and demanding format, not least for the viewer. In the eyes of the film trade, the average cinemagoer was reputed to prefer the comforting reassurance of a predictably linear narrative and a comparatively straightforward exposition of plot.

Stylistically Rossellini's method was to employ, once again, all those features he had introduced previously but to push them to greater limits. Thus, he shot on location (but more so than he had done before); some episodes were filmed almost entirely in long and medium shot to locate the characters firmly within their surroundings ('The actor must never be left alone', Rossellini stated, 'reveal the milieu'); and there was an increasing dependence on lesser known professional actors and non-professionals. Maria Michi (who

Figures 8/9.19 – 24 *Paisà*

Joe and Pasquale

Pasquale

Joe and Pasquale

Joe and Pasquale

Joe and Pasquale

Joe and Pasquale

had played Marina in the earlier film) was used in the role of the Rome prostitute; a couple of members of the imported American contingent claimed some acting experience. But most of the cast were chosen on the basis of their physical appearance rather than anything else. As the director explained: 'In order to choose my actors, I started by installing myself in the middle of the district where such or such an episode was to be shot. The passers-by then gathered around me and I chose my actors from amongst the crowd.' Thus, Rossellini claimed, with some measure of justification, '*Paisà* is therefore a film without actors in the true sense of the word'.

Given the self-contained nature of the six episodes, and the fact that you are to see episode two, the Neapolitan one, in its entirety, I do not intend to provide a synopsis of the complete film. What I want you to do, however, is to read the two quotations below (the first from Rossellini himself, the second from his assistant director and co-scriptwriter, Federico Fellini):

ROSSELLINI In *Paisà* there are two worlds which came into contact, each with a different psychology and mental structure. From this contact was born a great confusion; so much so that in the end there were neither victors nor vanquished, there remained only the everyday heroism of the man who clings to life. And who lives, despite everything, whether he is one of the victors or the vanquished.

FELLINI With *Paisà* I went all over Italy with Rossellini, because as you know the action of the film stretches right from Sicily to the Po, and it was a very exciting discovery, because the war had just ended, and we were surrounded by a whole new race of people, who seemed to be drawing hope from the very hopelessness of their situation. There were ruins, trees, scenes of disaster and loss, and everywhere a wild spirit of reconstruction. In the midst of which we did our tour. The troupe of people working on *Paisà* travelled through an Italy they scarcely knew, because for twenty years we'd been in the grip of a regime which had literally blindfolded us.

Exercise Watch Video-cassette 2, extract E. What were the film makers' intentions in regard to this episode, and by what means did they convey their intent?

Discussion Two things stand out for me as far as the film makers' purpose is concerned. First of all, the episode is plainly meant to show the hardship of everyday life and the awful realities of survival in the rubble of war-torn Naples. It is a devastating picture of the aftermath of war and its effects on ordinary people. The orphaned boy is compelled to eke out an existence by whatever devious means he can and forced to live in squalid conditions, along with the other displaced folk, in caves on the edge of the city. The lad's spirits remain high but poverty is rampant. And the black GI's astonished reaction on seeing such degradation and suffering speaks for us all. In this respect, the film makers achieve their desired effect by faithfully showing us the situation in as unsensational and unglamorous a manner as possible. The images are sufficiently powerful in themselves to evoke a sympathetic response, without recourse to much in the way of artifice or contrivance – notice the absence of background music on the soundtrack except, fleetingly, for emotional reinforcement in the few final shots.

In addition, however, the film is clearly attempting to broach a more philosophical theme: the encounter of two different cultures – Italian and American. This particularly fascinated Rossellini. It gave him the opportunity to pursue his personal brand of Christian humanism, so evident in his previous film, and to explore the extent to which solidarity might be created among people not only of differing backgrounds but also of differing nationalities.

In the first instance, as you see, there is a distinct clash of cultures. Language is a basic barrier; it limits communication and prevents deeper understanding. Then irony is used to great effect. The drunken Joe, the descendant of former slaves, is the subject of an auction among the very people he has been sent to liberate. Having acquired him by deceit, the boy Pasquale takes Joe to a puppet play where a black puppet features in the traditional role of villain. Subsequently, Joe and Pasquale strike up a friendship of sorts in the rubble of Naples. But Joe's equivocal position is stressed when, in the midst of his drunken reverie, he pours out his heart about returning home to no more than a rundown shack. Pasquale's ambivalence is emphasized with the warning to Joe not to fall asleep; if he does he is likely to lose his boots.

The final irony comes in the caves, of course. Once sober, and back in the MP's uniform which bestows so much authority, Joe apprehends Pasquale, recognizes him as the thief, and demands to see the boy's parents. But there are no parents. They have been killed in an Allied bombing raid, and there are only the folk in the caves. The boy's minor misdemeanour pales into insignificance against the immensity of suffering caused by the war. Joe flees the place.

At the end of this episode, then, the divisions between the two cultures appear as strong as ever. However, this has not prevented one American critic, Peter Bondanella, from arguing that 'Joe has taken the first step, that of understanding, towards becoming Pasquale's *paisà*' (*Italian Cinema*, p.46). Furthermore, for Bondanella the film demonstrates that 'the value of a man's life presupposes love for one's fellows' and that ultimately all the barriers – linguistic, cultural and otherwise – 'give way in the face of moral commitment' (p.50).

To my mind, this is reading too much both into this episode and the complete film. It is tempting to do so, given Rossellini's obvious intent with the earlier *Rome, Open City* to conjure an optimistic message out of a pessimistic narrative. But *Paisà* is a very different film, as audiences well recognized (it was a success but less so than its predecessor, reaching the ninth overall box-office position for the 1946–47 season).

The point of the episode we see, surely, is that Joe does flee the site of the caves. He may carry new-found sympathy in his heart for the dispossessed, as you would expect, but he flees just the same. We do not know the outcome of his experience, if, indeed, there is one. Rossellini raises the question of the two distinct cultures, he shows a clash and a modest rapprochement, but finally he resolves nothing. And the rest of the film is the same. The British critic, Roy Armes, is nearer the point when he states that '*Paisà* is not particularly profound in its handling of abstract concepts' and that Rossellini betrayed 'a certain vagueness of thought on wider issues'. This is because in *Paisà* 'the war is scaled down to a purely personal level'. Thus we get individual characters' 'dreams' but there is little of 'the ideological conflict' that was so evident in *Rome, Open City* (*Patterns of Realism*, pp.81 and 80).

The simple fact of the matter, of course, was that film makers were moving away from dealing exclusively with the Italian experience of the Second World War. As Rossellini admitted: 'It was the war which motivated me: war and resistance are collective actions by definition. If from the collective I then passed to an examination of personality – that was part of my natural evolution as a director.' ❑

It was this process of 'evolution', natural or otherwise, that increasingly gave rise to the charge of 'a betrayal of neo-realism', as we shall see with the next examples.

Caccia Tragica, 1947, and *Riso Amaro*, 1948

Both these films were directed by Giuseppe De Santis who, we have already noted, studied at *Centro Sperimentale*, worked as a critic for *Cinema* and as a scriptwriter on Visconti's *Ossessione*, and finally encountered problems with Andreotti's department. Indeed, after De Sica, he was reportedly next on Andreotti's list of targets over the years, and unsurprisingly so. Apart from his distinctly left-wing political credentials, De Santis was a leading advocate and exponent of neo-realist cinema. However, his long apprenticeship in film stood De Santis in good stead when he set about assembling production teams consisting of some of the best talent available. As you will see from the credits for these films (contained in *Cassette Notes 1*), his teams included scriptwriters old and new in Cesare Zavattini, Michelangelo Antonioni, Umberto Barbaro and Carlo Lizzani; the accomplished editor and Visconti's favourite, Mario Serandrei; and the most respected Italian cinematographer of the immediate post-war era, Otello Martelli.

Yet, paradoxically, De Santis is of special interest as the director who extended the boundaries of neo-realism, as these two films show. 'Though ideologically the most doctrinaire of the neo-realists in his militant commitment to the PCI', Millicent Marcus has observed, 'De Santis was the first major director to introduce heterodox elements into the new post-war film idiom'. He created a neo-realist hybrid and consciously so. His comments bear

Figures 8/9.25–30 *Caccia Tragica*

One of the gang

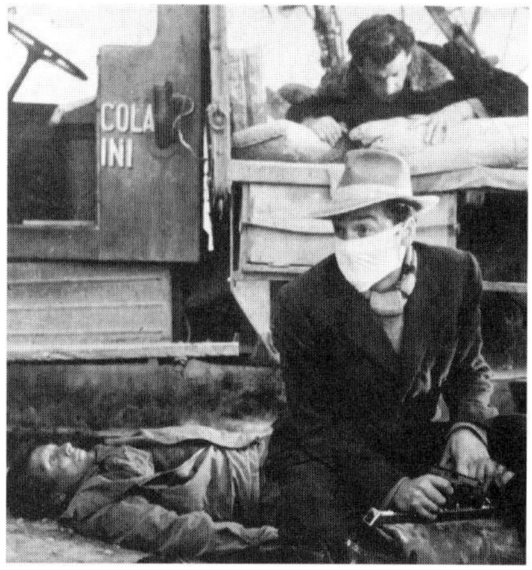

Gang members

Gang members flanking l–r Daniela, Alberto, Giovanna

Daniela

Alberto and Daniela

Giovanna, Alberto and Michele (standing above the crowd)

witness to what he sought to achieve and, incidentally, also bear fruitful comparison with De Sica's comments (as quoted on p.249):

> My position with regard to realism implies a transfiguration of reality. I do not entirely share Rossellini's theories – Art is not the reproduction of simple documents. By contenting ourselves with planting the film camera in the street or in the houses we can only attain a completely exterior realism. In my opinion, realism does not at all exclude a fiction, nor all the classically cinematographic means.

Yet, for De Santis, the starting point was still to be the events of everyday life and social reality. Thus, the genesis of *Caccia Tragica* ('Tragic Pursuit') lay in a news story published in the *Corriere Lombardo* recounting the trials and tribulations which beset an agricultural co-operative starting up in the Romagna in the months after the armistice. Similarly, *Riso Amaro* ('Bitter Rice') drew its inspiration from the experiences of the *mondine*, the thousands of women and girls who flocked annually to the rice fields to work under miserable conditions for a seasonal wage of 40,000 lire and 40 kilos of rice.

Both films, then, were plainly locked into reality at a time when agrarian struggles and reform were issues very much to the fore. 'By 1947 the first great wave of agrarian agitation in post-war Italy had clearly come to an end', Paul Ginsborg recounts in his talk on the topic, but 'between 1948 and 1950 another great wave of militancy swept through the rural areas' (Audio-cassette 5, side A). Yet both films, once completed, amounted to more than simple statements documenting the social problems of rural injustice. The reality they construed was undoubtedly transformed. And this was done by every cinematographic means at De Santis's disposal, as you will see.

Synopsis of Caccia Tragica

The film is set in the Romagna district, a few months after the Liberation. A lorry, carrying several million lire loaned by the government to an agricultural co-operative, is ambushed by bandits. Their leader is Daniela, nicknamed Lili Marlene because of her collaboration with the Germans during the war. Two young peasants, Michele and Giovanna, married only that morning, are travelling on the lorry. Michele recognizes one of the gang, Alberto, as a friend with whom he had been in a concentration camp. To ensure Michele's silence, Giovanna is taken as a hostage.

Learning of the theft, which means ruin for them, the members of the co-operative organize a hunt to capture the gang, recover the money and set Michele's wife free. Thus begins the 'tragic pursuit' of the title. Every farm collective in the region joins the hunt and a cordon is thrown around the district.

The farmers are soon in hot pursuit. They surround a house where the gang is hiding but because of Giovanna's presence, fail to prevent their getaway (extract F on Video-cassette 2). The gang separate. Alberto and two others decide to board a train usually crowded with black-marketeers but this time also filled with ex-servicemen on their way to a protest rally (extract G). Daniela makes for a hideout in the marshes taking Giovanna with her. Later, with police aid, the farmers hold up the train on which Alberto has already managed to exchange some of the stolen money for foreign currency. He gets away but is closely followed and caught by Michele who, angry at Alberto's attempts to bargain, beats him. Alberto, whose uneasy conscience has made him a prey to misgivings, promises to lead Michele to the hideout in the marshes where he will find his wife and retrieve the stolen money.

When they arrive, the farmers are again closing in. Alberto enters alone in the hope of convincing Daniela that the game is up and surrender is best. But she accuses him of treachery and threatens to blow up the fields which are landmined and the existence of which had been disclosed by the Germans. Failing to dissuade the crazed Daniela from her murderous course, Alberto shoots her, despite his horror of the deed.

He is taken by the farmers who immediately set up a summary court. Michele and Giovanna come to his aid and defend him, explaining the plight of the many unsettled and unemployed ex-prisoners of war. The farmers' livelihood is now secure with the return of the money and, also, the cattle which had been taken away by the corrupt henchmen of their absentee landlord. So, they give Alberto his liberty and he leaves their 'court room' with a new future before him (extract H).

Exercise Now watch the extracts (F, G and H) from *Caccia Tragica* on Video-cassette 2. While watching this material, identify those features that distinguish this film as neo-realist. What other elements and influences would you say were also evident? I will discuss these points after you have worked through *Riso Amaro*.

Synopsis of *Riso Amaro*

The railway station at Turin is crowded with thousands of women setting out for their seasonal work in the rice fields. Francesca is waiting for her lover, Walter, who has just stolen a diamond necklace. The police are already watching the station. Walter gives Francesca the necklace and escapes. Francesca finds herself on the train with the rice workers and makes friends with one of them, Silvana, whose outlook on life has been formed by cheap movies and even cheaper novelettes. Silvana suspects why Francesca is on the train. She helps her to get work in the rice fields with the *clandestine*, the 'outsiders', the non-union women who want work at any price and who are hated by the 'regulars'.

Walter is to join Francesca in the rice fields, so she must remain whatever the conditions and the difficulties. She becomes the ringleader of the *clandestine* and persuades them to work faster than the regulars in order to keep their jobs. By tradition the women may not talk while at work, but they can sing. The two sides abuse each other in song, and a fight develops in the flooded fields. The row is stopped by Silvana. She focuses everybody's anger on Francesca who, in panic, tries to flee. Marco, an army sergeant, appears with his men and his intervention brings peace (extract I on Video-cassette 2). He stops further quarrelling between the two girls but Silvana informs him that Francesca is a thief. Marco's kindly attitude influences Francesca to regret her past and Silvana to feel ashamed.

Figures 8/9.31–6 *Riso Amaro*

The mondine

Walter and Silvana

Silvana

Silvana

Francesca and Marco

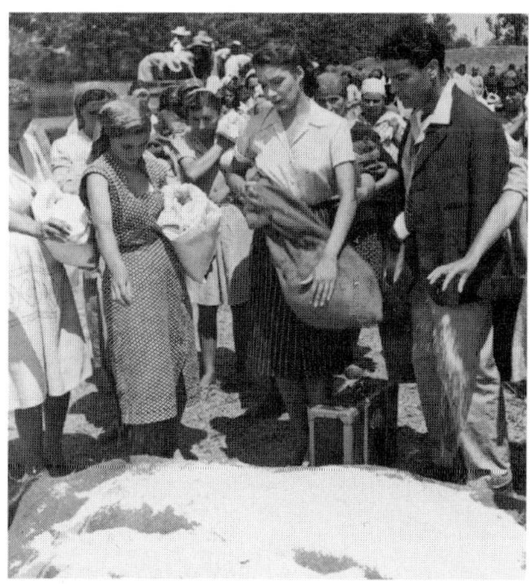

Scattering rice on Silvana's body

Walter turns up at the rice fields and one night, when the women are dancing, he joins Silvana, who attracts him. She is wearing the necklace. A fight develops between Marco and Walter, in which the latter gets the worst of it. He confides to Francesca that the necklace is false and explains that he will stay in hiding nearby because he plans another theft. He is also after Silvana, whom he seduces. Francesca is not blind to what is happening and is no longer interested in her lover.

The end of the rice season approaches and everyone looks forward to the harvest festival, when each worker receives a bonus of a sack of rice. Walter's plan is to flood the fields, with Silvana's help, and divert attention, then to steal the store of rice. Francesca discovers the plot and with Marco tries to prevent the theft. Marco and Walter again fight and Walter takes refuge in the farm's slaughterhouse. They are both wounded and the two girls take up the gun battle.

Silvana, who finds out the necklace is false, deliberately kills Walter to prevent his escape and, horrified by what she has done, ends her own life. The workers depart and each woman scatters a handful of rice over Silvana's body – to bestow a cherished possession is the ultimate symbol of forgiveness. Francesca and Marco start their lives together and once again the rice fields lie quiet.

Exercise Now watch Video-cassette 2, extract I, again looking out for what I asked earlier in relation to *Caccia Tragica.*

Discussion The most obvious neo-realist distinguishing feature is that both films undeniably adopt a social realist perspective: they raise genuine social problems for analysis, highlight a variety of social injustices, and posit a social solution which favours collective ideals and communal solidarity at the expense of individualism and self-advancement.

To emphasize this latter point, in particular, a series of simple contrasts is drawn, not least in the extracts you see: between, for example, Michele (who has suffered from his wartime experience but knows the way ahead lies in collective action) and Alberto (a fellow sufferer but one who has been led astray and is trying to go it alone); between, also, Silvana and the *mondine* – notice how you never actually see her working alongside them, how she takes to the horsedrawn cart to distribute the new rice shoots. Silvana is the cause of Francesca's victimization; when the *mondine* are reconciled with the *clandestine* and decide to present a united front to their overseers, Silvana stands apart and is left in the fields. The common cause is not for her.

Within these broad parameters, however, both films allow for a considerable degree of nuance in characterization. The murderous Daniela, blighted by the sin of collaboration, and the mindless thief, Walter, are summarily dispatched. But Alberto and Silvana have redeeming features and, besides, their failings are not wholly of their own making. Like the ex-servicemen on the train, Alberto could not find employment at the war's end. The former, united, tour the country and hold rallies seeking jobs and bread as well as long-term solutions to society's ills. Alberto sought only instant gratification and so took to a life of crime. But, when pressed, he cannot deny the fraternity of ex-comrades and fellow prisoners. He knows where his sympathies truly lie. And, as you see, he makes an impassioned and impressive speech on their behalf, apprising the people of their plight.

By the same token, Silvana is also a victim of circumstances. In her case, of course, the circumstances which gave rise to her problems arose largely in the period following Liberation. She is a victim of 'Americanization'. De Santis said as much when commenting that his purpose with Silvana was to 'criticize alienation, the American morality of *Readers Digest* and pin-up films'. He continued: 'I tried to show how certain sectors of the younger generation in Italy have become Americanized in outlook. These youngsters are incapable of understanding where their own interest lies. Instead of joining forces for the struggle, they drift into a life of facile pleasure which condemns them to extinction.' Thus America is a corrupting influence. But despite the force of that invective, De Santis's general attitude to the process of Americanization was clearly very ambivalent, as I trust you will have spotted (we shall elaborate on this shortly).

In the character of Silvana, however, De Santis made his intentions perfectly obvious. She is enamoured of everything North American, and the 'all-electric' life – unlike the good soldier Marco who prefers the prospect of life in South America. Though you do not see it in these extracts, Silvana reads avidly American pulp magazines, she dances wholeheartedly to the boogie woogie (a more alluring reprise of the opening scene on the train in *Caccia Tragica*, that you do see, where the makeshift combo plays a Glenn Miller tune), and she wins a Miss Mondina beauty contest (in the manner of every American beauty queen). Her facile nature invites extinction, then, according to De Santis's dictat. And she dies, at her own hand, on the platform which served as a dream throne in the beauty contest and now stands as a real scaffold. Her sin was betrayal of the ideals her community represented, her sentence a self-inflicted death.

In both films there is redemption for the guilty party, born of the magnanimity of the people. Alberto is ashamed and recants, while Michele speaks on his behalf at the trial. The final scene that we see shows the leaders of the collective pointing him in the direction of a likely job, and pelting him with handfuls of earth in a gesture that is both a rejection and a pardon. Similarly, Silvana recants, obviously so, and she gives up her life in the process. But, once again, there is forgiveness and the women proceed to cover her body with a shroud of the rice that is so precious to them.

In a very real sense, the films conclude, Alberto and Silvana are victims of society. Furthermore, in *Caccia Tragica*, De Santis had originally intended to emphasize that point with an ending that showed Alberto, once acquitted by the people's court, being subsequently arrested by the government police. His initial shooting script would have 'underlined the character of popular justice which sought to reintegrate into the workers' community an individual who was certainly guilty, but equally was also a victim of social conditions'. This proposal was rejected by the censors.

Both films, then, fall firmly within the neo-realist canon and I have only scratched the surface of their distinguishing characteristics at the thematic and stylistic levels. Doubtless you will have noticed a lot more. But I hope you will also have noticed something else, to which I have already briefly alluded. Both films owe a considerable debt to the genres and styles of the mainstream Hollywood cinema, not least the gangster film, the 'Western', and, even, the musical.

There is an epic sweep to both these films, with dynamic and aggressive editing and camerawork, and, in the case of *Riso Amaro* especially, more than a touch of overt eroticism – all of which are surely indebted to Hollywood. De Santis may well have anchored his films fairly and squarely in the Italian context, but the Hollywood influence is evident all the same.

'I like to immerse myself in tradition, express the current aspirations of the people through its traditions', De Santis claimed, and 'Besides, all of us, from time to time, happen to rediscover the Italian tradition of melodrama'. And we see ample evidence in *Caccia Tragica* and *Riso Amaro* of melodramatic and traditional touches – witness, as small examples of the latter, the collective whistling at Daniela's first hideout and the singing of the women in the rice fields. There are many melodramatic moments throughout both films which serve to heighten their overall dramatic impact.

However, De Santis was also a known admirer of the films of John Ford and King Vidor, and the acting of, among others, Joan Crawford, and the influence of the traditional Hollywood genres is much in evidence. Indeed, one might justifiably argue, they come to predominate. Thus, in the opening extract from *Caccia Tragica*, for example, we see the members of the farm collective advance on Daniela's hideout with their rifles at the ready, in archetypal Western fashion. It's the gunfight at Daniela's corral. When she appears, however, there is a distinct change of genre. She is dressed in typical gangster's garb – big coat, lapels turned up, hat pulled down, cigarette hanging from the mouth. She and her gang walk through the ranks of the assembled farmers and there is a customary exchange of 'tough talk' (harkening back to previous Resistance encounters, you will notice). Finally, they make their escape, guns blazing – with Daniela hanging out of the car window, firing her revolver, while her henchman is perched on the back of the car, machine-gunning all and sundry. De Santis knew his Hollywood iconography and how to mix his genres.

Riso Amaro also drew on the characteristics of the gangster genre but, as is particularly evident in the extract you see, it is notable most of all for drawing on the full panoply of cinematic eroticism. De Santis always denied any erotic intent, stating emphatically that he wanted 'to express man, woman and society in their ... natural primitive integrity'. But frankly, on this occasion, he was certainly being disingenuous – an understandable reaction in view of the public furore his film caused.

It is impossible not to see any erotic intent in a film which so obviously glories, as you see, in expressively depicting row on row of bare-legged and bare-thighed women, not to mention, during the fight in the water, the occasional glimpse of a bare breast. And there was also the little matter of a 'notorious' seduction scene in the rain, which you do not see. In Silvana Mangano, furthermore, De Santis discovered an actress who writers have variously described as 'a magnificent creature', 'visually opulent', or 'a stately counterpart of Rita Hayworth'. They are all evading the issue and conjuring euphemisms, as you might expect. A talented actress, Mangano was also beautiful and sexually attractive. De Santis may well have decried the influence of pin-ups on Italian youth, but he assuredly added to the vein and introduced the notion of the Hollywood *femme fatale* into neo-realism in a very obvious way. In this regard, the case has been well put by Millicent Marcus:

> Though neo-realism acknowledged the sexuality of its characters in the pre-marital pregnancies of Pina in *Rome, Open City* and of Maria in *Umberto D*, for example, it never made eroticism into one of the driving forces of the narrative action, nor did it parade the physical attributes of its protagonists, the way De Santis does in *Riso Amaro*.
>
> (*Italian Film in the Light of Neorealism*, p.79) ❑

Predictably, given its erotic attributes, the Church damned *Riso Amaro* outright and classified it 'forbidden to all believers'. De Santis also received a lot of criticism from the Italian left for the film's 'overt eroticism' and its 'indebtedness to American films', a final irony in view of his public pronouncements. Unsurprisingly, cinemagoers flocked to see it in droves. The film achieved fifth place in Italian box-office returns for the year 1949–50, and it went on to be an immense commercial success worldwide.

By contrast, the earlier *Caccia Tragica* was a resounding flop (though it won first prize at the 1947 Venice and Cannes Film Festivals). Whether that was because of its subject, its treatment, or the fact it did not star Mangano, we do not know. We do know that no Italian film distributor ever really tried to exhibit the film properly. Because the film had been financed by ANPI (the National Association of Italian Partisans), it was given a limited release through channels promoted by the PCI. They largely amounted to third-run cinemas where folk would not have expected to find a new film going out immediately on release. De Santis's personal brand of neo-realism clearly divided the industry as much as it divided the movement itself. He was at his most successful, commercially speaking, when he had something more to convey than social realism alone – very much like the neo-realist films generally.

Some of the issues raised in this study of De Santis's films, not least the question of Americanization and the depiction of women, will be further examined in later units (by Lesley Caldwell in Unit 13 and Arthur Marwick in Unit 15). Bear them very much in mind for future consideration.

La Terra Trema, 1948

Visconti's second film is often regarded as being both a masterpiece and the most 'revolutionary' film of the neo-realist movement. Indeed, 'revolutionary' is the word that occurs over and over again in critical commentaries on the film. For this reason, among many others, we must scrutinize it. Having said that, however, the film is 161 minutes long and does not have complete subtitles in English – a voice-over narration is translated throughout but not the actual dialogue spoken. It therefore poses problems: for me, when it comes to organizing discussion of the film in the limited space available within these units and on the video compilation; for you, in that you cannot be expected to analyse a film you might not fully understand. However, I hope to build on what I take to be your increasing confidence in knowing how to deal with this sort of material. I will, therefore, confine my role in this section to that of supplying you with the information that will enable you, when used in conjunction with your viewing, to form as full a picture of the film and its intentions as possible. I shall provide the supporting documentation and that alone. Interpretation will be largely of your own making.

La Terra Trema ('The Earth Trembles') was inspired by Verga's 1881 novel, *I Malavoglia* ('The House by the Medlar Tree'). It was intended to be the first part – hence the film's subtitle, *Episodio del Mare* – of a planned trilogy, set in Sicily, dealing with the fishermen, the peasants, and the workers in the sulphur mines, and charting their struggles to liberate themselves from oppression. But only this part was completed. It was initially financed with a small amount of money provided by the PCI, who expected that Visconti's trip to Sicily, in 1947, would produce a short documentary which would then be of use for propaganda purposes in their election campaign. Visconti stayed on for six months and *La Terra Trema* was the result.

After a trip to Catania in the region of Aci-Trezza in 1941, Visconti remarked:

> To me, a reader from Lombardy, accustomed by tradition to the limpid rigour of Manzoni's imagination, the primitive and gigantic world of the fisherman of Aci-Trezza and the herdsmen of Marineo had always seemed as if raised by the picturesque and violent tone of the epic; to my Lombard eyes ... Verga's Sicily appeared like a veritable island of Ulysses, an island of adventures and boiling passions. I thought therefore of a film taken from *I Malavoglia*.

Later, on reading the works of Antonio Gramsci, Visconti commented:

> The mythological vein which I had found in Verga no longer seemed adequate to me. I felt an impellent urge to find out for myself what were the historic, economic and social foundations on which the Southern drama had been built. Reading Gramsci I learned the truth that is still waiting to be resolved. Gramsci did not only convince me by the acuteness of his historical and political analysis but his teaching also explained to me the character of Southern Italy as a great social rupture and as a market for a colonialist type of exploitation by the ruling classes in the North. I saw in Gramsci ... something that is not to be found in other studies of the South's problems: the indications of a realistic, practical solution, in terms of the

> overall problem of the unity of our country; an alliance between the workers of the North and the peasants of the South, in order to break up the power of the agricultural and industrialist capitalist block.

On his planned trilogy about oppression in Sicily, Visconti said:

> I was seeking to express the whole dramatic theme as a direct outcome of economic conflict. The key to the understanding of the spiritual and psychological conflicts is always social, even if the conclusions I reach are always those which concern the individuals whose cases I am describing.

Roy Armes quotes Visconti on *La Terra Trema* and its position *vis-à-vis* neo-realism:

> The causes of *La Terra Trema* stemmed too, basically, from the perplexity which increased day by day within me, when I saw the movement going off course, losing its prestige. From which, at a certain moment, came the need to begin again from scratch, from pure truth, without any trickery. Without a pre-established script, without any real actors, relying completely on reality and truth ... At the time of *La Terra Trema* I remember that my professional conscience told me: you must do that, you must take the method to its extreme limit, you must make no concessions. You must demonstrate that this is the right course ... With *La Terra Trema* it seems to me that I really achieved realism.

(*Patterns of Realism*, pp.125–6)

Peter Bondanella elaborates further on Visconti's method when making this film:

> In many respects, *La Terra Trema* fits many of the traditional definitions of neo-realism better than any other work of the period. Absolutely no studio sets or sound stages were employed and the special lighting effects were used only during certain difficult night scenes at sea. Aci-Trezza provided the entire cast of the work: each morning, Visconti would explain the day's shooting to the villagers, describing the events to be filmed, and soliciting their opinions as to how they would respond in similar situations. Their spontaneous reactions were then incorporated into the script, which thus evolved as the film progressed. Unlike so many other Italian films during and since the neo-realist period, the popular technique of shooting without synchronized sound and dubbing the sound afterwards during the editing was rejected, as Visconti insisted on the authentic voices and sounds of the Sicilian environment. In this, he took a revolutionary cultural stance, refusing standard Italian (as well as the official culture it symbolized) for the dialect of the simple people he filmed, believing that the authentic expression of the people's emotions could only be achieved using their own language. Because this dialect was incomprehensible to most Italian audiences, he then chose to employ a voice-over, an objective narrative voice in Italian to provide an often ironic commentary to the storyline.

(*Italian Cinema*, p.68)

At the outset of *La Terra Trema* there is a prologue which recounts:

Figures 8/9.37–42 *La Terra Trema*

Lucia

Lucia and Mara

'Ntoni

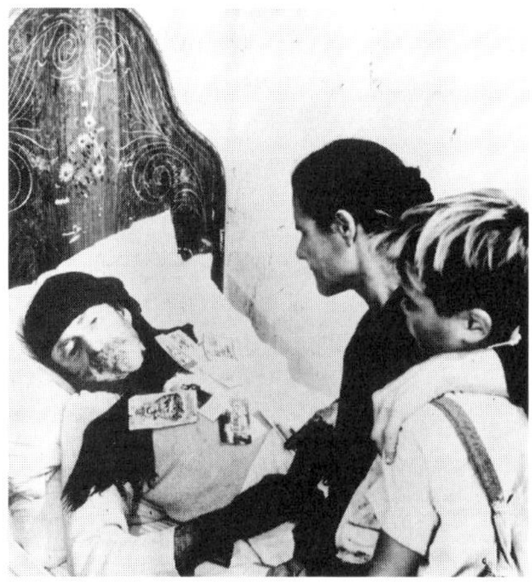

Grandfather, mother and Vanni

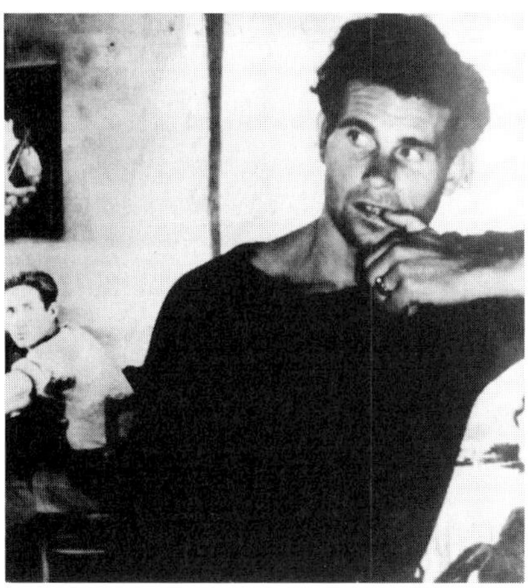

'Ntoni

'Ntoni

> The events represented in this film happened in Italy, more precisely in Sicily, in the region of Aci-Trezza on the Ionian sea near Catania. The story the film tells is one which has happened over and over again in all those countries where men exploit other men. The houses, streets, boats and the sea are those of Aci-Trezza. All the actors in the film were chosen from the inhabitants of the region: fishermen, children, labourers, masons, wholesalers. They knew no other language than Sicilian to express revolt, pain, hope. In Sicily, the Italian language is not the language of the poor.

Synopsis

The leading character 'Ntoni (Antonio), a young fisherman, is sick of being exploited by the wholesale fish dealers and decides to strike out on his own with just the help of his immediate family. They plan to catch and salt their own fish, and make their own arrangements for disposal of the same. But one stormy night the family boat is wrecked and they are deprived of their livelihood. 'Ntoni tries desperately to find work, but the wholesale dealers boycott him to punish him for his rebellious attitude and for initially inciting the other fishermen to revolt as well. When he is unable to meet the payments due on the mortgage taken out to finance their venture, the bank evicts the family from their home. The grandfather is taken ill. One sister, Lucia, allows herself to be seduced by the local chief of police and the other, Mara, feels unable to accept an offer of marriage. 'Ntoni resorts to drink. Finally, he is compelled to overcome his pride and, under humiliating circumstances, accepts work with the wholesalers once again. He now fishes on newly built boats which are collectively owned but directly controlled by the wholesalers.

The first extract on Video-cassette 2 (extract J) comes from early in the film and depicts the scene in which 'Ntoni leads the fishermen in general revolt. It speaks very much for itself and does not require further contextualization. The subtitling of the voice-over commentary is sufficient in this instance. Now watch this extract.

The next extract comes from a point in the film soon after the last one. Order has been restored and the fishermen's ringleaders jailed. But the wholesalers are compelled to seek their release when they realize that otherwise they too will be deprived of supplies of fish. The fishermen are freed, to everybody's delight. At this point 'Ntoni talks over with his family the prospect of going it alone. Before viewing this extract, read the script for the scene printed below.

> *Courtyard of Valastro house. Day.*
>
> *Lucia is peeling potatoes in front of the kitchen door. Inside the kitchen, the mother is standing at the stove. She picks up a pot and takes it into the dining room. Vanni [the youngest brother] is sitting in the doorway singing.*
>
> *Valastro house. Dining room. Day.*
>
> *Cola [the younger brother], Antonio, and the grandfather are seated at the table. Mara is sewing. The mother enters with the pot, which she places on the table. As Cola slices the bread, the mother fills the plates with soup. Vanni's song is heard in the distance. Antonio is about to start eating but then pushes his plate away.*

ANTONIO I don't want any.

MOTHER Why not, Antonio?

ANTONIO I don't want any.

He gets up from the table.

MOTHER Antonio, eat.

ANTONIO I don't want any.

GRANDFATHER
What do you get by not eating, Antonio?

Antonio lights a cigarette before answering.

ANTONIO Grandfather, that's not the point, eating or not. It's something else.

Cola and Mara turn to him.

GRANDFATHER
Well, what is the point, Antonio?

Antonio turns back to the table suddenly and speaks to the entire family.

ANTONIO Did you see? They put us in jail because the law says we committed a crime. But when it suits their purpose the law doesn't count any more. So they spring us! Can you understand what this means? I'll tell you!

Antonio takes a chair near the door through which Lucia now enters, stopping to listen. Antonio sits down at the table and continues to talk, growing increasingly excited.

ANTONIO It means they need us!

COLA (*bitterly*)
How can anyone need us? We're just draft animals, like Jano's donkey. Who could need us? The fish, to get themselves caught!

ANTONIO (*excited*)
I tell you they need us! So why do we always have to be under them? Let's forget them! And see how they do then! Let's see how far they get without us.

GRANDFATHER
Antonio, whoever leaves the old roads finds a worse road!

ANTONIO Grandfather, your proverbs were good once on a time but not any more! Don't think I've gone crazy. I think with my head, not with my feet! I don't want to hurt anybody. (*He hits the table.*) But I tell you we weren't born to be beggars, to not even hope to better our lives ... but to at least control our own lives and those of our families!

GRANDFATHER
Your father always worked and he never complained!

COLA Yes, but our father drowned, past Cape Mulini. Who ever thanked him? After he slaved all his life for other people! Who ever thinks of him now, or of all the other men who've died at sea slaving for other people? (*He hits the table and suddenly stands up and goes over to the window.*) Antonio's right! I'm not sure why, but Antonio's right! (*He leans against the wall and speaks to the whole family.*) If we worked on our own, everything we did would be for our house, for our mother and our sisters. When our father was alive he understood these things. He'd have gone along with Antonio. He sure wouldn't have wanted his sons to keep on like this!

Antonio hits his hand against the table and stands up, shouting.

ANTONIO You see, you understand too.

Vanni, off-screen, stops singing. Lucia comes to the table as Antonio walks toward the door.

ANTONIO If we all agree, we'll be rid of these bloodsuckers forever!

COLA What should we do, Antonio?

ANTONIO I want to get free of these 'dealer' crooks and free you all too! (*He turns around to face the family as the mother silently carries the pot back to the kitchen.*) We'll work on our own, with our own boat! (*Vanni enters from the courtyard to listen and leans against the doorway.*) And our women'll help salt the fish ... (*Cola comes over to his brother.*) And we'll sell it and go right to Catania!

COLA It'll take money to do that, and we haven't got any!

ANTONIO Don't worry, Cola; we have the house!

Antonio puts his hand on Cola's shoulder and goes out into the courtyard with him. Lucia, the grandfather, and Vanni watch them go.

Courtyard of the Valastro house. Day.

Cola and Antonio come out of the house into the courtyard.

COLA What d'you mean, we have the house? You want to sell it?

Antonio sits down under the tree; Cola follows him.

ANTONIO Not sell it, mortgage it: that's how we'll get the money! When we get the money we'll work for ourselves and little by little we'll pay off the debt.

COLA If the others agree, I agree too. (*Antonio, delighted to have been understood, slaps Cola's knee.*) The point is, if everybody agrees. (*At the kitchen door, the mother picks up the chair left by Lucia and brings it into the house.*) And our mother has to consent.

(from Visconti, *Two Screenplays*, pp.28–31)

Now watch Video-cassette 2, extract K.

The last extract comes from the end of the film. Once again, read the script below before viewing it on the cassette.

Drydock on the beach. Outside. Day.

A boat is being repaired. A woman is feeding a fire at the entrance. A little boy carrying a basket enters and goes up to the boat. A little girl, Rosa, runs up and hides at the entrance as if spying on someone. Sounds of workmen and of the sea.

Antonio comes up, hands in pockets; Rosa observes him. Two men are feeding another fire.

ROSA Hello, Antonio.

BASTIANO Hello, Antonio.

ANTONIO Hello, Bastiano.

Antonio goes off as the little girl steps out. A carpenter is repairing the Valastro boat. His hammering is heard throughout the scene. Antonio walks around the boat, examines it attentively, and sits down on it. Rosa, who has been following him, watches him as she leans against the gunwale. Antonio turns and sees her.

ANTONIO What do you want, little girl?

ROSA (*smiling*)
This is your boat, isn't it? And we're fixing it for you.

ANTONIO Yes, you're fixing it for me, but I haven't got any money to pay you for it. Did you know that?

ROSA Everybody says you're poor ... (*She walks around the boat, climbs up on to it and sits facing Antonio.*) ... but in the village they hate you.

ANTONIO (*sadly*)
I know it.

Rosa leans on her elbow and makes herself comfortable.

ROSA If I could help you ... I would!

She smiles at Antonio. He looks at her with a bitter smile.

ANTONIO Help me? How could you help me? The people who could do it don't because they're so jealous. But they should've understood that I did what I did for everybody, not just for myself. And now? You see how they've all walked out on me? And they'd like to eat me alive! (*He turns to look at the boat; Rosa lowers her eyes; he turns back to her and slaps the boat.*) This has been in my family for ages! See how wrecked it is? Everybody says it was my fault it was wrecked. (*He stares into the distance and seems to be talking to himself.*) But some day they'll all realize I was right! Then it'll be a blessing for everybody to lose everything like I did! (*Turning back to Rosa.*) We have to learn to stick up for each other, to stick together. Then we can go forward ...

He jumps down from the boat and goes off slowly. Rosa remains seated and removes her kerchief. Then she jumps down, too, and follows Antonio. She stops a little distance behind him. Antonio turns.

ROSA Antonio! Come back soon to see your boat!

Antonio goes off without answering, as Rosa sits down on the stones and watches him.

(from Visconti, *Two Screenplays*, pp.95–6)

Now watch Video-cassette 2, extract L.

In the end, then, as Geoffrey Nowell-Smith puts it, 'Ntoni 'articulates for the first time the lesson of his defeat: the failure of any individual attempt to go it alone, and the need for collective and concerted action if exploitation is to be brought to an end and the future secured' (*Luchino Visconti*, p.44). And Visconti's message, as expressed in the script – 'he has lost because he was isolated' – is made clear.

Yet for Nowell-Smith, in particular, *La Terra Trema* is not an unmitigated success. 'Visconti brought to the project a great amount of revolutionary fervour', he maintains, 'and an even greater ignorance of actual conditions'. As a consequence, his film was based on false premisses, both aesthetic and political:

> If the function of art is revolutionary (which, in a revolutionary period, is not an absurd premiss), and revolution was on the cards at any moment (which, from a Northern point of view, it certainly seemed to be), then a film of this pattern could fulfil its function by anticipating the cause it set out to further. Unfortunately, even in the balmy perspectives of 1947, the project was beset by contradictions. In the first place, the Sicilian proletariat was not going to rise, *en bloc*, against its oppressors, and if it did it was going to fail. The forces of reaction were too entrenched ... The political premiss was therefore false. Given even that the political premiss might have been true, there would still be something odd about a man of Visconti's temperament indulging in this sort of political wish-fulfilment, were it not clear from his later films that the initial formation of an abstract and often highly politicized schema is an integral part of his method of work. His initial scenarios have an ideological clarity and purity about them which is then systematically betrayed in the final elaboration.
>
> (*Luchino Visconti*, pp.39–40)

The 'betrayal' of clarity of ideological purpose in regard to *La Terra Trema*, for Nowell-Smith, inevitably followed from Visconti's 'search for complete realism'. Ironically, in one obvious respect it resulted from his idea of rendering the dialogue in Sicilian dialect and then consigning the explanation of events and what was being said to an overlaid Italian commentary:

> The pictorial style of the film was matched to the dialogue to form an audio-visual whole, while the more analytical content of the film was supplied by the commentary. This division of the film into a conceptual element and an element of 'pure' cinema was a necessary conclusion of Visconti's search for complete realism. But it was a conclusion that brought him straight up against an impasse ...
>
> Visconti had got too enmeshed in the documentary morass to withdraw from it so neatly. He had got the people of Aci-Trezza to speak their own parts in their own way. He had accepted and even exploited the limitations of their appreciation of their own situation. The method he chose to liberate himself from the impasse could not, however, transcend these limitations, it could only deny them, and at the same time deny or obfuscate the reality of the real lives with which he had involved himself.
>
> (*Luchino Visconti*, pp.53–4)

Thus Nowell-Smith found that 'The total effect is not realistic but lyrical', and he felt that, in all, *La Terra Trema* displayed a 'faint aura of aesthetic indulgence'. What do you think?

The criticism is not dissimilar to that levelled by Simon Hartog against *Bicycle Thieves* (see p.249) and, interestingly, both commentators were first publishing their critiques at much the same time – Nowell-Smith in 1967, Hartog in 1968. Hartog, you may recall, accused De Sica and Zavattini of a 'preliminary and incomplete consciousness' and of adopting 'an aesthetic posture'. Though by no means as virulent in his comments – he did, after all, recognize *La Terra Trema* as 'a great film, but not a flawless masterpiece' – Nowell-Smith, as you have seen, charged Visconti with betrayal of 'ideological clarity and purity' and with 'aesthetic indulgence'.

At the time of the film's original release, in 1948, few people got the chance to judge what they thought of it. It was shown in its entirety at the 1948 Venice Film Festival where it was unenthusiastically received and shared second prize. The Italian film critics gave it a predominantly hostile reception and it was cut by 4,000 feet. Even then it was considered too long for commercial release and was re-edited further, without Visconti's consent, to give a running time of 90 minutes, whereon it was put on limited release in selected cinemas.

Despite Visconti's best efforts to restore a measure of prestige to what he saw as an ailing movement, the neo-realist cinema was plainly finding it increasingly difficult to reach the very audiences for which it was intended. De Sica and Zavattini were to discover that matters had only got worse, for a variety of reasons, by the time they completed production of *Umberto D*.

Umberto D, 1951

Umberto D is a particularly apt film with which to conclude our viewing sessions and, indeed, to see in its entirety. It proved to be a turning point for the neo-realist movement in many ways. It marked a further peak of achievement, in purely aesthetic terms, but the beginning of the end, in strictly practical terms. As we have already noted, Giulio Andreotti thought the film did 'wretched service to the fatherland', and he publicly decried it in the most forthright manner (a matter to which we shall return shortly). The force of his reaction and the political support he mobilized did much to discourage other film makers from continuing in the same vein. As if to bear out his criticism, *Umberto D* fared disastrously at the box office. 'Not only did it flop financially in Italy but also abroad', admitted the director, Vittorio De Sica.

For De Sica and his long-time friend and scriptwriter, Cesare Zavattini, the film's lack of financial success was a profound setback and, in effect, put paid to their neo-realist ambitions. Together they had been responsible for some of the most accessible and internationally acclaimed films emanating from the neo-realist movement, including *Sciuscia* (1946), *Bicycle Thieves* (1948), and *Miracle in Milan* (1950). Despite the *Umberto D* débâcle, Zavattini declared the film was 'not ... a conclusion, but a point of departure'. He set about writing his theory of neo-realism, and he planned even more ambitious films for the future. But, in truth, within a few years he and De Sica were well and truly back within the mainstream of commercial film making, which was where they had

Figures 8/9.43–8 *Umberto D*

Umberto

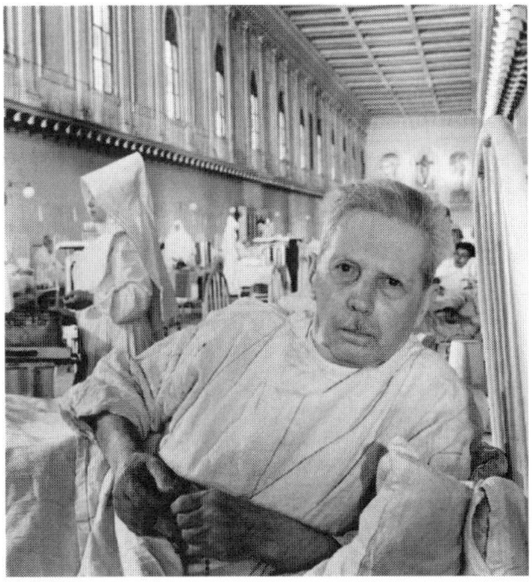

Umberto

Maria and Umberto

Maria and Umberto

Umberto's landlady and her coterie

The dog pound

both started their careers in the 1930s. Their fortunes picked up and prospered, but their ultimate goals remained unrealized. And neo-realism, for its part, was at an end.

Yet for all that, *Umberto D* did not pass unlauded. In June of 1952, André Bazin stated that it was 'in the forefront of neo-realism', it was 'most daring', and constituted an excellent example of 'total neo-realism' (quoted in Hillier, *Cahiers du Cinéma*, pp.180–1). Subsequently, another French critic, Pierre Leprohon, assessed the importance of the film as follows: 'Exemplary in its humanity, *Umberto D* is exemplary also in its neo-realist approach. It comes closer than any other film to Zavattini's ideal: the portrayal of life as it is lived from day to day, with no concessions made to abstract composition or conventional effects' (*The Italian Cinema,* 1966, p.131).

What, then, was there about the film of *Umberto D* that provoked such extreme reactions – what would prompt Andreotti to regard it as performing a 'wretched service', yet stir Bazin to praise its 'total neo-realism'? In what obvious respects did it accord with Zavattini's ideas on neo-realist cinema?

To answer those questions, I want you to read the reprint of Zavattini's article contained in *Documents and Texts 1*, item 24, and then to view Video-cassette 3 which contains *Umberto D* in its entirety. Clearly, there is a lot to be got through here and I do not expect you to tease out all the nuances in both written text and film text. But you have had a lot of experience in dealing with this sort of material by now and so you should be confident about proceeding. There are, though, one or two matters I would point out in advance.

Remember, for instance, that Zavattini was writing his account after this film had been made. It is therefore not only a summary of what he thought the pursuit of neo-realism entailed and what had been achieved, but also an outline of the way in which he felt the movement ought still to develop. It is prescriptive as well as being descriptive since Zavattini, like De Sica, was by no means fully satisfied with *Umberto D.*

Remember, furthermore, that while Zavattini and De Sica were very much of one mind when it came to their neo-realist intentions and they worked together in mutual harmony, there were occasional and inevitable differences between them. One point of difference is probably worth highlighting. De Sica, for example, maintained that 'neo-realism is poetry, the poetry of real life', and he drew a distinction between 'banal documentary' and the 'poetic transposition' of the reality he sought to convey. By contrast, as you will see, Zavattini put more emphasis on what he called 'the documentary spirit' (though that did not mean he wanted to make documentaries), and on keeping the artist's 'imagination' in check in order to increase the 'natural imaginative force' of the everyday situations he chose to analyse. As Zavattini puts it, 'the banal disappears, for it never really existed'.

I mention this to stress that the film you see was a genuinely collaborative effort and certainly not the work of Zavattini alone. That should be pretty evident anyway. However, to help you in identifying some of the features which might perhaps be more readily ascribed to Zavattini's influence, I suggest you pay particular attention to what he has to say in his essay on the following:

1 the 'task of the neo-realist artist';
2 the role of 'imagination';
3 the 'cinema of encounter' – 'direct contact with reality' and 'collective awareness';
4 transforming the 'ordinary' into 'spectacle';
5 the difference between 'illusion' and 'analysis';
6 the shortcomings of 'bourgeois synthesis' and 'moral allegory';
7 telling 'stories' and 'the documentary spirit';
8 the 'mythic idea' of the 'star';
9 the response to the attacks on neo-realism;
10 the problem with 'heroes', and the 'audience' as the 'true protagonist of life';
11 dispensing with 'technical-professional collaboration' and the prospect of 'the unique *auteur*';
12 the 'natural imaginative force' of 'situations'.

It is quite a long list, I appreciate, but you will find that Zavattini deals succinctly and briskly with some of the categories. His ideas are not difficult to grasp, given especially the visual expression which many of them receive in *Umberto D.*

When it comes to viewing the film, I want you to proceed in the usual fashion and to build up an impression of the overall intent, the themes, characterization, style, camerawork, and the like. But then concentrate your attention on the following four sequences for closer scrutiny: Umberto's preparation for bed on the first signs of illness; the maid doing her chores in the kitchen next morning; the attempted begging scene and Umberto's chat with the *commendatore*; the final night-time scene of Umberto in his bedroom, contemplating suicide.

Exercise Now read Zavattini's article and watch the film. Remember to bear in mind the questions that I raised: what in the film could have provoked the extreme reactions it did? In what ways does it fit with Zavattini's ideas about neo-realist cinema?

Discussion It is really not very hard to understand why Andreotti was so incensed by *Umberto D.* The simplest reading of the film would suggest it tells a sorry tale about a few days in the life of an irascible if faintly endearing old man and his dog. Beset by unfortunate personal circumstances and suffering from acute poverty, he is driven to attempt suicide as the only way out of his overpowering problems. 'An old man with all the faults of old age', as De Sica himself emphasized, Umberto Domenico Ferrari carries 'a whole weight of bitterness of past battles which makes him irritable and almost disagreeable'.

But there is obviously more to the film than just the story of one man and his dog. While by no means amounting to a searing indictment of political policies in regard to old-age pensioners, the film clearly lays the blame for the plight of the aged at society's door. De Sica, especially, disavowed expressions of political commitment and the making of political propaganda, stating 'Propaganda should be left to the newspapers, posters and election speakers'. Its twin themes of social injustice and old age are heralded right at the outset when we see the march of pensioners through the streets and the demonstration demanding an increase of their insufficient pensions ('We have worked all our lives', it reads on one of the protesters' placards). They are very easily broken up and dispersed, you will notice, first of all by a bus which ploughs its way through their midst (during the opening credits), and then by the arrival of the police. The police are society's tools and, in keeping with the author's other films, represent an obvious source of frustration and repression, along with petty officials and mindless bureaucrats. We see many examples of the two latter categories in *Umberto D* as well – witness the man who responds to the protesters, the unhelpful keepers at the dog pound, and the uncaring woman who administers the soup kitchen.

But thoughtless functionaries and officialdom are not the only targets singled out for attack in the course of the film. Those folk who profess a vocation, who claim to answer a higher calling and serve society's needs do not exactly escape unscathed – the doctors in the hospital are mocking and oblivious to the true nature of Umberto's condition. And the Church, in the form of the genial hospital nun, is all too willing to engage in hypocritical subterfuge provided Umberto puts on a show of Christian reverence and obeisance by asking for a rosary and dutifully reciting his prayers.

When it comes to hypocrisy, mind you, there is nothing to beat the newly emergent middle class of post-war Italy, personified in the landlady, her cinema-owning fiancé, and their opera-loving coterie. Their pretensions and aspirations are all too evident. The landlady yearns for marriage and respectability, yet she has no qualms about letting Umberto's room off for the afternoon as a lovers' nest and pocketing the proceeds. She gives Umberto notice to quit, kicks his dog out onto the street when he is in hospital, and as Maria recognizes, will do the same to her when her pregnancy becomes obvious. 'Umberto and Maria', as Millicent Marcus aptly comments, 'represent two disenfranchised social categories, the old and the "subproletariat" who suffer at the hands of the rising bourgeoisie'.

It is little wonder, then, that Andreotti took particular exception to the film. His public rebuke came in the form of a long open letter which was first published in *Libertas*, the Christian Democrat weekly, on 24 February 1952. There he admonished De Sica for failing to take sufficient account of the government's programmes for economic reconstruction and social welfare, and urged: 'We ask only of a man of culture to feel his social responsibility, which cannot be limited to describing the vices and miseries of a system and a generation but must help to conquer them.' He continued:

> And if it is true that evil can be combatted by baring its crudest aspects, it is still more true that if the world will be induced – erroneously – to think that the Italy of *Umberto D* is the Italy of the mid-twentieth century, then De Sica will have rendered a wretched service to his country, which is also the country of Don Bosco, of Forlanini, and of a progressive social legislation ... Let it not displease De Sica if we entreat him never to forget this minimum obligation to healthy and constructive optimism which truly helps humanity to hope and advance.

Accentuate the positive, eliminate the negative, and utilize the appropriate amount of social responsibility in between: that was Andreotti's message to De Sica.

By contrast, as we know, Bazin felt that *Umberto D* fulfilled the criteria of excellence he was expecting from a neo-realist film. 'Total neo-realism', he called it. Do you agree, after looking at those scenes I asked you to single out?

Well, there are no 'stars' in evidence, to begin with, but an abundance of non-professional actors. The man chosen to play the part of Umberto was Carlo Battisti, a university professor from Florence. And Zavattini, certainly, must have been well pleased with the scenes of Umberto's preparation for bed, and of the maid in the kitchen next morning – nothing happens of seeming significance, yet the ordinary is transformed into spectacle. The neo-realist import of these two scenes, in particular, has been well summarized by Millicent Marcus:

> ... the episode of Umberto's preparation for bed [is] an example of the *temps morts* that constitute so important a part of the film's dedramatizing technique. During this long sequence, which is interrupted by Maria's comings and goings, and a trip to the bookstall, nothing really happens to advance the storyline, yet its very dramatic insignificance concentrates our attention on the protagonist himself ... Without resorting to the more overt manipulative techniques of conventional cinema, De Sica and Zavattini succeed in drawing us into Umberto's interior world by making us cohabitants of his room – the room that has become an external expression of his innermost self ...
>
> The morning scene of Maria in the kitchen serves a similar interiorizing function ... The movement into her mind is done with delicacy and tact through a subjective camera shot which, when it returns to an 'objective' view of Maria, does so with new compassion and understanding. We merge with Maria's point of view early in the scene as she looks out the kitchen window onto the adjoining rooftops where she sees a stray cat – her momentary counterpart in its solitude and homelessness. When Maria returns to the stove and touches her breast to test for palpable signs of her pregnancy, we share with her the burgeoning realization of her desperate plight.

(*Italian Film in the Light of Neorealism*, pp.107–10)

Yet I wonder whether you think the two other sequences I asked you to consider are quite so 'pure' and 'total' in their adherence to neo-realist ideals? Don't they rather violate strictly neo-realist principles with their obvious manipulative approach? Or is that De Sica's more poetic instincts at work?

The use of humour, as we know, was a common enough neo-realist technique. It is also said that De Sica was a great fan of Charlie Chaplin and René Clair, just as Zavattini, for his part, was fond of the comic 'gag'. And there is certainly no lack of comic interjections throughout the film. Even the sombre scene of Umberto preparing for bed begins with comic antics as he loses the thermometer down his trouser leg. But the attempted begging scene definitely caps them all with its obvious piece of homage to Chaplin. Umberto finally summons up the courage to try begging and is on the verge of instant success when, duly embarrassed, he turns his hand palm down in a mock attempt to test for rain. Then, of course, he sets the dog to the task and the result looks very much like a circus routine. We are amused by Umberto and his dog. But does that not introduce too much distance between viewer and protagonist?

Subsequently, when the *commendatore* appears the humour is completely dissipated. But the manipulation continues, as Marcus notes:

> In a complex shot that reveals the *commendatore*'s flawed point of view, Umberto's image is reflected on the window of the bus which the other man has already boarded. Embarrassed because he has nothing to say, the *commendatore* stands at the window looking down, creating the optical illusion that he is contemplating Umberto's reflected image which, of course, we see but he cannot. The illusion is, however, an accurate indication of the *commendatore*'s attitude towards Umberto – both condescending and distorted – for he sees not the man, but his own version of this idle pensioner trying to make a claim on his reluctant attentions.
>
> (*Italian Film in the Light of Neorealism*, p.107)

By the same token, there is a considerable amount of artistic licence and cinematic contrivance at work in the final night-time scene of Umberto in his bedroom, contemplating suicide. At this point, as you see, his room is partly demolished in preparation for the landlady's redevelopment and redecoration. It reflects and reinforces Umberto's inner sense of disorder and chaos. The sudden zoom shot down to the tram lines and cobbles indicates his death wish in no uncertain terms. And though he does not go through with the suicide on this occasion, for his dog's sake, the subsequent hole-in-the-wall framing emphasizes the hopelessness of his plight. Umberto is lost and forlorn. And there is more than a hint he may yet try suicide as a way out of his problems. As we discover, he does finally try to kill himself.

It is all very effective and works exceptionally well. But is it not artifice? And don't moments like these, with their obvious resort to the 'grammar' and 'syntax' of film to convey their meaning, help explain why Zavattini felt neo-realism still had much to achieve?

One thing is clear, however: the ending of the film is very much in accord with what both authors intended. The film resolves nothing and there is no solution. De Sica scrupulously avoided advocating political answers, as we know. And Zavattini's theories, you may recall, proclaimed: 'As for solutions, it is not up to the artist to examine them. It is enough for him to make the need urgently felt.' In regard to *Umberto D*, furthermore, he maintained that 'the solution has to be given by the audience. The spectacle continues in the audience, the spectators are the authors of the dénouement of the drama.'

In that respect, as in so many others, we have come a long way from the heady days of Rossellini's first neo-realist efforts. 'Far from the future of solidarity and progressivism anticipated by Marcello's and Romoletto's activist stance, Umberto's present bears witness to the failure of social change and popular attempts at corrective action,' Marcus has argued. She concludes: 'De Sica's surrender to the isolation of the human condition and the impossibility of true solidarity marks the distance between *Rome, Open City* and *Umberto D*, between the harbinger of a new social order committed to the populist ideals of the resistance and the elegiac look back at the hope which history had failed to fulfil.'

Though it was not, in fact, the last neo-realist film, *Umberto D* effectively marked the end of the movement. It was both testament and testimony to what had been achieved. ❑

4 Conclusion

In October 1948 *L'Unità*, the Communist Party newspaper, launched an attack on *Riso Amaro* for its 'overt eroticism'. It objected, in particular, that De Santis's depiction of Silvana was not 'typical' of the Italian working woman. 'It is in the healthy men and women – mothers, wives, husbands, sons – who fight for their daily bread, that truth appears the richest,' wrote Antonello Trombadori. In February 1952, as we have seen, the Christian Democrat *Libertas* carried Andreotti's attack on the 'wretched service' done by *Umberto D* and his warning to De Sica to exercise 'social responsibility'.

In both instances, of course, we are witness to party political attempts to make the neo-realist film makers conform with what the rival politicians saw as being the proper role of the artist in society. And these demands for artistic conformity, with whatever political hue, were especially pronounced in the years between 1948 and 1952 when Cold War ideologies were rife (a matter already raised by Stephen Gundle in Unit 3 and one to which he will return in Unit 11). In such a context, inevitably, the politicians judged the neo-realist cinema strictly on its value to their respective causes and on its effectiveness in enhancing 'national prestige'.

Among critical commentators, at least initially, the criteria of excellence applied in judging the neo-realist films were very much the ones set forth at the outset by the neo-realists themselves. They stressed the originality of their movement and intentions, and their radical departure from the cinema of the Fascist era. In these respects, the critics largely concurred, neo-realism was indeed something new and different. No matter that it failed to woo the majority of Italian cinema-going audiences, so the argument went, the movement was an artistic and international triumph.

Subsequently, much has changed. Since neo-realism's demise, especially, we have witnessed a considerable revision of its achievements. This critical re-evaluation has tended to emphasize the links and continuities with the preceding era in Italian cinema. Furthermore, by carefully scrutinizing the careers of some of neo-realism's protagonists, as we have observed from the comments levelled at De Sica, Zavattini and Visconti, this revisionist tendency has found them to be wanting, not least in regard to their own aims and ambitions. How, then, should you best judge the legacy of neo-realism?

Well, to start with, you have Millicent Marcus to help. She argues, as you know, that the Italian cinema still owes it a 'lasting debt'. She would stress the importance of the movement in aesthetic terms and here I would recommend you re-read the final paragraphs of her introduction once again (*Documents and Texts 1*, p.22–3). Next, you should listen to Christopher Wagstaff on Audio-cassette 4, side B. He looks more closely at the Italian cinema industry in order to help locate neo-realism in its context. Finally, as you set about both these tasks, you should bear in mind the points raised in the following extract, which is taken from a seminal article by Geoffrey Nowell-Smith:

> Against the revisionist tendency it is worth reaffirming that neo-realism *was* different, though not necessarily quite in the way its protagonists saw it at the time (and have endlessly re-presented it since). It was different not only aesthetically but also – and principally – because political and economic conditions favoured and valorized its radical aesthetic. Allied occupation disrupted the industry ... creating opportunities for a new type of film making, responsive to the needs of the moment. Most importantly, however, neo-realism was a product of the Resistance, prepared for in the same way as the Resistance was prepared for; and it lasted for as long as the Resistance remained a force in Italian politics, rather than just a sentimental memory. Although the neo-realists exaggerated the importance and novelty of their achievement, they were substantially right in stressing that a break did occur. But this break was highly overdetermined. The idea of a new cinema could not have been enacted without the whole climate of the Liberation – not just the overthrow of Mussolini but the armed Resistance and the demolition of the capitalist and state-capitalist structures inherited from the regime. Equally, it could not survive beyond the point in the post-war settlement when the unity of the Resistance ceased to mean anything politically and when the Christian Democrat government (in the person of Giulio Andreotti) had enabled the film industry to regroup on capitalist lines. In the 1950s the Italian cinema – with certain exceptions – reverts to being a cinema very much like the one that Freddi had created in the mid-1930s. Once again the staple fare becomes comedies and dramas, often made by the same people as in the 1930s. The heritage of neo-realism splits into two: on the one hand a touch of populism added to comedies, dramas and low-life films; and on the other hand a striving after radical content in the 'art film', but less and less dependent on realism as an aesthetic.

('The Italian cinema under Fascism', pp.157 and 159)

To my mind, this is an admirable assessment of neo-realism and its legacy. What do you think?

Bibliography

ARMES, R., *Patterns of Realism*, London, The Tantivy Press, 1971.

BAZIN, A., '*Umberto D*', in J. Hillier (ed.), *Cahiers du Cinéma. vol.1, The 1950s*, London and New York, Routledge and Kegan Paul, 1985, pp.180–1.

BONDANELLA, P., *Italian Cinema: from Neo-Realism to the Present*, New York, Ungar, 1983.

CALVINO, I., 'Preface' to *The Path to the Nest of Spiders*, New York, The Ecco Press, 1976, pp.v–xxv.

DE SICA, V., *Bicycle Thieves*, translated with an introduction by S. Hartog, London, Lorrimer, 1968.

ELLWOOD, D., 'Italy: the regime, the nation and the film industry: an introduction' in K.R.M. Short (ed.), *Film and Radio Propaganda in World War II*, London, Croom Helm, 1983, pp.220–9.

HUACO, G.A., *The Sociology of Film Art*, New York, Basic Books, 1965.

LANDY, M., *Fascism in Film: the Italian Commercial Cinema, 1931–1943*, Princeton, Princeton University Press, 1986.

LEPROHON, P., *The Italian Cinema*, London, Secker and Warburg, 1966.

LIEHM, M., *Passion and Defiance, Film in Italy from 1942 to the Present*, Berkeley and Los Angeles, University of California Press, 1984.

MARCUS, M., *Italian Film in the Light of Neorealism*, Princeton, Princeton University Press, 1986.

MCCRAW, W.T., *Political Sponsorship of the Arts*, Stanford University, PhD., 1966.

NOWELL-SMITH, G., *Luchino Visconti*, London, Secker and Warburg, 1973, second edition (first published 1967).

NOWELL-SMITH, G., 'The Italian cinema under Fascism' in D. Forgacs (ed.), *Rethinking Italian Fascism: Capitalism, Populism and Culture*, London, Lawrence and Wishart, 1986, pp.142–61.

OVERBEY, D. (ed. and trans.), *Springtime in Italy: a Reader on Neo-Realism*, London, Talisman Books, 1978.

ROHDIE, S., 'Capitalism and Realism in the Italian Cinema', *Screen*, vol.24, nos.4–5, July–October, 1983, pp.37–46.

ROSSELLINI, R., *The War Trilogy*, trans. Judith Green, New York, Grossman, 1973.

VISCONTI, L., *Two Screenplays:* La Terra Trema *and* Senso, trans. Judith Green, New York, The Orion Press, 1970.

WAGSTAFF, C., 'The Italian cinema industry during the Fascist regime', *The Italianist*, no.4, 1984, pp.160–74.

WILLIAMS, C. (ed.), *Realism and the Cinema: a Reader*, London and New York, Routledge and Kegan Paul, 1980.